GREAT WOMEN OF
IMPERIAL ROME

"All women, because of their innate weakness, should be under the control of guardians," writes Cicero, curtly summarizing the status of women in Ancient Rome. Yet Roman women had more control than many believe. Stories of female artists, teachers, doctors, and even gladiators are scattered through the history of Imperial Rome; a Roman woman did not change her name when she married, her husband could not control her property or dowry, and she was free to divorce.

Royal women in particular – the wives, daughters, sisters and mothers of emperors – have made a profound impression on Roman history, long over-looked. This lively and attractive book vividly characterizes eleven such women, spanning the period from the death of Julius Caesar in 44 BC to the third century AD and with an epilogue surveying empresses of later eras. The author's compelling biographies reveal their remarkable contributions toward the legacy of Imperial Rome, often tinged with tragedy, courage, and injustice.

- A pregnant Roman princess saves a Roman army through an act of personal heroism.
- Three third-century empresses rule the most powerful state on earth, presiding over unprecedented social and political reform.
- Though revered by her husband, an empress is immortalized in history for infidelity and corruption by students of her greatest enemy.

Drawing from a broad range of documentation, Jasper Burns has painted portraits of these exceptional women that are colorful, sympathetic, and above all profoundly human. The women and their worlds are brought visually to life through photographs of over 300 ancient coins and through the author's own illustrations.

This book will be highly valuable to numismatists, students and scholars of Roman history or women's studies, and enjoyable to any reader.

Jasper Burns is a freelance author and illustrator. He has written numerous books and articles on ancient history, prehistoric history, and numismatics.

GREAT WOMEN OF IMPERIAL ROME

Mothers and wives of the Caesars

Jasper Burns

LONDON AND NEW YORK

First published 2007
by Routledge
270 Madison Ave, New York, NY 10016

Simultaneously published in the UK
by Routledge
2 Park Square, Milton Park, Abingdon, Oxon OX14 4RN

*Routledge is an imprint of the Taylor & Francis Group,
an Informa business*

© 2007 Jasper Burns

Typeset in Garamond 3 by
Florence Production Ltd, Stoodleigh, Devon
Printed and bound in Great Britain by
Antony Rowe Ltd, Chippenham, Wiltshire

Library of Congress Cataloging in Publication Data

British Library Cataloguing in Publication Data
A catalogue record for this book is available
from the British Library

ISBN10: 0–415–40897–0 (hbk)
ISBN10: 0–415–40898–9 (pbk)
ISBN10: 0–203–96707–7 (ebk)
ISBN13: 978–0–415–40897–4 (hbk)
ISBN13: 978–0–415–40898–1 (pbk)
ISBN13: 978–0–203–96707–1 (ebk)

To my father, James R. Burns
With thanks to Peter A. Clayton

CONTENTS

CONTENTS

ILLUSTRATIONS

FIGURES

ILLUSTRATIONS

MAPS

GENEALOGICAL TABLES

ACKNOWLEDGMENTS

Previous publishing experiences had taught me that getting a book into print can be a long and often frustrating process. However, the setbacks on this project made me wonder if the shades of the empresses were working against me. I can only hope that they are finally pleased.

To make a long and complicated story short, the book was to be published by the Rubicon Press. However, the unfortunate deaths of the principals of that company – Anthea and Robin Page – left the book in limbo. Enter Peter A. Clayton, who very kindly took the project under his wing. He introduced it to Richard Stoneman at Routledge, who successfully recommended it for publication. I am greatly indebted to both of these gentlemen for their interest in and support of my work.

My sincere gratitude is also due to the numismatists and dealers in ancient coins who generously gave permission for the use of their photographs of coins. I am obliged to Classical Numismatic Group, Inc., Edward J. Waddell, Ltd., Harlan J. Berk, Numismatik Lanz München, Freeman and Sear, Heather Howard, and Italo Vecchi. I believe that their pictures have greatly enhanced this volume. I am also indebted to them for the great majority of the coin attributions, though any errors are strictly my own.

I would also like to thank the editors of *The Celator: Journal of Ancient and Medieval Coinage* for serializing an earlier, much shorter version of the manuscript. The publishers of *The Celator* – Wayne G. Sayles and Kerry K. Wetterstrom – have also published many of my articles on ancient Roman art, coins, and history. I am grateful to them for their support and encouragement.

I owe an incalculable debt to the sculptors, *celators* (coin die engravers), historians, poets, and other ancient writers who left vivid records of these women, their associates, and their times. I am also greatly indebted to numerous modern historians, whose research and inspired accounts of the past have been my guides.

Especially valuable to me have been the works of Barbara Levick, Diana E. E. Kleiner, Anthony R. Birley, Anthony A. Barrett, J. P. V. D. Balsdon, Julian Bennett, John Bray, Michael Grant, Carlin A. Barton, Royston Lambert, and

Karl Galinsky. Also, this book would not have been possible without many fine translations of ancient texts, especially in the Loeb Classical Library, by scholars such as C. R. Whittaker, David Magie, Earnest Cary, H. W. Bird, Robert Graves, and many others. Thanks are due to Anthony R. Birley and Taylor & Francis Books/Routledge for permission to use translations from *Hadrian: The Restless Emperor*.

I would like to express my appreciation to my parents, James R. and Jaquelin Caskie Burns, for their unwavering support and encouragement. In addition, my father contributed many key translations of Latin texts and gave valuable suggestions and feedback. This book would certainly never have been written without the influence of his enthusiasm for Roman language and culture and his fostering of my childhood interest in ancient history.

Indispensable encouragement has also come from other members of my family, including my brothers David and Philip, my aunt and uncle, Marge and Rudolf Freund, and my cousins Mark and Pat Caskie, Jaqui Freund, and Martha Dabney Jones.

There are numerous friends and fellow students of classical culture who have provided encouragement and valuable suggestions. Heather Howard, Sandy Brenner, and Daniel Best – their enthusiasm for ancient coins and culture has inspired me. Vital support and encouragement have also come from Claude A. Ripley, Joan Ripley, Serena Nanda, Donald S. Miller, and Kim Harrell. And I would like to thank Jack Wilson for dragging me, kicking and screaming, into the world of computers.

Pliny the Elder wrote in his *Historia Natura* (2.V.18) that God is man helping man. Clearly, I have received my share of divine assistance in the preparation of this book.

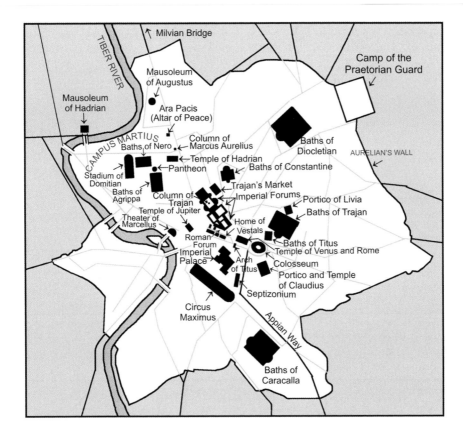

Map 1 City of Rome

Map 2 Central Italy

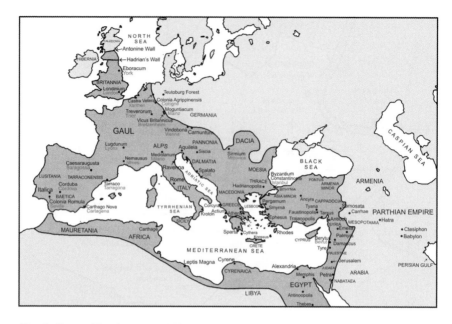

Map 3 Roman Empire, *c.* AD 150

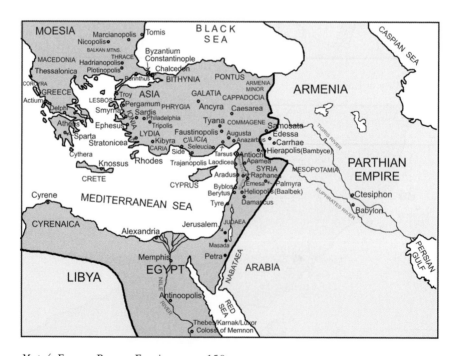

Map 4 Eastern Roman Empire, *c.* AD 150

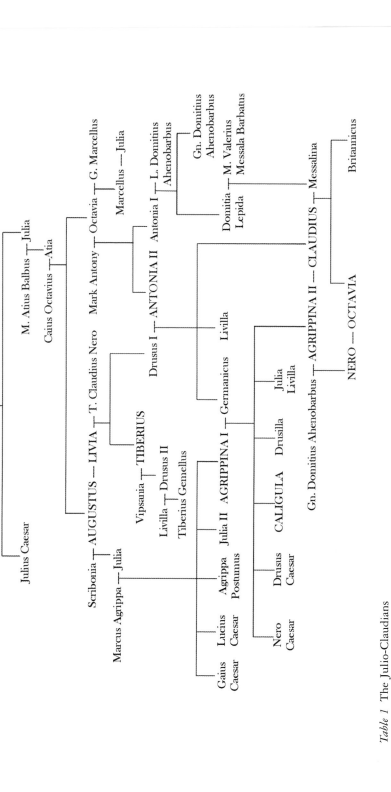

Table 1 The Julio-Claudians

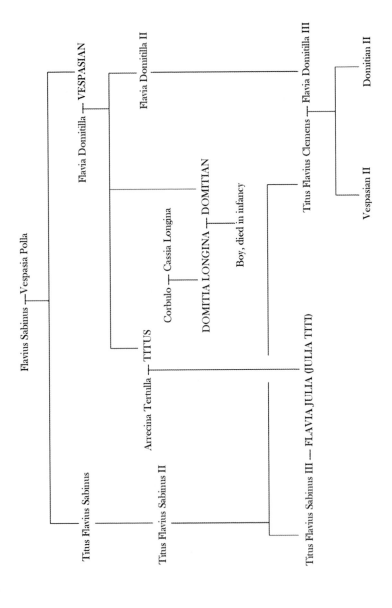

Table 2 The Flavians

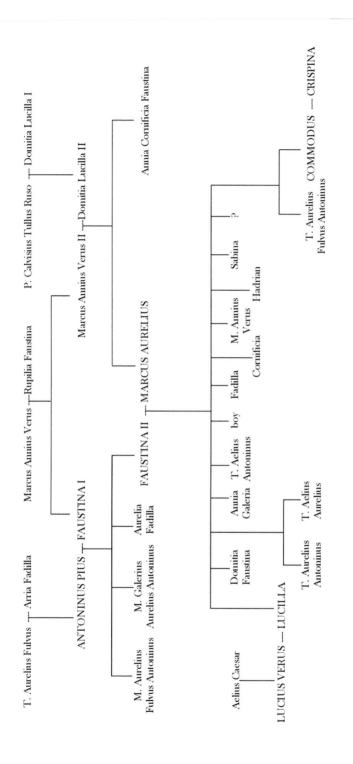

Table 3 The Antonines

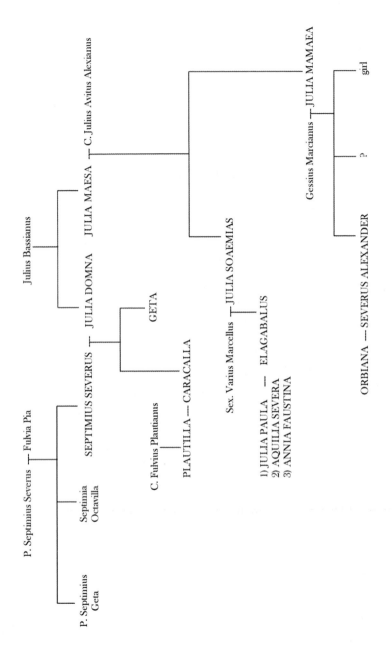

Table 4 The Severans

INTRODUCTION

The Roman Empire was one of the greatest political and cultural achievements in human history. Never before or since have people of so many different nationalities and cultural backgrounds been the willing members of a single state.

The story of how the ancient city of Rome gradually became the center of a vast empire is one of desperate battles, domestic sacrifices, courageous soldiers, ambitious politicians, and clever businessmen. Bit by bit, over a period of centuries, Rome gained control over all the countries that surrounded the Mediterranean Sea, and many of the lands of northern Europe as well.

During most of the time of Roman expansion, the city was a republic, ruled by the people, or, rather, by certain privileged groups of the people. There was no king or emperor and political power was in the hands of the free male citizens of Rome. Most positions of leadership were occupied by the senators, a class of wealthy aristocrats. Senators commanded the Roman armies and two of their number were elected each year to be the consuls, or co-leaders of the state. In times of emergency, a dictator might be elected to rule with supreme authority until the crisis had passed.

Among the most successful of Rome's military and political leaders under the Republic was Julius Caesar. He was a senator and consul who became more powerful than any of his predecessors. After defeating his rivals in war, he assumed supreme power on a permanent basis, receiving the title of "Perpetual Dictator." Naturally, this did not sit well with many of the other senators and, on the "Ides of March" (15 March) in the year 44 BC, Caesar was stabbed to death on his way to a meeting of the senate in Rome.

The death of Julius Caesar was followed by a violent struggle for control of the Roman world. The eventual winner was Caesar's great-nephew and adopted son, Octavian, who became known as Caesar Augustus, the first emperor of Rome. The golden age of the Roman Empire, which he inaugurated in 31 BC, lasted almost three centuries until AD 235 when fifty years of devastating war and political turmoil began.

The basic unit of Roman society was the *familia*, or household. It consisted not only of the members of an immediate family but also of relatives living

1

in the house, slaves, and freed slaves. In addition, the prosperous households commanded the loyalty of "clients." These were the less powerful people who looked to the household of a prominent family for support and protection.

At the head of the *familia* were the *pater familias*, the "father of the family," and the *mater familias*, "the mother of the family." Traditionally, both sons and daughters remained under their father's control as long as he lived. When a woman married, her name did not change and her husband did not control her property. He was entitled to any income that came from her dowry – the money her father provided for her when she married – but he could not touch the dowry itself.[1] A woman's relative independence from her husband also allowed her to divorce him without too much difficulty.[2]

The primary interest of the *pater familias* was in external affairs – the outside business of the household and its role in public life. The *mater familias* was concerned with internal affairs, overseeing social life and directing the education of the children of both sexes.

In an important sense, the Roman Empire at its height was run like an enormous household consisting of perhaps 50 million to 100 million people.[3] The emperor and empress were often called the *pater patriae* and *mater patriae*, or "father and mother of the fatherland." They were in effect the ultimate heads of the extended family of the Roman Empire, with all Roman citizens as their clients.

One of the benefits of the centuries of peace and prosperity during the golden age of the empire was the opportunity for women to enjoy an expanded role in public life, engaging in a wide variety of activities. For example, they worked as artists, shopkeepers, schoolteachers, doctors, dentists, nurses, weavers, bakers, beauticians, priestesses, actresses, real estate speculators, and even gladiators.[4] They attended the theater, bathed in the public baths, haggled in the marketplaces, ran their own businesses, and often acquired extensive property and wealth. All of this was in marked contrast to the societies of classical Greece, where respectable women were confined within the home and took almost no part in public life.

Why did women enjoy such an unusually high degree of freedom in the Roman Empire? One factor was the structure of the Roman family in which wives and mothers enjoyed unusual measures of influence and independence. Also, the last two centuries of the Roman Republic had seen dramatic changes in the position of women. They had gained an unprecedented degree of freedom from the control of their husbands and fathers or guardians, partly through their public protests against oppressive laws and customs.

For example, as early as 195 BC, Roman women successfully demonstrated *en masse* against a statute that limited their right to own and display wealth. They even blockaded streets and every entrance to the Roman Forum before the authorities capitulated.[5] In 42 BC, an attempt to confiscate the wealth of Roman women in order to finance a civil war was met with a public protest led by a woman named Hortensia. This was successful in reducing the amount of the tax and limiting the number of women affected by it.[6]

Though Roman women had gained the right to own and control property in their own names and took an active role in public life, they could neither vote nor run for office. Still, they attained a level of independence and economic power that was almost unparalleled in ancient times and is still unmatched in many modern societies. Their rising status was even reflected in the dining room. It had long been customary for them to sit at meals beside their men, who reclined on couches while they ate. Under the emperors, women also dined in the prone position.[7]

The sheer size and wealth of the empire had a role in opening up opportunities for women. Its administration and defense required many men to be absent from their families, leaving their wives in charge of the family business and household. Also, Roman conquests produced millions of slaves, who took over the menial housekeeping chores and freed many women to pursue personal interests and activities outside the home.[8]

This book focuses on the lives and times of the imperial women – the wives, daughters, sisters, and mothers of the emperors – during the golden age of Rome. The biographies begin with Livia Drusilla, the wife of the first emperor Augustus, continue through the first-century Julio-Claudian and Flavian dynasties into the world of the second-century adoptive and Antonine rulers, and conclude with the Severan empresses (AD 193–235) and a summary of their successors.

Fortunately, many artifacts, statues, and inscriptions survive that reveal details about the lives of these women and give us an idea of how they looked and lived. Even more valuable are the writings of the ancient historians, some of whom wrote from first-hand knowledge. Prominent among these are Tacitus (c. AD 55–117), Suetonius (born c. AD 70), Cassius Dio (wrote c. AD 200–220), and Herodian (early third-century). Their histories are often more colorful than factual, but they do provide much material that is certainly true, and they reveal how the empresses were perceived, at least by some Romans.

We can learn a great deal about the lives and aspirations of Roman women in general by studying the lives of the empresses. The Romans had no television or magazines or newspapers, but coins, paintings, and statues depicting members of the royal family – and stories about them – circulated throughout the Roman world. A Roman empress or princess was famous, rather like a royal personage, movie star, and religious leader all rolled into one. Her influence on Roman culture was often profound, and her impact on the course of Roman history should not be underestimated

Figure 1.1 Portrait of Livia by the author, adapted from a marble sculpture found in Egypt and now in the Ny Carlsberg Glyptotek, Copenhagen. The coin is a bronze dupondius minted under Tiberius (see Figure 1.19 for a similar specimen). Livia stands in the atrium of a Roman house, based on a dwelling in Pompeii. Her setting reflects her concern for domestic matters, especially related to the imperial family.

1

LIVIA

First lady of the empire

Rome had no history of great queens or powerful women in the political sense. Female rulers in foreign lands were generally regarded as symbols of weakness or decadence. Roman women who distinguished themselves in Roman society did so by displaying exceptional feminine virtue or by producing brilliant sons, not by wielding political power.

If the position of Roman empress was going to be something more than decorative, it would take an exceptional woman to set the precedent. As we shall see, Livia Drusilla, the wife of the first Roman emperor Augustus, was a woman of genius, restraint, and great personal dignity. To Rome's enduring good fortune, she gave the role a positive and often vital influence on the Roman world and set a lofty example for her successors to follow.

Nevertheless, despite her excellent qualities and achievements, Livia has gone down in history as one of the most ruthless women of ancient times. Her image as a scheming poisoner is deeply etched into the popular imagination, largely because of Robert Graves' novel *I Claudius*[1] and the superb television series of the same name. This impression, based on the writings of ancient historians who despised Livia and her son, Augustus' successor Tiberius, is almost certainly a wild distortion if not completely false. However, the true character of the first empress is somewhat elusive.

Livia's rise to the top of the Roman world was the result of an improbable series of events. In the years immediately following the assassination of Julius Caesar (44 BC), his great-nephew and heir Octavian (or Octavianus, later to be known as the emperor Augustus) struggled to secure power for himself and vengeance for Caesar's murder. In 42 BC, he and his allies defeated the army of the assassins at the Battle of Philippi in Thrace.

However, the destruction of Caesar's murderers and the defeat of their supporters did not bring an end to the struggle for control of the Roman state. By 40 BC, Octavian had fallen out with his chief ally, Mark Antony (famous as the lover of Cleopatra), and yet another civil war had begun. Antony's strength was concentrated in the eastern provinces and Egypt, while Octavian's was greatest in Italy and the West.

Livia was 16 years old at the time of Philippi, already married and expecting her first child, but under very difficult circumstances. Both her father and her husband had been firmly on the side of Caesar's assassins. Her father, Livius Drusus Calidianus, chose suicide[2] after the defeat at Philippi and her husband, a nobleman named Tiberius Claudius Nero, was one of Octavian's most prominent enemies. Though living in Rome, which was under Octavian's control, her husband chose to ally himself with Mark Antony.

Accordingly, in 40 BC, Tiberius Claudius Nero took Livia and their infant son Tiberius (born 16 November, 42 BC) to join Antony's allies at the stronghold of Perusia in central Italy (Umbria).[3] They soon found themselves besieged by Octavian's superior forces, and their leader, Mark Antony's brother Lucius Antonius, decided to surrender. This left Livia's husband in dire straits, as Octavian had marked him for death. Nero decided to take his family out of the country in an attempt to join Antony's supporters overseas.[4]

Thus began a year-long odyssey of escape from the wrath of Octavian. Livia and her family made their way to the port city of Neapolis (modern Naples, Italy), 200 miles to the south. Hotly pursued by Octavian's agents, they traveled at night on back roads. In Naples, the cries of little Tiberius nearly gave them away on two occasions, but they succeeded in boarding ship and sailing to the island of Sicily. They soon continued to Greece, where their family and Mark Antony had many clients and supporters. Nevertheless, they were far from safe.[5]

The Roman historian Suetonius tells the story of Livia's adventure while hiding in Sparta, in southern Greece. The people of that city, who were clients of her family, were entrusted with her protection. However, the approach of Octavian's henchmen during the night forced her to flee with little Tiberius into the countryside. As they hurried through the forest, a sudden fire engulfed them, scorching Livia's hair and robe.[6]

These experiences of life on the run, when Livia was a young mother in her teens, may have encouraged her opposition to republicanism, with its legacy of political instability, and left her determined to protect her family's interests at all costs. The chaos of the late Roman Republic had cost her father his life and nearly resulted in her own death and those of her son and husband. To Livia as empress, the exercise of absolute power was the best guarantee of security.

Finally, a truce between Octavian and Antony in 39 BC allowed Livia and her family to return to their home in Rome, though probably in reduced circumstances because of penalties imposed by Octavian.[7] It was at this time that Livia confronted Octavian, the arch-enemy of her husband and of her deceased father. Incredibly, it seems to have been love at first sight, at least as far as Octavian was concerned. This was despite the fact that he was already married and his wife Scribonia was pregnant.[8]

The 19-year-old Livia's attractions were many. She was a gifted woman, with intelligence and wit, and she was beautiful, with high cheekbones, a long straight nose, large brown eyes, and reddish blond hair. (Her eye and hair colors are known from residual paint on her statues.[9]) The Roman poet Ovid, who knew Livia personally, wrote that she had the "beauty of Venus [the goddess of love] and the character of Juno [the queen of the gods]."[10] She was also related to two of the noblest Roman families, the Livii (through the adoption of her father[11]) and the Claudii. A connection with Livia would give Octavian a significant boost in his rivalry with Antony, especially in the eyes of the Roman aristocracy.

Perhaps the most lasting of Livia's assets for Octavian was her remarkable political savvy. It is said that he came to value her opinion so highly that, when he consulted her on serious matters, he would read from prepared notes.[12] On her part, Livia kept all of her husband's written communications on file, archived and easily accessible.[13]

Octavian was so taken with Livia that he divorced Scribonia (on the very day she gave birth to his only child, a daughter named Julia[14]) and forced Livia's husband to release her.[15] Octavian was in his mid-twenties, somewhat small in stature, but handsome, with a well-proportioned physique, bright, penetrating eyes, and curly blond hair.[16] Despite his ruthlessness where politics were concerned, he had an easy, friendly manner and a lively sense of humor.[17] He was a gifted orator and writer who enjoyed gambling and giving dinner parties, though he was a light drinker.[18] His many interests included fishing and collecting coins and fossils.[19]

The marriage between Livia and Octavian took place on 17 January, 38 BC, 13 days before her twentieth birthday.[20] It all happened so quickly that one of Livia's servants couldn't keep up with events. At the wedding party, when he saw his mistress sitting next to Octavian rather than her former husband (who was required to be present in order to "give the bride away"[21]), he told her that she was sitting next to the wrong man.[22]

Three months after the wedding, Livia gave birth to a second son, Drusus, who was destined to be the father of the emperor Claudius. There was gossip that the baby was actually Octavian's[23] and, as the boy grew older, it was whispered that he resembled Livia's new husband far more than her old one. However, Octavian never claimed paternity, and the child must have been conceived before Livia's return to Rome.[24]

A couple of years after her marriage to Octavian, Livia gave birth to a stillborn child, but the couple were never able to have children of their own.[25] This would be both a personal disappointment and a political inconvenience.

Despite Livia's marriage to the most powerful man in Rome, custom dictated that her two boys remain in the household of their father, Tiberius Claudius Nero.[26] However, he died five years after their divorce and Livia's sons came to live permanently with her.[27] Each boy would serve their step-father well in a variety of official capacities during the coming years.

Octavian was a man with a vision for the future of Rome, which Livia soon came to share and influence. For a century, Roman politics had been in turmoil. Rivalry between powerful leaders had led to one disastrous civil war after another. Octavian believed that the only way to restore stability to the Roman government was to have all actual power under the control of one man while preserving the outward forms of republicanism. Naturally, he could think of no one better suited to rule under this system than himself. He set about removing his rivals and the political obstacles to his ambitions, relying on the support of his close friend Marcus Vipsanius Agrippa, who possessed the military genius that Octavian lacked.[28]

With Agrippa's defeat of Mark Antony at the battle of Actium in 31 BC, Octavian became the undisputed master of the Roman world. In 27, he was granted all the powers and titles that made his position official. His name even changed. He was no longer called Octavianus; he was Imperator Caesar Augustus.

"Imperator" was the title of a victorious general and is the source of the word "emperor." "Caesar" was the family name inherited from Julius Caesar, though it would become a title for future emperors and princes. "Augustus" meant "sacred" or "revered" and was also used by later emperors. Its feminine form, "Augusta," was bestowed as an honorary title on Roman empresses, beginning with Livia herself (though not during Augustus' lifetime).

Augustus concentrated on consolidating his position and improving the political and social fabric of the empire. He hoped to establish a stable government that would survive long after his death. The army was reformed so that the soldiers owed their allegiance to the emperor rather than to their local commanders.[29] A dramatic beautification of the city of Rome was begun. Augustus would later boast that he found the capital a city of bricks and left it a city of marble, though it is clear that both Livia and Marcus Agrippa had their share in this transformation.[30]

Livia and Augustus wanted to revitalize the ancient traditions of Roman religion and family life and bring about a return to old-fashioned morals and customs.[31] The divorce rate was up and the birth rate was down, particularly among Rome's ruling classes.[32] This meant a decrease in the number of aristocrats to help rule the empire. The emperor and empress were also concerned that a decline in moral behavior was robbing the Roman citizen of the toughness and self-discipline that had made him the master of so much of the known world.[33] They believed that one way to reverse these trends was to make the imperial family a model for all Romans, an example of conservative moderation that others would follow.[34]

Stiff penalties were imposed for adultery.[35] To encourage people to have large families, laws were enacted releasing the mothers of three children or more from the control of their fathers or guardians and giving their husbands special career advantages.[36] Augustus confirmed the traditional view that a woman who never divorced, known as a *univira*, or "woman of one man," was to be respected above her peers. However, widows under 50 were required to remarry within twelve months and divorced women within six months.[37]

Though he was the richest, most powerful man in the empire, Augustus displayed very simple personal tastes, which were mirrored by Livia. He wanted his family to live according to the traditional Roman values of austerity, obedience to the heads of the household, and respectful observance of the state and family religion. He preferred to wear clothes that had been made for him by Livia and the other women of his family from wool they had spun themselves.[38] Rather than move to a sumptuous palace, he and Livia continued to live in a modest house in Rome, which he made state property.[39] (This house, parts of which still survive, was apparently preserved in its original state by the Romans, much as George Washington's home is preserved in the United States today.[40])

Livia became the living symbol of the ideal wife and mother in Augustus' propaganda campaign. This was somewhat ironic as she was not a *univira* herself, having divorced her first husband while she was pregnant. Also, she qualified as an exalted "mother of three" on the technicality of having adopted two of her step-grandsons (Gaius and Lucius, the sons of Julia).

Just as ironic was the fact that Augustus had been married three times, divorced his wife Scribonia the day she gave birth to his only child, and was a habitual womanizer, even while married to Livia.[41] Livia is said to have turned a blind eye to her husband's infidelities.[42] Suetonius even claimed that she procured young girls for him to deflower.[43] However, his ultimate devotion to his wife was never doubted.[44] The fact that Augustus and Livia produced no children would have allowed him to dissolve their union at any time without provoking a scandal. The fact that he did not argues for his genuine affection.[45]

Despite the inconsistencies, Livia was assimilated in official art and propaganda to the goddess Ceres, the Roman symbol of fertility and the ideal womanly virtues of chastity and motherhood. Coins, gems, and statues were produced during and after Livia's lifetime depicting her in the guise of this deity, a connection that was emphasized when Augustus and Livia restored the Temple of Ceres, Liber, and Libera in Rome.[46] Portraits of Livia in the guise of other goddesses, such as Venus, Juno (see Figure 1.11), and Cybele were also displayed.[47]

The elevation of Livia into an icon had begun years before, during the struggle with Mark Antony and Cleopatra.[48] As queen of Ptolemaic Egypt, Cleopatra's position had religious overtones, which included status as a living goddess in the eyes of her people. Augustus could not elevate Livia to deification, but he could not allow his consort to be overshadowed in the propaganda war. Therefore, along with Augustus' sister Octavia, Livia was portrayed with divine associations as the ideal Roman matron. Augustus made the two women sacrosanct in 35 BC, giving them unprecedented independence and immunity from most of the laws that regulated women's public behavior.[49]

Augustus made this move partly so that he could legally wage war against Antony for his mistreatment of Octavia. She had been married to Antony in

40 BC as part of a truce, but had been abandoned in favor of Cleopatra.[50] Augustus granted Livia the same status as Octavia; it would not do for his sister to outrank his wife.

Livia, in particular, took advantage of this freedom to broaden her public activities. She pursued charitable and civic building projects on her own initiative, erecting numerous buildings, many with special significance to Roman women. Examples include public porticoes (covered columnar walk-ways to provide shade), shrines to Concordia (goddess of harmony) and *Pudicitia* (feminine modesty and chastity), and temples to Fortuna Muliebris (womanly fortune) and Bona Dea (a Roman fertility goddess).[51]

In the 20s BC, Augustus visited the far-flung provinces of the empire, touring first Gaul and Spain (27–24) and then the East (22–19). Livia may have accompanied her husband on both of these journeys; it is almost certain that she was with him on the second one.[52] This eastern trip took the imperial party to Sicily, Greece, Asia Minor, and Syria. The travelers stopped at the famous Greek shrine at Delphi, where Livia dedicated a Greek letter *epsilon*, inscribed in gold. The meaning of this gesture is unknown.[53] (Livia's knowledge of Greek was excellent, as shown by an extant letter to her from Augustus with long passages in that language.[54])

Stops were also made at Sparta and the island of Samos. Each of these had special connections with Livia and her family, and each received special privileges at her instigation. Augustus even granted Samos its symbolic freedom and exemption from taxes at his wife's request.[55] In Syria, it is probable that Livia met with her Jewish friends Salome and her brother Herod the Great, king of Judaea and a loyal client of Rome.[56]

During the earlier tour of Spain, Augustus had become seriously ill.[57] He suffered from poor health throughout his life.[58] Livia nursed him through several serious illnesses, including one in 23 BC that almost killed him.[59] He knew that the only way to preserve the peace he had achieved was to establish the right of his heir to rule when he was gone. Unfortunately, Augustus' male relatives had a habit of dying young.

In 25 BC, Augustus married his only child Julia, whose mother Scribonia had been his second wife, to his sister Octavia's son Marcellus. The young man seemed destined to succeed as emperor, but he died suddenly at the age of 20. Augustus promptly married Julia to his old friend Marcus Agrippa, and the couple produced two daughters and three sons. However, Augustus would live to see two of the boys (Gaius and Lucius) die in their twenties and be forced to exile the third (Agrippa Postumus) for outrageously bad behavior.[60]

After Agrippa's death in 12 BC, Julia was married for a third time – to Livia's older son Tiberius, now aged 30. This union was a disaster because Julia and Tiberius, whom Augustus had forced to give up a wife he loved, despised each other.[61] After losing her first husband when she was 16, Julia had been forced to marry a man her father's age, and now she was the wife of a man who loathed her.

Despite Julia's hardships, Livia and Augustus expected her to be a model of filial duty and modesty. After Agrippa's death, however, she broke into open rebellion. Julia had extravagant tastes and desires, as well as interests in literature and art, and she began to gratify them by living the life of a fashionable, wealthy princess.[62] As she put it, "My father may forget that he is Caesar, but I do not forget that I am the daughter of Caesar."[63] Nor is it likely that Julia forgot her father's repudiation of her mother on the day of her birth. This may account in part for their strained relationship.

As the *mater familias* of the imperial family, Livia would have had direct authority over Julia, even when she was married. Certainly there were clashes between the two women, whose tastes and demeanor were so different. The fifth-century author Macrobius describes the contrast in the types of men who accompanied Livia and Julia to a gladiatorial show. Livia's companions were respectable men of mature years, while Julia's were young and "extravagant." When Augustus pointed out the difference to his daughter, she replied that her friends would also be old when she was old.[64]

Augustus disapproved of Julia's vanity and increasingly frivolous lifestyle.[65] It is reported that, when she began to turn prematurely gray, she instructed her servants to pluck out her white hairs. When Augustus learned of this, he asked her, "Would you rather be bald or white-haired?" She replied, "White-haired." "Then why do your servants work so hard to make you bald?"[66]

Augustus also criticized his daughter for keeping company with men of loose morals and questionable politics. Then, in 2 BC, when Julia was 37, he discovered that she had taken lovers among them, though she was still married to Tiberius.[67] Stories circulated about her nocturnal revels when she drank heavily and committed numerous public adulteries in the Roman Forum, even selling sexual favors to strangers.[68]

The emperor was so infuriated by Julia's alleged behavior that he sent her to the tiny Mediterranean island of Pandateria, where she was forced to live in extreme deprivation.[69] Five years later he allowed her to move to a town in Italy, where she was treated less harshly (her mother Scribonia even came there to share her banishment[70]), but she would never return to Rome. Julia died in exile, just weeks after her father.[71]

The reasons for Augustus' severity extend far beyond the moral compunctions of a father. His ability to rule depended on his *auctoritas,* which roughly translates as his personal dignity, reputation, and authority, rather than on constitutionally defined powers. Any embarrassments caused by his family tended to diminish his *auctoritas* and, theoretically, his ability to lead the state.[72]

Despite Augustus' puritanical attitudes, the Romans were anything but bashful when it came to sex. Their homes, gardens, and public places were festooned with erect penises in bronze, stone, paint, and clay.[73] These were considered to be good luck charms. Statues and paintings of gods and humans

11

in the nude abounded in both public and private settings. Prostitution was legal and ubiquitous – even coins depicted naked and ithyphallic deities and scenes of sexual intercourse.

Augustus would not have questioned the sexual frankness of his times; sexual desire was considered sacred, a gift from the gods, and the human form a reflection of divine beauty. He himself was often portrayed as a naked hero in official art. However, he was opposed to licentious behavior and adultery as threats to toughness and the institution of the Roman family.

On Livia's forty-ninth birthday, 30 January, 9 BC, one of the great monuments of Augustan Rome was dedicated – the Ara Pacis Augustae (altar of Augustan Peace). Its decorations celebrated the highest principles of the new order and depicted the imperial family in religious procession, with Livia in a place of honor. The timing was a great tribute to Livia, underscored by the annual celebration of this occasion in years to come.[74]

Also in 9 BC came a personal tragedy for Livia in the loss of her younger son, Drusus, who was adored by the army and popular throughout the empire.[75] He fell from his horse while campaigning against the German tribes and died from his wounds at the age of 29.[76]

In an effort to console the empress, the senate voted to erect statues in her honor, and it was at this time that they enrolled her among the "mothers of three children."[77] At the public ceremonies conducted in Drusus' memory, Livia displayed her usual dignity and composure.[78] However, her stoicism was construed by some as indifference. Drusus was believed to have been in favor of a return to the republican form of government,[79] an attitude of which Livia would not have approved. Still, the author of a poem of consolation to the empress, in sympathy for her loss, refers to Livia's genuine grief.[80]

In fact, Livia was so distraught at the death of her younger son that she turned to the stoic philosopher, Areus Didymus of Alexandria, for consolation.[81] Areus, who was also admired by Augustus, gave advice with a decidedly modern ring to it. He advised Livia to share her feelings about her loss with her friends rather than keep them bottled up inside, to focus on the good memories and listen to the praises of her son's virtues and accomplishments. The somewhat reserved Livia benefited greatly from this counsel and was able to move on.[82] Livia's contemporary, the writer Seneca (born 4 or 5 BC), describes her continuing delight in praising Drusus and in displaying his image after his death, both publicly and privately.[83]

With Drusus' passing, the only remaining qualified candidate for the succession was Tiberius, but his relations with Augustus were not good. In 6 BC, Tiberius actually left Rome and his duties, against Augustus and Livia's wishes, and lived in self-imposed exile on the island of Rhodes.[84] Nevertheless, seven years later, Augustus recalled his 45-year-old stepson to the capital and adopted him as his heir.[85] The emperor was now in his mid-sixties and there was no one else ready to rule.

It must have been difficult for Augustus to settle on Tiberius as his successor. Whether or not the stories of their shared animosity are true, it is clear that Augustus had wanted to bequeath his power to a blood relative. One of the reasons for this was the importance of Julius Caesar. In 42 BC, the Roman senate had declared that Caesar was divine.[86] A temple was built in his honor with an altar in front of it for ritual sacrifices.[87] One of Augustus' most cherished titles was "son of the divine Julius."[88] He wanted his successor to be descended from the Julian clan, which Tiberius was not, and to share the blood of a "divine" predecessor.

It may seem strange that the Romans could conceive of a mortal man as being divine. The pharaohs of ancient Egypt had been worshiped as gods, and so had many Hellenistic kings and queens, starting with Alexander the Great and including Cleopatra. However, no recent Roman leader had received this honor. Still, many Romans believed that men had become gods in the past, such as Romulus, the founder of Rome, and Hercules. According to one popular theory (euhemerism), all of the traditional gods had originally been kings and heroes. It seemed possible that contemporary heroes, like Julius Caesar, could follow in their footsteps.

The Romans were accustomed to the idea that all men and women had a spark of divinity in them. Every man was believed to have a divine double, known as a *genius*, which was like a guardian angel. Similarly, each woman had her god-like counterpart, known as her *juno*.[89] One of the most important rituals of the Roman household was the worship of the *genius* of the *pater familias*.[90]

The concept of the divinity of Julius Caesar was something more than this, however. Some believed that he had joined the gods and goddesses in their heavenly realm and could intercede on behalf of his worshipers. If Augustus could convince the people of Rome that Caesar's divinity could be passed on in some way to his relatives, then they might be reluctant to accept a ruler who did not share his blood. However, the untimely deaths of all of the candidates from Augustus' family cancelled these ambitions. Nevertheless, Augustus' hope that the *genius* of the emperor would come to be worshiped by his subjects, as if all were members of his household, was realized.[91] Furthermore, the cults of deified emperors and empresses remained prominent in the religious life of the empire for the next three centuries.

Livia's role in Augustus' choice of a successor is not clear. She does seem to have persuaded Augustus to recall her son from his voluntary exile in Rhodes and may have begged him to adopt Tiberius as his heir.[92] There was gossip that she was so anxious to see Tiberius succeed her husband that she was responsible for the deaths of Marcellus and Augustus' two grandsons, Gaius and Lucius, as well as for the disgrace and eventual death of their brother, Agrippa Postumus.[93]

Years later, as we shall see in Chapter 3, Livia was also blamed by some for the death of another grandson, the popular prince Germanicus, allegedly removed because of his republican sympathies.[94] It was even whispered, after Augustus' death, that she had poisoned her husband with a fig.[95] Livia's grandson, the emperor Caligula, supposedly called her "Ulysses in a *stola* [woman's garment],"[96] alluding to her cunning and unscrupulous nature.

Most modern scholars dismiss the accusations of Livia's murderous intrigues for lack of reliable evidence.[97] The historians who recorded the charges were clearly biased against her. Tacitus, the main source of these allegations, nursed an intense hatred for Livia and Tiberius, even though he was born years after they had died. He called Livia a bully and a disaster for the nation and the family of the Caesars.[98] The other principal historian of this period, Suetonius, was all too ready to record any scandal or rumor, without much regard for its accuracy. Relying on these accounts would be like basing the study of a modern head of state on the claims of his or her political opponents, or on reports in tabloid newspapers.

In fact, the early deaths of so many members of the imperial family need not seem suspicious. Death of the young was a painfully common occurrence in Roman times. It is believed that the average life expectancy was only about 25–30 years, and that a 15-year-old Roman had about a 50–50 chance of living to be 25.[99] A study of funerary inscriptions in the Roman port city of Ostia, near Rome, suggests that only 20 percent of the population reached the age of 30.[100] The third-century Roman historian Cassius Dio, who records the rumor of Livia's role in the death of Marcellus, also points out in Livia's defense that a great many people died that same year because of unusually unhealthy conditions.[101]

Cassius Dio gives further evidence of a tradition that was favorable to Livia. He presents an extended conversation between Livia and Augustus (which was also referred to by Seneca[102]) in which she persuades her husband to be merciful to his enemies after an unsuccessful plot to assassinate him. While this dialogue may be a fabrication, it does show that history remembered a somewhat different Livia than the ruthless murderess described by Tacitus.

In Dio's account, Livia displays compassion, remarkable wisdom, and acute political insight. Some of the things that he has Livia say to her husband may be surprising:

> It is my opinion that many more wrongs can be corrected through kindness than through severity . . . Augustus, you should do more than just avoid acting unjustly; you should avoid the very *suspicion* of acting unjustly . . . Though a man can be made to fear another man, he should be made to love him instead . . . The highest glory is attained by being able to save all citizens, if possible, rather than by putting many of them to death.[103]

Whether or not these or similar words were ever actually spoken by Livia, it is significant that, nearly two centuries after her death, she was believed to have been capable of such thoughts. As it happened, Augustus took Livia's advice and pardoned the conspirators, even awarding their leader the consulship, and Livia was credited with having saved their lives.[104] Livia's contemporary, Velleius Paterculus, stated that she used her power only to protect and honor her subjects.[105]

Her wealth, power, and influence as empress and first lady of the Roman state were astonishing. Livia's personal staff consisted of over 1,000 slaves, agents, and functionaries.[106] She owned extensive properties in Italy and in provinces such as Egypt, Gaul, Sicily, Asia Minor, and Palestine.[107] She was given the right to erect statues of herself anywhere in the empire, many examples of which survive today, and a precinct of the city of Rome was named in her honor.[108] She received foreign embassies, commissioned the building of shrines, temples, and other public buildings (as we have seen), patronized the arts, gave public feasts, sponsored charities, and interceded on behalf of troubled cities and individuals in the interests of justice and mercy.[109] She was praised for supporting many children who had no one to look after them, and for providing destitute women with dowries.[110]

Among Livia's beneficiaries were the Vestal Virgins, in whom she had a special interest, even to the point of joining them in the performance of sacrifices.[111] The Vestals were a college of six celibate monastic priestesses of the goddess Vesta. They were enrolled before puberty for a period of thirty years and treated with the highest respect. It was believed that the welfare of the Roman state depended on their sanctity.

The Vestals were charged with tending a perpetual fire in the temple of the goddess, and engaged in special rituals and sacrifices. They enjoyed unusual privileges, including financial autonomy (unlike other women, they could make their own wills) and special seats at public events. If a Vestal encountered a condemned criminal, she had the right to commute his sentence.[112]

When Livia ventured out in public, it was in a *carpentum* (see Figure 1.17), a richly decorated ceremonial carriage, and she was permitted to sit in the seats reserved for the Vestal Virgins at public performances.[113] Livia's forbearance and dignity are illustrated by the story of a group of men who were condemned to death for appearing naked in her presence. She pardoned them, saying that, to a chaste woman like herself, such men seemed no more than statues.[114] Indeed, her contemporary Valerius Maximus praised her chastity and wrote of her "most holy marriage bed."[115]

Partly because of Livia's role as an icon for Augustus' social agenda, it is difficult to get a clear impression of the person behind the image. She was described as being more god-like than human in everything she did.[116] Her portraits show a reserved, serenely beautiful woman. She wore her hair in a variety of simple styles, inspired by classical Greek models. One of these is known as the "*nodus*" hairdo, characterized by an oval "bun" of hair gathered above the forehead.[117]

15

The Roman poet Ovid remarked that Livia was too busy to spend much time on her personal appearance.[118] While it is true that she generally appears simply dressed and without jewelry in most of her portraits, it is recorded that a large retinue of personal assistants were charged with attending to her person. These included hairdressers, keepers of her wardrobe, personal jewelers, a cobbler, and a masseuse.[119]

Certainly, Livia was accomplished and dignified, wise in the ways of state-craft and conscientious in the performance of her duties, public and private. Herod Agrippa, the great-nephew of Herod the Great and close friend of the future Roman emperors Caligula and Claudius, described Livia as being mentally gifted and extremely well educated.[120] Livia's control of her emotions was shown by her public composure after the loss of many family members, especially that of her son Drusus. Seneca described Livia as a woman who knew her own mind and was not easily swayed in her opin-ions.[121] He also wrote that she took special care to protect her reputation.[122]

Personal warmth, perhaps, is the quality least associated with Livia, though even Tacitus allowed that her graciousness in private life exceeded the norm.[123] Her affection for her family may be glimpsed in the tenderness of her relationship with Augustus, especially her patient nursing of him during his many illnesses.[124] She did what she could to relieve the sufferings of Julia's daughter (named Julia like her mother), who was also exiled by Augustus for adultery, and it is even possible that she assisted Julia herself.[125] When a favored great-grandson died in early childhood, Livia dedicated a statue of him dressed as a cupid to Venus, the goddess of love.[126] These stories may be contrasted, however, with Suetonius' claim that she treated her grandson Claudius, who was afflicted with some debilitating malady that affected his speech and movements, with scornful and unrelenting abuse.[127]

Livia had several close woman friends, some of whom benefited from her interventions when they or their husbands were in legal trouble. Her friend Urgulania, whose granddaughter was married to Livia's grandson Claudius, was said by Tacitus to be virtually above the law because of Livia's protec-tion. On one occasion, Urgulania ignored a legal summons and was supported in her defiance by the empress.[128] A woman named Plancina, who was impli-cated in the death of Germanicus, relied on her friendship with Livia to avoid punishment, which came only after her benefactress had died.[129] Within her own family, Livia enjoyed an especially close relationship with her daughter-in-law Antonia, the wife of Drusus. The two women continued to share a home for thirty-seven years after his death.[130]

At the time of his passing at age 75 on 19 August, AD 14, Augustus and Livia had been married for fifty-one years. His last words were spoken to her: "Never forget the happiness of our married life. Farewell!"[131] Augustus was given a magnificent state funeral, with unprecedented honors, culminating in a public cremation on the Campus Martius (or "Field of Mars"), a grassy field along the Tiber River in Rome.[132] Livia remained at the site of the funeral pyre for five full days, after which she gathered his bones and placed them in the same mausoleum (in ruins today) in which she would eventually be laid to rest.[133] After this, Livia held a three-day festival at her home on the Palatine Hill in Rome in honor of Augustus, an event that would be commemorated by subsequent emperors.[134]

Though his social policies had not been very successful, Augustus had restored order to Roman political life. His reign of forty-four years marked the beginning of a prolonged period of peace and prosperity, such as the Mediterranean countries have not seen since. Like Julius Caesar, Augustus was deified after his death.[135] Livia commissioned the building of the Temple of the Divine Augustus and assumed the role of priestess to her dead husband's spirit.[136] She also awarded a man who swore he had seen Augustus ascending to heaven the sum of 1 million sesterces (a very considerable sum – a Roman legionary only made 900 sesterces per year at this time).[137]

In his will, Augustus bequeathed even more of his wealth to Livia than the law allowed and adopted her into his own clan, giving her the name "Julia Augusta."[138] Tiberius was named as his successor and lived to rule for twenty-three years.

To see her son take Augustus' place must have been very gratifying to Livia. However, the historians tell us that her relationship with Tiberius deteriorated during the last few years of her life. When he left Rome for good in AD 26 to live in his lavish villa on the island of Capri near Naples, gossip spread that he had gone there to escape his nagging mother.[139]

Cassius Dio states that Livia openly claimed credit for her son's accession to the throne and sometimes behaved as if she had a full share in his power. The historian tells us that state documents were addressed to them jointly, and that, early in his reign, Tiberius' official correspondence bore his mother's name as well as his own.[140] The 55-year-old Tiberius resented these signs of his dependence on Livia. He reacted by limiting her role in public affairs and denying many of the senate's requests to honor her.[141] One of these must have been especially galling to him: they wanted to give Tiberius the official title "Son of Livia." [142]

Suetonius gives a vivid account of the bad feelings between Livia and the new emperor. He claims that, when Livia pressed Tiberius to make an appointment she favored, he agreed on the condition that the official records would show that he was forced to do so by his mother. She supposedly retaliated by threatening to expose letters from Augustus that revealed his dislike of Tiberius.[143]

Suetonius also writes of Livia's display of competence and courage when a fire broke out near the Temple of Vesta in Rome. She took it upon herself to direct and encourage the firefighters, with a degree of self-assertion that supposedly offended Tiberius. It was said that she was acting as if Augustus was still alive.[144] However, as Tiberius remained unmarried, Livia seems justified in continuing to perform the role of empress.

Despite these reported squabbles, Livia did retain the vast wealth she had inherited from Augustus and continued to wield enormous power from behind the scenes. She was respected and revered by the people of the empire, if not truly loved, and came to be known as *mater patriae*, or "mother of the fatherland," though Tiberius rejected the senate's attempt to make this title official.[145] After she nearly died from an illness in AD 22, he issued a coin bearing her image – something Augustus had never done (see Figure 1.19).[146] She was depicted on this coin as the personification of health (the goddess Salus), apparently celebrating her recovery.[147] Also, the senate decreed official prayers and ceremonies in hopes of speeding her return to health.[148] These honors, plus his haste to attend her sickbed, suggest that Tiberius still felt affection for his mother.[149]

We can get a glimpse of Livia's domestic world from the remnants of the places where she lived. Besides her home on the Palatine, which was decorated with stately *trompe-l'œil* architectural fantasies similar to those found in the buried city of Pompeii, she owned a villa at Prima Porto, nine miles from the capital.[150] Its contents included a magnificent marble statue of Augustus, which is believed to have kept the widowed Livia company in her old age.[151] Also surviving is a mural of a charming garden filled with birds, fruits, and trees, and with mountains looming in the distance. The mood of this painting, and the rural setting of the villa, suggests that Livia came here to escape the tumult and complexity of life in Rome.[152]

The painted greenery in Livia's villa also reflects her keen interest in horticulture. She was credited with having developed her own variety of fig, named "Liviana" in her honor.[153] In addition, a type of papyrus plant in Egypt was named for her,[154] and there was a famous story about her laurel grove at Prima Porto. It was said to have begun with a sprig from the beak of a white chick that fell into her lap from the talons of an eagle. Livia planted the sprig (and raised the chick), and her laurel bushes eventually produced all the wreaths worn by victorious generals during their triumphal processions through the streets of Rome.[155]

Livia was also interested in the medicinal properties of plants, and in health remedies and healthy living in general. Her knowledge of natural remedies was encyclopedic, and two of her recipes for herbal medicine were still in use four centuries after her death.[156] She adhered to a careful diet that featured the exclusive intake of wine from a particular rocky hill in Pucinum, on the Gulf of Trieste.[157]

Among Livia's domestic companions was a female dwarf named Andromeda. Pliny the Elder tells us that she competed with Augustus' granddaughter Julia for the privilege of having the smallest dwarf then known, a distinction Julia seems to have won with the male Conopas, whose height was two feet five inches (0.74 meters).[158]

The famous statue of Augustus from Prima Porto depicts him as a young man in full vigor, as he is shown in nearly all of his portraits produced both during and after his lifetime. Similarly, Livia is almost always portrayed as the young, beautiful, somewhat aloof symbol of perfect Roman womanhood, without a hint of advancing age.[159] This was a significant departure from the tradition of Roman portraiture, which was characterized by unflinching realism. Augustus chose to have the members of his family portrayed in an idealizing classical style like that favored by the royal houses of the Greek East. Apparently, the importance of the first imperial couple as icons for Roman society demanded that they appear to possess god-like beauty that did not decay, at least in official art. This idealization of rulers continued under Tiberius but broke down under subsequent emperors, most of whom were content to be portrayed with all their warts and wrinkles.

When Livia died in AD 29, aged 86,[160] youthful statues of her were in every town and city in the Roman world. The senate decreed that the women of the empire should observe a special period of mourning for her.[161] They also voted to erect an arch in her memory – a high honor never before given to a woman.[162] Unfortunately, Tiberius volunteered to pay for the arch himself, with the result that it was never built.[163] In fact, Suetonius claims that Tiberius only visited his mother once in the last three years of her life, did not attend her funeral, refused to allow her deification, saying that he was obeying her own wishes, and then, without acknowledging the contradiction, annulled her will.[164]

However, many of the honors denied by Tiberius were bestowed on Livia in later years. Her will was reinstated in AD 37 by her great-grandson, the emperor Caligula, who had delivered her funeral oration at the age of 17.[165] In 42, her grandson the emperor Claudius had Livia proclaimed to be divine, as Julius Caesar and Augustus had been after their deaths, and decreed that women should use her name when taking oaths.[166] Livia's statue was placed beside that of her husband in the Temple of Augustus, where the people paid homage to the deified Augusta, first empress of Rome (see Figure 1.22).[167]

By defining the role of a Roman empress through her actions and demeanor, Livia became the model for all of her successors. She established precedents for the exercise of considerable power and influence, based on the combination of enormous personal wealth and an exalted status that put her above the law.

Perhaps the most surprising example set by Livia, which was emulated with varying degrees of success by later empresses, was the prerogative to act on her own initiative. Freed from the control of a husband or guardian, she conducted business and diplomacy and exercised her patronage as she saw fit. It was within the sphere of a Roman *mater familias* to promote the careers and well-being of her dependants, to embellish the beauty and comfort of her home, and to support and encourage its religious observances. Livia fulfilled these duties in the time-honored tradition, both within her family and in the public arena. Her autonomy, in conjunction with her wealth and prestige, made Livia a force to be reckoned with.

It is interesting to note that Livia's ascendancy and the increased importance of women in Roman political life after her were to some extent the legacy of Cleopatra.[168] We have seen that Augustus' grant of sacrosanct status to Livia in 35 BC was the indirect result of his power struggle with the Egyptian queen and Mark Antony.[169] Augustus' conquest of Egypt brought him the wealth he needed to remodel the Roman state according to his vision.[170]

With the acquisition of Cleopatra's world came a greater familiarity with the Greek and oriental traditions of semi-divine rulers and the exercise of power by royal women. This influence would continue to grow in the coming years, during which three emperors (Caligula, Claudius, and Nero) and three Augustas (Antonia, Agrippina the Younger, and Nero's first wife Octavia), plus the empress Messalina, could trace their lineage directly to Mark Antony.

As much as Tiberius resented it, the imperial authority did reside in Livia's person and reputation. His rule *was* to an extent her gift, not only because of her influence over Augustus in his choice of successor but also because of her preeminence as the symbol of continuity for the new order he had established. Roman emperors were very concerned about what sort of men the women of their family married because a connection with a Roman princess was sufficient to make them potential rivals for the throne. This political potency of women was completely alien to the Romans before the remarkable career of Livia.

Figure 1.2 Lifetime portrait coin of Julius Caesar. Silver denarius, minted 43 BC, L. Flaminius Chilo, moneyer. RSC 26; courtesy Classical Numismatic Group, Inc.

Figure 1.3 Portrait coin of the young Octavian, later known as the emperor Augustus. Silver denarius, minted *c.* 30–27 BC. RIC I 271, BMCRE 633, RSC 124; courtesy Classical Numismatic Group, Inc.

Figure 1.4 Silver denarius of Mark Antony, minted in 41 BC. Crawford 517/2, Sydenham 1181, Sear 243, RSC 8; courtesy Classical Numismatic Group, Inc.

Figure 1.5 Portrait coin of Cleopatra VII, queen of Ptolemaic Egypt and consort of Julius Caesar and, later, Mark Antony. Bronze 80 drachmae, minted *c.* 51–30 BC. Svoronos 1871, SNG Copenhagen 419; courtesy Classical Numismatic Group, Inc.

Figure 1.6 Livia's elder son Tiberius as emperor on a silver denarius minted *c.* AD 14–37. RIC I 30, RSC 16a; courtesy Classical Numismatic Group, Inc.

Figure 1.7 Nero Claudius Drusus, the younger son of Livia. Gold aureus minted under Claudius, *c.* AD 41–42. RIC I 73 (Claudius), BMCRE 104 (Claudius), Cohen 5; courtesy Classical Numismatic Group, Inc.

Figure 1.8 (Left, obverse) Portraits of Augustus (right) and Marcus Agrippa (left) on a copper as or dupondius, minted in Nemausus, Gaul (Nîmes, France), *c.* 9–3 BC. This coin commemorates the capture of Egypt, symbolized by the chained crocodile on the reverse (right). RIC I 161, RPC 525; courtesy Classical Numismatic Group, Inc.

Figure 1.9 Copper coin (as) of the deified Augustus, minted posthumously under Tiberius, *c.* AD 31–37. RIC I 81 (Tiberius), Cohen 228, BMCRE 146 (Tiberius); courtesy Classical Numismatic Group, Inc.

Figure 1.10 Provincial portrait of Livia with a crescent moon above her head and a globe beneath her neck. Bronze dupondius minted in Colonia Romula (Seville, Spain) under Tiberius, *c.* AD 14–15. RPC 73; courtesy Edward J. Waddell, Ltd.

Figure 1.11 Livia as the Greek goddess Hera (Roman Juno), holding grain ears and poppies. A silver tetradrachm, minted in Tarsus, Cilicia, under Tiberius, *c.* AD 14–37. Prieur 749, RPC I 4005, Cohen 15; courtesy Classical Numismatic Group, Inc.

Figure 1.12 Octavian's sister Octavia with her husband Mark Antony. A silver cistophoric tetradrachm, minted in Ephesus, 39 BC. RPC 2202, RSC 3, Sydenham 1198; courtesy Numismatik Lanz München.

Figure 1.13 The goddess Diana, possibly with the features of Augustus' daughter Julia. Silver denarius minted 13 BC. RIC I 403, BMCRE 104, RSC 1; courtesy Freeman and Sear.

Figure 1.14 Julia's second husband, Marcus Agrippa. Copper as, minted under Agrippa's grandson Caligula, *c.* AD 37–41. RIC I 58 (Gaius), BMCRE 161 (Tiberius), Cohen 3; courtesy Classical Numismatic Group, Inc.

Figure 1.15 Julia, Augustus' daughter, with her sons, Gaius (right) and Lucius (left). Silver denarius minted *c.* 13 BC. RIC I 405, BMCRE 108; courtesy Edward J. Waddell, Ltd.

Figure 1.16 Augustus (center) with his grandsons, Gaius and Lucius. Bronze dupondius, minted in Caesaraugusta, Tarraconensis (Spain), *c.* 4–3 BC. Cf. RPC 319; courtesy Italo Vecchi.

Figure 1.17 Livia's ceremonial carriage, or *carpentum*, drawn by two mules. Bronze sestertius, minted under Tiberius, *c.* AD 22–23. RIC I 51 (Tiberius), BMCRE 76 (Tiberius), Cohen 6; courtesy Classical Numismatic Group, Inc.

Figure 1.18 Tiberius as emperor, seated on a curule chair, holding a *patera* (offering bowl) and scepter. Bronze sestertius, commemorating the restoration of cities after an earthquake in Asia Minor in AD 17, minted *c.* AD 22–23. RIC I 48, BMCRE 70, Cohen 3; courtesy Freeman and Sear.

Figure 1.19 Detailed portrait coin of Livia, probably commemorating her recovery from serious illness in AD 22. Bronze dupondius, minted under Tiberius, *c.* AD 22–23. RIC I 47 (Tiberius), BMCRE 82 (Tiberius), Cohen 5; courtesy Italo Vecchi.

Figure 1.20 Portrait of Livia on a provincial bronze coin (diameter 27 mm) minted in Augusta, Cilicia, under Tiberius, *c.* AD 14–37. The coin's legend is in Greek. RPC 4006, SNG Levante 1240, SNG von Aulock 5533; courtesy Classical Numismatic Group, Inc.

Figure 1.21 The deified Livia as Pax (Peace) on a bronze dupondius minted under Claudius, *c.* AD 41–42. RIC I 101 (Claudius), BMCRE 224 (Claudius), Cohen 93; courtesy Classical Numismatic Group, Inc.

Figure 1.22 Statues of the deified Livia and Augustus in their temple as depicted on a bronze sestertius, minted by Antoninus Pius (reigned AD 138–161), *c.* AD 157–158. RIC III 978, Cohen 803; courtesy Classical Numismatic Group, Inc.

Figure 2.1 Portrait adapted by the author from a statue found near Baiae showing Antonia as Venus, now in the Baia Museo, Baia, Italy. The coin is a bronze dupondius, minted by her son, Claudius (see Figure 2.5 for similar specimens). Antonia is shown by a road in the outskirts of Rome, which is lined with tombs. This signifies her devotion to the memory of her husband Drusus.

2

ANTONIA

"Supreme in beauty and mind"

Despite the scandals and tragedies that afflicted Augustus' household, it produced some of the most accomplished and respected personalities in Roman history. None of them were more distinguished than Antonia Minor, the younger of the two daughters of Augustus' older sister Octavia and his rival Mark Antony (Marcus Antonius).

The second-century Roman biographer Plutarch tells us that Antonia's mother Octavia possessed exceptional beauty and virtue and was much loved by Augustus.[1] His affection, however, did not stop him from using her as a pawn in his power games.

Octavia was married to Antony in 40 BC, within months of the death of her first husband Marcellus, with whom she had three children.[2] Octavia seems to have been a willing participant in this union, however, even working to reconcile her brother and new husband when their uneasy truce unraveled in 37 BC.[3] On his part, Antony honored Octavia by issuing numerous coins bearing her portrait (see Figure 2.3).[4]

Mark Antony was one of the most fascinating, larger-than-life personalities of his time. Famous as the handsome, extroverted general who became the captive of Cleopatra and the victim of his own vices, Antony was much more.[5] A competent soldier, adored by his troops for his courage, affability, and generosity, he was also an orator and a patron of the arts.[6] Julius Caesar valued his gifts so highly that he made him his spokesman in Rome during his prolonged absences from the capital.[7] When Caesar was killed, Antony's was a voice of moderation, even calling for an amnesty for the conspirators.[8] Despite his eventual defeat and humiliation by Octavian, Mark Antony remained an admired figure in Roman history, particularly in the eastern parts of the empire where he had held sway.

Octavia was admired for her loyalty to Antony despite his mistreatment of her. Even after her husband had married Cleopatra (a union not recognized by Roman law as she was not a Roman citizen), Octavia attempted to join him in the East, bringing gifts of troops and gold. A message from Antony intercepted her *en route*, accepting the gifts but instructing Octavia to return to Rome.[9] This snub outraged the Roman people and was exploited by Octavian in order to swing public opinion in his favor.[10] After Antony's death, Octavia further demonstrated her devotion to him, as well as her personal warmth and compassion, by assuming responsibility for raising his children by two of his former wives: Fulvia (who had died in 40 BC – see Figure 2.4) and Cleopatra herself.[11]

Marcia Antonia, named after her father (as was customary for Roman girls), was born on 31 January, 36 BC, three years after her sister of the same name. She never met Antony, who had left her mother for Cleopatra before she was even born. After being formally divorced in 32 BC, Octavia moved with her children into the household of Augustus and Livia, which already included Livia's sons from her first marriage, Tiberius, aged nine, and the five-year-old Drusus.[12]

Octavia and Augustus' wife Livia arranged for the education and betrothals of their swarm of royal offspring. Famous scholars were recruited to train them, both boys and girls, and most of the children were paired off for marriage within the extended royal family.[13] Their choice for Antonia was Livia's younger son, Drusus, whom she would marry in 18 BC when she was 18 and he was 20.[14]

Living together in the imperial household and knowing from an early age that they were destined for each other may have prepared the couple for a successful married life. Unlike most of the arranged marriages of the imperial family, the union of Antonia and Drusus survived and became legendary for its harmony, happiness, and fidelity.[15]

Another significant imperial marriage was that of Augustus' only child Julia to Antonia's older half-brother Marcellus. However, he died of fever (23 BC) at the age of only 20.[16] His mother Octavia abandoned herself to grief. She wore mourning clothes for the remaining twelve years of her life and spent long periods shut up in her darkened room. She couldn't even bear to hear her son's name mentioned or to see his portrait.[17] When the Roman poet Virgil mentioned the name "Marcellus" during a reading of the *Aeneid,* his epic poem about Rome's beginnings, Octavia was so overcome by emotion that she fainted away.[18] The spectacle of her mother's despair must have had a profound impact on the 13-year-old Antonia. Subsequent events would show that she inherited Octavia's intense family loyalty and highly emotional attachment to her loved ones.

The princesses of Rome, like princesses everywhere, were called beautiful almost as a matter of course. In the case of Antonia, however, the praise seems to have been warranted. The Greek poet Crinagoras called her "supreme in beauty and mind."[19] The Greek biographer Plutarch also celebrated her beauty and discretion, and the Jewish historian Josephus praised her chastity.[20] Pliny the Elder (born AD 23) said that her manners were so gentle and refined that even spitting was against her nature, and Valerius Maximus wrote that her "feminine merits" exceeded the "manly fame of her family," which was considerable.[21]

Antonia's statues and coin portraits (see Figures 2.1, 2.5) suggest a forbearing but firm temperament, a keen intellect, and a classic beauty, with large eyes, long straight nose, and a strong chin. She wore her hair in a very simple style, parted in the middle and with a queue in the back, which set off her striking features. While most of her portraits show her in idealized youthfulness, there are some that may document her appearance in later life. One sculpture that is tentatively identified as Antonia portrays an alert-looking elderly woman with pleasant features and a regal air.[22] There is some evidence that Antonia suffered from poor health, but she lived to a very good age for her time – 72 years.[23]

Antonia's husband Drusus was energetic and charismatic, and devoted to her.[24] His portraits suggest a robust, determined but agreeable sort of man. It is no surprise that he and his noble bride captured the imagination of Roman society. The idyllic wedding of the charming couple, which took place near Antonia's birthday, was even celebrated in poetry. The following is by Crinagoras:

> Roses once bloomed in spring; now our red buds burst open in winter, smiling brightly on the morning of your birth, so near your wedding – to grace the brow of the fairest of women is better than to wait for the sunshine of spring.[25]

We do not know how many children Drusus and Antonia had (the historian Suetonius says "several"), only that their first died in infancy and that three lived to adulthood.[26] These were the gifted and popular Germanicus, born in 15 BC; a daughter named Livilla, born a couple of years later; and the future Roman emperor Claudius, born in the province of Gaul in 10 BC.[27]

Duty called Drusus to command Roman armies in the field, and he was away at the wars much of the time from 15 BC on. He was a resourceful, adventurous general who, in tandem with his brother Tiberius, conquered the Alps and extended Roman control over many of the German tribes that threatened the empire's northwestern frontiers.[28] His courage in battle sometimes approached recklessness; he would put himself at risk by chasing after the enemy commander, trying to lure him into single combat.[29] Suetonius claims that Drusus was the first Roman general to sail the North Sea.[30]

According to ancient sources, Drusus also lived dangerously in his political views.[31] It was common knowledge that he favored a return to the republican form of government.[32] On one occasion, Drusus reportedly wrote to his brother Tiberius urging him to help persuade Augustus to renounce his powers and restore the republic.[33] Drusus is said to have openly proclaimed his intention to do precisely that should he ever come to power.[34] Though these attitudes might have alienated him from Augustus, his services to Rome were so great – and his personal qualities so excellent – that, to his credit, the emperor tolerated his opinions and felt much affection for his stepson.[35]

Antonia seems to have accompanied her husband on at least some of his assignments. We know that they were together in Gaul in 10 BC when Drusus was governor of that province because Antonia's son Claudius was born in the capital city of Lugdunum (modern Lyons, France).[36] However, Drusus spent much of his time fighting Germans in enemy territory, leaving Antonia behind.

In 9 BC, after his army had penetrated more deeply into German territory than ever before, Drusus fell from his horse and broke his leg.[37] The injured hero was taken to his army's summer camp, where his condition worsened. When news of Drusus' accident reached Rome, his brother Tiberius covered the 200 miles (320 km) to be with him in only 24 hours.[38] For thirty days after his fall, the 29-year-old general lived on while his countrymen prayed and sacrificed in vain for his recovery. Tiberius caught his dying breath and, walking the entire distance, accompanied his brother's body to Rome.[39] It was cremated in a public ceremony on the Campus Martius, and Drusus' ashes were interred in the mausoleum that had been built for Augustus and the members of his family.[40]

The circumstances of Drusus' death, as reported by the third-century historian Cassius Dio, are full of supernatural overtones. In Dio's version, Drusus died from a disease rather than an injury. Before his fatal illness, while pressing deep into Germany, an apparition in the form of a giant woman visited him and advised him to turn back. He heeded her warning, but soon became sick. Further apparitions haunted his camp (two youths on horseback and shooting stars), as well as the sounds of howling wolves and mourning women.[41]

It was customary for Roman historians to record (or invent) portents of the demise of Roman leaders, so Dio's tale, though unusually harrowing, was probably a later invention. However, if such stories circulated at the time of Drusus' death, they might have been very upsetting to the members of his family. Drusus' son Germanicus, who was only six at the time, was later known for his interest in the occult (he translated a Greek work on astrology into Latin[42]), and his own passing was accompanied by signs and omens and the suspicion of witchcraft.[43]

Tiberius was devoted to his brother and gave an oration at his funeral, as did Augustus.[44] The emperor also composed Drusus' epitaph and even wrote a biography of him.[45] Drusus was widely loved and admired and would be remembered long after his passing.

In her grief, Antonia took after her mother, who had died two years before in 11 BC. The Roman poet Ovid tells us that the 27-year-old Antonia screamed in agony like a madwoman, tore at her hair, even attempted suicide.[46] Despite her youth and pressure from Augustus, whose social

28

legislation required widows to remarry, Antonia refused to take another husband.[47] She was a true *univira* – a "one-man woman." Indeed, she lived for the remaining forty-five years of her life in the very same quarters at Livia's house that she had shared with Drusus.[48]

However, Antonia did not withdraw from the world as her mother had done. She had three young children to raise and had inherited from her parents and husband enormous wealth, which made her the second richest woman in the empire after Livia.[49]

Augustus had allowed Antonia and her sister to inherit much of their father's wealth.[50] They also retained many of his contacts, particularly in the provinces and client kingdoms of the East.[51] She owned extensive real estate in several places, especially Egypt, where her holdings included vineyards, palm groves, pastures for sheep and goats, even a fleet of fishing boats.[52] With these assets came tremendous responsibilities, and Antonia was one of the most responsible people in Rome.

When she wanted a holiday from her busy life in the capital, Antonia often stayed at her villa at Bauli in Campania, two days away on the magnificent Bay of Baiae near Naples. It was there that she kept her pet fish, a lamprey to which she was so devoted that she had earrings made for it.[53] This fish became famous and attracted crowds of sightseers.[54] (Antonia's luxurious villa later became the property of her granddaughter, Agrippina the Younger, the mother of the emperor Nero, who was murdered there by her son's agents in AD 59[55] – see Chapter 4.)

Each of Antonia's three surviving children grew up to play an important role in Roman history. Her elder son Germanicus, who married Augustus' granddaughter Agrippina, followed in his father's footsteps as a daring and successful general and became even more popular with the Roman people. Augustus regarded him so highly that, when he designated Tiberius as his heir, he compelled him to adopt Germanicus and place him next in line to the throne, though Tiberius had a grown son of his own.[56]

Antonia's daughter Livilla was first married to Gaius, the grandson of Augustus, who died in AD 4, and then to Tiberius' son, Drusus the Younger. Tacitus informs us that Livilla was unattractive as a child, but became a great beauty as a grown woman.[57] She and Drusus had a daughter and, in AD 19, Livilla gave birth to twin sons – an event that was commemorated on coins (see Figure 2.13).[58] She also left another, infamous mark on history, as we shall see.

Antonia's youngest child Claudius was afflicted with a serious ailment that affected his speech, walking, and general demeanor. He stammered when he talked and dragged his right foot when he walked. His head and hands shook slightly and his nose ran when he was angry.[59] Obviously, he was not what Augustus had in mind for an imperial role model, so Claudius was kept out of public view and did not pursue a public career.

The ancient historians praised Antonia for her gentleness and compassion, but these qualities were apparently not always in evidence where Claudius was concerned. She is said to have called him "a monster of a man, whom Nature began but left unfinished."[60] Her standard insult for stupidity was to call someone "even more of a fool than my son Claudius."[61]

Despite Antonia's remarks, there is evidence of her concern for her son. When Claudius, who was a historian and scholar of considerable ability, decided to write a history of Rome, his mother (as well as his grandmother Livia) warned him to skip over controversial periods in Augustus' early career, probably saving him from getting into trouble.[62]

As the mother of three children, under Augustus' new legislation, Antonia was free to administer her affairs without the need for a male guardian. The way in which she handled the duties and opportunities that her position gave her left a profound mark on the future. Her contacts throughout the ancient world made her one of the most important people of her time. She had very close connections with the Jewish elite of Egyptian Alexandria, and with the client kingdoms of Palestine and African Mauretania (the latter through its queen, her half-sister Cleopatra Selene, the daughter of Mark Antony and Cleopatra).[63]

Antonia also raised and supervised the education of numerous foreign princes and princesses who were sent or brought to Rome from places such as Judaea, Thrace, Commagene, Mauretania, even Rome's arch-enemy Parthia.[64] She Romanized her royal charges, and they took her influence and their loyalty to her and to Rome back to their countries when they were grown. Prime examples were the three young sons of the Thracian king Cotys – Rhoemetalces, Polemo, and Cotys II – who were sent to Antonia after their father's murder. They eventually grew up to rule Thrace, Pontus and the Bosphorus, and Armenia Minor, respectively.[65]

Several prominent Romans also benefited from Antonia's patronage, including the senators Valerius Asiaticus and Lucius Vitellius.[66] Asiaticus was of German extraction and may have known Antonia when she was staying with her husband in the north. He rose to be consul and provincial governor before succumbing to the empress Messalina in AD 47.[67] Lucius Vitellius served as consul three times as well as being governor of Syria. When Claudius went to Britain to oversee its conquest, he left Lucius in charge of affairs in Rome.[68] Vitellius' son Aulus even enjoyed a brief reign as emperor in 69 after the death of Nero.

Antonia was nearly 50 in AD 14 when her uncle Augustus died and her brother-in-law Tiberius became the second emperor of Rome. Her son Germanicus was 28 and already a successful general with many victories over the Germans under his belt. Now he was first in line to the throne.

In 17, after celebrating a triumph in Rome for his success in Germany, Germanicus took his family with him on a new assignment to the eastern provinces. Antonia seems to have accompanied him for the first part of his journey.[69] She visited Athens, where her mother had lived for a time with Mark Antony. Emotions must have run especially high when the party visited Actium, the site of Antony's defeat at the hands of Augustus and Agrippa.[70] Germanicus, the grandson of Antony, was now married to Agrippina, Agrippa's daughter and Augustus' granddaughter – the old rift had been healed.

The party was welcomed enthusiastically in Greece and the other eastern provinces.[71] These parts of the Roman Empire had long been accustomed to the idea that their rulers were chosen by the gods and possessed semi-divine qualities. Also, they were disposed to favor the descendants of Mark Antony, whose memory they still revered.

Apparently, Antonia returned to Rome before Germanicus completed his travels in the East and settled at his headquarters in Syria.[72] We can imagine her anxiety when, in AD 19, she received news that her son was dangerously ill – and her despair when she heard that he had died.

The circumstances of his death were alarming; Germanicus himself believed that his enemies were poisoning him.[73] It was rumored that Tiberius resented the popularity of his nephew, and many believed that the emperor had ordered his death.[74] These suspicions only increased when neither he nor his mother Livia attended Germanicus' funeral in Rome.[75]

The death of Germanicus sent shock waves through the empire and had no small effect on the political history of the next half-century, as we shall see in the following chapters. The gossip about Tiberius' role put Antonia in a difficult position. She was on friendly terms with the emperor, she lived with his mother Livia, and her daughter Livilla was married to his son.[76] Also, Antonia knew that the future prospects of her family depended on the emperor's good will. While Germanicus' widow Agrippina was outspoken regarding her suspicions of Tiberius, Antonia remained silent.

Tacitus relates that, like Tiberius and Livia, Antonia failed to attend the public observances of her son's passing. He suggests that her absence was due to the influence or coercion of Tiberius, or, alternatively, to ill health or incapacitating grief.[77] Antonia's extreme reaction to the death of her husband Drusus, which recalled her mother's despair at the death of Marcellus, might argue for the last explanation. However, there is evidence in the form of an inscription that Tacitus got it wrong and that Antonia was a participant in the ceremonies after all.[78] It is difficult to believe that she would have missed them.

In 26, Tiberius left Rome for good, settling on the island of Capri. He was now in his late sixties and relying heavily on a man by the name of Lucius Aelius Sejanus to handle the business of running the empire. Sejanus was in command of the Praetorian Guard, the emperor's bodyguard and the only fighting force near the city of Rome. This gave Sejanus considerable power, which he used to persecute Tiberius' enemies, including Agrippina and the friends of Germanicus.[79]

It seems likely that Livia, in her eighties, had been protecting her grandson's family because, soon after she died in 29, Sejanus quickly imprisoned Agrippina and her grown sons.[80] Germanicus' younger children, including the future emperor Caligula, came under the care of their grandmother Antonia.[81] She must have watched in desperation as the ambitious Sejanus systematically destroyed her son's family.

Sejanus also moved to overcome his modest origins by connecting himself to the royal family. He arranged for Antonia's son Claudius to marry one of his relatives and even asked Tiberius for permission to marry Antonia's daughter Livilla, whose husband had recently died.[82] It seemed that Sejanus intended to succeed the aging Tiberius as emperor. He had carefully removed nearly all of his potential rivals in the royal family. Only Caligula, 18 years old and under Antonia's protection, stood in his way.

Antonia must have been anxious about her grandson's safety, and relieved when the means were finally found to destroy Sejanus. In 31, she obtained documentary evidence that he was plotting to remove Tiberius, murder Caligula, and take the throne for himself.[83] However, the emperor's trust in Sejanus, whom he called "the partner of my labors,"[84] was almost complete. Sejanus controlled access to him on Capri and filtered his mail. How could a warning be given to Tiberius in a way that he would believe it?

Antonia was the only person whom the emperor might trust even more than Sejanus; her reputation for prudence and honesty was beyond reproach. Indeed, this may explain why the proof of Sejanus' conspiracy found its way to her in the first place. Antonia dictated a letter to her maidservant Caenis and instructed her slave Pallas to deliver it to the emperor under cover of darkness.[85] When Tiberius became aware of the schemes and ambitions of his lieutenant, he carefully engineered his downfall, pretending to promote him to new heights and then suddenly condemning him to death.[86]

Antonia's essential role in the downfall of Sejanus was made public and Tiberius treated her with even greater respect than before.[87] Her servants, who had participated in the mission to warn the emperor, were rewarded with their freedom. Both lived to achieve greatness: Caenis as the beloved mistress of the future emperor Vespasian; Pallas as the rich and powerful advisor of the emperor Claudius.[88]

However, Antonia's relief must have been short-lived. In the aftermath of Sejanus' fall it was revealed that, eight years previously, he had poisoned the emperor's son (Drusus the Younger) with the connivance of Livilla, Drusus' wife and Antonia's daughter.[89] This information came in the form of a letter to Tiberius from Sejanus' divorced wife Apicata, who then committed suicide in despair over the murder of her children with Sejanus. Apicata had been jilted in favor of Livilla and had ample reason to detest her, but the charge was taken seriously, investigated, and proven to be true.[90]

32

Antonia was now 66 years old. With Livia gone and Tiberius unmarried, she was the first lady of the imperial family and the richest woman in the Roman world.[91] She had received public recognition for saving the lives of both the reigning emperor and the emperor to be. However, Antonia's glories could do nothing to change the fact that Sejanus had succeeded in eliminating her daughter-in-law (Agrippina) and two of her grandsons (Caligula's older brothers Nero and Drusus). Nor could they erase the shame of her daughter's love for Sejanus and murder of her own husband.

Livilla's crime must have been particularly heinous in the eyes of Antonia, whose devotion to her own husband was legendary. However, if Livilla's actions were inspired by loyalty to the man she loved, then perhaps the apple did not fall so far from the tree. It seems unlikely that Livilla was motivated by political ambition as she was married to the heir apparent and her personal expectations and hopes for her children were not improved by eliminating her husband. Her murder of Drusus may have been a crime of passion rather than political expediency, committed for the sake of her lover, Sejanus.

Though Tiberius spared Livilla in deference to her mother, Cassius Dio claims that Antonia punished her daughter by starving her to death.[92] If this is true, Antonia must have acted from a sense of moral duty as a *mater familias* of the old school. In Roman custom, the head of a family had the power of life and death over the members of a household and could act as judge and jury in the punishment of their crimes.[93] Such a severe punishment of Livilla would be consistent with Antonia's lifelong adherence to traditional Roman values.

One of Antonia's closest personal attachments was to a Judaean prince by the name of Herod Agrippa. He was the son of Antonia's close friend Berenice, who was the niece of the Judaean king Herod the Great and the daughter of Livia's friend Salome.[94] Herod Agrippa, who was raised in Antonia's home with her son Claudius,[95] lived a fast and dangerous life and Antonia often bailed him out of trouble. The historian Josephus describes some of her efforts on his behalf.

On one occasion Herod was arrested for unpaid debts to the emperor Tiberius. Antonia lent him the money (300,000 drachmae, roughly 1,000 kg of silver) to get out of this predicament.[96] Herod repaid Antonia with money he borrowed elsewhere and cultivated a friendship with her grandson, the future emperor Caligula. Then, in AD 36, he was overheard telling Caligula that he wished Tiberius would die so that Caligula could succeed him. Herod was thrown into prison by the understandably irritated emperor. Antonia was unable to get him released, but she used her influence to secure him good food, a daily bath, comfortable clothes, and gentle guards. This went on for six months until March, 37, when Tiberius died at the age of 78 and Herod was set free.[97]

Antonia's obvious affection for a character like Herod Agrippa demonstrates that, despite her own impeccable standards of dignity and integrity, she could be tolerant of the shortcomings of others. Considering the accounts of her grandson Caligula, who now succeeded Tiberius as emperor, this quality must have been exercised frequently.

Caligula was only 24 when he ascended the throne. As the son of the legendary hero Germanicus, he began his reign with enthusiastic public support. However, Caligula soon began to indulge in the extremes of behavior that have made his name synonymous with insanity, cruelty, and depravity, and which would lead to his assassination after only four years of rule.

It is impossible for us to know how many of the crimes attributed to Caligula actually happened and how many were invented by hostile historians. In some ways, he was ahead of his time in his vision of an absolute monarchy with semi-divine overtones, similar to the forms of kingship that his family had encountered in the eastern provinces.[98] However, after only two previous emperors, both of whom had endeavored to maintain the appearance of republican forms, Rome was not ready for the trappings of despotism that Caligula seems to have displayed, though many of these would become customary in the not-so-distant future.

For Antonia, now 72 years of age, Caligula's reign began with a flood of honors. In one fell swoop he awarded her all of the titles accumulated by Livia in her long career.[99] She was granted the rank of Augusta (though she may have refused this title) and the privileges of a Vestal Virgin.[100] She was also made high priestess of the cult of the divine Augustus.[101] Her status in the empire, already high in the last years of Tiberius, rose even higher.

But within six weeks of Caligula's rise to power, Antonia was dead. Suetonius reports that rumors swirled around Rome that she had fallen out of favor with her grandson and that he had driven her to suicide, or even poisoned her.[102] It was said that he had grown tired of her advice and refused even to see her without his officials.[103] On one occasion, when she warned him about his behavior, he supposedly replied in a threatening tone that he could do anything he liked and to anyone.[104]

Did Caligula turn against his grandmother so soon after honoring her so extravagantly? Or do these stories arise from the vicious, often exaggerated charges made against Caligula after his death? Certainly Antonia knew his character well. He had lived in her household since Livia's death in 29, probably with two of his sisters.[105] Suetonius even reports that Antonia had caught the adolescent Caligula in bed with his sister Drusilla, though this story is unlikely to be true.[106] However, it may be that Antonia knew that Caligula was mad and preferred suicide to living under his rule.[107]

The truth is that Antonia saw very little of Caligula the emperor.[108] He was out of Rome during much of his early reign, spending no more than three weeks in the city between 18 March, 37, when he assumed the throne, and Antonia's death on May 1. This was a very short time to erase a lifelong relationship that seems to have been amicable. Caligula continued to celebrate Antonia's birthday and refer to her as Augusta after her death.[109] Her remains were cremated publicly in the Campus Martius, site of her husband's funeral forty-five years before,[110] and she was probably buried with her husband in the mausoleum of Augustus.[111]

Though we cannot be certain of the circumstances of her passing, it seems unlikely that Antonia died at Caligula's hands. Her prestige as the most respected member of the royal family made her a valuable symbol of continuity and legitimacy for the young Caligula. However, it is more difficult to dismiss the rumors that Antonia ended her own life, especially when the timing of her death is considered – barely six weeks into a reign that would prove disastrous. Antonia's treatment of Livilla demonstrated her willingness to make the grand gesture in support of her scruples.

Antonia's life and the qualities for which she was admired demonstrate the high status and widening role of women in Roman society. She was both Augustus' ideal of the traditional Roman matron and a model for the new woman who could exercise considerable power and freedom. She was simultaneously celebrated for her old-fashioned feminine virtues of beauty, chastity, and devotion to her husband and family, and for her strong will, independent spirit, and competence in managing her family's complex affairs. It is interesting that these varied qualities were praised with no sense of contradiction or irony. When Antonia asserted herself publicly in the Sejanus affair and in diplomatic relations with the client kingdoms, she was seen as fulfilling the proper role of a *mater familias*, especially one without a husband or male guardian, by protecting and furthering the interests of her household and her nation.

When her son Claudius became emperor in 41, Antonia's memory was accorded many new honors. He re-conferred the title of Augusta and introduced annual games on her birthday.[112] During similar games that he instituted for his father, Claudius had an image of Antonia paraded in a carriage for all to see.[113] He also issued gold, silver, and brass coins in her honor, though he minted none for his wife, the empress Messalina. Some of these coins portrayed Antonia as the goddess Ceres (see Figure 2.19), a mark of special veneration.[114] She was also depicted in statues in the form of other goddesses, such as Juno and Venus Genetrix, the mythical ancestress of the Roman people.[115] Claudius instituted public sacrifices to the spirits of Antonia and Drusus,[116] and may have had a temple built for his mother in Rome, suggesting that he also arranged for her deification.[117]

Claudius' tributes to his mother may be surprising, considering the ridicule that she was said to have heaped on him. However, he would have benefited from honoring Antonia, even if he didn't like her, by being seen as a dutiful son to a noble parent. The circumstances of his accession to power made it necessary for him to advertise his family connections in support of his claim to the throne. (Claudius had been discovered hiding behind a curtain in the palace by the Praetorian Guard, who thrust him into power, at least partially to avoid unemployment.) However, the duration and scale of Claudius' tributes to Antonia argue for his having had a genuine affection for her. Whatever his private feelings may have been, Claudius couldn't go wrong in praising one of the most beloved and respected women in Roman history.

Figure 2.2 Portrait of Antonia's father Mark Antony on a gold aureus, minted 41 BC. Sydenham 1180, Cohen 7, BMC (East) 98; courtesy Classical Numismatic Group, Inc.

Figure 2.3 Octavia, Antonia's mother, portrayed on a silver cistophoric tetradrachm minted in Ephesus in 39 BC. RPC 2201, RSC 3, Sydenham 1197, RSC 2; courtesy Numismatik Lanz München.

Figure 2.4 Fulvia, Mark Antony's first wife, who died *c.* 40 BC. Bronze coin (diameter 18 mm) minted *c.* 44–40 BC. BMC p. 213, 20; courtesy Classical Numismatic Group, Inc.

Figure 2.5 Two posthumous coin portraits of Antonia on brass dupondii minted under her son Claudius, *c.* AD 41–50. RIC I 92, BMCRE 166, Cohen 6; both courtesy Classical Numismatic Group, Inc.

Figure 2.6 Posthumous portrait of Antonia's husband, Nero Claudius Drusus, on a bronze sestertius minted under his son Claudius, *c.* AD 42–43. RIC I 109 (Claudius), BMCRE 208 (Claudius), Cohen 8; courtesy Freeman and Sear.

Figure 2.7 Posthumous portrait of Antonia's elder son, Germanicus, on a copper as minted under his brother Claudius, *c.* AD 42–43. RIC I 106, BMCRE 215, Cohen 9; courtesy Freeman and Sear.

Figure 2.8 Expressive portrait of Antonia's younger son Claudius as emperor on a silver cistophoric tetradrachm, minted in Ephesus, *c.* AD 41–54. RIC 118, BMCRE 229, Cohen 30; courtesy Classical Numismatic Group, Inc.

Figure 2.9 Bronze sestertius showing a triumphal arch erected on the Appian Way near Rome in honor of Drusus, Antonia's husband. The arch is topped with an equestrian statue of Drusus (relative size exaggerated) between trophies made of enemy arms. Minted under Claudius, *c.* AD 41–42. RIC I 98, BMCRE 121–122, Cohen 48; courtesy Classical Numismatic Group, Inc.

Figure 2.10 Antonia's brother-in-law, the emperor Tiberius. Copper as, minted *c.* AD 36–37. RIC I 64, cf. Cohen 14, BMCRE 136; courtesy Freeman and Sear.

Figure 2.11 Drusus the Younger, the son of Tiberius and husband of Antonia's daughter Livilla. Copper as minted under Tiberius, *c.* AD 22–23. RIC I 45 (Tiberius), Cohen 2; courtesy Classical Numismatic Group, Inc.

Figure 2.12 Coin issued in the name of Drusus, Antonia's grandson, in honor of Pietas, possibly with the features of his mother, Tiberius' first wife Vipsania. Bronze dupondius, minted under Tiberius, AD 23. RIC I 43, BMCRE 133, 98, Cohen 1; see "Vipsania on Roman Coins," by the author, *The Celator*, May 2004.

Figure 2.13 Antonia's twin grandsons, Tiberius Gemellus and Germanicus Gemellus, on a bronze sestertius minted under Tiberius, *c.* AD 22–23. RIC I 42 (Tiberius), BMCRE 95 (Tiberius), Cohen 1 (Drusus); courtesy Classical Numismatic Group, Inc.

Figure 2.14 Cleopatra Selene, daughter of Mark Antony and Cleopatra VII. She was the half-sister of Antonia and queen of Mauretania. Silver denarius, minted *c.* 25 BC–AD 23. SNG Copenhagen 566, Mazard 366; courtesy Classical Numismatic Group, Inc.

Figure 2.15 Rhoemetalces I, king of Thrace, protégé as a boy of Antonia, with his wife Pythodoris (behind). Bronze coin (diameter 23 mm), minted *c.* 11 BC–AD 12. Youroukova 206, RPC 1711; courtesy Classical Numismatic Group, Inc.

Figure 2.16 Aulus Vitellius, the son of Antonia's protégé Lucius Vitellius, as emperor in AD 69. Silver denarius, minted AD 69. RIC I 73, BMCRE 7, RSC 20; courtesy Classical Numismatic Group, Inc.

Figure 2.17 Herod Agrippa I, king of Judaea and Antonia's protégé. Bronze (diameter 21 mm), minted AD 42–43. Hendin 555; courtesy Classical Numismatic Group, Inc.

Figure 2.18 Antonia's grandson Gaius "Caligula," as emperor on a copper as, minted *c.* AD 37–38. RIC I 38 (Tiberius), Cohen 27, BMCRE 46; photo courtesy Classical Numismatic Group, Inc.

Figure 2.19 Antonia as the goddess Ceres, wearing a wreath of corn ears. Silver denarius, minted under Claudius, *c.* AD 41–54. RIC I 66 (Claudius), BMCRE 111 (Claudius), RSC 2; courtesy Classical Numismatic Group, Inc.

Figure 3.1 Portrait of Agrippina the Elder by the author, based on a sculpture in the German Archeological Institute in Rome. The coin is a bronze sestertius issued by her son Caligula (see Figure 3.3 for a similar specimen). Agrippina stands on a fortification above the Rhine River on the German frontier.

3

AGRIPPINA THE ELDER
Heroine of the Rhine bridge

After her first husband Marcellus died in 23 BC, Augustus' only child Julia married the emperor's old friend and ablest military commander, Marcus Vipsanius Agrippa. Despite the difference in their ages (twenty-four years) and its political motivation, the marriage seems to have been successful, producing five children. There were three boys: Gaius (born in 20), Lucius (17), and Agrippa Postumus (born after his father's death in 12); and two girls: Julia (born in 19) and Vipsania Agrippina (born about 14 BC), known as Agrippina the Elder or Senior to distinguish her from her famous daughter.

At least three and arguably all five of these grandchildren of Augustus would succumb to the perils of life in the imperial family. Perhaps none would experience its ups and downs more dramatically than Agrippina. After losing her father at age 2, she saw her mother banished by Augustus when she was 10 and both of her older brothers perish under suspicious circumstances before she was 18.

By the time she was 22, her remaining siblings, Julia and Agrippa, had followed in their mother's footsteps: exiled by Augustus. Julia was accused of the same crimes as her mother – indulgence in luxury and wanton sexual behavior. She gave birth while in exile, but Augustus refused to recognize the child or allow it to be reared.[1] Her brother Agrippa was also banished for bad behavior and was executed immediately after Augustus' death in AD 14.

Whatever the traumatic effects of these events on her character, Agrippina as a grown woman was known for her volatility, obstinacy, and unbridled ambition.[2] The historian Tacitus, who admired Agrippina, used surprising adjectives to describe her: "fierce; harsh; arrogant; and power-hungry."[3] She had a stunning, severe beauty, with a somewhat triangular face, large, widely spaced eyes under a straight brow, and a long, narrow nose. In a letter to her, Augustus praised Agrippina for her intelligence, but warned her "to avoid affectation" in her speech and writing.[4] Agrippina was well educated; she understood and probably spoke Greek.[5] She was also courageous, with a boldness and thirst for adventure that some said were excessive for a woman,[6] but which were perhaps to be expected in the daughter of the greatest general of the age.

Agrippina's father, called the noblest of men,[7] deserved much of the credit for Augustus' rise to power because of his generalship during the war with Antony. His marriage to Julia made him the emperor's son-in-law and marked him as heir to the throne. Though about the same age as Agrippa, Augustus suffered from chronic ill health and did not expect to outlive his friend, though he would do so by twenty-five years.

Agrippa was an energetic builder, whose numerous constructions included the Pantheon in Rome (later drastically remodeled by the emperor Hadrian) and the magnificent bridge and aqueduct at Nemausus in Gaul (modern Nîmes, France) known as the Pont du Gard, which still stands today.[8] (See the background of the drawing of the empress Plotina, Figure 6.1 in this volume.) Agrippa was renowned for his courage, wisdom, and unassuming nature, and for his public benefactions, which included baths that he arranged to be open free of charge to the Roman people, even after his death.[9]

In AD 4 or 5, when she was 17 or 18, Agrippina was married to her second cousin Germanicus, the son of Antonia and Livia's younger son Drusus.[10] She and Germanicus had grown up together in Augustus' household and were probably intended for each other from an early age.

As an adult, Germanicus was perhaps the most popular man in the Roman Empire.[11] If the people had been allowed to elect their emperor, he would probably have been their choice. He was handsome and brilliant; a brave and charismatic soldier who also wrote comedies in Greek and was an effective and popular advocate in the Roman courts of law.[12] The historian Josephus comments on his easy manner and his ability to interact with either senators or common folk as if he were their equal.[13] Germanicus also seems to have been highly emotional.[14] On at least two occasions, he had to be restrained from committing suicide when faced with difficult but surmountable problems.[15]

Germanicus and Agrippina soon began a large family. She would bear nine children in all, six of whom lived to adulthood and played important roles in the life of the imperial court.[16] In order of appearance, these were Nero (born about AD 6), Drusus (7 or 8), Gaius (the future emperor "Caligula," born 31 August, 12), Agrippina junior (born 6 November, 15, mother of the emperor Nero), Drusilla (born in 16), and Julia Livilla (born in 17 or 18).[17] Augustus was so pleased by the size of Agrippina's brood that he showed them off in public as part of his campaign to encourage Roman aristocrats to marry and have more children.[18]

During the later years of Augustus' reign, Roman armies were engaged in the conquest of the German tribes. Livia's sons Tiberius and Drusus became famous generals in this struggle as their legions gradually broke down the resistance of the enemy. However, in AD 9, the Roman army was staggered by its worst defeat in over two centuries.

A commander named Publius Quinctilius Varus was leading three legions – perhaps 30,000 soldiers and camp followers in all – through the Teutoberg Forest in occupied Germany. Varus was confident that he had nothing to fear from the German warriors, but they had been secretly rallied by a chief named Arminius and were preparing an ambush. Using training he had formerly received as a Roman soldier, Arminius launched a surprise attack that led to the almost complete annihilation of the Roman forces. This was a catastrophe beyond the worst fears of Augustus. Three of the total of twenty-eight legions in the entire Roman army had been wiped out.[19]

In the five years that followed, a new generation of generals, including Agrippina's husband Germanicus, tried to repair the damage to Roman prestige.[20] Fortunately for them, Arminius lost control of the German tribes, who were once again bickering among themselves. Nevertheless, the situation on the German frontier remained precarious. The confidence of the Roman soldiers was low and many of the troops, enlisted against their will after the Varus disaster, were clamoring for release.[21]

Agrippina was pregnant in the spring of AD 14 when she journeyed to join her husband at his post in Roman Gaul (modern France and Belgium). Germanicus commanded a vast army of eight legions (consisting of 40,000 men, plus an equal number of auxiliary troops) that was stationed along the Rhine River, the border between the Roman Empire and barbarian Germany.

Some months after her arrival at her husband's camp, Agrippina was joined by her son Gaius, not quite 2, who had been sent to her from Rome by Augustus. The aging emperor showed his affection for the young family in a letter he wrote to Agrippina at this time, part of which survives. Augustus makes a gift of one of his doctors (a slave) and closes his letter with the words: "Goodbye, my dear Agrippina. Keep well as you return to your Germanicus."[22]

It was probably Agrippina's idea to dress Gaius in a miniature soldier's uniform, complete with plumed helmet and tiny hobnail boots, during his sojourn with the army of the Rhine. He became a sort of mascot for the troops and earned the nickname "Caligula" ("Little Boots"), which would stay with him for the rest of his life.[23]

Soon after Caligula's arrival came the startling news that Augustus had died on August 19 (AD 14), after ruling for forty-four years. The Romans had never faced the death of an emperor before. Germanicus' uncle Tiberius, long the virtual co-ruler with Augustus, was the successor. Augustus had previously arranged for Tiberius to adopt Germanicus, making Agrippina's husband first in line to the throne – just ahead of Tiberius' somewhat younger natural son, Drusus.[24]

Tacitus tells a vivid tale of the events that confronted Germanicus and Agrippina on the German frontier following Augustus' passing.[25] Though Tiberius was respected by the troops as a fine soldier, he was also feared as a severe and tight-fisted commander. The disgruntled soldiers of the Rhine legions saw an opportunity to air their grievances.

When Germanicus got wind of the army's rebellious mood he acted quickly, calling all of the nearby troops and local tribal leaders together at his headquarters. He swore allegiance to Tiberius in their presence and called on the soldiers and tribesmen to do the same. They complied, but with some reluctance, and Germanicus knew that the soldiers in other camps were also restless.[26]

Indeed, a full-scale mutiny soon broke out at one of the camps, involving four full legions. Their demands echoed those of the troops at his head-quarters: lighter work details, higher pay, and discharges for the older veterans. The soldiers even attacked some of their officers, tossing them into the Rhine.[27]

Germanicus hurried to quell the uprising. Surprisingly, Agrippina and Caligula went with him. Perhaps it was hoped that the sight of Augustus' granddaughter and her child would shame the soldiers into obedience. When Germanicus and Agrippina approached the mutinous camp, they found the troops quiet, many with their heads bowed, as if ashamed of their rebellion. But as soon as Germanicus entered the entrenchments, a throng of angry soldiers surrounded him. One legionary reached for Germanicus' hand, as if to kiss it, and then thrust it into his own toothless mouth – his point being that he had grown old in service and his discharge was long overdue. Other veteran soldiers displayed the signs of their age and begged to be released.[28]

The rebellious soldiers complained of harsh treatment by their officers and asked Germanicus to pay them the money promised in Augustus' will.[29] They also urged him to overthrow Tiberius and become emperor himself.[30] Horrified, Germanicus refused the offer and, with a gesture of disgust, tried to withdraw, but the soldiers blocked his path. Germanicus raised his hand for silence, saying that he would rather die than betray the emperor, the senate, and the people of Rome. He drew his sword and pointed it at his own chest. The officers rushed to disarm him, but a few of the soldiers told him to go ahead and strike. One man even offered his own sword to Germanicus, saying, "Try mine, Caesar, it's sharper."[31]

This dramatic scene left the soldiers confused and quarrelling among themselves. Germanicus withdrew to his tent, where he conferred with Agrippina and his officers. They learned that the rebellious legions were plan-ning to send delegations to the rest of Germanicus' army, urging them to join the uprising. There was even talk of abandoning the German frontier and plundering the cities of Roman Gaul. If this happened, Rome itself would be in danger.[32]

In this desperate situation, Germanicus resorted to deception. He had recently received a letter from Tiberius in Rome. He now pretended that it instructed him to discharge the soldiers who were beyond normal military age and to pay every man double the money promised by Augustus.[33] The

soldiers accepted this offer on the condition that it was made good immediately. Germanicus replied that he lacked the funds to pay them then and
there, but promised to do so after the men had returned to their winter
camps. Two of the legions accepted his word, but the other two refused.
Germanicus and his officers pooled all of the cash they could lay their hands
on, including tax money he had recently collected in Gaul. The troops were
paid and agreed to call off the mutiny and take the oath of allegiance to
Tiberius.[34] Germanicus was forced to promise the same terms to the rest of
his legions, in exchange for their oaths of loyalty.

It seemed that the situation was under control, until the inopportune
arrival of a senatorial delegation sent from Rome by Tiberius. The soldiers
learned from the senators that the letter from the emperor had been a hoax
and that Tiberius had agreed to none of their demands. The troops rebelled
once again and took the senators into custody. They even barged into
Germanicus' headquarters and confiscated the sacred emblems of his army –
the golden eagles and standards – symbolically stripping Germanicus of his
command.[35]

It was decided, apparently despite her protests, that Agrippina, Caligula,
and the wives and children of the officers should be sent out of the camp.[36]
They would be safe among the local Gauls, who were proving more loyal to
Rome than the Roman army. Tacitus records that Agrippina's departure was
the turning point in the crisis. The soldiers watched in disbelief as the women
and children, led by Agrippina and Caligula, climbed into the carriages:
a Roman princess and her son, driven into flight by a Roman army. The
sight of "Little Boots" trembling as he clung to Agrippina's skirts was intol-
erable. Some of the soldiers became afraid of the consequences; when Tiberius
heard of this disgrace, he would certainly punish them. Defiance melted into
fear. The soldiers swarmed around the carriages, grabbing the horses' reins.
They would not let the party leave camp. Many averted their eyes from
Agrippina's glare.[37]

The third-century historian Cassius Dio tells a somewhat different story.
He claims that Agrippina and Caligula were indeed sent away for their safety,
but were then seized by the rebellious soldiers. He states that they released
the pregnant Agrippina at Germanicus' request, but held Caligula hostage.
Finally, a change of heart led them to release the boy and even turn on the
leaders of the mutiny, some of whom they executed.[38]

Agrippina's thoughts and feelings during this crisis can only be imagined.
She must have been reluctant to leave Germanicus, but may have realized
that her presence would serve to protect the other women and children as
they took flight. Perhaps she anticipated the effect her departure would have
on the troops – perhaps it was even her idea. In any case, she must have found
her experiences in the army camps invigorating, so different from her previous life spinning wool in Augustus' court in Rome. However, the traumatic
effects of these events on her young child Caligula were attested by future

events. When he became emperor, he attempted to massacre the soldiers who had rebelled against his father, though a quarter century had passed.[39]

What followed the mutiny's end is a testament to the brilliant leadership of Germanicus. Now that the army was ashamed of its actions, Germanicus gave them the chance to redeem themselves – by attacking the Germans.[40] A bridge was quickly built across the Rhine and the legions marched into enemy territory, catching the German warriors unprepared. They were surprised at festivals or at their dinner tables or half-asleep. All of the emotion of the past weeks was spent in murdering Germans, in destroying their homes and temples and fortifications.[41]

While Germanicus was in Germany, Agrippina suffered three terrible blows. First, her baby girl died soon after birth. Then came news that her exiled mother Julia had been starved to death by Tiberius and that her brother, Agrippa Postumus, had also been killed, apparently at Tiberius' order.[42] These must have been bitter pills for her to swallow after all of the risks that she and Germanicus had taken on behalf of the new emperor.

The winter passed into spring (AD 15) and Germanicus again led his army into Germany to continue the war. Messengers brought stories of his personal bravery, fighting hand to hand with the German warriors, trying to inspire his troops to victory. And the victories were being won. One of the "eagles," a legionary standard that had been captured by the Germans during their massacre of Varus' army, was recovered. This was a tremendous boost to Roman morale.[43]

Germanicus pushed deep into the German forest, even reaching the spot where Varus had been ambushed five years earlier. The open ground was littered with the bones of men and horses, gathered in heaps where groups of soldiers had made their final stands. The trees were festooned with white and pinkish skulls, hung there by the victorious enemy. Most horrible of all were the altars where the Germans had sacrificed the captives to their gods. After Germanicus and his men gathered the bones and built a funeral mound, they held a memorial ceremony in honor of the dead.[44]

During the following weeks, Agrippina received news of many battles with Arminius, who was leading the fight against the Roman invasion. The Germans were conducting guerrilla warfare in the woods, helped by floods that destroyed some of the Roman fortifications and temporary bridges. Then came a report that they had attacked a detachment of the army that was making its way back to the Rhine bridge. The Romans were trapped in a swamp and some of them were deserting. It sounded like the Varus disaster all over again.[45]

This report spread panic in Roman Gaul. Many believed that a victorious German army was on its way to cross the river and invade the province.[46] A mob of terrified soldiers and civilians rushed to the Rhine bridge at the Roman stronghold of Castra Vetera (modern Xanthen), intent on destroying it before the Germans could come across.[47]

It was at this moment that Agrippina proved herself to be one of the most courageous of all Romans. She realized that the destruction of the bridge would condemn any returning Roman soldiers to death, so she placed it under her personal protection.[48] She refused to budge from the bridge before all of the Roman soldiers had returned to safety. The crowd backed down. No one dared to defy the princess. She ordered that food and bandages be made ready for the returning troops.

Finally, the rattle and clang of approaching soldiers could be heard. But were they Romans . . . or Germans? They were Romans. Hard pressed by Arminius, they had beaten him off in the end. As the exhausted troops passed by on the bridge, Agrippina and her servants distributed food and clothing, and tended to the wounded. She also praised the returning soldiers and thanked them for their courage.[49]

Tacitus relates that Agrippina assumed the duties of a general at this time, inspecting troops, attending the standards, even distributing bonuses.[50] She remained in charge until Germanicus returned by ship on the Rhine with his detachment of the army.

Agrippina's heroism becomes even more impressive when we realize that she was as much as seven months pregnant at the time.[51] The story of her bravery made her famous and admired throughout the empire. Tiberius, however, was not pleased by this display of leadership by a woman.[52]

During the next two years, Germanicus invaded Germany repeatedly. He experienced some setbacks, including the loss of a fleet during a storm at sea. This disaster inspired another suicide attempt, again thwarted by his men.[53] However, his campaigns were successful for the most part, recapturing at least one more of the eagles that had been lost by Varus.[54]

Tacitus' account of Germanicus' exploits in Germany was intended to show the young man's courage and exceptional leadership. However, it appears that he only averted military disaster and personal dishonor through the interventions of his wife.[55] It was Agrippina who brought an end to the mutiny, possibly through her own initiative, and her defense of the Rhine bridge saved Germanicus from disgrace and possible defeat at the hands of the German tribes. In contrast, her husband's efforts to end the mutiny had been almost laughable, involving a pathetic gesture of suicide, deceits that were exposed, and false promises, some of which were never honored. In his defense, Germanicus was a young man (28) in very difficult circumstances and his overall conduct of the war in Germany does seem to have been both courageous and effective.

Germanicus' involvement in Germany was over by AD 17 when Tiberius recalled him, out of jealousy some said, and posted him to the eastern provinces. Arminius was later killed by enemies among his own people, but Germany never was conquered by Rome. The Rhine River remained the boundary of the empire until, 400 years after the death of Germanicus, German tribesmen crossed it and conquered Rome itself.

Germanicus did his best to stay on good terms with the new emperor, and he enjoyed a genuine friendship with Drusus, Tiberius' son and second in line to the throne.[56] However, the high-spirited Agrippina, who had ample reason to dislike Tiberius for his role in her mother's and brother's deaths, was often at odds with him. She did not get along well with his mother Livia either.[57] The reserved dowager empress preferred a low-profile, domestically oriented image for women of the imperial court. Agrippina's love of adventure and insistence on accompanying her husband on his missions — even living in the army camps with him — must have created friction between the two women.

Despite the ill feeling at court, Germanicus was honored on 26 May, AD 17 for his military achievements with a triumph in Rome.[58] This celebration, reserved for members of the royal family by this time, was traditionally awarded to a Roman military leader who had scored an especially significant victory. It consisted of a magnificent procession through the streets of Rome to the Temple of Jupiter on the Capitoline Hill in the center of the city. In front of the parade were the standard bearers of the army, followed by various floats, statues of the gods, and paintings of scenes from the successful campaign. Groups of enemy prisoners were displayed, as well as samples of captured booty. Priests led enormous white bulls to be sacrificed in gratitude for Roman success. Far back in the procession came the victorious general, riding in a gilded chariot drawn by four horses and followed by his troops. (In his triumph, Germanicus allowed five of his children to ride in his chariot with him.[59]) At the end of the triumph, handouts of grain and coins were made to the public, and a lavish feast was served to all comers.

Still basking in their glory, Germanicus and his family sailed east. His new assignment gave him authority over all of the governors of the eastern provinces of the empire. He was even empowered to appoint kings for neighboring countries that were allied with Rome and to establish new provinces. Germanicus granted relief assistance to cities in eastern Asia Minor that had been devastated by an earthquake the year before.[60] Suetonius tells us that he also crowned a new king of Armenia and made Cappadocia a Roman province.[61]

There was the sense that Germanicus' journey was a sightseeing and public relations tour. His party, which included Agrippina and most of their children, as well as his mother Antonia, visited numerous cities, historical monuments, and religious centers.[62] The people of the eastern empire, accustomed to treating their rulers as gods, greeted Germanicus and Agrippina with extravagant enthusiasm.[63]

Agrippina paused in her travels at the Aegean island of Lesbos, famed as the home of the early sixth-century BC Greek poetess Sappho, and visited at some length by Agrippina's father Agrippa.[64] The reason for her stop was to give birth to the last of her nine children, a girl named Julia Livilla.[65] This was the third girl born to Agrippina in three years. Her three boys, Caligula (now 6), Nero (12), and Drusus (10), brought the number of her living children to six, three others having died.

After recovering from childbirth, Agrippina joined Germanicus and the rest of their party in the province of Syria. The Roman governor there, a man by the name of Gnaeus Calpurnius Piso, disliked Germanicus and resented being under his authority. The ancient writers describe Piso as an arrogant, violent, irritable, and inflexible man.[66] His wife Plancina, a woman of great wealth and high birth, shared her husband's dislike for Germanicus and detested Agrippina. When Piso and Plancina accompanied Germanicus' party to Petra, a city in the kingdom of Nabataea south of Judaea, Germanicus and Agrippina were presented with heavy golden crowns. Piso resented this intensely, rejecting the lighter crown that he was given and protesting that it was inappropriate for them to accept such gifts.[67]

Plancina reportedly made insulting remarks to Agrippina and Germanicus on numerous occasions. In what may have been an attempt to upstage her rival, she attended military maneuvers, though this was considered unbecoming for a woman. Nevertheless, it won her some support among the local troops and may have been her answer to the stories of Agrippina's exploits in Germany.[68]

Despite these provocations, Germanicus continued in his efforts to get along with Piso and his wife. Their differences, however, were extreme. While Germanicus showed an interest in eastern customs and mingled freely with the people, Piso lectured them on their ignoble past and criticized Germanicus for showing them too much respect.[69] In Piso's view, a Roman was far above his Greek subjects and should remain aloof from them, an attitude in stark contrast to Germanicus, who often "went native" and even dressed as a Greek.[70]

Agrippina and Germanicus journeyed to Egypt, which had been a province of the Roman Empire since the deaths of Antony and Cleopatra.[71] Egypt was of vital importance to Rome as the source of much of the grain that fed the people of the capital city. Whoever controlled Egypt could starve Rome if he chose, so Augustus had decreed that no person of senatorial rank (which Germanicus was) could enter the province without the permission of the emperor.[72] However, Egypt was suffering from famine and Germanicus went there without consulting Tiberius.[73] He also took the initiative of opening the public granaries to relieve the hungry Egyptians.[74]

While in Egypt, Germanicus and Agrippina sailed up the Nile River and saw the famous monuments of that country's past. They visited the temples of Karnak and Luxor, where Germanicus had the priests translate the hieroglyphic inscriptions for them. He traveled casually as a tourist, wearing Greek dress and using no bodyguard.[75] When Tiberius heard about all of this, he publicly criticized Germanicus for going to Egypt without his permission and for dressing in an undignified manner.[76]

Germanicus returned to Antioch in Syria and discovered that Piso had cancelled his orders while he was gone.[77] Furious, he lashed out at the insubordinate governor, who responded in kind. Suddenly, Germanicus fell ill and claimed that Piso and Plancina were poisoning him. He uttered a traditional formula signifying the formal renunciation of their friendship and ordered Piso to resign his post and leave the country.[78]

Germanicus' condition gradually worsened as Piso delayed his departure, awaiting the outcome of his enemy's illness. On his deathbed, Germanicus asked his friends to avenge his death, to demand justice and stand up for his wife and children as the victims of a terrible crime.[79] Before he died, Germanicus spoke to Agrippina, begging her to control her "harsh manner" and be willing to compromise with those more powerful than she, especially Tiberius.[80] Other words were whispered to her, which have not been recorded. He knew that she was fearless and outspoken and that he would not be there to protect her.[81]

The rumor spread that Piso and Plancina, known for their interest in black magic, were responsible for Germanicus' death. According to Suetonius and Cassius Dio, there were signs of poisoning – dark stains on his body and foam on his lips – though Tacitus disputes this.[82] A search of his room reportedly uncovered curse tablets, remains of human bodies, and charred and blood-smeared ashes – all signs of a plot to destroy Germanicus through supernatural means.[83]

Germanicus' passing in AD 19 at the age of 33 shook the empire no less than it devastated Agrippina. Temples were stoned and household gods were thrown into the streets, for it was said that if the gods could allow such a death they did not deserve to be worshiped.[84] Businesses shut down in a spontaneous gesture of mourning; even Rome's enemies displayed their grief.[85] There were grumblings that Piso and Plancina had murdered Germanicus on the orders of Tiberius and Livia, who were said to be pleased by his passing.[86]

Agrippina took the urn containing her husband's ashes and headed home.[87] Her somber journey had an electrifying effect on the people of the empire. Although it was winter, when the seas were unsafe for travel, she sailed for Italy, pausing for a few days on the island of Corcyra to compose herself.[88] A vast throng gathered at the Italian port of Brundisium to meet her ship, including many veterans from her husband's army.[89] With awe-inspiring dignity, Agrippina disembarked, carrying the urn in her hands and accompanied by her younger children.[90]

It was 300 miles (480 km) to Rome. Along the way, crowds came to the roadside to pay their respects to the great hero and his heartbroken family. Tiberius sent an honor guard to accompany Germanicus' remains to the capital.[91] It was high drama, and Agrippina's role in it captured the public's imagination. When the procession arrived in Rome, sacrifices were made to the spirit of Germanicus. The streets filled with mourners and at night there was a torchlight vigil. Agrippina placed her husband's ashes in the mausoleum of Augustus and was acclaimed by the crowds as the "glory of her country" and the "only true descendant of Augustus."[92]

The rumors of Tiberius' guilt grew stronger when he failed to attend the interment or even to honor Germanicus with a state funeral. And then, after some days, it was Tiberius who declared that the mourning had gone on long enough and it was time to get back to business as usual.[93]

Agrippina had not only lost her beloved husband, she had lost her hopes of becoming an empress, for which her entire adult life had been a preparation. She had witnessed 30,000 Roman soldiers beg Germanicus to replace Tiberius as emperor. She had seen him ride in triumph through the streets of Rome and be welcomed as a god in the eastern provinces. She had seen the full measure of devotion the people felt for him and had herself been hailed as Augustus' only true heir. And yet, suddenly, she was nothing more than the widow of a dead Caesar, completely out of the line of succession. It was as if her destiny had passed her by.

Eventually, Piso was charged before the Roman senate with having conspired to murder Germanicus.[94] At one point in the trial, he implied that he had written instructions from Tiberius concerning the matter, but this document was never produced.[95] Finally Piso saw that, without Tiberius' open support, his cause was hopeless. He committed suicide by cutting his own throat. Livia intervened to protect Plancina, which must have confirmed Agrippina's enmity for the empress.[96]

But then destiny took another turn. Only four years after the death of Germanicus, Tiberius' son Drusus, the new designated heir to the throne, also died in his mid-thirties. Through a sudden reversal of fortune, Agrippina's family again stood in line to rule. Her teenaged sons Nero and Drusus were the likeliest candidates to succeed the aging Tiberius.

There were many in Rome, including Agrippina, who were impatient to see this transfer of power take place. Germanicus' reputation had rubbed off on his sons, and the unpopular Tiberius, now in his mid-sixties, was semi-retired and relying ever more heavily on his brilliant but brutal lieutenant, Lucius Aelius Sejanus, to run the empire for him.

Sejanus, who had been secretly responsible for the murder of Tiberius' son, was determined to remove Agrippina's family and clear his own way to the throne.[97] He warned the insecure Tiberius that Agrippina had become the focal point for a circle of supporters who opposed the emperor and wanted to see him replaced by a son of Germanicus.[98] He even induced some of her associates to encourage her to be more outspoken in her criticism of Tiberius.[99] The emperor was so alarmed by reports of Agrippina's opposition that he gave Sejanus permission to begin removing important members of her circle of friends.[100]

Among the first targets were Agrippina's woman friend Sosia Galla and her husband Gaius Silius, Germanicus' friend and fellow soldier. Silius, accused of treason, saw that his cause was hopeless and committed suicide.[101] Sosia was sent into exile. Sejanus then turned against Claudia Pulchra, Agrippina's cousin and dear friend. She was accused of plotting to kill the emperor with poison and sorcery.[102]

Desperate to save Claudia, Agrippina confronted Tiberius himself.[103] She found him sacrificing to an image of the deified Augustus. Agrippina chastised the emperor for persecuting her friends and relatives and called him a hypocrite for worshiping Augustus even as he punished his descendants. She declared that, as Augustus' granddaughter, she embodied his celestial spirit more perfectly than the statue Tiberius was worshiping and accused him of attacking Claudia Pulchra only because she had dared to remain Agrippina's friend.[104] Unmoved, Tiberius took Agrippina's hand and quoted a famous line from Greek literature: "And if you are not queen, my dear, have I done you wrong?"[105] Claudia Pulchra was condemned.[106]

Somewhat later, when Agrippina was ill, the emperor came to see her. Perhaps remembering her husband's deathbed warnings, she tried to make peace with Tiberius, complaining that she was ill and tired. She asked him to allow her to marry again, but Tiberius, perhaps aware that a new husband of Agrippina could be a potent rival, gave no answer. (The story of this exchange, Tacitus reports, came from the memoirs of Agrippina's daughter, Agrippina the Younger.[107])

According to Suetonius, this was the last conversation between Tiberius and Agrippina.[108] Her invitations to dinner also ended when she insulted the emperor by refusing to eat fruit that he offered to her, implying that she suspected him of trying to poison her.[109] Tacitus explains that Sejanus' agents had aroused her suspicions by posing as her friends and warning her that Tiberius planned to get rid of her in that way.[110]

At this point, Agrippina's life must have seemed a living hell. But even more devastating blows were on the way. In AD 29 Sejanus succeeded in persuading her second son, Drusus, to turn against Agrippina and her oldest son Nero. Sejanus convinced Drusus that he would succeed Tiberius if Nero was eliminated. Jealous of his older brother, who was first in line to the throne and Agrippina's favorite, he conspired with Sejanus to destroy him.[111]

Agrippina's dismay over her son's defection can be imagined. Her despair must have been deepened still further by the news of her sister Julia's death after twenty years in exile.[112] Then came the death of Livia (AD 29). Though she and Agrippina were often at odds with each other, the events that followed Livia's passing suggest that she had been protecting Agrippina from Tiberius' full fury. Almost at once, a letter was made public charging Nero with perversity. Tiberius then attacked Agrippina in the senate, accusing her of insolence and disobedience.[113]

Nevertheless, many of the people remained loyal to the family of Germanicus. A crowd gathered outside the senate house, carrying images of Agrippina and Nero and claiming that the letter was a forgery.[114] Tiberius disregarded their protests and ordered both Agrippina and Nero to be exiled. When she protested, he had her flogged. The soldier beat her so severely that she lost the sight of one eye.[115]

Mother and son were sent to separate islands off the coast of Italy. Agrippina went to Pandateria, the place of her mother's banishment thirty years before. Whenever she was moved from one place of imprisonment to another, she traveled under armed guard in a closed litter, with her wrists and ankles bound.[116] The conditions of her imprisonment were harsh. Suetonius claims that she tried to kill herself by abstaining from food, but her guards forced open her mouth to feed her.[117] Finally, on 18 October, 33, after four years in exile (and two years to the day after the death of her tormentor, Sejanus[118]), Agrippina died of starvation, either forced or by her own will, at about the age of 46.

When Agrippina died, Tiberius claimed that he had been lenient in her case as the usual punishment for treason was to be strangled or thrown to one's death down a flight of stairs. He heaped fresh insults on her, accusing her of committing adultery with an elderly senator named Gaius Asinius Gallus, who had recently also died of starvation in exile.[119] Tacitus rejected this accusation, saying that Agrippina was preoccupied by masculine ambition and lacked the "feminine weakness" implied by the charge.[120]

Tiberius' claim, though probably false, is interesting. Gallus was a very prominent figure during the reign of Tiberius. Even Augustus had noted his ambition to rule the empire and Gallus had long been a thorn in Tiberius' side, asking him embarrassing questions in the senate.[121] He had married Tiberius' first wife Vipsania after Augustus had compelled Tiberius to divorce her against his will.[122] Vipsania was a daughter of Marcus Agrippa by an earlier marriage and was thus Agrippina's half sister, making Gallus her brother-in-law.

However, it was Gallus who had proposed the banishment of Agrippina's friend Sosia, and Germanicus' enemy Piso had even asked him to speak in his defense in the senate, though Gallus declined.[123] Furthermore, Gallus had cultivated the friendship of Sejanus and publicly encouraged Tiberius to accuse Agrippina of plotting against him and to allow her removal.[124] Given these facts, it seems very unlikely that Gallus and Agrippina were lovers, or even friends, though they certainly shared a dislike for Tiberius.

Agrippina's death, allegedly by suicide, came shortly after the death of Gallus, allowing Tiberius to insult two of his enemies at once by claiming that Gallus' death had taken away Agrippina's will to live.[125] However, it seems very unlikely that Agrippina died by her own hand. She had seen many turns of fortune in her life and must have been bolstered by the survival of her son Caligula and her three daughters, Drusilla, Julia Livilla, and Agrippina. With Tiberius in his seventies, she had reason to hope for the future.

Agrippina's reasons for detesting Tiberius are obvious. It may be less clear, however, why a man who ruled peacefully and competently for twenty-three years should have been so universally reviled. His most unrelenting critic, Tacitus, calls him cunning and cruel, a perverse criminal and tyrant of the worst kind.[126] Suetonius describes a savage, sadistic man who clearly suffered from severe depression and self-loathing.[127]

Tiberius' reputation did not improve with the passage of time. In the third century, Cassius Dio described him as peculiar, deceitful, and malicious.[128] More than a century later, Eutropius accused the second Roman emperor of laziness, cruelty, and greed, and declared that his death delighted everyone.[129] The late Roman emperor Julian II (reigned AD 360–363) depicted Tiberius in his satire *The Caesars* as solemn, grim, and suffering after death from countless sores in punishment for a life of cruelty and self-indulgence.[130]

Some modern scholars have taken a more positive view of Tiberius, giving him credit for building on Augustus' accomplishments and continuing an era of unprecedented prosperity and stable government.[131] His excesses, if real, would only have affected a tiny minority of the people, the majority of whom benefited from his just and steady rule.

Agrippina had seen three brothers, a husband, and two sons cheated of their rights to the throne. Both of her older sons had died in prison before her – the disloyal Drusus even resorted to eating the stuffing of his mattress in a futile attempt to ward off starvation.[132] As the proud granddaughter of Augustus she would have remembered his wish to be succeeded by those who shared his blood. She probably considered Tiberius merely the caretaker of a throne that belonged by rights to her family. It is ironic that in 37, only four years after her death, one of her sons (Caligula) became emperor after all.

Immediately after his accession, Caligula went to Pandateria – the scene of his mother's imprisonment and death – and collected her ashes, reverently transferring them to an urn with his own hands. He then carried them back to Rome in a procession that recalled his mother's journey with the ashes of Germanicus. Caligula's ship flew a special banner and the urn was carried through the capital by an entourage of distinguished Romans to the mausoleum of Augustus where she was laid to rest (her tombstone still survives).[133]

An annual day of funeral sacrifices was instituted in Agrippina's honor, as well as circus games, where her image was carried in a ceremonial carriage (*carpentum*), depicted on many of the coins that Caligula minted in his mother's memory (see Figure 3.11).[134] Further, the young emperor (24 years old) annulled the legal measures taken against Agrippina and his brothers, punished their persecutors, and recalled those of their friends who were still alive in exile.[135]

Agrippina continued to be honored during the reign of Caligula's successor Claudius, who was the brother of Germanicus. This was especially true after his marriage in 49 to Agrippina's daughter (and his own niece), Agrippina the Younger. A fresh issue of coins with Agrippina's likeness was released (see Figure 3.13), probably at the request or in honor of the new empress. Also produced at this time was an exquisite cameo that has come down to us, depicting the two Agrippinas with their husbands, Germanicus and Claudius, each of whom emerges from a cornucopia.[136] Agrippina the Elder is shown wearing a helmet, perhaps alluding to her military exploits in Germany and identifying her with the personification of the city of Rome. Years later, almost half a century after Agrippina's passing, the emperor Titus also honored her memory, even issuing coins with her portrait.[137] She had become a legendary figure, both as heroine and victim.

Tacitus, who wrote some seventy years after Agrippina's death, would have us believe that she was guilty of little more than high spirits and inordinate pride. He portrayed her punishment by Tiberius as an injustice perpetrated by a cruel man whose principal motivation was jealously. However, it seems likely that Tiberius had the goods on Agrippina – that she had been guilty of plotting to overthrow him after all. Considering Agrippina's fearlessness and ambition, and the tragic circumstances of her life, an involvement in a conspiracy would not have been surprising. Tiberius paid a heavy price in public opinion for his condemnation of the popular princess. As a sober and skillful politician, he was unlikely to have acted unless he perceived Agrippina as a genuine threat to his rule.

Germanicus expected Agrippina's high-strung personality to get her into trouble. Even her grandfather Augustus warned her to control her sharp tongue. She was clearly lacking in tact and discretion, both of which were vital for survival in Roman political life. Agrippina's inability to hide her feelings played into the hands of her enemies. But, whatever her shortcomings, she also possessed remarkable courage, dignity, and steadfastness. She would back down from nobody, which once saved the army of the Rhine but ultimately cost the brave princess her life.

Figure 3.2 Provincial portrait of Marcus Agrippa, Agrippina's father, on a copper as, minted under his grandson Caligula, *c.* AD 37–41. RIC 58 (Gaius), BMCRE 161 (Tiberius), Cohen 3; courtesy Numismatik Lanz München.

Figure 3.3 Superb portrait of Agrippina the Elder on a sestertius minted by her son Gaius "Caligula," AD 37–41. RIC I 55 (Caligula), Cohen 1 (Agrippina Senior), BMCRE 85 (Caligula); courtesy Classical Numismatic Group, Inc.

Figure 3.4 Copper as of Germanicus, minted under his son Caligula, *c.* AD 37–41. RIC I 35 (Gaius), BMCRE 49 (Caligula), Cohen 1; courtesy Classical Numismatic Group, Inc.

Figure 3.5 Agrippina's elder sons, Nero and Drusus, as commemorated by their brother Caligula. Bronze dupondius minted *c.* AD 37–38. RIC I 34 (Gaius), BMCRE 44 (Caligula); courtesy Classical Numismatic Group, Inc.

Figure 3.6 Agrippina's nemesis Tiberius as emperor on a copper as, minted *c.* AD 22–23. RIC I 44, BMCRE 91, Cohen 25; courtesy Freeman and Sear.

Figure 3.7 Legionary eagle between two military standards on a silver cistophoric tetradrachm, minted under the emperor Nerva, AD 97. RIC II 119, BMCRE 80, RSC 44a; courtesy Classical Numismatic Group, Inc.

Figure 3.8 Germanicus holding an eagle-tipped scepter on a bronze dupondius minted under Caligula, *c.* AD 37–41. RIC I 57 (Gaius), BMCRE 94 (Caligula), Cohen 7; courtesy Italo Vecchi.

Figure 3.9 Germanicus in his triumphal chariot (*quadriga*, with four horses) on a bronze dupondius minted under Caligula, *c.* AD 37–41. RIC I 57 (Gaius), BMCRE 94 (Caligula), Cohen 7; courtesy Classical Numismatic Group, Inc.

Figure 3.10 Caligula portrait on a bronze sestertius, minted AD 37–38. RIC I 37, Cohen 24, BMCRE 38; courtesy Classical Numismatic Group, Inc.

Figure 3.11 Agrippina the Elder's honorary *carpentum*, drawn by two mules, on a bronze sestertius minted by her son Gaius "Caligula," AD 37–41. RIC I 55 (Caligula), Cohen 1 (Agrippina Senior), BMCRE 85 (Caligula); courtesy Classical Numismatic Group, Inc.

Figure 3.12 Caligula shown addressing the troops on a bronze sestertius, minted AD 39–40. RIC I 40, Cohen 2, BMCRE p. 156 (asterisk); courtesy Classical Numismatic Group, Inc.

Figure 3.13 Posthumous Agrippina the Elder portrait on a bronze sestertius minted under her brother-in-law Claudius, AD 42–54. RIC I 102, BMCRE I 219, Cohen 3; courtesy Classical Numismatic Group, Inc.

Figure 3.14 A caricature-like portrait of Agrippina the Elder on a silver denarius minted by her son Gaius "Caligula," AD 37. RIC I 8 (Caligula), Cohen 1 (Agrippina Senior), BMCRE 8 (Caligula), RSC 4; courtesy Classical Numismatic Group, Inc.

Figure 4.1 Portrait of Agrippina the Younger, adapted by the author from a marble sculpture in the Ny Carlsberg Glyptotek, Copenhagen. The coin is a silver denarius. Behind Agrippina is an impression of the Bay of Baiae where her son Nero's henchmen attempted to murder her using a collapsible boat.

4

AGRIPPINA THE YOUNGER
Sister of Caligula, mother of Nero

After years of persecution, the family of Germanicus and Agrippina the Elder finally came into its own in March, 37, when Tiberius died at the age of 77 and the 24-year-old Caligula became Rome's third emperor. A son of Germanicus was on the throne, and his three daughters – Agrippina, Drusilla, and Julia Livilla – graced the imperial court. It seemed to the jubilant Roman people that justice had been done at last.

The long years of anxiety and the loss of their parents and older brothers had made Caligula and his sisters very close – malicious gossip said unnaturally close.[1] The new emperor honored his siblings with the rights of honorary Vestal Virgins[2] (though all three were married and the eldest, Agrippina, was pregnant), and had them included in the oaths made to the emperor. The consuls began each senate meeting with the declaration, "Favor and good luck to Gaius (Caligula) and his sisters!"[3] They were even depicted and identified by name on coins. A magnificent large brass sestertius was issued with Caligula's portrait on one side and images of Agrippina, Drusilla, and Julia Livilla on the other as the personifications the divine qualities of Security, Harmony, and Fortune, respectively (see Figure 4.2).[4]

During the last years of his reign, Tiberius had assigned husbands to the three sisters. His ambivalence toward the family of Germanicus had been evident in the choices he made. The men were all of noble birth, but with qualities that limited their prospects and consequently those of their families. Drusilla and Julia Livilla were given to men with little energy or ambition.[5] Agrippina, born 6 November, AD 15, was married at the age of 13 to a wealthy but disagreeable character named Gnaeus Domitius Ahenobarbus. He was her second cousin, the grandson of Octavia and Mark Antony and son of their first daughter, Antonia Major.[6]

Tiberius arranged for Agrippina's marriage to be publicly celebrated in Rome in AD 28, and her husband was honored with the consulship in 32.[7] However, the stories of his various misdeeds make one wonder how he treated his young wife. Ahenobarbus is said to have executed one of his freed slaves for not drinking as much as he was told.[8] Once, he intentionally ran over and killed a young boy with his chariot, and he reportedly gouged out the eye of a man in the Roman Forum because he didn't like what he had to say.[9] He was also reputed to be dishonest, reneging on his debts and cheating charioteers of their prize money.[10]

Agrippina and Ahenobarbus had been married for nearly ten years before their only child was born on 15 December, 37, almost exactly nine months after Caligula's accession. This son grew up to be one of the most detested men in history: the emperor Nero. Nero would probably never have come to the throne without his mother's machinations. Her ruthlessness has won her almost as bad a reputation as her son's, but Agrippina's actions must be understood in the context of her life and her family's tragic history. She understood that the only way to ensure the safety of her family was for one of its members to rule. Agrippina was determined to stay as close to the seat of power as possible, an ambition that would determine the course of her life.

Agrippina's name and political ambition were but two of many traits that she shared with her mother. She also possessed courage, a keen intellect, and an iron will. Tacitus, who clearly loathed the younger Agrippina (though he was only a toddler when she died), accused her of "masculine despotism" and unbounded greed for money. He described her as austere in her habits, and chaste, unless power could be gained through seduction.[11]

Agrippina was as highly strung as her mother had been, and as beautiful, admired for her elegant, aristocratic bearing and her magnificent dress.[12] She had her mother's large eyes and straight brow and her father's slight over-bite and prominent chin. In later life, she wore her hair in the elaborate style of the day, with clusters of tight curls framing her face and coiled tendrils loose about her neck. According to Pliny the Elder, Agrippina had a double set of canine teeth on the right side of her jaw, an anomaly that was believed to be auspicious.[13]

In public, Agrippina was reserved and arrogant; in private, determined and domineering.[14] She worked tirelessly to broaden her influence and secure the advancement of her family and supporters. Agrippina played the role of the highborn princess as she had learned it from her mother and kept an ever-watchful eye on her own welfare and that of her son. Perhaps it was no accident that on Caligula's "three sisters" coin Agrippina was portrayed as the embodiment of security (Securitas).[15]

With the beginning of Caligula's reign, the problem of family security seemed to have been solved. Not only was the new emperor popular and ruling well but his whole family, including even his awkward uncle Claudius, was being treated with honor.[16] Caligula pleased everyone by abolishing the treason trials through which Tiberius had removed so many of his mother's supporters.[17] He also won friends in the senate by showing it respect and courtesy. Even more importantly, Caligula was adored by the army as the son of Germanicus, and he pleased the troops by paying numerous tributes to his parents. His issued coins in their honor, as well as for his two dead brothers, Nero and Drusus (see Figure 3.5). He also brought his mother's remains to Rome and gave her a magnificent funeral.[18]

The pregnant Agrippina must have felt optimistic about her baby's prospects during the early days of Caligula's rule. However, he became seriously ill several months into his reign, and, though he recovered a month or two later, his behavior had become unpredictable and strange.[19] He began spending the enormous surplus of money that Tiberius had left him, irresponsibly and with alarming speed.[20]

The new emperor also began to reveal his personal eccentricities in public. He lived and dressed flamboyantly, often wearing women's clothes and openly displaying his bisexual affections.[21] When he attended a wedding late in his first year of rule, he liked the bride so much that he claimed her for himself, married her, and then discarded her soon afterwards.[22] He began to torture and execute people for seemingly trivial reasons.[23] Tiberius had named his teenaged grandson Gemellus joint heir with Caligula, who had obligingly adopted the boy. Now Caligula abruptly ordered Gemellus' execution, as well as that of his own close advisor Macro, the commander of the Praetorian Guard.[24]

In the summer of 38, Caligula's favorite sister Drusilla died at the age of 20. This loss seemed to unhinge him even further. His moods became more erratic and his actions perverse.[25] He declared that his most cherished personal quality was his "shamelessness."[26] He gave incredibly sumptuous banquets and entertainments and masqueraded in public as one of the gods or goddesses, including Neptune, Bacchus, Venus, and Juno.[27]

Caligula also indulged his passions for chariot and horse racing, theatrical shows, gambling, and gladiatorial contests.[28] He even competed as a gladiator now and then, once killing an opponent in a rigged match.[29] His enthusiasm for horse racing produced the famous story of Incitatus, the horse that lived in a marble stable, was invited to banquets, and was even promised (but never given) a consulship.[30] Suetonius claims that Caligula made his surviving sisters, Agrippina and Julia Livilla, available to his friends as sexual partners.[31]

Though these stories may be exaggerated, they probably have some basis in fact. Agrippina must have witnessed the changes in her brother with trepidation. She believed in conservative behavior for members of the Roman nobility, emphasizing the quality known as *gravitas*, which implied a serious, dignified demeanor and austere lifestyle.[32] Her brother's extravagance and erratic behavior were very far from this ideal.

Caligula's support among the established senatorial families was weakening. Agrippina realized that growing opposition could lead to his overthrow and jeopardize her own safety and that of her son. She seems to have decided not to leave matters to chance. Suetonius reports that in 39 she was accused of plotting with her sister Julia Livilla and Drusilla's widowed husband, Marcus Aemilius Lepidus, to remove Caligula from the throne and put Lepidus in his place.[33] Caligula executed Lepidus, accused both of his sisters of committing adultery with him, and banished them to Ponza, an island off the coast of Italy.[34]

Before Agrippina was taken away, Caligula forced her to participate in a macabre parody of their mother's famous procession to Rome, in which Agrippina the Elder had carried the ashes of Germanicus. Now her daughter had to carry the remains of Lepidus into the capital, where they were discarded without burial.[35] While Agrippina languished in exile, her 3-year-old son Nero stayed in Rome with his wealthy but ailing father, who died the following year. Nero's entire inheritance was grabbed by Caligula, who also confiscated all of Agrippina's and Julia Livilla's possessions.[36]

Agrippina was following all too closely in the tragic footsteps of her mother. She was confined to a small island and separated from her son, with little hope of seeing him again. Caligula even sent menacing notes to his sisters, reminding them that he owned swords as well as islands and that he could have them killed whenever he wished.[37]

Agrippina had learned a new lesson – it wasn't enough to have a member of the family on the throne. To be safe from the emperor, one must *be* the emperor – or control him completely.

As it turned out, Agrippina's exile may have been a blessing in disguise. Caligula's behavior became more and more extreme until finally, in January of 41, one of the many plots to assassinate him was successful.[38] His wife Caesonia and baby girl Drusilla were also killed,[39] and it is likely that, if Agrippina had remained in Rome and on good terms with her brother, she would have been a victim of the coup.

In the wake of Caligula's murder, many of the senators hoped to restore the republic and do without an emperor altogether. However, while they were arguing in the senate building, the real power in Rome was choosing the new ruler – Agrippina's uncle Claudius. The soldiers of the Praetorian Guard found him hiding behind a curtain in the imperial palace. In need of an emperor to protect, and with no better candidate for the job at hand, the soldiers forced the senate to accept Claudius as Caligula's successor.[40]

All at once, Agrippina's fortunes were reversed. One of Claudius' first acts was to recall his nieces from exile and restore the value of the property that Caligula had stolen from them.[41] Despite their mistreatment by Caligula, Agrippina and Julia Livilla gave his remains a proper burial, probably in the mausoleum of Augustus.[42] Such was their devotion to family.

At the time of his accession, Claudius was married to his third wife, his 21-year-old cousin Valeria Messalina, who soon gave birth to a son named Britannicus. She is described as a jealous, lustful, and unscrupulous woman, who used her powers as empress to indulge her whims and passions.[43] Messalina reportedly took many lovers and tolerated no rivals.

Before long, Agrippina's sister Julia Livilla fell foul of the empress, supposedly for daring to possess exceptional beauty and on suspicion of flirting with

Claudius.[44] Julia Livilla was also accused of committing adultery with a rising young senator, the famous writer and philosopher Lucius Annaeus Seneca.[45] Both were sent into exile and Julia Livilla was executed in 42.[46]

Agrippina seems to have learned from her sister's misfortune and managed to avoid banishment or worse at Messalina's hands. Still, Tacitus states that the empress persecuted her, for which Agrippina won popular sympathy.[47]

Agrippina now turned her mind to the matter of choosing a new husband. She and her son would need a powerful protector, and she was certainly not going to wait for someone to choose her. Her first candidate was a distinguished 43-year-old general by the name of Servius Galba, who had been a favorite of the empress Livia. Galba was, however, primarily homosexual and a married man to boot.[48] This did not deter Agrippina from pursuing him, but Galba resisted and his mother-in-law was so outraged by the attempted seduction that she slapped Agrippina in public.[49] (Though her bid for Galba failed, Agrippina's ability to pick a rising star was demonstrated when Galba rose to become emperor of Rome in 68.)

Agrippina now set her sights on another promising man, one of Rome's best-known wits and leading politicians, Passienus Crispus. He is best remembered as the man who said of Caligula, "there was never a better slave nor a worse master."[50] Passienus, like Galba, was already married – to Domitia Lepida, Messalina's mother. She was also the sister of Agrippina's first husband, Ahenobarbus. Nevertheless, Crispus shared Agrippina's ambition and apparently found a connection with the house of Germanicus more attractive than one with the empress's mother. He divorced his wife and married Agrippina.[51]

Passienus Crispus, who was considerably older than Agrippina, was a very capable man. Both Caligula and Claudius favored him, despite his teasing comments about them. He once remarked that while he would prefer to enjoy the esteem of certain men, like Augustus, than to receive gifts from them, in Claudius' case he preferred the gifts.[52] Seneca admired Crispus and called him the most "subtle" thing he had ever encountered.[53]

Agrippina's new husband also had an unusual capacity for fun, demonstrated by the story that he once pretended to have fallen in love with a beech tree on one of his estates. Crispus made a show of embracing and kissing the tree, and even poured wine over its trunk.[54] Though Agrippina is not remembered for her sense of humor, her choice of Crispus as husband suggests that she had one.

Passienus died after a few years of marriage, during which Agrippina seems to have accompanied him to the eastern provinces.[55] She was later blamed for having caused his death, largely because she benefited so much from it.[56] Not only did she inherit his vast wealth, but she was also freed for an even more advantageous marriage, as we shall see.

Agrippina's ambitions for herself and her son were ultimately blocked by the presence of the ruthless Messalina, who was removing any young man of royal blood who might be a potential rival to her son Britannicus.[57] Her remarkable influence over her husband made it easy for her to seduce or eliminate almost anyone she chose.

However, Messalina's ability to deceive and control Claudius finally made her reckless. She took a lover by the name of Gaius Silius, said to be the handsomest man in Rome,[58] and plotted with him to kill Claudius and put her son Britannicus in his place. She even went through a mock marriage ceremony with Silius while Claudius was out of town.[59] When the emperor was told of his wife's actions, he ordered Silius' execution, and Messalina was either killed or driven to suicide.[60]

Claudius was so outraged by the affair that he swore to the Praetorian Guard he would never marry again – and that they could kill him if he ever broke his word.[61] Fortunately, the soldiers ignored this promise, for within three months, in January, 49, Claudius remarried. His advisors persuaded him that an emperor, especially one who had just been made to seem a fool, must have an empress. Furthermore, Claudius needed an influential, respected bride who could enhance his image.

Each of his closest advisors – the freedmen Narcissus, Callistus, and Pallas – supported a different woman.[62] Narcissus argued in favor of Aelia Paetina, to whom Claudius had previously been married, while Callistus preferred Lollia Paulina, a former wife of Caligula.[63] Pallas, who had been the slave of the emperor's mother Antonia (the very man who had carried her warning to Tiberius about Sejanus[64]), suggested that he marry Agrippina.[65] He argued that she possessed beauty, proven fertility, and a son (Nero) who was worthy of royal rank. Pallas also pointed out that it would not be wise to allow her to transfer her considerable prestige to the house of another man.[66]

Claudius accepted the arguments in favor of Agrippina, but how could he marry his own niece? The wheels began to turn. Lucius Vitellius, one of Agrippina's advocates in the senate, addressed his colleagues on the necessity for an emperor to have a wife to share his burden. He argued that Agrippina's nobility and virtue qualified her for this role. He disposed of the difficulty of incest by pointing out that uncle/niece marriages were permissible in other countries, and that marriages between first cousins, once illegal in Rome, had become commonplace.[67]

Taking their cue, many of the senators and the Roman mob began to demonstrate in favor of the union. The senate obligingly cancelled the law against uncle/niece marriages and begged the emperor to take Agrippina as his wife.[68] The people of Rome demanded it, they said. Who could make a better empress than a daughter of the great Germanicus?

For Agrippina, this union was an opportunity to control her own destiny. Claudius married her because she was well qualified to help him rule. Accordingly, she took an active role in all aspects of government. She persuaded Claudius to recall Seneca from exile.[69] Banished at Messalina's instigation eight years before, he was one of the most learned Romans alive and

Agrippina wanted him as a tutor for Nero. Then, in 50, she convinced Claudius to adopt her son.[70]

Agrippina also acquired unprecedented honors for herself. She became the first wife of a reigning emperor to be given the title "Augusta" and to be honored on the imperial coinage (see Figure 4.3). Coins were also issued bearing the images of her mother and father (see Figures 2.7, 3.13).[71] Agrippina's public appearances set a new standard for imperial grandeur. She traveled through Rome in a special carriage (see Figure 4.13) and wore dazzling jewelry, lavishly embroidered robes, and a shimmering cloak of golden threads.[72] The place of her birth, a provincial capital in Roman Germany (the modern city of Cologne), was renamed Colonia Agrippinensis, or "the Colony of Agrippina." (Tacitus tells us that, half a century after her death, the citizens of this city still honored her memory by calling themselves "Agrippinenses.")[73]

Agrippina was openly involved in the official business of the empire, receiving embassies on a raised dais, just like Claudius.[74] Her status as Claudius' partner on the throne was demonstrated when the emperor pardoned the Celtic chieftain Caratacus, his chief adversary in the ongoing conquest of Britain. Caratacus and his family displayed their obeisance and gratitude to both emperor and empress on their adjacent thrones.[75] Tacitus even reports that Agrippina proclaimed her right to share the throne that her ancestors (including Augustus and Agrippa) had won.[76]

The empress was determined to concentrate as much power as possible in her own hands. She stocked the Praetorian Guard with her supporters and had her man, Burrus, made its sole commander.[77] She removed people whose support she could not count on, often by "rewarding" them with promotions to posts that got them out of the way.[78] She also conspired with Pallas to undermine the emperor's other advisors, making Claudius ever more dependent on her.

Agrippina nursed a particularly strong dislike for Claudius' advisor Narcissus. When Claudius was choosing a wife, he had championed the emperor's ex-wife Aelia Paetina (a relative of her family's nemesis Sejanus[79]). In 52, she found a spectacular opportunity to attack him.

Claudius and Agrippina (wearing her golden cloak) attended a celebration for the completion of a waterway designed to drain the Fucine Lake in the hills east of Rome. The finances of this enormous project had been under Narcissus' control. Before the opening of the waterway, games were given involving 19,000 combatants in a mock sea battle. However, when the waterway was opened, it failed to work. This was an embarrassment to the emperor and did no credit to Narcissus. Then, after some modifications had been made, another gathering watched in horror as the waterway worked too well, nearly washing away the spectators, including Claudius and Agrippina.[80]

Agrippina accused Narcissus of corruption, claiming that he had profited by embezzling funds that had been needed to do the job properly. Narcissus countered by accusing the empress of being dictatorial and excessively ambitious.[81] Though Claudius did not punish Narcissus for these remarks, Agrippina had her revenge after the emperor's death by having Narcissus imprisoned and driven to suicide.[82]

To illustrate Agrippina's ruthlessness, Tacitus claims that she destroyed a former governor of Africa, Titus Statilius Taurus, simply because she coveted his gardens. Taurus was accused of extortion and black magic and, anticipating the verdict, committed suicide.[83] Female opponents were as vulnerable to the empress as male ones. Agrippina reportedly punished a noblewoman named Calpurnia for having caught the emperor's eye.[84] This alone was not a capital offense, however. The ultimate punishment was reserved for those women whom she perceived as serious threats to her position.

One such victim was Lollia Paulina, one of the three candidates for Claudius' hand after the fall of Messalina. As Caligula's former wife, she had once been Agrippina's sister-in-law. Lollia was now charged with conspiring with astrologers and magicians. Claudius himself spoke against her, praising her noble lineage but claiming that her activities constituted a threat to national security.[85] She was exiled without a chance to defend herself and forced to commit suicide.[86] The historian Cassius Dio claims that, after her death, Lollia's head was brought to Agrippina, who inspected the teeth to confirm her identity.[87]

The most prominent of Agrippina's alleged female victims was her rival Domitia Lepida, the sister of her first husband, ex-wife of her second, and mother of Messalina. As Nero's aunt, she enjoyed a strong influence over him. While Agrippina tried to discipline her son and imbue him with the quality of *gravitas*, his aunt Lepida encouraged his more frivolous tendencies, which his mother tried to suppress.[88] This interference was resented by Agrippina, as were Lepida's wealth, beauty, and power. The empress charged her rival with conspiring to kill her with black magic and with threatening the peace by failing to control her slaves.[89] In order to please his mother, Nero testified against his aunt at her trial.[90] Despite the vehement support of Narcissus, Lepida was found guilty and sentenced to death.[91]

Though Tacitus implies that Agrippina's violence toward Lollia and Domitia was motivated by "feminine jealousy,"[92] there were more compelling reasons for their removal. Claudius' hold on power was very precarious. He had been something of a laughing-stock before his rise because of the physical symptoms of a disability from which he had suffered all his life. This condition made him walk with a limp, drool uncontrollably, and stammer when he spoke. Also, it caused his head to jerk involuntarily from a nervous tic.[93]

As a result of his ailments, Claudius' family had not considered him fit to pursue the usual princely career.[94] Unlike his brother Germanicus, he had never commanded armies or governed provinces and had only attained the consulship late in life at the whim of his nephew Caligula.[95]

Claudius had been thrust onto the throne by the Praetorian Guard, even as the senate was making a serious but unsuccessful bid to regain power and eliminate emperors altogether. It is not surprising that, early in Claudius' reign, the idea was current among leading members of the nobility that if Claudius could become emperor so could they. Suetonius tells us that numerous attempts were made to remove him, by individual rivals, conspiracies, and even a short-lived civil war.[96] The stability of Claudius' regime had been shaken still further by the conspiracy of Messalina and Gaius Silius. Indeed, the winning argument for his union with Agrippina seems to have been that she was too important to be allowed to marry anyone else. His choice may have been a simple one: marry your niece or get rid of her. He had already got rid of her sister Julia Livilla for the mundane crime of adultery.[97]

These factors do not necessarily exonerate the empress for the removal of her enemies, but they do suggest that political considerations, and the concerns of Claudius and his advisors, were involved. The emperor's insecurity is shown by the executions of a great many senators (35) and knights (either 221 or 300) during his reign.[98] When Lollia Paulina was charged it was Claudius himself who denounced her, and his reason was that she presented a threat to the nation (meaning his control of it). Clearly, there was much more than "feminine jealousy" involved here. The long-term consequences of Agrippina's rise and the purge that followed seem to have been positive. Relations between Claudius and the senate were improved and the emperor's position became much more secure. It is likely that Agrippina deserves some of the credit for this.[99]

Despite the extent of her influence, Agrippina realized that her position ultimately depended on the aging Claudius. If she was going to survive his passing, she would have to pick his successor. The royal family at the time of Agrippina's marriage to Claudius in 49 included her 12-year-old son Nero and the emperor's two children by Messalina. These were Britannicus, almost 9 and the logical choice to succeed Claudius, and a 10-year-old daughter named Octavia. To the astonishment of many, Claudius soon began to show obvious signs of preferring Nero to Britannicus.

Claudius adopted Nero in 50 and, in 51, gave him the title "Princeps Iuventutis" ("Prince of Youth"), which clearly marked him as the heir apparent. Nero appeared at the games wearing triumphal robes while Britannicus remained dressed as a boy.[100] Britannicus' portrait disappeared from the imperial coinage (though not from all provincial issues) while Nero's portrait remained (see Figure 4.14).[101]

Why did Claudius prefer his stepson to his natural son? While Nero was older than Britannicus by a little more than three years, Claudius' actions perplexed the ancients no less than they do modern scholars. Many writers have tried to explain them as the result of pressures brought on him by Agrippina and by her accomplice, the finance minister Pallas. It has even been argued that Claudius, aware of Messalina's infidelities, suspected that Britannicus was not his own son.[102] Is it possible that Claudius believed that Nero *was*?[103]

Though this possibility does not seem to have occurred to previous historians, there are a few intriguing bits of evidence in support of the idea. The first stumbling block, of course, is the blood relationship between Claudius and Agrippina, making their union incestuous. However, it should be remembered that the sexual activities of the Julio-Claudian court were extremely complex and unpredictable. Claudius was married four times, Agrippina three, and both were famous for their extramarital exploits.

Agrippina was reputed to have been the lover of, among others, Pallas, Seneca, both of Nero's praetorian prefects, and even her own son.[104] She and her sisters, Julia Livilla and Drusilla, were believed to have committed incest with their brother Caligula.[105] Also, Ahenobarbus, Agrippina's husband at the time of Nero's birth, was charged with treason, adultery, and incest with his sister at the end of Tiberius' reign – just before Nero's conception.[106] It was only the old emperor's death and the accession of Caligula that rescued him from prosecution.[107]

After Nero's birth, Ahenobarbus, who suffered from dropsy and was a near invalid, acknowledged the boy as his own. (He was not likely to have accused the new emperor's sister of adultery, even if he had suspected it.) However, he supposedly remarked that any result of a collaboration between himself and Agrippina was bound to "have a detestable nature and become a public danger."[108] This was a heavy curse to lay on one's own son. Ahenobarbus died when Nero was 3.

As was customary, Nero's family gathered nine days after he was born for a purification ceremony and the choice of a name. Ordinarily, a first-born son was named after his father. However, in the Ahenobarbus family males were given the names Lucius or Gnaeus in alternating generations.[109] Therefore, Nero would be expected to receive the name Lucius Domitius Ahenobarbus.

The emperor Caligula was present at this naming ceremony, as was Claudius. Agrippina asked Caligula to choose a name for her baby. The historian Suetonius tells us that the emperor, known for his ironic sense of humor, looked at Claudius, grinned, and said: "I name him Claudius."[110]

Agrippina ignored the suggestion and chose "Lucius Domitius" after all. Everyone assumed that Caligula was just being mischievous by choosing the name of his laughing-stock of an uncle.[111] However, was he alluding to a family secret by choosing the name of the boy's *real* father?

There is a story about the young Nero involving an attempt by Messalina to have him killed by hired assassins. This tale may have come from the memoirs published by Agrippina when she was married to Claudius and working to secure the succession for Nero.[112] Suetonius' version states that the assassins entered Nero's room intending to strangle him as he slept, but were frightened off by a snake that emerged from under his pillow. A sloughed snakeskin was later found, which Agrippina mounted in a golden bracelet worn as a talisman by Nero for many years.[113] The historian Tacitus mentions a version involving more than one snake, but tells us that Nero himself confirmed the one-snake story.[114]

This tale may be relevant for a couple of reasons. First, if true, it shows Messalina's determination to eliminate Nero as a possible rival to her son Britannicus. While she is said to have taken pains to remove or disgrace several of her husband's male relatives, she seems to have taken an unusually direct approach with Nero.[115] Could she have known or suspected that he had a special relationship to Claudius?

The other intriguing aspect of this story is more romantic. The tale of Nero and the serpent(s) is reminiscent of a legendary story of the baby Hercules (see Figure 4.15). According to the Greek myth, Hercules was the son of the mortal woman Alcmene and the god Zeus, who assumed the form of her husband Amphitryon to make love to her. The goddess Hera, Zeus' wife, was so jealous of Alcmene that she sent two snakes to destroy Hercules and his twin brother Iphicles in their sleep. However, the superhuman Hercules woke up and strangled the snakes, revealing his divine paternity.

Now, if we see Nero as Hercules, Claudius as Zeus, Agrippina as Alcmene, and Messalina as Hera – and remember that Agrippina is believed to have told this story while promoting Nero's claim to succeed as emperor – we might reasonably wonder if it contains a hidden message.

It has been assumed that Agrippina's marriage to the 58-year-old Claudius was no love match, that he was only capitalizing on her popularity as Germanicus' daughter and that she was using her uncle to further her own ambitions. It is true that, though Agrippina was only 33 at the time of their marriage, she and Claudius had no children. However, the story also circulated that Agrippina had seduced the emperor by using her status as his niece to gain private access to him and then flirted with him "inappropriately," kissing and caressing him.[116] Sexual relations between the two were taken for granted by Tacitus.[117]

Suetonius tells us that Claudius had a long-standing affection for Agrippina. Shortly before their marriage, he described her as "my daughter and adopted child, virtually born and raised in my own lap."[118] After the law was changed to make their marriage possible, two weddings took place between uncles and nieces.[119] The fact that Claudius and Agrippina attended one of them might suggest some sentimentality on the subject.[120]

There is an interesting story concerning the adoption of Nero, which comes from Suetonius. As an example of Claudius' "scatterbrainedness and short-sightedness," he reports that: "Shortly before he adopted his stepson Nero – as though this were not bad enough, as he already possessed a grown up son of his own – Claudius proudly announced more than once that nobody had ever been adopted into the Claudian family."[121]

The question here is: Why did Suetonius find this remark strange? Were there previous adoptions into the clan that Claudius forgot about? Not according to Tacitus, who confirms the emperor's statement.[122] Was it because he was showing insensitivity to Britannicus' obvious misfortune in losing his place as the eldest son? Or was it because Claudius was unaccountably bragging about an ancient family tradition just as he was preparing to break it? If so, then the fascinating question arises: Was Claudius hinting that Nero's adoption was not an exception to the rule after all, as he was really a Claudian by birth?

Admittedly, the evidence is open to interpretation. However, it is interesting that all of the suggestive passages seem to originate from the people most likely to have known the truth about Nero's parentage – his mother Agrippina, Claudius, and Caligula. Also, the strongest argument in favor of this theory is not open to question: Claudius did prefer Nero to Britannicus, and treated the two boys as if there were no difference between them but age.

There is no sign that the ancients suspected that Nero was Claudius' natural son. It seemed that his elevation could only be explained as a sign of Agrippina's powerful influence over the aging emperor. In 53, Nero was married to Claudius' daughter Octavia (she was legally transferred to another *gens*, or clan, to avoid legal incest). According to Tacitus, Agrippina had planned this union even before her marriage to Claudius.[123] Ironically, she made it possible by having a trumped-up charge of incest brought against the man who was already betrothed to Octavia.[124]

It was believed that, as the years went by and Britannicus approached the age of legal manhood, Claudius changed his mind about favoring Nero.[125] However, this seems unlikely to be true, as Claudius certainly would have realized that a change so late in the game would only invite civil war. If he did reconsider, and if Agrippina became aware of it, she would have seen all of her plans for the future about to collapse. The fact that Claudius died suddenly in 54, just before Britannicus reached the age of legal manhood (14), convinced many that Agrippina had murdered her husband.

Stories circulated that Agrippina had retained an expert on poisons, a woman named Locusta, to help her assassinate Claudius.[126] It was claimed that, at a family dinner in the palace on the evening of 12 October, either Agrippina or Claudius' taster, acting under her instructions, fed the intoxicated emperor a poisoned mushroom.[127] However, Claudius was so drunk that the poison had less than the desired effect. Undeterred, Agrippina made the court physician administer another dose by sticking a poisoned feather into his throat under the pretense of helping him to vomit.[128] After a night of agony, the 63-year-old Claudius finally died. Agrippina withheld the news for several hours, until the Praetorian Guard had been prepared to receive Nero as the new emperor.[129]

Various versions of this story were so widely accepted that Nero was even reported to have joked about the murder, calling mushrooms the "food of the gods," as Claudius had eaten one before his death and deification.[130] The official story announced by Agrippina and Nero was that Claudius had died at noon on 13 October from an attack of fever while watching a pantomime.[131] It is true that he had suffered from digestive illness for the previous four years, and had nearly died from it in 52 and again in 53.[132]

Whatever the truth was, no one doubted that Agrippina was capable of doing away with the emperor, nor that she and Nero were now in control. Tacitus reports that Claudius' will was not read publicly to avoid drawing attention to the obvious injustice to Britannicus.[133] It may be, however, that the will was not read either because it named Britannicus as joint heir or because it failed to name Nero unequivocally as the sole heir.[134]

Claudius' funeral was observed with much pomp and ceremony. He was deified, unlike his two predecessors on the throne, and Agrippina became the priestess of his cult.[135] The funeral rites recalled those of Augustus in scale, and Agrippina strove to emulate Livia in the tributes she paid to her dead husband.[136] She began construction of a temple in his honor, which Nero nearly destroyed but which was finally completed by the emperor Vespasian (reigned AD 69–79).[137]

And so Agrippina entered into a new "partnership in power," this time with her 16-year-old son, and her control of Nero initially gave her the upper hand. For the first time in Roman history a woman was the leading political force in the empire. When she rode or was carried in a litter around Rome, Nero rode with her or walked along beside her.[138] His first watchword for the military was "Best of Mothers."[139] As no woman was allowed in the senate chamber, it was arranged for senate meetings to be held in the palace so that Agrippina could listen in, concealed behind a curtain.[140] Coins were minted with their busts facing each other (see Figure 4.17). However, her titles were on the more important "heads" side of the coin (obverse), and written in language that seems to indicate that the coins were issued under her authority rather than his.[141]

With the assistance of her allies – Pallas, the Praetorian Guard commander Burrus, and Nero's tutor Seneca – Agrippina ran the empire. She had realized the ultimate goal of her maneuvering and plotting and influence peddling. However, she was also a woman, and neither the senate nor the imperial advisors, nor even Nero, would tolerate her dominance for long.

Nero is one of the most intriguing personalities in history. His popular image as an extravagant, cruel, and debauched tyrant is probably the reason why he continues to fascinate. He is seen as the ultimate unbridled ego: a grotesque example of what happens when a person with virtually unlimited wealth and power is free to indulge his whims and appetites without legal or moral restraints. This impression is not entirely fair to Nero, but it has enough basis in fact (or at least in legend) to be enduring.

In contrast to the usual caricature of him, Nero did enjoy many successes during his reign. The later emperor Trajan (one of the so-called "good" emperors) reportedly said that no emperor could surpass Nero's conduct during the first five years of his rule.[142] Surprisingly, Nero was extremely tolerant of criticism. Even when people were reported for slandering him, or dared to ridicule him to his face, he was invariably lenient and forgiving.[143]

One possible explanation for his forbearance is the Roman belief that it was unsafe to appear too successful. It was feared that the gods might become jealous and bring about some adjustment in circumstances. Accordingly, it was customary for eminent Romans (including emperors) to employ jesters (e.g. the *derisor*) to ridicule and mimic their masters, especially at dinner parties or other social gatherings.[144] It was hoped that this abuse would deflect any divine resentment.[145] Perhaps Nero reasoned that the more idle criticism he received, the less the gods would envy him. On the other hand, like his mother, Nero was conditioned to be wary of any serious threat to his life or position, and would lash out viciously at anyone suspected of plotting his overthrow.

Nero was the only surviving male descendant of the beloved Germanicus, which made him tremendously popular. As a boy he had been shy, with good manners and unusual intelligence, and he had been given a severe, "old-fashioned" upbringing. He must have been marked by having his mother sent away from him when he was not quite 2, and then losing his father a year later. His aunt Domitia Lepida, who raised Nero until Agrippina returned from exile, reportedly chose a barber and a ballet dancer to look after the boy.[146] This could only have increased the shock when his formidable mother returned and put him in the charge of two demanding new tutors, Beryllus and Anicetus. Then, when Nero was 12, Agrippina brought in the intellectual senator Seneca to teach her son how to make speeches and understand the ways of the world.[147]

We have previously met Seneca as the man sent into exile by Claudius at Messalina's instigation for his alleged dalliance with Agrippina's sister Julia Livilla. He was an adherent of the philosophical system known as Stoicism and was one of the ablest and most accomplished men of his age. We may gain an impression of his character and beliefs from his writings, which include satires, letters, poems, and moral essays. Though it is not known to what extent Agrippina shared his views, it is instructive that she wanted her son to be exposed to them.

Seneca was against slavery, the gladiatorial games, and cruelty in any form.[148] He believed in a benevolent, moral God who represented the unity of all the various deities and who loved mankind. In his own words, taken from his letters to his friend Lucilius:

> Therefore, we must search for that which is beyond change. What is that? It is the soul, but one that is upright, good, and great. What can you call a soul like this, other than a god inhabiting a human body? Such a soul may descend into a Roman knight, or a freedman's

son, or a slave. These are only names born out of ambition or from injury to others. One may leap into heaven from any position in life.[149]

God is close to you, he is with you, he is within you . . . A holy spirit sits within us, observing our bad and good deeds, and watching over us. This spirit behaves towards us as we behave towards it. In truth, no man can be good without God's help . . .[150]

Do, therefore, the one thing that has the power to make you truly happy: discard and trample underfoot the things that glitter on the outside . . . Look to the true good and delight only in that which comes from within you. And what do I mean "from within you"? I mean from your own self, from the best part of you.[151]

Little is known of Agrippina's religious beliefs or activities other than her ceremonial role in the state religion. However, her personal interests might be reflected in the special attention paid to the cult of Cybele, the Great Mother goddess, during her husband's reign. It was under Claudius that Attis, Cybele's emasculated consort, was officially admitted into the Roman pantheon and that Roman citizens were first allowed to join her priest-hood.[152] Cybele was an omnipotent goddess, worshiped as the author of the universe, who dominated her male associates, both human and divine. These qualities may have had a special appeal for Agrippina, who was no shrinking violet herself.

According to Suetonius, Nero had little interest in the gods with the exception of Atargatis, a Syrian goddess whose rituals and iconography had very strong affinities with those of Cybele.[153] The cults of both deities featured mystery rites, frenzied forms of worship, lion attendants, emascu-lated transvestite priests, and divine but subordinate male consorts. Nero's devotion to Atargatis may be an echo of his mother's interest in a very similar cult. Suetonius claims that Nero eventually lost his faith in Atargatis, even urinating on her statue, and eventually replaced her in his devotions with the statuette of a girl, given to him by one of his subjects as a talisman against conspiracies.[154] Nevertheless, he showed a persistent interest in variant forms of sexuality like those associated with the cults of both Cybele and her Syrian counterpart.

For example, Nero frequently assumed female personae for theatrical performances and, like his uncle Caligula, often wore female or feminizing attire. Suetonius tells us that he donned masks bearing the features of his current female lovers for the stage, and Dio describes a performance in which the emperor pretended to be giving birth.[155] The British queen Boudicca, who led a devastating but unsuccessful rebellion against Roman rule during his reign, referred to Nero as "Mistress Domitia-Nero" because "he beauti-fies himself and sings and plays the lyre like a woman."[156]

After the death of his second wife, Nero reportedly castrated a male look-a-like named Sporus, dressed him as a woman, married him, and treated him as his empress.[157] As proof of Nero's versatility, he is also said to have assumed female attire and married a man named Pythagoras.[158] The nuptials were performed according to custom, with Nero even mimicking the cries of a virgin bride on her wedding night.[159]

Despite his later excesses as emperor, Nero seems to have received the best possible education as a prince. Seneca's surviving writings include a moral essay addressed to the young man, expounding on the virtue of mercy and encouraging his natural inclinations in that direction.[160] Much of the credit for Nero's early success as a ruler has been attributed to the guidance of Seneca and Burrus, both of whom had been hand-picked by Agrippina.

From early in his life, all things artistic fascinated Nero: painting, sculpture, dance, music, poetry, and all forms of theater.[161] Agrippina allowed him to study these things on the understanding that they were not to be taken too seriously. It was acceptable for a prince to appreciate the arts, but not to become an artist himself. In Roman society, artists and actors were often famous, but they remained near the bottom of the social scale.

Nero was also enthusiastic about Greek athletics and horse and chariot racing and would later show a taste for philosophy.[162] However, Agrippina discouraged these interests, presumably because sports were beneath his dignity and philosophy might weaken his resolve to act in his own best interests.[163] The tragedy of Nero's life was that his nature made him an artist, but his birth (and Agrippina's determination) made him an emperor. Though he would try heroically, he couldn't be both.

In contrast to Nero's exuberance and passion, Agrippina was reserved and practical, and she criticized his flamboyant impulses as unsuitable for a man in his position. During the early part of his reign she kept him firmly under her thumb. However, with the encouragement of Burrus and Seneca, Nero soon began to untie the apron strings. There may have been a hint of this in the second issue of coins that were minted under Nero (see Figure 4.18).[164] They still showed both portraits, but now the emperor's bust was placed in front of Agrippina's – as if she had been eclipsed by him – and his titles were shown on the "heads" side of the coin, while hers were relegated to the reverse. This would be the last time that Agrippina would even appear on the Roman imperial coinage.

Agrippina tried to keep a grip on things, but the system was against her. Much of the important business of the empire was conducted between the emperor and the senate. Though Agrippina had arranged to witness these meetings from behind a curtain in the palace, she could not intervene when some of Claudius' edicts of which she approved were overturned with Nero's consent.[165] Seneca and Burrus, though indebted to Agrippina for their positions, took advantage of Nero's resentment of his mother's strictness to increase their influence over him at her expense.

No matter how much Nero owed to Agrippina, he was the emperor and was ultimately in charge. This fact was underscored only a couple of months into the new reign in dramatic fashion. An important delegation from the kingdom of Armenia had come to Rome and was addressing Nero, who sat on his dais in the palace. Agrippina entered the room and, rather than take a seat on a separate platform as she had done under Claudius, headed straight for Nero. Clearly, she intended to join the emperor and sit beside him. In the protocol of the court, this was as good as saying that she shared the throne with Nero as his equal. Seneca saw the scene unfolding and acted quickly. He told Nero to rise from his seat and meet Agrippina before she could ascend the platform. He did so, and greeted his mother warmly. Agrippina had not been insulted, but the line had been drawn.[166]

Her hold on Nero loosened even further in 55 when he fell in love with a former slave by the name of Acte.[167] His loveless marriage with Octavia had been no threat to Agrippina's emotional control of her son, but this liaison was something different. From fear of his mother, Nero tried to hide the affair from her. When Agrippina discovered it, she scolded him violently for giving so much importance to a person of low birth.[168] However, her opposition only increased Nero's attachment to Acte and he began to flaunt his feelings openly. At 18, with the encouragement of Seneca and his friends at court, the emperor was declaring independence from his mother.

Agrippina changed her tactics. In a desperate attempt to remain the central figure in her son's life, she apologized to Nero and dropped her objections to Acte. Knowing that wealth without power was nothing, Agrippina placed her riches at his disposal. She also showered him with affection and encouragement – gossips even claimed that she tried to seduce him.[169] (Sexual relations between Agrippina and Nero were often rumored. He is said to have once selected a lover because of her resemblance to his mother.[170])

Anxious for peace, Nero reconciled with Agrippina. He sent her a priceless jeweled garment from the wardrobe of a previous empress. However, Agrippina, perhaps thinking too soon that she had recovered her extraordinary power over her son, scoffed at the gift as an insignificant fraction of what he owed her.[171]

Now Nero showed that he had a temper. He fired Pallas, Agrippina's closest ally at court, the man who had virtually ruled the empire with her during the last five years of Claudius' reign.[172] Furious, Agrippina reportedly threatened to present Britannicus, now almost 14, to the Praetorian Guard as a better candidate for the throne.[173] Terrified that she might be serious, Nero apparently had Britannicus poisoned at a family dinner.[174] Whether the emperor was responsible for his death or not, Britannicus was out of the way.

However, Agrippina would not be intimidated. She transferred her support to Nero's neglected wife Octavia and worked to consolidate her own influence, especially among the officers of the Praetorian Guard. She was rumored to be raising a large sum of money, as if she was preparing to overthrow her son and put someone else in power.[175] Nero was alarmed, but he held all the cards now. He stripped Agrippina of her personal bodyguard and forced her to move out of the palace and into the old residence of Antonia, where she would be remote from the circles of power.[176] When he made his brief visits to see his mother, he always came with an escort of armed guards.[177]

Now that Agrippina's fall from grace was evident, her enemies saw their chance for revenge.[178] Junia Silana, a former woman friend whom Agrippina had offended by scaring off one of her prospective lovers, joined forces with Nero's *other* aunt Domitia – the sister of Domitia Lepida.[179]

Late one night, Domitia's freedman warned Nero that Agrippina was planning to depose him. He claimed that she would marry Rubellius Plautus, a descendant of the emperor Augustus, and take over the empire.[180] Nero went into a panic at the news and demanded the immediate deaths of his mother and the other conspirators. With difficulty, he was persuaded by Burrus to give Agrippina a chance to answer the charges, but Nero insisted that she would be executed if found guilty.[181]

Whether there was any truth to the allegations or not, Agrippina handled the situation calmly and brilliantly. She pointed out that if Junia Silana had ever had any children, she would realize how ludicrous it was to suggest that a mother would assassinate her own son.[182] She contrasted her tireless promotion of Nero's interests with his aunt Domitia's preoccupation with beautifying her fishponds.[183] Agrippina also insisted that if anyone other than Nero was on the throne she would be far more vulnerable to her enemies. Then she managed to see her son and won him over so completely that he punished her accusers and rewarded her supporters.[184]

Agrippina had escaped, but her days of running the empire were clearly over. She spent her time away from the mainstream of political life, visiting her many properties and managing her still considerable wealth. She openly criticized her son's "undignified" behavior.[185] He had taken to roaming the streets of the capital at night in disguise and indulging with his companions in all sorts of rowdy behavior.[186] Even his fondness for Greek culture, his deepening passions for sports and the arts, showed a lack of good old Roman *gravitas* in Agrippina's view. She knew that the same tendencies in her brother Caligula had contributed to his downfall.

Agrippina's relations with Nero continued to deteriorate. Each was wary of plots that might be hatched by the other. Though still married to Octavia, Nero had a new woman in his life, the beautiful and ambitious Poppaea Sabina, whose mother had been killed by Messalina.[187] Poppaea chided the emperor for still being under Agrippina's control, claiming that the only thing that kept him from divorcing Octavia and marrying her was his fear of his mother.[188]

Nero finally resolved to get rid of Agrippina. However, Burrus told him that the soldiers of the Praetorian Guard would never cooperate in the murder of a daughter of Germanicus. Though Agrippina's ruthlessness had made her unpopular, there was no telling what the public reaction to her murder would be. Nero hesitated, but when an emperor wanted something to happen, there was always someone who would seek his favor by providing a way.[189]

One of Nero's boyhood tutors, a freed slave by the name of Anicetus, was now the commander of the Roman fleet at the Italian port of Misenum on the Bay of Naples. Anicetus suggested a way Agrippina could be killed that would look like an accident. A ship could be constructed for her use that would be designed to collapse at sea. If she didn't drown on her own, his sailors would make sure that the "accident" proved fatal. This idea appealed to the theatrically minded emperor, and all was arranged.[190]

First, Nero made a show of forgiving his mother, saying that children should humor and tolerate their parents, even when they find themselves at odds with them. He invited Agrippina to join him at the annual festival of the goddess Minerva in Baiae, near Misenum. On a calm, starlit night in late March of 59, they met for a magnificent feast. Nero treated his mother with great courtesy and affection. It seemed that reconciliation was possible after all. When the party was over, Nero directed Agrippina to a lavishly decorated ship that he had prepared in her honor to take her across the bay to her villa.[191]

Not suspecting Nero's intentions, Agrippina stepped on board with two female companions and sailed for home. As she sat on a couch talking with the women, the heavy roof of the ship suddenly collapsed, killing one of her friends instantly. The raised sides of their couch, which caught the falling weight, saved Agrippina and the other woman. The ship was supposed to disintegrate at this point, but it held together. The sailors who were in on the plot tried to capsize the vessel by throwing their weight to one side. However, other sailors cancelled their efforts by working to stay afloat.[192]

Agrippina's surviving woman companion made the fatal mistake of calling for help, claiming that she was Agrippina. Her cries were answered by a series of blows delivered by Anicetus' men, using their oars and poles. Realizing by now what was happening, Agrippina jumped overboard and, though she had sustained an injury to her shoulder, managed to swim to a nearby sailboat that ferried her ashore.[193]

Tacitus describes the confusion that ensued as reports of Agrippina's mishap spread. A crowd gathered by torchlight along the waterfront near her villa, wailing and offering prayers for her safety.[194] Agrippina must have known that Nero had tried to kill her, but she decided to feign ignorance. She sent her confidential freedman Agerinus to Nero with news of the misfortune and assurances that she was safe. By now Nero was beside himself, afraid that Agrippina would find a way to strike back, and desperate to be rid of his mother once and for all. He, or one of his men, dropped a sword at Agerinus' feet and claimed that he had been sent by Agrippina to assassinate the emperor.[195]

Nero sent Anicetus and his soldiers to Agrippina's villa to finish her off. The troops surrounded the house and Anicetus burst into the villa with his officers. Agrippina was with a slave girl, who ran off in terror as her mistress called after her, "Do you abandon me, too?"[196] The soldiers found Agrippina alone in her bedroom. She guessed their mission but protested that she did not believe her son would order them to kill her. One of the officers, a naval captain, hit Agrippina on the head with a club. Realizing that the end had come, and that Nero had ordered her execution, she pointed to her womb, where she had carried her only child, and said, "Strike here!" A centurion struck with his sword and Agrippina was dead. She was 43 years old.[197]

Some said that shortly after the murder Nero gazed on his mother's corpse and praised her beauty.[198] That very night, her body was cremated on a dining-room couch.[199] Her ashes were buried along the road from Baiae to Misenum.[200]

The emperor must have tried very hard to believe the official story that he announced in a letter to the senate: Agrippina had sent her servant to kill him and had paid the penalty. She had conspired to take control of the government and had committed innumerable crimes, dating back to the days of Claudius. Nero added that he could hardly believe he was finally safe from her. Still, it took him six months to summon the courage to return to Rome for fear of the reaction to his crime, and his matricide would haunt him for the rest of his life. Suetonius reports that Nero confessed to being haunted by Agrippina's ghost and even employed Persian magicians to placate her.[201]

Despite Nero's fears, there seems to have been no outcry against the murder of Agrippina, though rumors of the emperor's guilt seem to have been rampant.[202] Tacitus reports that when Nero did enter the capital he was greeted with celebrations reminiscent of a triumph.[203] Cassius Dio writes that the people pulled down Agrippina's statues upon his entry into the capital.[204] Nero was congratulated for having foiled a plot against his life and the security of the empire. Annual games were decreed to mark the anniversary of its discovery and Agrippina's birthday was officially declared to be inauspicious.[205]

Similar outpourings of relief and thanksgiving had occurred in the towns of Campania near the scene of Agrippina's murder. Though Tacitus claims that Nero's courtiers had staged these demonstrations,[206] it does appear that Agrippina's death was greeted with considerable rejoicing. It is true that many of her alleged victims had been popular and distinguished: Domitia Lepida (the great-niece of Augustus), Lollia Paulina, and even Claudius, whose death was universally laid at Agrippina's door. She had made many enemies during her career, and her supposed crimes and haughty manners must have undermined her popularity with the people.

The question must be asked – did Agrippina attempt to kill Nero after all? Realizing that he had resolved to murder her, did she send Agerinus to kill him first, hoping that her prestige would allow her to choose his successor? Agrippina's chances of survival after Nero's death would not have been very good. However, the emperor's closest advisors, Seneca and Burrus, owed their positions to her, and the government and Praetorian Guard were still stocked with her favorites. She may have decided that her chances would not be worse than they were with Nero alive.

The calm manner in which Agrippina met her death must have impressed her former protégé, Seneca. A noble death was one of the philosopher's preoccupations and he revered those men and women who had resigned themselves to execution or taken their own lives with dignity. He once wrote, "Death consecrates those whose end is praised even by those who fear it."[207] Nero gave Seneca the opportunity to live up to his own words only six years later when he drove his former teacher and advisor to suicide.[208]

History has condemned Agrippina, probably the most famous of the empresses, for her excessive ambition to gain power and for the unscrupulous means she used to keep it. However, she believed that this was the only way for her to survive. Given the tragic history of her family – and her own horrible end – who could argue with her? As a woman, she could never occupy the throne; she could only rule through the men in her family. This she did more successfully under Claudius than under Nero. In the end, she was subject to the whims of the emperor, just like everyone else.

When Nero was forced to commit suicide at the age of 30, nine years after the murder of Agrippina, he was the last surviving descendant of Augustus. Most of the once-numerous members of the royal family had lost their lives through politically motivated executions or forced suicides. Agrippina understood the game of life at the top of Roman society very well: power was everything. Her life was an endless struggle to obtain it, hold on to it, and pass it on to her son. It is said that, when she was expecting Nero, it was foretold that he would live to become emperor, and to kill his mother. Agrippina's response: "Then let him kill me, so long as he rules!"[209]

Figure 4.2 Gaius Caligula's sisters – (left to right) Agrippina (as Securitas), Drusilla (as Concordia), and Julia Livilla (as Fortuna). Bronze sestertius minted under Caligula, AD 37–38. RIC I 33, BMCRE 37; courtesy Classical Numismatic Group, Inc.

Figure 4.3 Agrippina the Younger portrait on a gold aureus minted under Claudius, AD 51. RIC I 80, BMCRE 72, Cohen 3; courtesy Classical Numismatic Group, Inc.

Figure 4.4 Nero as Caesar at the age of 13 or 14, on a silver cistophoric tetradrachm, minted in Pergamum, *c.* AD 50–51. RIC I 121 (variety), BMCRE 236, Cohen 82; courtesy Classical Numismatic Group, Inc.

Figure 4.5 Dramatic portrait of Agrippina's brother Caligula on a silver denarius, minted in AD 37. RIC I 2, BMCRE 4; courtesy Classical Numismatic Group, Inc.

Figure 4.6 Caligula making a sacrifice in front of a temple dedicated to his great-grandfather, the deified Augustus. Bronze sestertius, minted AD 37–38. RIC I 36, BMCRE 41, Cohen 9; courtesy Classical Numismatic Group, Inc.

Figure 4.7 Agrippina the Younger's uncle Claudius as emperor. Bronze sestertius, minted *c.* AD 41–50. RIC I 115, BMCRE 192, Cohen 85; courtesy Classical Numismatic Group, Inc.

Figure 4.8 Crude portrait of Messalina, Roman empress and wife of Claudius, on a bronze coin (diameter 21 mm) minted in Knossus, Crete, *c.* AD 48. RPC 1001–1002; courtesy Classical Numismatic Group, Inc.

Figure 4.9 Portrait of Britannicus, Claudius' son by Messalina, on a bronze sestertius, minted in the Balkans under Claudius, *c.* AD 50–54. RIC I p. 130 note, BMCRE 226 (Claudius) and 306 (Titus), Cohen 2; courtesy Classical Numismatic Group, Inc.

Figure 4.10 Messalina, wife of Claudius, holding miniature figures of her children, Octavia and Britannicus. Billon tetradrachm, minted in Alexandria, Egypt, AD 43–44. BMC 72, Köln 81, Dattari 185; courtesy Harlan J. Berk, Ltd.

4.11

4.12

4.13

4.14

Figure 4.11 Galba, Roman emperor in AD 68–69, who was unsuccessfully wooed years earlier by Agrippina the Younger. Bronze sestertius, RIC I 389, BMCRE p. 319, RSC 223; courtesy Classical Numismatic Group, Inc.

Figure 4.12 Expressive portraits of Claudius and Agrippina the Younger on a silver cistophoric tetradrachm minted in Ephesus, *c.* AD 50–51. RIC I 119, BMCRE 231; courtesy Classical Numismatic Group, Inc.

Figure 4.13 Agrippina and her *carpentum*, or ceremonial carriage, on a bronze sestertius minted under Claudius, *c.* AD 50–54. RIC I 103; courtesy Numismatik Lanz München.

Figure 4.14 Nero as Princeps Iuventutis, the "Prince of Youth," on a silver denarius minted under Claudius, *c.* AD 51–54. RIC 79 (Claudius), BMCRE 93 (Claudius), Cohen 97; courtesy Numismatik Lanz München.

Figure 4.15 The infant Hercules strangling the serpents sent by Hera to kill him. Silver nomos, minted in Kroton, Italy, *c.* 370 BC. SNG ANS 384–386, SNG Lockett 631, SNG Lloyd 618, Jameson 433, Dewing 513; courtesy Classical Numismatic Group, Inc.

Figure 4.16 Portraits of Nero (left) and Claudius (right) on a silver tetradrachm, struck under Nero at an uncertain mint in Syria, *c.* AD 54–68. RPC 4123, RSC 2, Sydenham 65 (Caesarea); courtesy Classical Numismatic Group, Inc.

Figure 4.17 Silver denarius struck soon after Claudius' death showing Nero facing his mother Agrippina, with her titles on the obverse of the coin, his on the reverse. Minted in Lugdunum, Gaul (Lyons, France) in AD 54. RIC I 2, BMCRE 3, RSC 7; courtesy Classical Numismatic Group, Inc.

Figure 4.18 Nero and Agrippina, with his titles on the obverse, hers relegated to the reverse. Silver denarius, minted in AD 55. RIC I 7, BMCRE 8, RSC 4; courtesy Classical Numismatic Group, Inc.

Figure 4.19 The Mother Goddess Cybele, enthroned, holding a tympanum (drum) and patera (ceremonial offering bowl), with lions at her feet. Her cult was favored during Claudius' reign. Bronze coin (diameter 26 mm) of Tomis, Moesia Inferior, minted under Philip I, *c.* AD 247–249. Pick 3604.

Figure 4.20 Nero facing his first wife Octavia, the daughter of Claudius and Messalina, on a bronze coin (diameter 27 mm) minted in Knossus, Crete, *c.* AD 54–62. RPC 1006, Svoronos, Crete, p. 95, 217; courtesy Classical Numismatic Group, Inc.

Figure 4.21 Portrait of Poppaea, Nero's second wife, on a billon tetradrachm, minted in Alexandria, Egypt, AD 63–64. Köln 157/158, BMC 122/123, Milne 217–221, Curtis, 138–142; courtesy Classical Numismatic Group, Inc.

Figure 4.22 Roman ship on a coin of Tranquillina, Roman empress from AD 241–244. Bronze coin (diameter 24mm) minted in Hadrianopolis, Thrace. BMC Thrace p. 122, 46 variety, Mionnet Supplement II p. 334, 809; courtesy Classical Numismatic Group, Inc.

4.23   4.24

4.25

Figure 4.23 Portrait of Agrippina the Younger on a silver drachm, minted under Nero in Caesarea, Cappadocia, *c.* AD 54–59. (There is a later countermark to the right of the portrait.) RPC 3637.5, Howgego 850, Sydenham 78 (variety); courtesy Classical Numismatic Group, Inc.

Figure 4.24 Portrait sestertius of Nero, minted in Rome AD 64. RIC I 178, cf. BMCRE 131 note, Cohen 38; courtesy Classical Numismatic Group, Inc.

Figure 4.25 Statilia Messalina, third and final wife of Nero, on a bronze coin (diameter 19 mm) minted in Ephesus, *c.* AD 66–68. RPC 2632; courtesy Classical Numismatic Group, Inc.

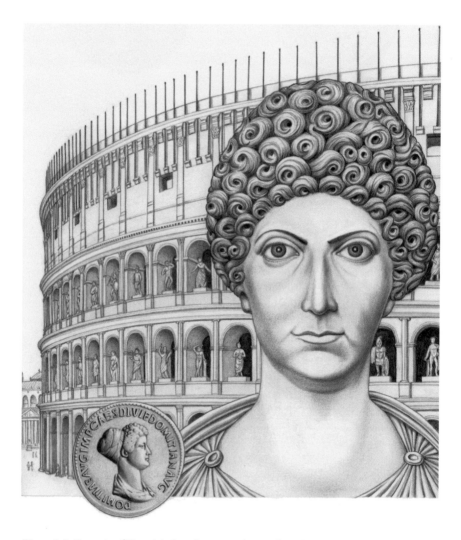

Figure 5.1 Portrait of Domitia based on a sculpture from Terracina, Italy, now in the Museo Nazionale delle Terme, Rome. The coin is a rare bronze sestertius. Behind Domitia is the Flavian Amphitheatre, or Colosseum, which was completed during her husband Domitian's reign.

5

DOMITIA LONGINA

The survivor

At the time of his mother's death in 59, Nero still enjoyed a reputation as a reasonably efficient and successful ruler. This was largely due to the efforts of others, including his chief advisors, Seneca and Burrus, and the most famous and successful general of the day, Gnaeus Domitius Corbulo. As we shall see, Corbulo would pay the price for excellence under Nero, but his daughter Domitia Longina would survive to become an empress and to play a pivotal role in Roman history.

Corbulo, born about the year AD 1, or a few years earlier, had an impressive appearance and was a master orator. He was known for his wisdom, graciousness, and his blunt sense of humor. (He once called a man a "plucked ostrich" to his face in the senate, driving the man to tears.) Corbulo achieved significant military successes in Germany under Claudius, and in Armenia under Nero, and much of Nero's record of success in foreign affairs was due to his accomplishments.[1]

Domitia's father was also a paragon of physical strength. If one wanted to stress the weight of an object, one might say "even Corbulo" could not lift it. A gifted writer, he produced letters and memoirs that were widely read but are now unfortunately lost.[2]

As with many others, Corbulo's undoing was the result of Nero's insecurity, which became extreme after his misrule led to a series of plots and uprisings. The emperor's grip began to loosen in 62, when Burrus died and Seneca retired soon after. Nero replaced Burrus as praetorian prefect with Ofonius Tigellinus, an unscrupulous man who corrupted the conduct of government while encouraging the emperor to act out his artistic and sexual fantasies.[3]

A major setback to Nero's prestige came in the form of a catastrophic fire that ravaged Rome in July, 64, destroying much of the city, including part of the imperial palace.[4] Nero was out of town when the blaze started, but hurried back to deal with the disaster. His measures to relieve the victims and restore order to the city were generous and prompt.[5] However, any credit he might have received was cancelled by the rumor that he sang about the sack of Troy while watching the city burn.[6] And when he claimed a large portion of the ruined area for himself and built a sprawling pleasure palace known as the Domus Aurea (House of Gold), people suspected that the fire had been set at his command.[7]

Nero also found himself increasingly at odds with the senate. In 65, and again in 66, conspiracies arose involving prominent senators intent on removing him from the throne. The second, more serious plot seems to have been led by Annius Vinicianus, a son-in-law of Corbulo.[8] Apparently, Vinicianus hoped to replace Nero with his father-in-law, the famous general.

Corbulo may have been unaware of his son-in-law's plans for him – at least he was not punished when the conspiracy was exposed. However, Nero could not tolerate a man who had been singled out to rule in his stead.[9] Several months after the incident, in the winter of 66/67, he summoned Corbulo to join him in Greece, ostensibly to receive a new assignment, and ordered his death.[10] When Corbulo received the sentence, he uttered one Greek word: "*Axios*" ("deserved"), grabbed a sword, and killed himself.[11] No one knows whether he meant that he deserved to die for plotting against Nero, for being foolish enough to trust the emperor, or for having served him in the first place.[12]

Nero executed many of Corbulo's friends and relatives during the final years of his reign.[13] Among the fortunate survivors was his teenaged daughter Domitia, born on 11 February in the early to mid-fifties.[14] She had grown up in a very wealthy, very noble senatorial family. Little is known of her mother Longina. She may have been the daughter of a distinguished jurist and descended from Cassius Longinus, one of the assassins of Julius Caesar.[15]

Under the emperors, Domitia's family held a prominent place in the "loyal opposition" to the monarchy. Though they often served the Caesars with distinction, these aristocrats opposed the inherited rule by one man that deprived them of their traditional powers.

Domitia's relations on her father's side included some remarkably independent spirits. Her grandfather, the elder Corbulo, was a quarrelsome senator from the Italian countryside who complained so bitterly about the state of the roads in Italy that Caligula gave him a commission to supervise their repair.[16] However, his actions in this office were so severe that Claudius was forced to make restitution to his victims.[17]

This man's wife, Vistilia, Domitia's grandmother, married six times and gave birth to five children in the seventh month of pregnancy, one in the eighth month, and one in the eleventh month.[18] Her seven children included Domitia's father Corbulo and his half-sister Caesonia, the last wife of the emperor Caligula. Another Vistilia, possibly a niece of Domitia's grandmother, showed the family individualism by proclaiming herself to be a prostitute rather than fall foul of the laws against adultery. However, her high birth made this ruse legally unacceptable and she was banished from Rome.[19]

As a young girl in a privileged family, Domitia would have received a fine education. She seems to have developed an interest in literature,[20] which was entering a period of high achievement and creativity in the Rome of her youth. At an early age she was married to a man with the formidable name of Lucius Aelius Lamia Plautius Aelianus. Lamia (for short) had a son from a previous marriage, was witty, with a good voice and a love of music, but had very little energy.[21]

The death of Corbulo did not bring Nero's troubles to an end. Another uprising came in March of 68, led by Julius Vindex, the governor of one of the provinces in Gaul. Vindex stood little chance of success until he was joined by Servius Sulpicius Galba, the governor of the largest province in Spain and one of the noblest and most experienced of Roman leaders. Nevertheless, Vindex was quickly defeated by troops loyal to Nero, who might have survived the challenge from Galba if he had kept his composure. Instead, he panicked and tried to flee to the eastern part of the empire. The Praetorian Guard abandoned him, and on 9 June, 68, after reigning for nearly fourteen years, the last of the so-called Julio-Claudian emperors committed suicide with the assistance of his private secretary. Among Nero's last words was the famous phrase: "What an artist the world is losing in me."[22]

Domitia must have welcomed the end of the tyrant who had caused her father's death. The new emperor Galba was a dignified, severe-looking man of 70 who seemed capable of restoring order to the empire. However, he quickly made some crucial mistakes. He offended many of his supporters and, far worse, the legions in Germany by failing to reward their support as generously as they had expected. Within three months of his arrival in Rome in October, 68, Galba had been murdered and the empire was plunged into civil war.[23]

A former friend of Nero's, Marcus Otho (who had lost his wife Poppaea Sabina to the emperor), took command in Rome; at the same time, a provincial governor, Aulus Vitellius, was proclaimed emperor by the legions in Germany. By April of 69, Otho had been defeated and committed suicide.

It must have seemed to many that the matter was settled. The new emperor Vitellius was from a very distinguished family and had been a favorite of Tiberius, Caligula, Claudius, and Nero.[24] He did not, however, have a good reputation. Vitellius was infamous for his gluttony, his shameless flattery of the Julio-Claudian emperors, and for his Nero-like tastes for chariot racing, acting, and sexual escapades.[25] His assumption of the throne had been due to the initiative of the legions in Germany, not to his own qualities or energetic actions.[26] Furthermore, the dizzying events of the past year had demonstrated that anyone with ambition and an army behind him could claim the throne. Accordingly, on 1 July, 69, Titus Flavius Sabinus Vespasianus (better known as Vespasian), the governor of the province of Judaea and the leading general in the East, made his play for power.

Vespasian was a capable, 60-year-old soldier with wide experience of government and military matters. Nero's confidence in him was shown by his assignment to Judaea, where he confronted a serious rebellion, known as the First Jewish Revolt. This uprising would not be completely put down until the fall of the fortress of Masada in the year 73.

Vespasian's candidacy for the throne was enhanced by his having two grown sons capable of succeeding him as emperor. (His wife and daughter, both named Flavia Domitilla, had previously died.[27]) The elder son, Titus, was nearly 30 and had already commanded a legion in Judaea. His younger brother, the 17-year-old Domitian, was in Rome, living with his father's older brother Titus Flavius Sabinus.

Vespasian's brother Sabinus still held the high office of prefect of the city of Rome that he had received from Nero. It speaks well for Vitellius that he did not persecute the relatives of Vespasian who were in the capital and under his power. Tacitus, however, attributes this restraint to Vitellius' concern for his own relatives who were living outside his area of control.[28]

One can imagine the atmosphere in Rome as reports of Vespasian's actions filtered in. He had dispatched a force under the command of his ally, Caius Licinius Mucianus, to move on the capital.

As Mucianus' army and other supporters of Vespasian approached the city, chaos reigned in the streets. Vitellius, realizing that his cause was lost, was nearly persuaded by Vespasian's brother Sabinus to abdicate. However, his supporters would have none of it. They besieged and captured Sabinus and many of Vespasian's supporters on the Capitoline Hill and hauled them before Vitellius in chains.[29] The mob insisted on execution; Sabinus himself was beheaded.[30] Fortunately, Vespasian's son Domitian had been hidden by the caretaker of the Temple of Jupiter on the Capitoline, which was destroyed by fire in the attack.[31] Domitian took refuge among the worshipers of the goddess Isis and, the next day, was smuggled to safety wearing the linen robes of a priest.[32]

On 20 December, 69, Vespasian's forces fought their way into the city. Vitellius was captured, tortured, and killed. Domitian came out of hiding, was hailed as "Caesar," and escorted by the soldiers to his father's house.[33]

With Vespasian in Egypt and his older brother Titus in Judaea, Domitian emerged as his father's figurehead in the capital. He was very young (18), and it was primarily his father's lieutenant Mucianus who exercised power in the capital as Vespasian's representative.[34] Nevertheless, it was nearly a year before Vespasian came to Rome and his younger son became accustomed to the trappings of power.

Domitian had also become the most eligible bachelor in Rome. Even his enemies admitted that he was an unusually handsome man. Tall and well built, he had a slight overbite and a florid complexion, which together gave him an air of modesty and sincerity, though he was often rude and quick-tempered.[35] His deep voice served him well in public recitals of his own poetry.[36] He also seems to have inherited his father's talent for one-liners (of which more later). For example, Domitian once said of a man known for his vanity, "My, to be as handsome as Maecius thinks he is!"[37]

Domitian was reputed to be highly sexed, with an insatiable appetite for what he called "bed-wrestling."[38] His new position as Caesar greatly enhanced his powers of seduction, and the young prince became famous for his many affairs.[39] However, Domitian soon fell passionately in love with a married woman: Domitia Longina.

Domitia was still in her teens and might well have been impressed by the good-looking young prince. It seems that she shared his enthusiasm for literature,[40] and she may have been unhappy in her marriage to Lamia. It is possible that her husband was so anxious to please the new ruling family that he encouraged the attachment as a way to advance his career (he did eventually attain the consulship).[41] If so, Domitia can hardly have regretted losing such a husband.[42] On the other hand, Cassius Dio and Suetonius report that the infatuated prince took Domitia from Lamia by force. In any case, they were married about the time of Vespasian's arrival in Rome in late 70.[43]

The surviving portraits of Domitia, which consist of statues and images on coins from the reign of Domitian, are somewhat confusing. Most of the sculpted likenesses and the busts on large bronze coins (see Figure 5.1) show a plumpish, pleasant-looking woman with an oval face, arched brows, a small mouth, somewhat pointed nose, and a strong chin. However, many of the gold and silver coins of Domitia depict a masculine-looking woman with a heavy brow, protruding chin, and large, blunt nose (see Figures 5.9, 5.10). In fact, she looks very much like her husband Domitian in drag. Presumably, these coin portrayals came from the imagination of engravers who had never seen Domitia or a competent portrait of her.

Domitia's character is equally elusive. Suetonius remarks that she was guilty of many misdeeds and that she openly boasted of them, suggesting that she was a defiant and outspoken woman.[44] However, in the mid-sixth century, after the fall of Rome and the western half of the empire, the Palestinian writer Procopius described Domitia as a discreet woman of noble character who never harmed anyone and was beloved by the Roman people.[45] Though Procopius is not considered to be a reliable source, his account tells us something of how Domitia was remembered. Her popularity with the Roman people is also attested by Cassius Dio.[46]

Vespasian certainly must have approved of his son's choice for a wife. In fact, despite the stories of Domitian's uncontrollable passion and abduction of his bride, it is quite possible that the union was arranged for political purposes. Vespasian wanted to distance himself as much as possible from Nero and would have welcomed a connection with the daughter of Corbulo, one of Nero's most famous and admired victims. Also, the dead general's family far exceeded Vespasian's in prestige and nobility.[47]

The emperor's arrival in Rome in 70 must have been a bit of a shock to Domitian and his bride. There were stories that Vespasian disapproved of the liberties taken by Domitian in exercising his powers, even that he sarcastically thanked his son for allowing him to keep his throne.[48] For nearly a year, the young prince had enjoyed the status of a virtual emperor in Rome; now he was merely second in line behind his brother Titus.[49]

Also, Domitian the poet,[50] who had grown up in an atmosphere of aesthetic refinement and innovation under Nero, must have been disconcerted by his father's rough, conservative new image of royalty. Vespasian wanted to found a dynasty with a less pretentious style than the previous one and emphatically rejected the image of emperor as a sophisticated, eccentric autocrat.

Vespasian, who was from the Sabine country in Italy, intentionally fostered the impression of being a down-to-earth, almost peasant-like soldier from the old school who spoke with a country accent and got where he was through plain hard work.[51] He wore a crew cut rather than an elaborately styled hairdo like Nero's and made himself unprecedentedly available to his subjects. He was even seen carrying a load of soil like a common laborer during the renovation of the fire-damaged Temple of Jupiter in Rome.[52]

The image that Vespasian cultivated was something of a lie. He, his father, and his elder brother had been consuls, and his son Titus had been educated at the palace with the emperor Claudius' son Britannicus.[53] Vespasian had commanded a legion during Claudius' conquest of Britain, and had been honored by Tiberius, Caligula, and Claudius before becoming a member of Nero's inner circle. He accompanied the emperor on his "artistic tour" of Greece, and the story that Vespasian angered Nero – by falling asleep while the emperor was singing – may well have been invented or exaggerated to make him seem one of Nero's victims rather than one of his cronies.[54]

However, Vespasian's image as "a regular guy" was enhanced by stories of his affability and humorous remarks. Fortunately, many of these anecdotes have come down to us and serve to make him seem more human than most of the men who ruled the Roman Empire.

For example, in expressing his contempt for the luxurious lifestyle of his rival for the throne, Vespasian said: "Vitellius uses more ointment in his bath than I do water. If he was pierced by a sword, more ointment would run out of him than blood."[55] In a similar vein, when a heavily perfumed young man came to thank Vespasian for a commission he had received, he found the appointment revoked by the disgusted emperor. Vespasian said, "I wouldn't have minded so much if you had only smelled of garlic."[56]

Many of Vespasian's witticisms had to do with sex. One example describes his encounter with a female admirer. The woman threw herself at Vespasian, claiming that she loved him madly, and walked away from his bed 4,000 gold pieces richer. When the emperor's accountant asked him how to enter the expense in the books, Vespasian replied, "Charge it to passion for Vespasian."[57]

When his son, the future emperor Titus, complained to his father about his new tax on lavatories, Vespasian made Titus sniff a coin that had been earned from the tax and asked him if it smelled bad. Titus replied that it did not, and Vespasian declared, "And yet it comes from urine."[58]

A delegation from the senate informed Vespasian that a colossal statue of him costing a million sesterces had been voted in his honor at public expense. The emperor stuck out his hand, palm upward, and said "Here's the pedestal, give me the money."[59]

Perhaps the best proof of Vespasian's sense of humor was his ability to take a joke. He had a very solid, compact build, and the knobby features of his deeply furrowed, square face gave him the appearance of a perpetual grimace. When he asked a famous wit to make a joke about him, Vespasian apparently laughed as well as anyone when the man replied, "I will when you have finished relieving yourself."[60]

Whenever anonymous insults to the emperor were posted in public, Vespasian would simply post a reply in kind, as if to say "Same to you, buddy," and bear no further grudge.[61] Similarly, when the Cynic philosopher Demetrius snubbed and insulted Vespasian, he replied, "Good dog!" punning on the derivation of "cynic" from the Greek word for dog.[62]

Though the stories of Vespasian's lack of pretension and homespun habits endeared him to his subjects, they projected an image that was alien to the refined and autocratic Domitian. Finding himself shut out from the exercise of real power and out of step with his father's court, he withdrew. He and Domitia spent most of their time at their magnificent villa in Alba, some 12 miles (19 km) from Rome, pursuing their artistic interests and beginning a family.[63] Though continuing to perform his ceremonial role in public, he took little part in governing the empire.

Domitia's household at this time probably included her niece, Flavia Julia, the motherless daughter of Domitian's brother Titus.[64] She was about 6 or 7 when Domitian married in 70, and her unmarried father was away from Rome until June of the following year. When Titus returned to the capital in 71, he would have been preoccupied with his duties at court and Julia probably continued to stay with her uncle. She remained close to him for the rest of her life and, as we shall see, there is some reason to believe that she was devoted to Domitia as well.

There is much confusion about Domitia's children. In 73, when she was about 20 (or, alternatively, as much as ten years later), she seems to have given birth to a son, who died at 2 or 3 years of age.[65] Suetonius records that Domitia also had a daughter, but, if she ever existed, she left no other mark on the historical record.[66] There is also a controversial bit of evidence in a poem of Martial that Domitia was pregnant in 90, when she was in her mid-thirties.[67] However, this potential child also remains unknown to history, suggesting that Domitia suffered a miscarriage, though some scholars think that Martial was merely wishing out loud.[68]

The death of Domitia's son must have been a cruel blow to the imperial family. His passing was observed on coins, including a silver denarius of 81–84, the reverse of which shows Domitia seated beside her boy (see Figure 5.12).[69] Gold and silver coins were also issued, depicting the chubby infant sitting on a globe, reaching out to the stars (see Figure 5.13).[70] The child was deified and, in a touching passage by Martial, he is described as sprinkling snow from heaven onto the head of his father, who smiles with pleasure.[71]

The production of heirs was the most important duty of a princess, and Domitia's failure must have weighed heavily on her. The pressure probably increased in 79 when Vespasian died after almost a decade of rule. According to Suetonius, he delivered the most famous of his one-liners on his deathbed. Realizing that the end had come and anticipating his inevitable deification, he said: "Dear me, I'm turning into a god!"[72]

Suddenly, Domitian was heir to the throne. His older brother Titus was emperor, but was unmarried and had no sons. The new emperor looked to his only daughter Flavia Julia and to his brother to provide him with heirs. With Domitia apparently unable to bear viable children, Titus suggested that Domitian divorce her – and marry Julia.[73]

In effect, Domitian had to choose between his wife and supreme power. If he did not marry Julia, then she would certainly be married to someone else, and one of her children would eventually replace him as Titus' successor. However, he loved Domitia and refused his brother's request.[74]

Domitian is said to have admired the emperor Tiberius and to have enjoyed reading his memoirs.[75] He may well have remembered Tiberius' bitter regrets over having bowed to the will of Augustus in divorcing his wife Vipsania to marry another Julia, the daughter of the first emperor. He was determined not to make the same mistake, even if it meant that he would never rule.[76]

Somewhat grudgingly, Titus married Julia to her cousin instead. But, before they could provide him with an heir, Titus died at the age of 41 after a reign of only 27 months. Suddenly, Domitian was emperor after all, taking the throne on 14 September, 81, at the age of 29.

Titus had been a robust, charismatic, and kind-hearted man, and his subjects mourned him sincerely.[77] As emperor, he was extremely popular, though he had earlier gained a reputation for severity as praetorian prefect under his father.[78] Domitia might well have resented Titus' efforts to make her husband divorce her and marry his daughter. However, Titus had himself relinquished love for the sake of duty. After divorcing Julia's mother (his second wife) in 64 or 65, he fell in love with the beautiful Jewish queen Berenice.[79] She visited him in Rome twice, but Titus sent her away both times because of public opposition to the match.[80] Interestingly, he never remarried after his divorce, though he desperately wanted an heir.

When Titus died, he reportedly said that he regretted just one of his actions.[81] There has been much speculation about what he meant by this. Domitian supposedly claimed that Titus regretted having failed to share the throne with him, as he believed Vespasian had intended.[82] Cassius Dio preferred the view that he regretted not having killed Domitian before he could rule.[83] Both Dio and Suetonius mention another startling theory: that he was remembering his alleged adultery with his sister-in-law Domitia (an affair she vehemently denied ever happened). However, it seems most likely that Titus felt remorse for having repudiated Berenice, the woman he loved, for political reasons.

Domitia Longina now filled the role of empress that had been vacant under both Vespasian and Titus, neither of whom had been married while they ruled. There is little evidence that she exercised the political influence enjoyed by her Julio-Claudian predecessors, such as Livia or Agrippina the Younger. However, her input might be seen in Domitian's candidates for the consulship.

This was the highest position available to a Roman citizen other than the emperor. Vespasian and Titus had kept this office within the family to an unprecedented degree. However, while Domitian was consul more often than any other man in Roman history (seventeen times), he also broke with family tradition by awarding the post to many senators from the old aristocratic families, including several of his staunchest opponents. The fact that Domitia's family belonged to this group, and that she had many connections within it, raises the possibility of her involvement in her husband's choices.[84]

Domitia received the title of Augusta[85] and appeared on coins wearing a new hairstyle that set the standard of fashion for Roman women (see Figure 5.14). It consisted of a high crown of tight curls above the forehead that would grow ever taller as the years passed until it became almost a tower, requiring the support of a wire frame.[86] The rest of the hair was arranged in braids that were gathered into a queue, or sometimes a bun, at the back of the head. This hairstyle required a significant amount of skill and time for an *ornatrix*, or hairdresser, to create. We know the name of one of Domitia's *ornatrices* – a young woman named Telesphoris who died at age 25 and whose husband honored her memory with a marble plaque.[87]

The Roman satirist Juvenal joked about the illusion of great height created by this hairdo: "She builds her head high with so many curls that she looks like Andromache (a towering mythological woman) from the front. But she is not so tall from behind – you would take her for someone else."[88] Soon, every Roman woman who could afford it was wearing the hairdo. As Juvenal put it: "What woman will not follow where an empress leads?"[89]

While Domitia played the role of empress, something was going terribly wrong in her marriage. After eleven years of sharing a semi-retired life with her husband, she was losing Domitian to his new job. Also, there are several contradictions in Domitian's character and behavior that suggest he was difficult to live with.

For example, the young Domitian displayed a profound distaste for blood-shed; he objected to the eating of beef and even drafted an edict forbidding the sacrifice of oxen.[90] When passing sentence against criminals, he shied away from death by flogging as being too horrible. Yet he was also famous for his pastime of killing flies with a sharp pen, for his acts of extreme cruelty, and his enthusiasm for gladiatorial contests.[91] He even staged torch-lit matches at his Alban villa, pairing cripples, dwarfs, and women, and requiring the combatants to use especially sharp swords. Though he loathed the castration of boys and made the practice illegal, he was openly devoted to his eunuchs, one of whom, named Earinus, the poet Papinius Statius celebrated for his beauty.[92] Domitian was a loner who enjoyed solitude and was uncomfortable with people, yet his court was as lavish and crowded with toadies and concubines as Nero's had ever been.[93]

It is tempting to speculate about Domitia's personality on the basis of her husband's apparent taste for aggressive women. He promoted women's sports (footraces for girls in the arena and combats between female gladiators) and was particularly devoted to the warrior goddess Minerva (often shown with shield, spear, and helmet). His term for sexual intercourse ("bed-wrestling") is also suggestive. Perhaps the character of Domitia, the daughter of a paragon of strength and courage, fit into this pattern in some way.

Cassius Dio describes a bizarre scene that, if factual, reveals something of Domitian's darker side. The emperor gave a nocturnal feast to the leading senators and Roman knights in a room that was completely black, with black furnishings and naked slave boys as waiters, also painted black. Beside each guest was a silver gravestone, inscribed with his own name. Food was served on black plates in a manner that recalled offerings to the dead. Meanwhile, Domitian spoke of death and slaughter. His terrified guests were finally dismissed and later rewarded with the silver "tombstones" and the slave boys, washed and adorned as gifts.[94] Dio does not tell us if Domitia was present at this affair; it seems likely that she was.

Whatever strains Domitian's quirks might have put on the imperial marriage, matters came to a head in 83. The couple separated and Domitia left Rome. The explanation for this startling event, recorded by Roman historians years later, runs like this: Domitian discovered that his wife had fallen in love and committed adultery with a famous actor by the name of Paris.[95] He divorced the empress and murdered Paris in the streets of Rome.[96] Suetonius even claims that Domitian executed one of Paris' young students for resembling his teacher too closely and banished the author of a farce that seemed to refer to the emperor's divorce.[97] Domitian was supposedly tempted to have Domitia executed, but was dissuaded by an imperial relative, a man named Lucius Julius Ursus, and sent her into exile instead.[98]

Shortly after the divorce, Domitian's niece Julia moved into the palace, her husband having been executed by Domitian.[99] Cassius Dio claims that tongues began to wag about an incestuous relationship between them.[100] To silence this gossip – or perhaps because he missed the woman he truly loved – the emperor recalled Domitia after a brief separation, remarried her, and reinstated her as his empress. He is supposed to have said that he recalled his wife because "the people demanded it."[101] Suetonius provides the detail that the emperor referred to Domitia as being "called back to my divine bed."[102]

Some historians believed that Domitian really did have an affair with Julia.[103] It was even claimed that it continued after Domitia's return and that, when Julia became pregnant by him in the late 80s, the emperor insisted that she have an abortion, which proved fatal.[104] (Abortions were generally performed skillfully in the Roman Empire, and were legal until the end of the second century.[105])

Modern scholars have questioned the story of Domitian's reaction to his wife's alleged affair with Paris because he was a notorious stickler for the rules.[106] Augustus' laws against adultery gave him the right to kill his wife's lover, but only if he divorced her and never took her back. In fact, Domitian punished a Roman knight who took his wife back after divorcing her for adultery.[107] By remarrying Domitia (a ceremony for which there is no record), the emperor would have been breaking a law that he clearly supported and become technically guilty of murder.

One possible reason for a separation was Domitia's failure to provide an heir. Domitian may have divorced her reluctantly for the good of the dynasty, then taken her back without adequate explanation. This would have left the door open for imaginative gossip to supply the reasons.[108]

Another possibility is that Domitia left her husband of her own free will. The story of her unfaithfulness may be doubted. While most empresses were accused of habitual promiscuity, the ancient writers charged Domitia with only two lapses in this regard: the affair with Paris, and the supposed liaison with Titus mentioned by Suetonius.[109] She denied the accusation of adultery with her brother-in-law so solemnly that even the scandal-loving Suetonius believed her.[110]

The tale of Julia's affair with Domitian is also rejected as fantasy.[111] The fact that Domitia returned to her husband soon after his niece moved into the palace suggests that Julia had a role in the reconciliation and argues strongly against any affair between her and her uncle. The story of Julia's abortion is also unlikely to be true. The emperor was so desperate for an heir that he would certainly have found a way to explain and accept his niece's child, especially as nothing would have prevented him from legally marrying Julia, thanks to the precedent of Claudius and Agrippina.

Also, even after Julia's death between 87 and 90,[112] there were still hopes that Domitia might produce an heir. The court poet Martial wrote a fantasy about her having a son named Julius after the deceased and deified Julia, who would serve as a sort of celestial guardian for the infant.[113] It seems unlikely that Martial would have written such a thing if he had heard stories of an affair between Julia and Domitian.[114]

Whatever really happened, Domitia resumed her place at her husband's side, probably in 84, within a year of their separation. Coins minted during the following year or later celebrate Concordia August, or the concord of the imperial couple. However, Domitia would not appear on any coins of the imperial mint during the last decade of her husband's rule.[115]

Interestingly, Domitia's disappearance from the coinage coincided with the turning point in his reign. From 85 on, Domitian became more autocratic and oppressive and his enemies multiplied in number.

Domitian's regime is one of the most controversial in Roman history. Though there is persuasive evidence that he was a gifted ruler and accomplished many positive things, the ancient historians detested him and described him as a vicious, bloodthirsty tyrant. Much of this negative press comes from the Roman writers Pliny and Tacitus, both of whom served under Domitian and benefited from his patronage.[116] Writing under the succeeding dynasty, they were anxious to explain away their cooperation with him and to justify the claims of their new rulers to have restored justice and liberty to the empire.

Also, these and other writers were members of the group of senators who were often at odds with Domitian and who had seen many of their friends banished or executed by him. Pliny himself was charged with treason shortly before Domitian's death and would probably have been executed had the emperor not died first.[117] When Domitian's enemies had the opportunity to get revenge with their pens, they took full advantage of it.[118]

The dynasty established by Domitian's successor (Nerva) remained in power (in name, though not in reality) from 96 until 235, so it remained politic for Domitian to be regarded as an ogre who had deserved to be replaced. Any other view would have reflected on the right of his successors to rule. It is only in recent years that scholars have taken another look at his reign and recognized his substantial abilities and achievements.[119]

A balanced view of Domitian reveals him as a vainglorious but hardworking and conscientious emperor, determined that his government would be administered efficiently and with as little corruption as possible. Even his enemies conceded that government officials were never more honest than under Domitian.[120] Though he alienated many people, particularly among the ruling classes, he was a competent and effective ruler.

Domitian saw himself as a "new Augustus," responsible for the moral climate of the empire as well as its security and prosperity. Like the first emperor, he stiffened laws against adultery and encouraged traditional religious practices whenever possible.[121] He clamped down on the behavior of the Vestal Virgins, insisting on their chastity and executing those who were found guilty of "incest" (as they were daughters of the state, sexual intercourse between a Vestal and any Roman was considered incest).[122] He ordered that a chief vestal, Cornelia, receive the traditional punishment for this crime – live burial, with her supposed lovers being clubbed to death.[123]

Domitian also enforced the Scantinian Law against homosexual acts with freeborn males, outlawed castration, restricted the performance of mimes and farces (which were generally quite vulgar), forbade the use of obscene language by satirical poets, and even exiled a senator for being too fond of acting and dancing.[124]

Domitian's desire to play the role of the glorious Roman ruler meant that he had to be successful as a soldier. On five occasions he left Rome to fight on the northern frontiers of the empire, spending a total of three years on military campaign.[125] None of these wars were won as conclusively as he would have liked and his armies even suffered defeats on several occasions. Still, he succeeded in securing the empire's borders and gained the opportunity to cover himself in military honors.

Personally, Domitian was very religious and profoundly devoted to the goddess Minerva, the Roman equivalent of the Greek Athena (see Figure 5.16).[126] He even claimed to be her son and had a shrine dedicated to her in his bedroom.[127] He was also assiduous in honoring other ancestral Roman deities. The Temple of Jupiter on the Capitoline Hill in Rome, which the supporters of Vitellius had destroyed, had been rebuilt by Vespasian, only to burn down again in 80. Now Domitian restored it in unprecedented grandeur, spending the enormous sum of 288 million sesterces (nearly one-quarter of his annual revenues) in gilding it.[128]

His religious interests also embraced some of the so-called oriental cults, which were steadily gaining acceptance and adherents in Rome. Specifically, the Egyptian gods Isis and Serapis and the Anatolian Great Mother Cybele were honored by Domitian and celebrated on his coins.[129] The rising status of these foreign religions is reflected in the story of Domitian's escape from the followers of Vitellius in 69 by disguising himself as a worshiper of Isis. Forty years before this event, the writer Valerius Maximus described an almost identical case in which a Roman nobleman had escaped his enemies in 42 BC by impersonating a priest of the same goddess.[130] However, while Maximus criticized this man for demeaning himself by associating with a disreputable cult, Domitian's adventure was reported without a hint of disgrace.

Domitian's consular appointments and his support of traditional Roman values and customs should have won him support among the conservative aristocracy in Rome. However, any credit he might have gained was canceled by his conduct toward the senate. His father's philosophy of government had been absolute rule by the emperor, with very little power in the hands of the senators. But both he and Titus had disguised this attitude by observing the old formalities, attending senate meetings regularly, and behaving modestly and without display.

Domitian inherited their ideas of absolute rule, but not their willingness to show deference to the senate.[131] He rarely attended its meetings and carried on business as usual while out of the capital, without referring matters for senatorial consideration.[132] He also began to appoint non-senators as governors of key provinces and as commanders of armies in the field – positions that had traditionally been reserved for senators alone.[133] He made no attempt to hide the fact that real power rested entirely with him and the imperial court.

To add insult to injury Domitian made no pretense of living simply, as his father had done. He built a magnificent palace on the Palatine Hill in Rome – so magnificent that all future emperors were content to live in it. With a full stadium in its grounds, Domitian's new house towered above the city with walls 10 feet thick. It was gracefully decorated in the grandiose baroque style of the day with colossal statues, mosaics, frescoes, colored marbles, soaring domes, and countless columns. This rich and colorful decoration of the palace may reflect Domitia's tastes as well as the emperor's. The throne room was 138 feet (42.1 meters) long, 105 feet (32 meters) wide, and had a ceiling that towered 98 feet (29.9 meters) above the floor. Domitian's throne occupied the position that would ordinarily have been reserved for a likeness of one of the gods.[134]

Clearly, this was not the home of a humble man. Even his coins show a change in Domitian's image. Under his father and brother, Domitian was shown with the typical family features of hooked nose, double chin, heavy brow, and short, thick neck (see Figure 5.7). Now that he was emperor, Domitian gave himself a facelift. He was determined to look every inch the magnificent autocrat that he intended to be. His coins show an elegant, proud-looking man with a long stately neck, a strong chin, and a carefully arranged coiffure (see Figure 5.18).

This last feature is somewhat surprising as we know that Domitian was rapidly losing his hair.[135] He even wrote a book called "On the Care of the Hair," which he dedicated to a balding friend.[136] His statues reveal that he had learned to comb his dwindling locks forward to hide his baldness. All things considered, it is not surprising that the satirist Juvenal called Domitian "a bald-headed Nero."[137]

Domitian offended many conservative aristocrats by turning his old family home into a magnificent shrine and by renaming his birth month of October "Domitianus."[138] He inaugurated Greek-style games in Rome and appeared at the splendid festival in honor of Capitoline Jupiter wearing Greek dress, including a purple robe and a golden crown that bore images of Jupiter, Juno, and Minerva. His celebrations featured poetical and oratorical contests, horse races, musical competitions, gymnastics, even a footrace for girls.[139] Domitian capped some of his spectacles by distributing gold coins to the crowd, or by scattering little clay balls that were inscribed with the names of valuable prizes that could be claimed by their lucky recipients.[140]

When he and Domitia arrived at the stupendous new amphitheater that his father had begun and that he had completed (known today as the Colosseum), they were hailed as *Dominus et Domina,* or "Lord and Lady."[141] Domitian was behaving precisely as what he was: an absolute monarch. However, his ostentation only made those senators whose traditional powers he monopolized resent him more.

On 1 January, 89, Domitian had to face the rebellion of a provincial army. This revolt was quickly stamped out, but the emperor responded by clamping down heavily on his opponents. Informers were rewarded for reporting critics of Domitian or potential conspirators. There were numerous treason trials, leading to executions, banishments, and the confiscation of property.[142] Philosophers who spoke out against the emperor were sent into exile – in fact, Suetonius claims that all philosophers were banished from Italy.[143]

Domitian even executed his cousin Titus Flavius Clemens and banished his wife, Domitian's own niece Flavia Domitilla, apparently for their religious beliefs.[144] Flavia was the daughter of Domitian's sister, who had died before Vespasian came to power. Flavia's sons, named Vespasianus and Domitianus, were the designated heirs to the throne.[145] According to Cassius Dio, both Clemens and Flavia were charged with "atheism" for having converted to "Jewish ways," a possible reference to Christianity.[146]

The victims of Domitian's purges also included close associates of the empress and her family. Her ex-husband Lamia was killed, supposedly for making insulting remarks against the emperor.[147] Years before, when Titus had urged him to remarry after losing his wife to Domitian, Lamia had quipped "What, are you looking for a wife as well?"[148] Also, he had once credited his fine singing voice to the celibacy forced on him by Domitian.[149] It seems that Lamia finally went too far with his witticisms.

It should be stressed that Domitian's government remained fundamentally sound and efficient throughout his reign.[150] Though he largely ignored the senate when making decisions, he relied on an excellent team of advisors, including two future emperors, Nerva and Trajan. The army adored Domitian, both for having raised their pay by one-third and for spending more time at the frontiers, fighting Rome's enemies, than any previous emperor.[151]

Nevertheless, opposition to Domitian continued to grow. He was increasingly afraid of plots and complained that no one believes an emperor who suspects his enemies are planning to assassinate him until he has been slain.[152] On 18 September, 96, his paranoia was finally justified. The 44-year-old Domitian was stabbed to death in the palace by a group of his low-ranking courtiers.[153]

Suetonius reports that the first blow was struck by a steward named Stephanus.[154] The emperor struggled but was overcome by four other assassins, who stabbed him seven times.[155] His body was cremated and his ashes mingled with those of Julia by his nurse Phyllis, who had raised them both.[156]

While his enemies celebrated, Domitian's supporters were outraged. The army demanded his immediate deification (in vain),[157] and the Praetorian Guard eventually revolted against the new emperor Marcus Cocceius Nerva. The Guard stormed the palace and forced Nerva to hand over two of the assassins, who were brutally killed. Nerva felt so threatened by the indignant troops that he adopted the popular general Trajan as his son and heir in an effort to win them over.[158]

The ancient writers claimed that Domitia knew about the plot in advance, and even that she was one of the conspirators.[159] Cassius Dio wrote that she came across a "hit list" prepared by Domitian and warned the intended victims, who killed the emperor before he could kill them.[160] The fact that the empress survived her husband's death and retained much or all of her wealth argues that, at the least, she accepted Domitian's removal without too much protest.

Domitia was in her early forties when the assassination took place, and still had at least thirty years to live. (We know that she was alive in 126, but had passed away by 140.[161]) She retired to her villa near Gabii, 12 miles (19 km) east of the capital, but remained an important figure in Rome. Josephus acknowledged receiving her patronage, even after Domitian's death.[162] Bricks have been discovered in the vicinity of Rome that were manufactured in 123 at a factory owned by the widowed empress long after the assassination. We know where they were made because they are stamped "from the brickyards of Domitia, wife of Domitian."[163]

These bricks offer a startling insight into the mind and heart of this mysterious woman. They demonstrate that she never remarried, and that she remained loyal to the memory of her husband.[164] After Domitian's death, the senate decreed a *damnatio memoriae*, meaning that his name and image were to be destroyed everywhere in the empire. His name was struck from public monuments and his portraits were demolished, recycled, or melted down.[165] While Domitia could easily have avoided using his name on her bricks, she defied the senate and called herself the "wife of Domitian."[166] The fact that she continued this practice over a long period of time proves that the senate did not dare to reprimand her.

This remarkable deference to Domitia raises an interesting question. Did Domitian's successors treat her with such respect because she had made the ultimate sacrifice? Did Domitia cooperate in the murder of a man she truly loved for the good of the empire? It is intriguing that men of low status committed the crime: a steward, imperial gladiator, head chamberlain, subaltern, and freedman.[167] These were all men who, as residents of the palace, would have been known by Domitia and under her authority. Could she have realized that her husband's situation was hopeless, and therefore conspired, possibly with Nerva, to bring about a relatively bloodless change of government? If so, it is easy to see why the new dynasty treated her so well.

Domitia was never stripped of her title of Augusta by succeeding emperors. In 140, her freedmen erected a shrine at Gabii in her honor and donated funds to pay for an annual feast in celebration of her birthday. An inscribed marble tablet from this shrine has been found, with a dedication to "Domitia Augusta, daughter of Gnaeus Domitius Corbulo." No mention is made of Domitian – apparently, only Domitia could get away with that.[168]

According to Procopius (whose sixth-century writings are full of errors and must be read with caution), Domitia disapproved of her husband's actions but remained devoted to him.[169] He claims that she was summoned by the senate after the assassination and offered whatever she might wish. She asked for her husband's body, which he says had been cut into pieces, so that she might bury it. She also asked to be allowed to set up a single bronze statue in Domitian's honor.[170]

At this point, Procopius claims that, like Isis in the legend of Osiris, Domitia reassembled the parts of her husband's body and had a sculptor model a statue from it. Despite the *damnatio memoriae,* this likeness of Domitian was set up in a prominent place near the Capitol in Rome. Procopius claimed to have seen it himself, and noticed the lines where the body had been put back together.[171] It has been surmised that the marks Procopius saw probably indicated where the statue itself had been reassembled from fragments, not Domitian's body. Indeed, the story of Domitian's dismemberment probably arose from the appearance of the statue.[172]

If Domitia was permitted to pay such a tribute to her husband, then it must be seen as a remarkable concession made by a senate that hated him, perhaps in return for a great service rendered. Whether or not Procopius' tale has any basis in fact, the testimony of the bricks argues that at least some concessions were made to Domitia regarding her husband's memory. Whatever her role in Domitian's removal, she emerged from the palace *coup* unscathed and lived to a ripe old age with her prestige – and her independence – intact.

Figure 5.2 Caricature-like portrait of Galba, Roman emperor in AD 68–69, on a silver denarius minted in Tarraco, Spain. RIC I 45, BMCRE 187, RSC 223; courtesy Classical Numismatic Group, Inc.

Figure 5.3 Silver denarius of Otho, emperor for a brief period in AD 69. RIC I 8, BMCRE 17, RSC 17; courtesy Classical Numismatic Group, Inc.

Figure 5.4 Portrait sestertius of Vitellius, emperor for a brief period in AD 69. RIC I 115, BMCRE p. 376 note, Cohen 61; courtesy Classical Numismatic Group, Inc.

Figure 5.5 Superb portrait of Vespasian on a bronze sestertius, minted AD 71. Cohen 554; courtesy Classical Numismatic Group, Inc.

Figure 5.6 Flavia Domitilla, wife of Vespasian, who died before her husband became emperor. Silver denarius minted under Titus or Domitian, *c.* AD 79–84. RIC II 71 (Titus), BMCRE 137 (Titus), RSC 3; courtesy Classical Numismatic Group, Inc.

Figure 5.7 Portrait of Domitian as Caesar under Vespasian on a silver denarius, minted AD 79. (Compare to portrait on Figure 5.18.) RIC II 243 (Vespasian), BMCRE 265 (Vespasian), RSC 384; courtesy Classical Numismatic Group, Inc.

Figure 5.8 Portrait of Domitian's older brother Titus as Caesar on a bronze sestertius minted under Vespasian, AD 72–73. RIC II 636 (variety) (Vespasian), BMCRE 651a (variety) (Vespasian); courtesy Edward J. Waddell, Ltd.

Figure 5.9 Domitia Longina shown with her husband Domitian on a silver didrachm struck in Caesarea, Cappadocia, *c.* AD 92–93. Apparently unpublished; courtesy Numismatik Lanz München.

Figure 5.10 Portrait of Domitia Longina on a silver denarius, minted AD 81–84. RIC II 212 (Domitian), BMCRE 61 (Domitian); courtesy Classical Numismatic Group, Inc.

5.11   5.12

5.13   5.14

5.15   5.16

Figure 5.11 Flavia Julia, also known as Julia Titi, the daughter of Titus. Silver denarius, minted under Titus, *c.* AD 80–81. RIC II 56 (Titus), BMCRE 141 (Titus), RSC 14; courtesy Classical Numismatic Group, Inc.

Figure 5.12 Domitia, enthroned, with the smaller figure of her deceased son beside her. Silver denarius, minted AD 81–84. RIC II 214 (Domitian), BMCRE 65 (Domitian); courtesy Classical Numismatic Group, Inc.

Figure 5.13 Domitia's son, who died in infancy, seated on globe surrounded by seven stars. This reverse type normally appears on coins of Domitia. However, in this case the obverse is of Domitian. Silver denarius minted *c.* AD 82–83. Cf. RIC II 209a; courtesy Classical Numismatic Group, Inc.

Figure 5.14 Domitia Longina with the towering hairdo that became popular during her reign. Provincial bronze coin (diameter 22 mm) minted by Ephesus and Smyrna, Ionia, in alliance, *c.* AD 81–96. BMC Ionia p. 112, 414/415, SNG Copenhagen 544, SNG von Aulock 1938; courtesy Classical Numismatic Group, Inc.

Figure 5.15 Julia Titi, daughter of Titus, on a bronze dupondius minted during her father's reign, *c.* AD 80–81. RIC II 180 (Titus), BMCRE 257, Cohen 18; courtesy Classical Numismatic Group, Inc.

Figure 5.16 Domitian sacrificing at a shrine of Minerva, to whom he was especially devoted. Bronze sestertius, minted AD 85. RIC II 256, BMCRE 296, Cohen 491; courtesy Classical Numismatic Group, Inc.

5.17

5.18

5.19

5.20

5.21

Figure 5.17 The Egyptian deities Isis and Serapis, both of whom were honored by Domitian. Silver tetradrachm, minted in Egypt under the Hellenistic king, Ptolemy V, *c.* 221–205 BC. Svoronos 1124, SNG Copenhagen 197; courtesy Classical Numismatic Group, Inc.

Figure 5.18 Splendid portrait of Domitian as emperor on a bronze sestertius, minted *c.* AD 95–96. (Compare the earlier portrait of Domitian in Figure 5.7.) RIC II 416, BMCRE p. 407 and note, Cohen 531; courtesy Classical Numismatic Group, Inc.

Figure 5.19 The Flavian Amphitheater, or "Colosseum," begun by Vespasian and completed by Domitian. Bronze sestertius of Titus, minted *c.* AD 80–81. RIC II 110 (variety), BMCRE 190 (variety), Cohen 400 (variety); courtesy Numismatik Lanz München.

Figure 5.20 Nerva, Domitian's successor as emperor, on a bronze sestertius, minted AD 97. RIC II 60, BMCRE 107, Cohen 67; courtesy Classical Numismatic Group, Inc.

Figure 5.21 Domitia Longina (right), with her husband Domitian on a provincial bronze coin (diameter 23 mm) struck in Kibyra, Phrygia, *c.* AD 81–96. SNG von Aulock 3731, BMC Phrygia p. 138, 43, Howgego 444; courtesy Classical Numismatic Group, Inc.

Figure 6.1 Portrait of Plotina, adapted by the author from a head found in Ostia, Italy, now in the Museo Nazionale delle Terme, Rome. The coin is a gold aureus (see Figure 6.16 for a similar specimen). Behind Plotina is the famous aqueduct known as the Pont du Gard near her home city of Nemausus (Nîmes, France) in southern Gaul.

6

PLOTINA
The new Livia

Under the republic and the early emperors, the conquests of Rome were primarily administered by Italians for the benefit of Italians. As time passed, however, the status of provincial subjects improved as many served in the army, attained Roman citizenship, and even entered the senate. An important step in this process came in AD 98 when the emperor Nerva was succeeded by Marcus Ulpius Traianus (better known as Trajan) – the first emperor not to have grown up in Italy. Trajan was from the city of Italica in the province of Baetica in southern Spain, and his wife, Pompeia Plotina, probably came from Nemausus (modern Nîmes, France) in southern Gaul.[1]

The Romans' first experience of rule by provincials was a resounding success. Trajan was celebrated in his lifetime as Optimus Princeps, or "the best of princes,"[2] and Plotina became one of the most praised women in Roman history, honored for her dignity and simplicity and many other qualities. She was so respected that she became a model for succeeding empresses, and has been called a "new Livia."[3]

Plotina, the daughter of Lucius Pompeius, was probably born in the early 60s.[4] Her native city, whose full name was Colonia Augusta Nemausus, was wealthy and thoroughly Romanized. Originally a Celtic center,[5] it became a Roman colony in the middle of the first century BC and was expanded and beautified under Augustus. His lieutenant, Marcus Agrippa, settled many veterans from the wars with Mark Antony there.[6]

Agrippa's Nemausus was laid out as a well-appointed, spacious city with a population of about 25,000. Its walls had ten gates, embraced ninety towers, and enclosed an area one-tenth the size of Rome, though the capital contained forty times as many people.[7] Some of the buildings that graced Nemausus in Plotina's day still survive, including a lovely temple, the Maison Carrée (dedicated to Augustus' grandsons, Gaius and Lucius). An amphitheater, built shortly before or during Trajan's rule, is still used today for bullfights and other activities.[8] Fresh water was brought to the city from a source 50 miles away by a magnificent aqueduct (the famous Pont du Gard), which still looms 155 feet (47 meters) high as it crosses the Gard River on its way to the city (see Figure 6.1). This impressive structure, built by Agrippa, was originally painted red.[9]

Trajan was born on 18 September, most likely in the year 56 (or possibly a few years earlier).[10] Like Nemausus, his birthplace of Italica had been a home for retired Roman soldiers. It was established in 206 BC as a residence for wounded veterans of the Second Punic War, the struggle against Carthage that featured the heroics of Rome's enemy Hannibal.[11]

Trajan's family, known as the Ulpii, had risen to prominence in Italica by at least the first century BC, and his father, also named Marcus Ulpius Traianus, commanded a legion under Vespasian during the First Jewish Revolt (AD 66–73).[12] Vespasian made the senior Trajan a consul and promoted his son, the future emperor, to the senate.[13] (It is possible, but not certain, that Trajan's family was related by marriage to Vespasian's son Titus.[14])

The young Trajan, whose hero was Julius Caesar, pursued a military career, serving under his father in Syria in the mid-70s.[15] He was transferred to Germany in 77 and it was probably during this assignment that he married Plotina, who was still in her teens.[16]

All of the existing portraits of Plotina seem to have been created when she was in her forties or older. Only eleven sculptures are known,[17] in addition to a comparatively limited variety of rare portrait coins. However, the high quality of many of these representations allows us to get a good idea of her appearance, and maybe even her personality.

Plotina had a long face (made to seem even longer by the towering hairstyles of the day), long nose, rather thin neck, receding chin, and large, expressive eyes. Taken together, the portraits give the impression of a calm, gentle, somewhat austere woman with more than her share of common sense. Some modern critics have looked at Plotina's portraits and described her as "plain, sober, strait-laced," and even "dull."[18] Certainly, she seems to have possessed more character than glamour.

Plotina's husband was tall and well built, with an even temper and affable nature.[19] Trajan grew prematurely gray, which seems only to have enhanced his impressive appearance.[20] Portraits on coins and sculptures show that he had a large round head, thin lips, a short chin, and a rather prominent brow (see Figure 6.2). He wore his hair in a simple style, reminiscent of Augustus, and combed it forward in bangs.

As emperor, Trajan was one of the few men to rule the Roman Empire without the aid of a personal astrologer.[21] However, he did consult the oracle at Heliopolis in Syria about his future shortly before he died (the signs were not favorable[22]), and he championed the traditional Roman religion. He was also tolerant of other religions (including the "eastern" cults), which continued to grow in popularity during his reign.[23]

Trajan does not seem to have been artistically or intellectually inclined.[24] He delighted in the soldier's life and enjoyed gladiatorial displays, hunting, and dining with friends.[25] He often drank wine to excess, though he instructed his servants to stop serving him when he became drunk.[26]

Trajan also indulged a passion for young boys.[27] Though this taste would be scandalous today, it was common and more or less acceptable in Trajan's time, especially in the Roman upper classes. Pederasty was but one of the many aspects of Greek culture wealthy Romans embraced and made fashionable.[28] Nevertheless, Trajan became unusually identified with this form of homosexuality. Two hundred and fifty years after his death, the Roman emperor Julian II joked that the god Jupiter should be careful or Trajan's ghost would steal his pretty boy Ganymede from him.[29]

It is likely that if Trajan had been an unpopular emperor or failed to show respect to the senate, his drinking and sexual exploits would have been ridiculed. Instead they were excused. Pliny even congratulated him on being without "any kind of vice," and Cassius Dio insisted that his dalliances with boys "harmed no one."[30]

Plotina's reaction to her husband's love for boys is not recorded. She probably tolerated it as a common practice that threatened neither her position nor her loving relationship with her husband. Despite their lack of children, all accounts agree that Plotina and Trajan were happily married and devoted to each other.[31]

Trajan continued to climb the career ladder under Domitian, who posted him to the command of a legion in Spain.[32] In January of 89, Domitian showed his confidence by ordering Trajan to take his troops all the way to Germany (a journey of 700 miles (1,125 km)) to put down the rebellion of a Roman general named Saturninus.[33] The uprising was quashed before Trajan arrived on the scene, but he was praised for his loyalty and the promptness of his response, which involved crossing both the Alps and the Pyrenees.[34] Domitian rewarded Trajan with a consulship for the year 91.[35] This was the pinnacle of the professional career for a Roman senator and general, and was very likely capped by an appointment to the governorship of one of the key northern provinces.[36]

Trajan was probably stationed near the Danube River when news came of Domitian's assassination (on Trajan's fortieth birthday) and Nerva's accession to the throne.[37] As an emperor without strong ties to the military, Nerva was in a precarious position. The Praetorian Guard even rebelled soon after his accession, stormed the palace, and compelled Nerva to punish Domitian's assassins.[38] The emperor desperately needed the support of the army, so he adopted Trajan, the most popular and respected soldier of the day, and designated him as his heir.[39] This was no temporary gesture; Nerva was in his sixties, childless, and in ill health. It may have occurred to him that, with the largest army near Rome behind him, Trajan could take control of the empire whenever he wished.[40] He gave Trajan powers almost equal to his own and, when Nerva died on 28 January, 98, the new reign began without incident.

Nerva's sudden adoption of Trajan had surprised and delighted the army and most of the Roman people.[41] The wisdom of his choice was soon apparent: Trajan became one of the most successful rulers in Roman history, taking the empire to new heights of prosperity and territorial expansion and ruling with a mildness and evenhandedness that became legendary. It became traditional after his death to wish that each succeeding emperor would prove to be "better than Trajan, more fortunate than Augustus."[42]

Though he became emperor in January of 98, Trajan did not come to Rome until September of the following year, lingering in the northern provinces to strengthen their military defenses.[43] He may have been somewhat reluctant to leave the army camps and take his place in the center of Roman society. Trajan was a soldier by experience and inclination, with simple tastes and a strong sense of camaraderie with his men. He is said to have known a great many of his soldiers not only by name but also by their humorous camp nicknames.[44]

In Rome, the new emperor made himself more accessible than any of his predecessors.[45] Rather than remain aloof from his old friends, he visited them in their homes when they were sick and exchanged dinner invitations with them.[46] When he traveled by carriage, he often took guests on board, though he usually preferred to walk from place to place.[47] Plotina was also praised for walking rather than being carried in a litter.[48] The imperial family dined publicly, welcoming visitors and mingling with their guests more or less as equals.[49]

Trajan was occasionally criticized for being too familiar with his subjects, but he said that he wished to behave toward others as he had wished previous emperors would behave toward him.[50] It is also true that Trajan could afford to be more accessible to his people than the emperors of the past because he was much more heavily guarded. Remembering the recent sticky end of Domitian and the uprising of the Praetorian Guard against Nerva, he established a sort of "secret service" and a mounted bodyguard to protect him.[51] Nevertheless, he once brandished a sword in the presence of the praetorians and said: "Take this sword so that you may use it for me if I rule well, or against me if I rule poorly."[52]

Plotina's feelings about her sudden elevation were expressed in a little speech she made to the people who watched her enter the palace for the first time. The historian Cassius Dio tells us that she turned around at the top of the stairs, faced the crowd of onlookers, and said: "I enter this place as the sort of woman that I would like to be when I leave it."[53] Plotina's remark spoke volumes about her values, confidence, and level-headedness – and her preference for a simple, unpretentious way of life. Cassius Dio assures us that she lived up to her words, "conducting herself throughout her husband's reign in a manner that was above reproach."[54] The senator Pliny the Younger praised Plotina for her modest, unassuming demeanor in public, her simple dress, and the moderate number of her attendants.[55]

Despite her comments on the palace steps, Plotina certainly *was* changed by her role as empress. She took an active interest in her husband's policies and exerted her influence in telling ways. When corruption began to take hold among Trajan's officials in the provinces, Plotina scolded him for allowing them to hurt his good name and pressed him to punish infractions more severely.[56] She persuaded him to simplify the procedures by which private citizens could resolve disputes with the imperial treasury.[57] She even managed to convince her husband to take the side of a Jewish legation from Alexandria in a dispute with the Greeks of that city – before Trajan had even conducted a hearing on the subject.[58]

The couple's childlessness may have inspired their special concern for the welfare of needy and maltreated children. Trajan passed laws freeing abused sons from the control of their fathers and tightening the regulation of guardians.[59] In ancient times it was common for unwanted babies to be exposed, allowing anyone to claim them and raise them as their own. Trajan decreed that those abandoned babies who had been freeborn could assert their freedom as adults without having to repay their foster parents.[60] The disadvantaged children of Italy also benefited from the *alimenta* system, which had been instituted as a government program under Nerva but was expanded by Trajan.[61] When he lent large sums of money to rural districts in an effort to reverse the decline of Italian agriculture, he stipulated that the 5 percent interest on the loans would be used to feed poor children.[62]

Although Plotina and Trajan had no offspring, the empire was not without a royal family. Ulpia Marciana, Trajan's widowed older sister, her daughter Matidia, and at least two of Matidia's daughters, Sabina (the future empress) and Matidia the Younger, lived in the palace. The remarkable relationship between Plotina and Marciana must go down as one of the wonders of the ancient world. Despite the fact that they shared the running of the imperial household, equal shares of Trajan's esteem, and equivalent titles and status, there is no hint of any rivalry or even friction between them.[63] They seem to have been united in their devotion to Trajan and to Marciana's daughter and granddaughters, and in unwavering affection for each other.[64]

Pliny relates that when the senate offered Plotina and Marciana the title of Augusta at the beginning of Trajan's reign both women refused it, citing the emperor's initial rejection of the honorific *Pater Patriae*, or "Father of the Fatherland."[65] However, both women had accepted the honor by 105, after Trajan had accepted his.

If Plotina lacked the quality of glamour, as her portraits suggest, then her female in-laws made up for this shortcoming. Marciana's portraits show an unfortunate resemblance to her brother, which she overcame by wearing fantastically elaborate hairstyles, imitated by her daughter and granddaughters. These coiffures captured the imagination of fashionable, well-to-do Roman women, who copied them enthusiastically. The complicated, multi-tiered constructions involved plaited, twisted, and rolled hair, plus assorted pieces of "hair furniture"[66] such as metal crowns and tiaras. In profile, the hairdos vaguely resembled sleeping swans perched on women's heads, with their tail feathers arching high above the women's brows (see Figures 6.6, 6.7). Plotina's coiffure was decidedly less impressive, with plenty of lift in front but only a queue of braids in the back, and fewer bothered to copy it.[67]

In AD 100 a consulship was awarded to Pliny the Younger (Gaius Plinius, born in 61 or 62), who expressed his appreciation to the emperor in a speech of praise. Pliny later published an expanded version, known as the *Panegyricus*, which is one of our best sources of information about Trajan's reign. As we might expect, he laid his accolades on a bit heavily. Still, this glowing account was not contradicted by other writers of the time, though Trajan and his immediate successors allowed remarkable freedom of speech. Indeed, Trajan was still remembered for his clemency and mildness more than two centuries after his death.[68]

Besides complimenting the emperor on his excellent rule and god-like qualities, Pliny congratulated him on his choice of a wife.[69] He called Plotina an example of virtuous Roman womanhood in the ancient tradition and the sort of woman fit to be the wife of the chief priest of the state religion (a role Trajan filled as Pontifex Maximus).[70] Both Plotina and Marciana were lauded in the *Panegyricus* for their upright living, absolute devotion to Trajan, and the exceptional harmony that existed between them.[71] It is interesting, however, that Pliny attributed Marciana's excellent qualities to her birth, while Plotina's were the result of careful training by her husband.[72]

This reminds us that Roman women were usually very young when they married (Plotina was probably about 15 or 16) and were often assumed to have been "raised" to some degree by their much older husbands. It may also point to a disparity in the status of Plotina's and Trajan's families. On the other hand, the existence in Herculaneum (one of the cities buried by the eruption of Vesuvius in AD 79) of a woman named Ulpia Plotina has led to speculation that Plotina and Trajan were related to each other in some way, as the woman's name suggests a link between the two families.[73]

Aside from the *Panegyricus*, much of Pliny's correspondence survives, including a letter referring to Plotina as a "most virtuous woman" (*sanctissima femina*).[74] There also exist some letters between Pliny and Trajan. The most famous of these concerns Pliny's request for guidance from the emperor regarding the treatment of Christians in the province of Bithynia (in northern Turkey), where Pliny was governor. Trajan instructed him as follows:

> They are not to be searched out. If they should be handed over to you, and if charges against them should be proven, they must be punished, but with this proviso: That if anyone denies being a Christian, and gives clear evidence by praying to our gods, then he

shall be pardoned on the basis of his repentance, no matter how suspiciously he had behaved in the past. Written complaints submitted anonymously really must have no role in any accusation, for this sets the worst possible precedent and does not fit in with the spirit of our times.[75]

Another of Pliny's letters offers an interesting description of the imperial villa at Centumcellae on the Mediterranean coast, about 50 miles (80 km) northwest of Rome. He describes the house as extremely beautiful, facing the sea and surrounded by green fields.[76] There was a bay in front, which Trajan converted into a substantial harbor, with a man-made island at its entrance to act as a breakwater. This villa's remote location must have offered Trajan and Plotina some respite from their hectic lives in Rome.

While visiting at the villa, Pliny witnessed Trajan's "friendliness, a quality that is most fully revealed in his country retreat":[77]

> You see how creditably and seriously we spent our days; but the most pleasant relaxations followed. We were invited to dinner every day. It was modest, considering his position as emperor. Sometimes we heard entertaining recitations, and sometimes we passed the night in the most delightful conversations. On our last day, gifts were sent to us as we were leaving – so thoughtful was Caesar in his kindness![78]

Something of the resort atmosphere at Centumcellae might be glimpsed in Pliny's account of his own seaside villa, which was located a few miles to the south:

> There are porticos laid out to resemble the letter D, enclosing a very small but pleasant space. They afford an outstanding little refuge from storms, for they are protected by window panes and, much more, by overhanging roofs . . . There is a rather beautiful dining room that runs out to the seashore, and whenever the sea is driven by the African wind, the room is lightly sprayed by the breaking waves . . .
>
> The drive, which encircles the garden, is bordered along its outer edge by boxwood and, where the boxwood does not thrive, by rosemary. The inner edge of the drive is bordered by a tender and shady vineyard, soft and yielding even to bare feet. The garden is densely planted with mulberry and fig trees . . .
>
> At the end of the walkway and garden portico is a suite of rooms that is my favorite, my very favorite: I had it built there myself. When I have retreated to this little world, I don't even seem to be present in my own villa, and I take great pleasure in this, especially during the Saturnalia, when the rest of the place is booming loudly

with the freedom and festive clamor of those days; for neither do I
myself disturb the celebrations, nor do they disturb my studies.[79]

The Saturnalia, which Pliny mentions, was an annual festival celebrated
for several days in December in honor of the god Saturn. The greatest Roman
holiday of all (and the Roman calendar observed well over a hundred holidays each year[80]), it featured outrageous levity and license, including the
reversal of social roles. Masters and mistresses served their slaves at table,
there was extravagant feasting, gambling in the streets, and people exchanged
gifts with each other. This last observance has survived in the traditions of
Christmas.[81]

As adored and successful as Trajan was in Italy, the old soldier must have
been secretly pleased when trouble with the neighboring kingdom of Dacia
(roughly modern Romania) required him to join his army along the Danube.
Between 101 and 106, the emperor led the Roman legions in two major
wars that ended with the destruction of the enemy and the addition of Dacia
to the Roman Empire. The spoils of victory added no less than 5 million
pounds of gold and 10 million pounds of silver to Trajan's treasury.[82] The
celebration in Rome lasted for 123 days and involved the sacrifice of 11,000
animals and combats between 10,000 gladiators.[83]

The conquest of Dacia was celebrated on the 125-foot (38.1-meter) tall
Trajan's Column, which still stands among the ruins of his magnificent forum
in Rome. This complex of buildings and open squares, designed by the architect Apollodorus of Damascus, included an enormous basilica and two
libraries, one for works in Greek, the other for those in Latin.[84]

The column (see Figure 6.8), which stood between the libraries, has a
helical, over 800-foot-long (240 meters) frieze carved on its surface, depicting
episodes from the Dacian wars.[85] Originally colored and decorated with
bronze spears, the scenes include 2,500 human figures, sixty of these being
of Trajan himself. The column is hollow, with a 185-step spiral staircase that
leads to the top, where a gilded statue of the victorious emperor once stood
(it was replaced in 1588 by a statue of Saint Peter).[86]

The booty from the Dacian wars allowed Trajan to embark on a spectacular building program.[87] Besides the forum and column, he built or
improved harbors, bridges, roads, aqueducts – even a shopping mall in the
capital with 150 indoor shops.[88] Triumphal arches were erected in many parts
of the empire, some topped by statues of Trajan with Plotina and Marciana.[89]
Trajan's name adorned so many buildings in Rome that he was compared to
a vine or creeper.[90]

One of Plotina's contributions to the beautification of the capital seems to
have been the restoration of the altar known as the Ara Pudicitia.[91] Pudicitia
was the personification of feminine modesty and chastity – virtues that the
empress exemplified – and coins were issued in Plotina's name bearing her
image and that of the newly dedicated shrine (see Figure 6.10).[92]

Never before had the Roman Empire enjoyed such prosperity and military strength. By 112, its borders had expanded even further with the annexation of the province of Arabia (the modern Sinai Peninsula and much of Jordan).[93] It must have seemed that Trajan could do no wrong.

In August of 112 Trajan's sister Marciana died, probably in her early sixties. A city near the Black Sea was named Marcianopolis in her honor, and her title of Augusta was passed on to her daughter Matidia.[94] Then, in the fall of 113, problems with Rome's long-time enemy Parthia required the aging emperor to head east and take the field of battle once again. This time, Plotina went with him, making Antioch in northern Syria her base.[95] Trajan's operations in the East would occupy him for the rest of his life.

In December, 115, while Trajan was wintering with Plotina in Antioch between campaigning seasons, a catastrophic earthquake hit the region. The loss of life and destruction of property were extensive. A Roman consul was killed, and Trajan himself was injured and forced to escape from a damaged building by crawling through a window.[96] It was said that the entire empire suffered from this calamity as emissaries from all of the provinces were in Antioch attending the emperor.[97] No doubt Plotina and Trajan were active in providing assistance to the victims of the disaster.

The Parthian war brought Trajan his greatest triumphs and his greatest tragedies. His armies swept all before them, conquering Armenia and Mesopotamia and occupying Ctesiphon, the Parthian capital. At the mouth of the Tigris River on the Persian Gulf, the emperor, now in his late fifties, watched a merchant ship sail for India and wished that he was as young as Alexander the Great had been so that he, too, could lead his army there.[98] However, Trajan had already overextended himself. While he daydreamed at the Gulf, his new conquests were in rebellion, killing or expelling their Roman garrisons.[99]

Trajan's forces were still trying to restore order in Parthia when news came of a serious revolt of the Jews living in Cyrene, Cyprus, and Alexandria.[100] There was long-standing animosity between the Greek and Jewish populations in the eastern provinces, largely because of religious and cultural differences. The destruction of Jerusalem and its temple by Titus in 70 had left a legacy of Jewish resentment against the Romans as well. Cassius Dio claims that the Jewish rebels massacred nearly half a million Greeks and Romans in Cyrene and Cyprus, and committed other atrocities in Egypt before the revolt could be put down.[101]

Trajan tried desperately to regain control of the situation. Faced with a new Parthian invasion of Armenia, he was forced to acknowledge client-kings there and in Parthia itself rather than formally annex them to the empire as he had hoped to do. Then his attempt to recapture the desert fortress of Hatra, crucial to the control of Mesopotamia, ended in failure.[102] The siege of this city exposed Trajan and his men to thirst, terrible weather, and hosts of flies that covered their food and drink and spread disease.[103]

Clearly, the emperor's luck had changed. He rejoined Plotina in Antioch at the end of 116, planning to march into Mesopotamia again the following year.[104] However, by the spring of 117 his health had begun to fail. Trajan fell ill soon after the failure at Hatra – perhaps a late victim of the flies – and suffered a stroke that left him partially paralyzed.[105] His extremities became swollen and he suffered from other ominous symptoms.[106] It was probably the empress who convinced him to put away his sword and return to Rome.[107]

Trajan must have been deeply troubled as he set sail in July of 117 with Plotina and Matidia, leaving Syria and his dreams of eastern conquest behind for good. He imagined that he was being poisoned, and blamed this for his sickness.[108] Three hundred miles into the journey, off the coast of what is now southern Turkey, Trajan's health took a serious turn for the worse. His ship put in at the nearest port, the city of Selinus (afterwards known as Trajanopolis), where he died on or about the 9th of August, not quite 61 years of age.[109] Trajan's body was taken back to Syria, where it was cremated. Plotina and Matidia carried his ashes in a golden urn to Rome, where they were placed in the base of his famous column.[110]

Plotina's role in Trajan's last moments and in his choice of a successor would be the subject of much controversy. The senate received a letter from the emperor, written from his deathbed, naming his cousin and ward, Publius Aelius Hadrianus (better known as Hadrian), as his adopted son and heir. However, Plotina signed the document rather than Trajan, presumably because his paralysis prevented him from writing. This raised the possibility that Hadrian had not been the emperor's choice at all, but Plotina's.[111]

A century later, Cassius Dio repeated a story his father had told him, charging that the empress had concealed her husband's death for some days and retained an actor who impersonated Trajan. The imposter supposedly announced the adoption of Hadrian, speaking in a weak voice in a darkened room.[112] The convenient death of Trajan's valet at the age of 28, just days after the emperor's demise, seemed to add credence to this story.[113]

This gossip originated from Hadrian's enemies, however, and is almost certainly without foundation. Soon after he became emperor, Hadrian alienated certain hawkish Roman senators by relinquishing Trajan's conquests in the East, thus depriving them of lucrative administrative posts in the new territories.[114] Then, before he had even arrived in Rome, four distinguished senators were executed for plotting Hadrian's overthrow.[115] Though he swore publicly that he was not responsible for these deaths and that he would never put a senator to death without a proper trial, the damage to his reputation had been done.[116]

Hadrian, born in 76, was the son of Trajan's first cousin on his father's side. When Hadrian lost his father at the age of 10, he became the ward of Trajan and another man.[117] Plotina took a deep interest in the boy and helped arrange his marriage to Trajan's great-niece Sabina in 100 with the support of the girl's mother and grandmother.[118] Hadrian's enemies would later claim that Trajan himself had opposed this match, but this seems unlikely to be true.[119] The marriage to Sabina was a clear sign of imperial favor and was followed by numerous honors, including the consulship in 108.[120]

At the time of Trajan's death, Hadrian was governor of the critical province of Syria with a large army at his command.[121] Clearly, Trajan trusted him to handle the dangerous situation in the East when his own health was failing. The emperor had previously given Hadrian a diamond that he had received from Nerva, perhaps to signify his designation as successor.[122] There is little doubt that Hadrian was Trajan's choice to succeed him; he had left no one else in a position to challenge for the throne.

Plotina enjoyed a close relationship with the new emperor, who continued to issue coins bearing her image.[123] For all of Trajan's many virtues, intellectual refinement was not one of them.[124] Hadrian, on the other hand, was probably the most intellectually accomplished of all Roman emperors. His stimulating company seems to have filled a void in Plotina's life; some of Hadrian's enemies even claimed that there was a love affair between them.[125] Their surviving letters argue against this. He addressed her as "my dearest and most honored mother,"[126] to which she replied "my own dear son."[127] These are hardly lovers' greetings. It seems appropriate that the childless Plotina came to look upon the attractive Hadrian as her son, which he was by adoption.

A letter from Plotina to Hadrian survives, inscribed in stone, which reveals her interest in the Greek philosophy known as Epicureanism.[128] She writes asking the emperor to allow "our" school of Epicurus in Athens to choose leaders who are not Roman citizens.[129] The text of her letter is paraphrased below:

> Master, you know how interested I am in the sect of Epicurus. Your help is needed regarding the succession of its leaders. The range of choice is presently very narrow as only Roman citizens are eligible. I ask in the name of Popillius Theotimus, the present successor at Athens, that you will allow him to write the part of his disposition that deals with the succession in Greek and permit him to fill his place with a non-citizen, if a candidate's qualifications make this advisable. Also, that you let future successors enjoy the same right. This will ease the choosing of the best man as the choice will be from a larger group.[130]

Epicurus was an Athenian of the fourth to third century BC who maintained that the universe consisted of nothing but space and atoms; that neither the gods nor death should be feared; and that the goal of human life should be happiness. Contrary to the modern popular impression of Epicureanism, this happiness was not to be attained by indulging sensual appetites. Rather, it required the elimination of anxiety and agitation by acquiring knowledge of the Truth. In this system, men and women are not the slaves of fate but, as the offspring of heavenly seed and divine mother earth, can accomplish anything through the exercise of free will.

We know that Hadrian agreed to Plotina's request because his favorable response – and her letter conveying the good news to the school – was also commemorated in stone. Plotina wrote her fellow Epicureans in Greek: "Plotina to all the friends, Greeting. We have what we were so eager to obtain."[131] She went on to say that she and they owed a debt of gratitude to Hadrian, "the benefactor and overseer of all culture," whom she loved as an "outstanding guardian and a loyal son."[132] She also advised the members of the school to avoid abusing the privilege by choosing leaders on the basis of merit rather than personal favoritism.[133]

A letter from Hadrian to Plotina has also been preserved which, if authentic, provides a glimpse of the warmth of their relationship. Purportedly written in January of 120 or 121, near the end of Plotina's life, it is an invitation from the emperor to dine with him on his birthday:

> [To my] best and dearest mother, As you make many prayers to the gods for me, so also I pray to them for you. For your piety and dignity can achieve everything. But I am glad, by Hercules, that everything I do pleases you and wins your praise. You know, mother, that today is my birthday and we ought to dine together. If you wish, then, come in good time after the bath, with my sisters, for Sabina has set off for the villa – but has sent a present of her own. Be sure to come early so that we can celebrate together.[134]

Plotina's financial independence after her husband's death is attested by stamped tiles from her brickworks near Rome, which bear her name and are dated to 123.[135] It is interesting that she followed the empress Domitia in this business – it must have been an especially lucrative one. Clearly, the famous boast of the emperor Augustus that he found Rome made of brick and left it made of marble did not signal the end of the local brick business.[136]

Plotina probably died in 123 when she was about 60 years of age.[137] After her passing, Hadrian commented that "though she asked a great deal of me, I refused her nothing."[138] This not only showed his esteem and affection for Plotina, but also the fact that, in his opinion, her requests were always reasonable.[139] The emperor honored her memory by composing hymns to her, by wearing black for nine days after her passing, and by dedicating a basilica to her in Nemausus.[140] The Temple of the Divine Trajan in Rome was rededicated to include the newly deified empress, and her ashes, placed in a golden urn like her husband's, were also deposited in the podium of Trajan's Column.[141]

Hadrian's enduring affection for Plotina may be suggested by an issue of gold coins minted in 136, only two years before his death. On the obverse is a portrait of the emperor, surprisingly shown as a young man of about 20; on the reverse are portraits of his adoptive parents, the deified Plotina and Trajan.[142] At the least, these coins demonstrate the continuing prestige of Trajan and Plotina. However, Hadrian's youthful portrayal seems to imply some sentimentality on the part of the emperor, who was 60 years old at the time.

Unlike most Roman empresses, Plotina went down in Roman history as a paragon of moral rectitude and seemly behavior and a benevolent force for justice and mercy. Even her one alleged indiscretion – her favoritism for Hadrian and maneuvering to secure his succession – turned out for the best. He was a gifted and effective ruler, remembered in history as one of the series of "five good emperors," the others being Nerva, Trajan, and Hadrian's two successors, Antoninus Pius and Marcus Aurelius.

Plotina certainly realized her ambition of leaving the palace as "the same sort of woman" as when she entered it, though also as a far more accomplished and respected one. Her career established the new standard of behavior for the empress of the second century; she was perhaps less independent than her predecessors under the Julio-Claudians had been, more confined to the shadow of her husband.[143]

Though her political authority had decreased, the empress remained a potent figure in Roman society, probably more visible and accessible to the people than ever before. Her influence was most keenly felt in the cultural sphere, in the encouragement of the arts and of religious and philosophical sects, and in the support of children and the disadvantaged. She also acted as a sort of conscience for her husband, making him aware of injustices or causes that needed his support. In many ways, this was a return to the example set by Livia.

Trajan's reign was followed by a long period of peace, prosperity, and cultural integration among the peoples of the Roman Empire. Plotina and her protégé, Hadrian, better symbolized the values and trends of this new golden age than Trajan, the last of the great conquering generals.

6.2   6.3   6.4

6.6   6.7

6.5   6.8   6.9

Figure 6.2 Portrait of Trajan on a bronze sestertius, minted AD 105. RIC II 577, BMCRE 863, Cohen 549; courtesy Classical Numismatic Group, Inc.

Figure 6.3 Portrait of Plotina on a bronze sestertius minted AD 112. RIC II 740 (Trajan), BMCRE 1080 (Trajan), Cohen 12; courtesy Classical Numismatic Group, Inc.

Figure 6.4 Posthumous portrait of Trajan's deified father, Marcus Ulpius Traianus, on a gold aureus, struck AD 115. RIC II 764, BMCRE 506 note, Cohen 3; courtesy Classical Numismatic Group, Inc.

Figure 6.5 Bronze sestertius of Trajan commemorating the *Alimenta* system, which benefited disadvantaged Italian children. Annona, representing the corn harvest, holds the hand of a small child. Minted in AD 111. RIC II 459, Cohen 7; courtesy Numismatik Lanz München.

Figure 6.6 Posthumous portrait of Marciana, Trajan's sister, on a silver denarius, minted AD 112. RIC II 743 (Trajan), BMCRE 650 (Trajan), RSC 4; courtesy Classical Numismatic Group, Inc.

Figure 6.7 Portrait of Trajan's niece Matidia the Elder, the daughter of Marciana and mother of Sabina, the wife of the emperor Hadrian, on a silver denarius, minted *c.* AD 112. RIC II 759 (Trajan), BMCRE 660 (Trajan), RSC 10; courtesy Classical Numismatic Group, Inc.

Figure 6.8 Trajan's Column, celebrating the emperor's conquest of Dacia, on a bronze dupondius minted in AD 115. A statue of Trajan (relative size exaggerated) stands on top of the Column, which has two eagles at its base. Hill 684; courtesy Classical Numismatic Group, Inc.

Figure 6.9 View of the façade of Trajan's Forum in Rome on a gold aureus minted AD 115. RIC II 256, BMCRE 509, Cohen 168; courtesy Classical Numismatic Group, Inc.

6.10

6.11   6.12   6.13

6.14   6.15   6.16

Figure 6.10 Silver denarius of Plotina showing the Altar to Pudicitia, the personification of feminine modesty and chastity. A statue of Pudicitia standing on an honorary curule chair is depicted on the altar. Minted AD 112. RIC II 733 (Trajan), RSC 7, BMCRE 529; courtesy Classical Numismatic Group, Inc.

Figure 6.11 A seated Pudicitia pulling a veil over her face. Bronze sestertius of the empress Otacilia Severa, minted under Philip I *c.* AD 244–249. RIC IV 209a, Cohen 55; courtesy Classical Numismatic Group, Inc.

Figure 6.12 Trajan (seated) with Parthamaspates (kneeling) – his choice to rule defeated Parthia. Bronze sestertius, minted in AD 116. RIC II 667, BMCRE 1046, Cohen 328; courtesy Classical Numismatic Group, Inc.

Figure 6.13 Trajan is shown standing and holding a spear and *parazonium* (sword) over the mourning figure of Armenia personified (to his nearer left), with the river gods Tigris and Euphrates on either side. Bronze sestertius minted *c.* AD 114–117. RIC II 642, BMCRE 1033, Cohen 39; courtesy Classical Numismatic Group, Inc.

Figure 6.14 Trajan (seated) shown addressing his troops on a bronze sestertius, minted *c.* AD 115–116. RIC II 658, BMCRE 1019; courtesy Classical Numismatic Group, Inc.

Figure 6.15 A provincial portrait of Trajan, on a silver tetradrachm minted in Antioch, Syria, *c.* AD 98–117. Wruck 141; courtesy Classical Numismatic Group, Inc.

Figure 6.16 Plotina on a gold aureus, minted in AD 112. RIC II 730 (Trajan), BMCRE 525 (Trajan); courtesy Numismatic Lanz München.

6.17   6.18

Figure 6.17 A portrait of the young emperor Hadrian on his earliest bronze sestertius issue, minted in AD 117. RIC II 534a, BMCRE 1101, Cohen 523, Hill 10; courtesy Classical Numismatic Group, Inc.

Figure 6.18 Trajan (left) presenting a globe to Hadrian. Bronze sestertius, minted under Hadrian, AD 117. RIC II 534a, BMCRE 1101, Cohen 523; courtesy Classical Numismatic Group, Inc.

Figure 7.1 Author's portrait of the empress Sabina, based on a veiled sculpture in the Museo Nazionale delle Terme, Rome. The coin is a bronze sestertius (see Figure 7.14 for a similar specimen). Sabina stands before the so-called Pool of Canopus, or Scenic Canal, at Hadrian's Villa in Tibur (Tivoli), east of Rome.

7

SABINA

Wife of "the Greekling"

Vibia Sabina, the younger of the two known daughters of Trajan's niece Salonia Matidia, was born sometime in the mid-80s.[1] At about age 15, in about the year 100, she married her 24-year-old second cousin, the future emperor Hadrian.[2]

Very little is known about Sabina, but she is generally supposed to have languished in a miserable marriage to a man who scorned her. However, the rich documentation of her husband's career provides many insights into what her life as empress must have been like, and suggests a somewhat happier fate.

Sabina's father, an obscure but promising senator by the name of Lucius Vibius Sabinus, died soon after holding the consulship in 97, probably a couple of years before his daughter's wedding.[3] Her marriage to Hadrian was arranged by her mother, grandmother, and Trajan's wife Plotina for the political purpose of singling Hadrian out as the heir apparent.[4] It is interesting that Sabina's older sister, Mindia Matidia (probably her half-sister), who lived to a ripe old age, seems never to have married.[5]

Remnants of paint on Sabina's statues show that she had brown eyes and brown hair.[6] (The fact that classical Greek and Roman sculptures were originally painted may come as a surprise as they are most familiar today as pale stone, devoid of color. Though residual coloration is rarely preserved, this was the standard decoration of stone statues and buildings in the ancient world.[7]) Sabina wore her hair in a variety of styles. These included elaborate upswept constructions like those favored by her mother and her grandmother, Trajan's sister Marciana. However, she also broke away from extravagance in coiffure by wearing simpler styles that were copied by succeeding empresses and Roman women in general.[8] These included a parted arrangement, based on classical Greek models, with the hair in a bun at the nape of the neck (see Figure 7.5), and a very simple hairdo in which the hair was pulled back into a ponytail-like queue (see Figure 7.14).

Sabina's facial features in her portraits on coins and statues are smallish, except for a prominent, somewhat pointed nose. Modern critics have criticized her "sour expression and grim hairdo," "tight little button of a mouth," and "listless, feckless" expression.[9] However, criticisms of Sabina's personality by the ancient historians probably inspired these comments more than her features on surviving portraits. Indeed, some of her likenesses suggest a delicate beauty and an attractive tenderness and vulnerability, and she was called lovely in her own time, though admittedly by a close friend.[10]

Hadrian, to whom Sabina was married for more than thirty-five years, was one of the most talented and active rulers in history. Born 24 January, 76, he was tall, robust, and elegant in his dress and grooming, with fair skin and piercing, close-set, gray-blue eyes that were "luminescent."[11] He wore a neatly trimmed beard in the Greek style (which set the fashion for emperors for the next century) and had his hair curled with a comb, as Nero and Domitian had done.[12]

Hadrian was probably the best educated of all Roman emperors, and the most enamored of Greek culture and history.[13] He dressed in Greek clothing in private, even when in Italy.[14] In fact, the only known statue of a Roman emperor in Greek attire is of him.[15]

Hadrian's array of talents and cultivated abilities is astonishing. He was a gifted poet, writer, painter, and sculptor, an innovative architect, master astrologer, accomplished mathematician, singer, and musician (specializing in the flute).[16] His memory was prodigious; like Trajan, he was able to remember the names of countless soldiers in his army.[17] He loved mountain climbing and was an avid hunter, risking his life in the pursuit of boars, bears, and lions.[18] His mastery of the military arts and sciences ranged from the broadest defensive strategy to the tiniest details of a foot soldier's equipment and battle tactics.[19]

However, Sabina's husband could be unpredictable and exasperating.[20] Though usually affable and accessible to the common man,[21] he was sometimes aloof and arrogant. He was jealous of experts in the many fields where he possessed some expertise and intolerant of rivals, though he rewarded and supported them as readily as he humiliated them.[22] According to an anecdote in the *Historia Augusta*, the skilled rhetorician Favorinus was once criticized for not defending himself when the emperor had falsely accused him of misusing a word. Favorinus' response was revealing: "You are mistaken, my friends, in urging me not to consider the commander of 30 legions the most learned of men."[23]

Hadrian seems to have measured himself against some of the most formidable minds of his day. Besides Favorinus, he probably matched wits with the brilliant Stoic philosopher Epictetus, the famous Greek writer and biographer Plutarch, the noted historian Arrian, and the influential Greek sophist Polemo.[24] His interactions with the architect Apollodorus of Damascus, designer of Trajan's magnificent Forum in Rome, are recorded by Cassius Dio. Dio claims that the architect's ridicule of Hadrian's efforts in architectural design so infuriated him that he eventually had Apollodorus executed.[25] However, modern scholars doubt that Hadrian was guilty of such a crime.[26]

Hadrian could be alternately playful and stern, merciful and cruel, modest and vainglorious.[27] Many of his qualities and interests seem contradictory, but also show an unparalleled versatility. For example, he was a practical man with a strong interest in astrology, mysticism, and magic.[28] Though a calculating politician, he was also a romantic dreamer, given to sentimental outbursts that opened him up to ridicule.[29] He was a dandified *bon vivant* who delighted in lavish banquets and yet seemed perfectly content with the harsh living conditions and simple food of the common Roman soldier.[30] Though a refined, highly educated intellectual, Hadrian loved to mingle naked with the common folk at the public baths, sharing their coarsest jokes.[31]

Hadrian relished a good dinner party, where he could enjoy philosophical discussion as well as musical, literary, and theatrical performances.[32] As important lights in Roman society, he and Sabina attended and gave countless banquets. These occasions could be fairly dignified, like the one described in a letter from Pliny the Younger to Septicius Clarus, Hadrian's future Praetorian Prefect (who had failed to attend the party):

> These foods had all been prepared: One head of lettuce, three snails, and two eggs for each of us; pasta and honeyed wine chilled with snow; and olives, beets, cucumbers, onions, and a thousand other items no less sumptuous. You would have heard comic actors, or a reader, or a musician, or (such is my generosity!) all of these ... How much fun, laughter, and learning we would have had![33]

Some dinner parties were fabulously extravagant affairs, as described in the classic scene of Trimalchio's banquet in Petronius' novel *Satyricon*, written shortly before Hadrian's birth. This feast began with white and black olives, and dormice dipped in honey and rolled in poppy seeds. Then came sausages on a silver grill over pomegranate seeds and damsons and a variety of hors-d'œuvres. At a musical signal, singing servants whisked the lighter dishes away and wine was brought in, for the washing of hands as well as for drinking. Four dancers revealed the next course: on a dish decorated with the twelve signs of the zodiac, with foods symbolic of each, was an assortment of fowls and sows' bellies, and a hare in the middle, sporting wings in imitation of Pegasus.[34]

Later, an enormous roasted boar was brought in on a tray, wearing a *pileus*, or cap of freedom, and surrounded by suckling pigs made of simnel-like cake. A large man with a beard opened the boar's side with his hunting knife and a flock of birds escaped and flew around the room. Eventually, a beautiful boy made up to look like Dionysos distributed grapes to the guests from a small basket.[35]

(Though menus such as these may make Roman food seem merely exotic or even grotesque, the preparation of food was extremely sophisticated.

Roman wines were varied and often superb, and the use of herbs, spices, and sauces reached the level of an art form. Only its offspring, French cuisine, rivals Roman cooking in the European tradition.[36])

Hadrian was first and foremost a lover of all things Greek. As a young man, he earned the nickname "Graeculus" ("the Greekling") for his obsession with Greek culture.[37] From his personal appearance to his religious tastes, he patterned himself after the heroes of classical and archaic Greece. He also participated in the Hellenic custom of man–boy love, in which an adult male entered into a romantic, sexual, socially sanctioned relationship with an adolescent boy. Though this practice was alien to Roman tradition, it had become well established among the upper classes by Hadrian's time. As we shall see, Hadrian's attachment to one young man, a Bithynian named Antinous, would become famous.

Hadrian's enthusiasm for Greek culture would have affected Sabina in several ways. She was probably accepting of his relationships with boys; her great-uncle Trajan had indulged in them freely and she seems to have been on good terms with Antinous.[38] She also appears to have shared her husband's interest in Greek religion, art, and literature.[39] However, Greek customs tended to restrict the freedom and influence of women. Accordingly, Sabina seems to have had a less independent role in the life of the court than some of her predecessors, possibly reflecting the emperor's Greek-influenced attitudes about "a woman's place." An intimate friend of Hadrian's once responded to his wife's complaints about his infidelities with the remark, "Let me have my fun, for to be a wife is an honor, not a pleasure."[40]

Soon after Sabina's marriage to Hadrian, he was elevated to the senate.[41] His travels and official assignments under Trajan took him to various parts of the empire, including Pannonia on the Danube River, Greece, Asia Minor, and Syria. Sabina is believed to have been with Hadrian at most or all of these places; she was probably with him in Syrian Antioch in 117 when Trajan died and Hadrian became emperor.[42]

Hadrian's long, prosperous reign was marked by a series of grand tours, during which he visited at least thirty-eight and probably all but one of the forty-four provinces of the empire.[43] His travels occupied nearly two-thirds of his twenty-one years on the throne.[44] Sabina accompanied him on the majority of these journeys. She was certainly with him in Britain, Gaul, Greece, Asia Minor, Syria, Palmyra, and Egypt.[45] The imperial retinue included senatorial advisors and other members of the royal family, as well as poets, pages, hunting partners for the emperor, and woman friends of the empress.[46]

Sabina's traveling companions included her unmarried sister Matidia and her husband's sister, Domitia Paulina.[47] Paulina, who was married to Julius Servianus, a distinguished senator more than thirty years her senior,[48] is an obscure figure who certainly did not receive the official attention from her brother that Trajan had bestowed on his own sister, Marciana. Paulina seems to have died while touring Egypt with Hadrian and Sabina in 130, and Cassius Dio claims that Hadrian was ridiculed for being slow to honor her passing.[49]

Despite the amiable company, these visits to the provinces were far more than sightseeing trips. The entourage also included architects, builders, and stonemasons, for Hadrian restored old buildings and built new ones wherever he went.[50] He also founded cities and encouraged local artistic, cultural, and religious institutions.[51] In fact, the emperor's activities prompted the Greek writer Pausanias, writing a generation later, to credit Hadrian with "having done more to increase the happiness of each of his subjects than any other ruler in history."[52]

Hadrian inspected and drilled the army in the provinces he visited.[53] Surviving examples of his speeches to the troops reveal a meticulous attention to detail and concern for morale.[54] He concentrated on defining and defending the existing boundaries of the empire, constructing permanent barriers on several borders.[55] These included an extensive wooden palisade along the German frontier, stone and mudbrick walls along the southern boundaries in Africa,[56] and, of course, Hadrian's Wall in northern Britain. Hadrian's Wall was 14 feet (4.2 meters) high and built of stone, with a small fortress every mile and two lookout towers in between. It extended for 73 miles (117 km) from coast to coast, with a 40-mile (64 km) extension along the western shoreline.[57]

We can only speculate about Sabina's activities during her years of travel. Coins that commemorate the imperial visit to Egypt show her sacrificing to the gods and sitting on a throne, as if she is receiving embassies or hearing entreaties from local subjects.[58] No doubt she took a special interest in the cultural and religious life of the places she went, in keeping with the example of her predecessors. Locally minted coins, inscriptions, and statues in her honor have been found in several places she visited – for example, Greece, Egypt (see Figure 7.8), Asia Minor, and Palmyra – presumably in gratitude for her benefactions.[59]

The empress' initiatives in public building and patronage are not well documented. However, we do know that she erected a structure in the capital for the benefit of Roman matrons, which the empress Julia Domna restored a century later.[60] The city of Sabratha in Libya expressed its gratitude to Sabina for some unspecified service on an inscription in the Roman Forum.[61] Also, Hadrian's distribution of largess to the poor children of Rome, depicted on a monument to Sabina that was erected after her death, may point to one of her special concerns.[62] In addition, his increased appropriations for the state support of poor children and the raising of the maximum age for eligibility may reflect her influence.[63]

A concern on Sabina's part for the welfare of women in the empire might have inspired some of her husband's edicts. In Rome, he prohibited men from visiting the public baths in the mornings so that women could bathe in privacy.[64] He also altered the practice, started by Nero, of tossing into mixed crowds small wooden balls, inscribed with the names of prizes such as slaves, silver plate, or joints of meat.[65] Obviously, these distributions caused chaos, in which women were often trampled or out-competed. Hadrian decreed that there would be separate events for men and women.[66] He also bestowed sums of money on impoverished subjects, which the *Historia Augusta* claims helped many women to survive.[67]

Hadrian's attitude toward and treatment of women may be glimpsed in a few anecdotes. A collection of sayings for Roman schoolchildren survives that includes one from Hadrian in which he reproves a young man for not honoring his mother: "Unless you recognize this woman as your mother, I won't recognize you as a Roman citizen."[68] On another occasion, Hadrian was accosted by a woman who had a request to make of him. He replied that he was too busy to stop, prompting her to cry out, "Then stop being emperor!" He paused and gave her a hearing on the spot.[69] When a case was brought to Hadrian accusing a woman of promiscuity because she had given birth eleven months after the death of her husband, the emperor consulted physicians and literary sources and decided that an eleven-month pregnancy was possible. The woman was therefore acquitted.[70]

That a woman could be prosecuted for alleged "promiscuous" behavior after her husband's death is surprising, given the abundant evidence of sexual freedom during the empire's golden age. However, Augustus' laws, which attempted to regulate public moral behavior, especially for the upper classes, remained in effect and made individuals liable to prosecution for their sexual behavior, in or out of wedlock. Adultery, homosexuality, and seduction were illegal, and conviction could bring penalties ranging from public censure to disqualification for inheritance to banishment or even death. A husband could legally accuse his adulterous wife, while a woman required a third party to act as her agent in accusing her adulterous husband. Though the literature makes it clear that the prohibited forms of behavior were widespread and seldom punished, this story demonstrates that a woman could be charged with extramarital sexual relations and face trial under the law.[71]

Hadrian said that the administration of the empire should "combine justice with human kindness."[72] He backed up his words with numerous edicts that were intended to protect his subjects, especially those most vulnerable. For example, he passed several laws protecting the rights of slaves, making it illegal for them to be killed by their owners.[73] Sweatshops for slave or free workers were banned and slaves could not be sold to fight as gladiators or to work as prostitutes unless their owners could show just cause.[74]

Unfortunately, at least one of Hadrian's well-intentioned edicts was spectacularly ill-advised. When Hadrian made circumcision illegal, considering it to be a barbarous practice similar to castration, it sparked a rebellion in Judaea (AD 132), known as the Second Jewish Revolt, that cost at least half a million lives before it was put down.[75]

Hadrian's building projects were numerous and prodigious.[76] He had a passion for architecture and the means to indulge it. His restored version of the Pantheon in Rome remains one of the most magnificent buildings in the world, with a dome that soars 140 feet (43.2 meters) above the temple floor. His villa at Tibur (modern Tivoli) near Rome was certainly one of the most extravagant personal residences ever built. This complex of gracefully designed structures covered an area of 1,000 by 500 yards (900 by 450 meters).[77] It included several dining halls, numerous guest rooms, theaters, baths, and countless fountains and pools – even underground corridors intended to represent Hades.[78]

The villa was everywhere decorated with colorful paintings, mosaics, and innumerable sculptures.[79] These were of such quality and variety that the residence has been called the world's first museum.[80] No imperial couple collected works of art more extensively than Hadrian and Sabina, and no society in history has had a greater enthusiasm for art than the Roman Empire.[81] Romans of all social strata[82] adorned themselves with gorgeous jewelry and their homes with paintings, mosaics, textiles, pottery, sculptures (in stone, metal, and clay), silverware, and glassware, and their cities with graceful and richly decorated architectural wonders.

Our most complete impressions of art in the Roman world come from the fossil cities of Pompeii and Herculaneum, which reveal its astonishing quality and abundance. It has been said that no society in history has enjoyed such a high level of "visual civilization."[83] Even humble homes were decorated with paintings of high quality.

Roman art drew its main inspiration from Classical and Hellenistic Greek forms, but also incorporated Egyptian, oriental, Celtic, and native Italian traditions. The masterpieces of Greco-Roman art have never been surpassed. Indeed, their rediscovery inspired perhaps the most brilliant period in subsequent European art, the Renaissance, when artists strove to emulate the ancient masters.

The ornate decoration of the villa at Tibur, replete with delicate floral designs, has been called "lighthearted," even "feminine."[84] Perhaps this indicates Sabina's taste and active involvement in the design and furnishing of what was, after all, her home as well as Hadrian's. The astounding beauty and variety of "Hadrian's Villa" might be better understood if it is also seen as "Sabina's Villa."

The domestic quarters at Tibur have been excavated. As was usual in Roman dwellings, there were separate bedrooms for master and mistress, each with an anteroom and single-person lavatory.[85] Roman homes allotted equal space to the husband and wife, in contrast to classical Greek homes, where men's quarters were superior to women's in both size and quality of decoration.[86]

Hadrian spent as much of his time as possible in Greece, visiting the shrines of her magnificent past and striving to promote the glory and influence of Greek culture. He embellished city after city with temples, libraries, and other buildings.[87] Hadrian even founded a Greek-style university in Rome, the first such institution in the western part of the empire.[88] He also established a confederation of Greek cities – the Panhellenion – that revived the ancient dream of a united Greek world.[89] Perhaps the most personally significant of Hadrian's experiences in Greece – shared enthusiastically by Sabina and her sister Matidia – was initiation into the Mysteries of Eleusis.[90]

Religion in the Roman Empire was undergoing significant changes during the second century. The traditional worship of the Olympian gods was losing ground to mystical religions from the East, which emphasized personal salvation and the promise of a blissful afterlife. These included the cults of mother goddesses like Isis and Cybele, and of gods such as Mithras, Dionysos, Jesus, and Jehovah. Conservative Romans still viewed the so-called "oriental cults" with suspicion, but the ancient Mysteries of Eleusis, located near Athens, offered the best of both worlds. They were open to all, male or female, slave or free, and were respected as part of the classical Greek tradition. Like many eastern cults, they were centered on the worship of an archaic mother goddess (Demeter) and a god who died and was resurrected (Demeter's daughter, Persephone).

Part of the secret ritual at Eleusis involved the identification of the initiate with Demeter or Persephone. (The third-century Roman emperor Gallienus even seems to have had himself represented in the guise of Persephone on his coins after his participation in the Mysteries.[91]) After his experiences at Eleusis, Hadrian issued coins describing himself as "reborn."[92] Sabina was celebrated in Eleusis as "the new Demeter," and a temple was erected there in her honor.[93] Hadrian participated in the Mysteries at least three times, attaining the status of an *epoptes*, or "one who has seen." He was so impressed with the rites that he tried to establish a version of them in Rome toward the end of his reign.[94]

In 128, the imperial party was in Greece, where a learned noblewoman by the name of Julia Balbilla joined the empress in her travels.[95] Sabina had probably already met this woman, an intellectual and an accomplished poet, in Rome or Athens before her husband became emperor.[96] Balbilla was the granddaughter of the last king of Commagene (see Figure 7.7), who had been deposed by Vespasian.[97] Her literary interests, which Sabina probably shared, are shown by a series of four poems that Balbilla inscribed on the foot of the Colossus of Memnon in Egypt.[98]

The Colossus, one of a pair of seated statues nearly 70 feet high, was erected by the Egyptian pharaoh Amenhotep III in the fifteenth century BC The Greeks identified it with Memnon, a hero of the Trojan War, who was said to have been the Ethiopian son of Eos, the goddess of the dawn. Ancient tourists made a point of witnessing a strange phenomenon associated with the Colossus. When the morning sun shone on the statue, it gave out a strange, musical sound "like the sound of a lyre string when it breaks."[99] As the third-century Greek writer Philostratus described it, "When the sun strikes Memnon's lips, like a plectrum on the strings of a lyre, they seem to speak . . ."[100]

After initial failures, Sabina, Hadrian, and Balbilla all heard this sound during their visit in November of 130.[101] Unfortunately, only a fragment of an inscription left on the Colossus by Sabina herself survives.[102] However, Balbilla's poems record the experience and praise the empress: "Yesterday, Memnon received the spouse in silence so that the fair Sabina might come back again – for the lovely form of the Queen delights you."[103]

Balbilla claimed that Memnon finally spoke "lest the King [Hadrian] be vexed at you, since for a long time you have been detaining his revered wedded wife."[104]

One of Balbilla's poems, which states that she came with "lovely Queen Sabina," was written in the style of the Greek poetess Sappho (born *c.* 630 BC), famed for her love affairs with women.[105] This has led to speculation that there was a sexual relationship between the empress and her learned friend.[106] However, imitation of Sappho's poetry was no guarantee of lesbianism, and the evidence is far too slight for any conclusions to be drawn. In any case, it seems unlikely that Balbilla would have left clues to such a liaison on a public monument.

The most famous member of Hadrian's entourage in Egypt was his boyfriend, Antinous. Hadrian made no effort to hide his extreme attachment to this young man, who was probably born around the year 110.[107] As numerous portraits of him show, Antinous was physically beautiful (with a passing resemblance to Elvis Presley – see Figures 7.10 and 7.12) and seems to have personified for Hadrian the Greek ideal of male perfection in body, mind, and spirit. He joined the emperor on his travels and hunting expeditions and became an established member of the imperial court. Other Roman emperors had pursued their love of boys without scandal and there is no indication of the relationship being ridiculed during Hadrian's lifetime.[108] What set Antinous apart from previous boyfriends of Roman emperors was what happened after he died.

Less than a month before the visit to the Colossus of Memnon, the imperial party was traveling up the Nile by boat when Antinous drowned under mysterious circumstances.[109] The emperor insisted in his memoirs (which have not survived) that it was an accidental death and nothing more.[110] However, the extreme honors paid to the young man, including deification and the founding of the city of Antinoopolis where he had died, encouraged a variety of fantastic rumors. It was claimed that he had been sacrificed, or had sacrificed himself, for the benefit of the emperor, his life being an offering to extend Hadrian's time on earth.[111]

Whatever the actual circumstances, there is no doubt that Antinous was deified and became the object of a popular new cult.[112] His supposed resurrection was believed to offer the same sort of hope for the faithful that was to be found in Eleusis or the stories of Dionysos and Jesus. The parallels to Jesus were so close that later Christian writers targeted Antinous for criticism, calling him an unworthy rival of Christ.[113]

Perhaps the most enduring legacy of Antinous' life and death was an outpouring of highly artistic portraits of him. Hadrian was said to have wept "like a woman" after the loss of his beloved,[114] and he commemorated Antinous in at least twenty-two statues that have been discovered at his villa at Tibur (only two of Sabina have been found there[115]). The young man's place of burial is not known for certain; Antinoopolis, Rome, and Tibur have all been suggested.[116] An obelisk in Rome that seems to have come from his funeral monument honors Sabina, apparently confirming her good relations with the boy. Its dedication puts the following words into the mouth of the deified Antinous: "[To] the great royal lady beloved by [Hadrian], Sabina, who lives, is safe and in health, the *Augusta*, who lives forever."[117]

Partly because of Hadrian's close relationship with Antinous, there is a long-standing tradition that he and Sabina had a terrible marriage.[118] It has been claimed that Hadrian was exclusively homosexual, with no sexual interest in Sabina or any other woman.[119] In support of this view is the fact that Sabina remained childless.

However, the emperor's Greek-style relationship with Antinous does not necessarily imply any aversion to women. In fact, the ancient writers accused Hadrian of numerous adulterous affairs with the wives of other men.[120] The third-century Christian writer Origen even chided Antinous for his inability to distract Hadrian from the opposite sex.[121]

It is true that many of the direct references to Sabina in the historical literature paint a horrifying picture of a woman caught in a loveless marriage to a man who despised and mistreated her. The *Historia Augusta* quotes Hadrian as saying that if he had been a private citizen he would surely have dismissed her because of her moody, difficult nature.[122] For her part, Sabina is supposed to have complained publicly of being treated no better than a slave by her husband.[123] She reportedly said that she took steps to avoid pregnancy by Hadrian, thereby sparing mankind the curse of a child from such an evil man.[124] Not surprisingly, Hadrian's alleged bitterness toward Sabina inspired rumors after her death that he had poisoned her or driven her to suicide.[125]

However, it is important to consider the sources of the claims of bad relations between Hadrian and Sabina. The accounts come from two surviving texts: the *Historia Augusta* and the anonymous writings known as the *Epitome de Caesaribus*. Both of these date from the late fourth century – 250 years after their deaths – and are biased against Hadrian. They are believed to have been based on the writings of one Marius Maximus, a high official who was born in about 160 (more than twenty years after Hadrian passed away) and wrote a scandalous, gossipy history of the Caesars in the 220s or 230s.[126]

Maximus' account is now lost, but it was called unreliable by the author of the *Historia Augusta*, which has itself been called a model of unreliability.[127]

If we look for corroborating evidence of trouble between Hadrian and Sabina, we find just the opposite. For example, far more coins were issued in honor of Sabina, both by the imperial mint and in the provinces, than for any previous empress.[128] She was granted the title of Augusta and other honors, and was promptly deified upon her death.[129] In fact, the beautiful relief that commemorates this event, showing Sabina borne aloft into heaven by a winged female, is the first official depiction of the apotheosis of a woman in Roman art and the first imperial monument to have a woman as its central figure.[130]

The fact that Hadrian took Sabina with him on almost all of his journeys also seems to deny a bad relationship. It has been suggested that he didn't trust the empress and wanted to keep an eye on her.[131] However, he had set the precedent of including her on his missions long before he became emperor, and he could have kept her out of mischief in other ways. Also, she participated in his official receptions with full honors and clearly had her own agenda as empress during her travels.[132]

One of the most interesting episodes regarding Sabina took place in about 122. While the emperor was in northern Britain, probably giving instructions for building Hadrian's Wall, Sabina seems to have stayed in Londinium (London) with members of the entourage. These included two high-ranking officials: Septicius Clarus (the man we have met previously as Pliny's errant dinner guest) and Tranquillus Suetonius, the historian and author of *The Twelve Caesars*. Hadrian abruptly fired both men, as well as many others, for behaving less formally toward Sabina than court etiquette demanded.[133] The uncertain wording of this account,[134] recorded by the *Historia Augusta* and therefore suspect, leaves open the possibility that the behavior had offended Sabina as well as her husband.

Septicius Clarus and Suetonius were not mere insolent servants; they were two of the most important men in Hadrian's court. Clarus was a prefect of the Praetorian Guard and Suetonius was Hadrian's chief secretary. They were also gifted, accomplished men of high status. The letters of Pliny the Younger, who was a friend of both men, may reveal something of their character. Suetonius is described as polite, scholarly, perhaps even introverted, while Clarus emerges as probably more outgoing and cavalier in his behavior, suggesting that he was the more likely instigator.[135]

There are many questions about what actually happened between Sabina and Hadrian's officials in Britain. The fact that Hadrian is said to have banished "many others" in addition to Suetonius and Clarus makes the nature of the offense even more mysterious. It is tempting to imagine some sort of wild "office party" during which excessive liberties were taken. Whatever transpired, the story does suggest that the emperor held Sabina in high regard and was protective, perhaps even jealous, of her.

There are other hints of at least tolerable relations between the imperial couple. Hadrian was devoted to Sabina's mother Matidia, who died in 119 in her early fifties when Sabina was in her thirties.[136] In his funeral oration to Matidia, Hadrian praised her extravagantly, citing her "great beauty, chastity, gentleness, tenderness, amiability, and modesty."[137] He deified his "most-beloved" mother-in-law, erected a temple to her – perhaps the first ever erected solely for a woman in Rome – and distributed spices to the people in her memory.[138] In the course of his speech, Hadrian referred to his wife as "my Sabina."[139] Also, when he laid out the ten divisions of Antinoopolis, he named one for Sabina, associating her with "harmony," and another for Sabina's mother Matidia, calling her "the mother of beautiful children."[140]

While the above deeds and comments were meant for public consumption, the fact remains that Hadrian *did* remain married to Sabina, though her childlessness put him in a difficult position regarding the succession and gave him a pretext for divorcing her if he wished. Her death came in 136 or 137 when she was about age 50, after thirty-six years of marriage. Only a year or two later, on 10 July, 138, Hadrian passed away at the age of 62.[141] Their remains were placed in a new mausoleum built for Hadrian and his family, which survives today as the Castel Sant' Angelo.[142] Unfortunately, the urns containing their ashes were looted by the Goths during their sack of Rome in 410.[143]

Whatever her marital relations were like, Sabina must have had a full and fascinating life. She saw more of the world than any previous empress, and her documented experiences in Eleusis and Egypt show that she took an active interest in the places and customs she encountered. The Roman Empire that Sabina toured was at its zenith in prosperity and political stability.[144] It embraced a staggering variety of cultures, languages, and religions, mostly coexisting and cross-fertilizing each other in harmony. Of all the women who reigned over the Roman Empire, none could have had a better understanding of what that empire was in terms of real people and real places than Vibia Sabina.

7.2   7.3   7.4

7.5   7.6   7.7

7.8

Figure 7.2 Sabina's mother, Matidia I, with her daughters, Sabina and Matidia II, on a bronze sestertius of Matidia I, minted by Trajan, AD 112. RIC II 761, BMCRE 1088, Cohen 11 (Matidia); courtesy Numismatik Lanz München.

Figure 7.3 Portrait of Sabina showing one of her more elaborate hairstyles. Bronze sestertius, minted AD 128. RIC II 1019, BMCRE 1879, Cohen 69; courtesy Classical Numismatic Group, Inc.

Figure 7.4 Vigorous portrait of Hadrian as emperor on a bronze sestertius, minted *c.* AD 132–134. RIC II 706, cf. BMCRE 1394ff., Cohen 663; courtesy Classical Numismatic Group, Inc.

Figure 7.5 Sabina with one of her simpler hairstyles on a copper as, minted AD 129. RIC II 1037, BMCRE 1889, Hill 415a; courtesy Classical Numismatic Group, Inc.

Figure 7.6 Hadrian (far right) with his troops on a bronze sestertius, minted AD 137. RIC II 747, BMCRE 1485, Cohen 544; courtesy Classical Numismatic Group, Inc.

Figure 7.7 Coin of King Antiochus IV of Commagene, reigned AD 38–72. He was the grandfather of Sabina's friend Julia Balbilla. Bronze coin (diameter 28 mm). AC 199, RPC 3856; courtesy Classical Numismatic Group, Inc.

Figure 7.8 A provincial portrait of Sabina. The reverse shows the empress as Demeter, the goddess of grain. Billon tetradrachm, minted in Alexandria, Egypt, *c.* AD 130–131. Köln 1261, BMC 918 (variety), Dattari 2065 (variety); courtesy Classical Numismatic Group, Inc.

Figure 7.9 Sappho, as envisioned in Roman times, shown playing a lyre on a bronze coin (diameter 27 mm) minted in her home city of Mytilene, Lesbos, *c.* AD 150–200. BMC Troas etc. p. 200/165; courtesy Classical Numismatic Group, Inc.

Figure 7.10 Hadrian's Bithynian friend Antinous on a bronze hemidrachm, minted in Alexandria, Egypt, *c.* AD 134–135. Dattari 2080; courtesy Freeman and Sear.

Figure 7.11 The personification of the Nile River in Egypt, with a child and hippopotamus in the background. Bronze sestertius of Hadrian, minted AD 136. RIC 781f (variety), BMCRE 1772–1773 (variety), Cohen 1377 (variety); courtesy Freeman and Sear.

Figure 7.12 Artistic portrait of Antinous, Hadrian's boyfriend, on a bronze coin (diameter 34 mm) minted in Ancyra, Galatia, after his death in AD 130. Waddington 6607 (variety); courtesy Classical Numismatic Group, Inc.

Figure 7.13 Hadrian's portrait on a bronze sestertius minted in AD 128. RIC II 970, BMCRE 1370, Cohen 817; courtesy Classical Numismatic Group, Inc.

Figure 7.14 Portrait of Sabina on a bronze sestertius, minted *c.* AD 117–138. RIC II 1035, BMCRE 1885, Cohen 82; courtesy Classical Numismatic Group, Inc.

Figure 7.15 The deified Sabina wearing a veil and corn wreath on a bronze sestertius minted by Hadrian, *c.* AD 136–138. BMCRE 1906, Cohen 33; courtesy Harlan J. Berk, Ltd.

Figure 8.1 Portrait of Faustina the Elder based on a statue in the Museo Capitolino, Rome. The coin is a bronze sestertius. Behind Faustina is a view of the city of Rome, reflecting the fact that she and her husband, the emperor Antoninus Pius, remained in the capital during most of their reigns. To the left are statues of her preferred deity, Cybele, the Great Mother of the Gods, and Cybele's consort, Attis.

8

FAUSTINA THE ELDER

The eternal empress

The childless Hadrian was forced to adopt his successor, a task he put off until late in his life. His first choice, announced in 136 when the emperor was 60, was a handsome young noble to whom he gave the name Aelius Caesar. However, Aelius died of tuberculosis on New Year's Day, 138, and Hadrian was forced to find another man. He promptly (24 January) selected a very distinguished 51-year-old senator with the ample name of Titus Aurelius Fulvus Boionius Arrius Antoninus.[1]

Antoninus was reluctant to assume the purple and deliberated for a whole month before accepting the honor.[2] Because of his advanced age, many expected that his reign would be a short one. Instead, it lasted longer than that of any emperor since Tiberius – twenty-three years. His wife Faustina would die after only two years as empress, but she remained an important figure throughout the entirety of her husband's reign because of his unceasing tributes to her memory.

Annia Galeria Faustina was born in October, probably in the late 90s, into a wealthy, noble family from Ucubi, Spain (modern Espejo, near Cordova) with probable ties to the families of Trajan and Hadrian.[3] Faustina's father, Marcus Annius Verus, was the most honored man in the empire after Hadrian; his three consulships equaled the number held by the emperor himself.[4] He is described as "quiet and steady" and was one of the richest men in the empire.[5] Faustina's mother, Rupilia Faustina, might have been the half-sister of the empress Sabina,[6] which would help explain her husband's high position. Faustina had two brothers: Verus, the father of the future emperor Marcus Aurelius, who died when Marcus was 3 or 4; and Libo, who served as consul in 128.[7] There may also have been a sister named Annia.[8]

A total of fifty-odd surviving portrait sculptures[9] and innumerable coins show Faustina to have been a very agreeable-looking woman, with oval face, full, rounded lips, a prominent nose, large, expressive eyes, and, in middle age, somewhat fleshy cheeks and jowls. Her coin portraits especially seem to reveal her lightheartedness and amiability (see Figures 8.5, 8.11).[10] Her most common type of hairstyle has been called the "turban,"[11] consisting of numerous thin braids or tresses that were wound or looped gracefully around the head and tied up together into a nest-shaped coil on top. It is likely that the braids were sometimes decorated with ribbons or jewelry to create what must have been a very elegant and dignified effect.[12]

It is obvious that Faustina spent a great deal of time with her hairdresser. Other than means of beautification, elaborate hairdos were status symbols: only upper-class women could afford the time and money needed for their creation. It was fitting that some of the most complicated and painstaking styles of all should appear on the heads of the empresses. One ancient satirist (Lucian of Samosata) poked fun at Roman women for the trouble they took in styling their locks.

Lucian claimed that most of their energy went into dressing their hair. "Not being satisfied with Nature's endowments," they used pigments to dye their hair red or yellow, as with colored wool. He said that even those who were content with their natural color spent their husbands' fortunes on perfumes from Arabia to scent their hair. Iron instruments warmed in a fire were used to curl the locks into ringlets. The styled hair was then brought down to the eyebrows, obscuring the forehead, while the tresses at the back were allowed to cascade to the shoulders.[13]

Faustina's husband Antoninus was tall, bearded, and physically strong, with a noble bearing but unpretentious manners.[14] His numerous portraits show a mild, earnest-looking man, with pleasant features and a yearning look that is reminiscent of later depictions of the Christian saints. He was born 20 miles (32 km) south of Rome on 19 September, 86, and grew up at his family home at Lorium, 10 miles (16 km) west of the capital, where he would build a palace in later years.[15] His parents' families were wealthy and distinguished and seem to have come from southern Gaul – perhaps from Nemausus (modern Nîmes, France), the home of Trajan's wife Plotina.[16]

The written accounts of Antoninus' life are short on historical detail, but long on praise for his many good qualities. His contemporaries described him as nothing less than a paragon of virtue. He was friendly, intelligent, thrifty, forgiving, peace loving, prudent, compassionate, and kind.[17] Antoninus was curious about many things, and enjoyed hunting, fishing, and attending the theater.[18] He was praised for treating the senate with respect and for reducing the imperial pomp "to the utmost simplicity."[19] He lived modestly, even participating in the grape harvest like a private citizen.[20]

Nevertheless, Antoninus knew how to give a good show. The marriage of his younger daughter (which unfortunately occurred after her mother's death) was a major spectacle.[21] Also, in celebration of the 900th anniversary of the founding of Rome (traditionally dated to the equivalent of 753 BC), he gave lavish games in the arena, involving elephants, rhinos, crocodiles, and hippos, and as many as a hundred lions and tigers in one event.[22]

Antoninus seems to have possessed a dry sense of humor. He once summoned a man named Apollonius from Chalcedon in Bithynia (in northern

Turkey) to tutor his nephew Marcus Aurelius in Rome. When Apollonius
was asked to come to the palace to meet his student, he replied, "A master
should not come to a pupil, but a pupil to the master." Antoninus laughed
and said, "It was easier for Apollonius to come from Chalcedon to Rome
than from his house to the palace."[23] On another occasion, when a foppish
philosopher complained that the emperor was not paying attention to him,
Antoninus responded, "I do pay attention, and I am very familiar with you.
You are the one who is always fixing his hair, cleaning his teeth, and doing
his nails, and who always reeks of myrrh."[24]

His compassionate nature is shown by a remark made when the palace
servants admonished the young Marcus for shedding tears over the death of
a tutor: "Allow him to be just a man this time; neither philosophy nor imperial power removes feelings."[25] Antoninus often quoted a line attributed to
the Roman hero Scipio: "I would rather save a single citizen than slay a thousand foes."[26] His concern for the slave population of the empire was shown
by edicts forbidding their cruel or abusive treatment.[27]

The highest praise of Antoninus comes from those who knew him best
of all. For example, the rhetorician Marcus Cornelius Fronto, who was
Antoninus' friend and the tutor of his adopted sons, called the emperor a
"god-like man," whose outstanding qualities excelled those of all other
rulers.[28] Marcus Aurelius, writing privately rather than for public consumption, exhorted himself to be the disciple of Antoninus in all things and to
emulate his "rationality, even temper, piety, serenity, sweetness, patience,
forbearance, simplicity, industry, and open-mindedness."[29] No wonder
Antoninus was more genuinely mourned than any other Roman emperor.[30]
Two hundred years after his passing, the Roman historian Ammianus
Marcellinus referred to him simply as "Antoninus the Good."[31]

Faustina and her excellent husband were probably married about the year
110 and would have four children.[32] The eldest, a daughter named Aurelia
Fadilla, lived long enough to marry a man named Lamia Silanus, but died
in the early 130s before her father had come to the throne.[33] Two sons,
Aurelius Antoninus and Galerius Antoninus, also died young, probably in
early childhood.[34] Another daughter, named Annia Galeria Faustina for her
mother, grew up to marry Marcus Aurelius and become empress of Rome
(see Chapter 9).

Unlike her two predecessors, Plotina and Sabina, Faustina does not seem
to have had to share her husband's affections with male lovers. Antoninus
was apparently opposed to pederasty and was even praised by Marcus
Aurelius for suppressing the practice.[35]

Antoninus' public career contrasted sharply with those of Trajan and
Hadrian in its lack of travel and military experience. He is only known to
have left Italy once in his life, sometime between the years 133 and 136, to
serve as the proconsul (governor) of the province of Asia (modern western
Turkey).[36] Faustina probably accompanied her husband on this trip.[37] Their

elder daughter, Aurelia Fadilla, had quite recently died and they may well have sought solace in each other's company.[38]

There are a couple of interesting stories about Antoninus' sojourn in Asia that reflect his humble and forgiving nature. When his party arrived in Smyrna, they were settled in the finest house in the city, which happened to belong to the orator Antonius Polemo. Polemo, who was out of town at the time, was said to think so highly of himself that "he talked to the gods as his equals."[39] When he unexpectedly returned late at night and found his house occupied, he raised such a fuss that Antoninus was forced to vacate the premises.[40]

On another occasion, when traveling by carriage on a narrow mountain road, Antoninus was nearly forced into a ditch by the carriage of another rich, arrogant orator. This man, named Herodes Atticus (whom we will meet again in Chapter 9), was even said to have struck Antoninus during the incident.[41] Despite these indignities, Antoninus bore ill will toward neither man and honored them both when he became emperor.[42]

After Hadrian's death on 10 July, 138, Antoninus assumed power and asked the Roman senate to deify his predecessor. However, the deceased emperor was so unpopular that the request was denied.[43] The senators even threatened to cancel the decrees of Hadrian, as had been done after the deaths of "bad" emperors such as Caligula and Domitian. Antoninus insisted on due honors being paid to Hadrian, pointing out that if his acts were cancelled, then his own adoption and succession would become null and void.[44] The senate relented, and, probably because of his dutiful efforts on Hadrian's behalf, bestowed the name "Pius" ("the pious one") on the new emperor.[45]

As it happened, Hadrian had not been content with naming his own successor – he named Antoninus' successors as well. He had required the new Caesar to adopt as his sons and heirs Lucius Verus, the 8-year-old son of Aelius Caesar (his first choice as successor), and Marcus Aurelius, Antoninus and Faustina's 17-year-old nephew.[46] (Their own sons had probably died by this time, or passed away soon after Antoninus came to power.[47]) Hadrian's arrangements for the future were inspired: Antoninus and Marcus Aurelius proved to be two of the finest rulers in history.

The imperial family also included Antoninus' daughter Faustina the Younger, now probably in her early teens. Before Hadrian's death she had been betrothed to Lucius Verus, though he was several years her junior. Antoninus realized that his daughter was better suited in age to marry Marcus Aurelius, and, as he intended for Marcus to succeed him on the throne, he was anxious for his daughter to rule with him. Marcus, however, was already betrothed to Lucius Verus' sister. Deferring to his wife's authority as *mater familias*, Antoninus asked Faustina to approach Marcus Aurelius about changing these arrangements.[48] Marcus agreed to his aunt's request and, in 139, Marcus and Faustina the Younger were formally betrothed.[49]

(Lucius Verus, deprived of marrying Faustina the Younger, eventually married her daughter, Lucilla.)

The empress' concern for the welfare of her complicated family may be shown by a couple of anecdotes. The *Historia Augusta* claims that, after Antoninus' adoption by Hadrian, she complained to him that he was not being sufficiently generous to the members of his family in regard to some minor matter. Antoninus was said to have replied, "Silly woman, we have even lost what we had before, now that we have gained the empire!"[50]

Similar concerns are revealed in a letter purportedly written much later by Faustina the Younger to her husband, the emperor Marcus Aurelius. She remarked that, years before during the rebellion of a man named Celsus (otherwise unknown), her mother had urged Antoninus to put the welfare of his own people first and foremost, "for an emperor is not righteous who ignores his wife and children."[51]

If Faustina put her family's well-being above the principle of imperial impartiality, this was consistent with old aristocratic attitudes against the very idea of an emperor. Antoninus' grandfather had actually offered his *condolences* to Nerva on his elevation to the throne, and Antoninus himself had delayed for a month before reluctantly accepting Hadrian's adoption.[52] Faustina may have initially argued against his assuming the throne, and then accepted the appointment as a necessary evil.

Whatever Faustina's attitude toward imperial status, the senate did not hesitate to honor her with the title of Augusta,[53] and she appeared on the imperial coinage from early in her husband's reign. However, after only two years as empress, Faustina died from unknown causes, probably in October or November of 140.[54] She was most likely in her early forties.

Antoninus was heartbroken. He showed his undying devotion to his wife throughout the remaining twenty years of his rule by continuing to honor her memory in a variety of ways. Faustina was deified and called "Diva Faustina" on the enormous imperial coinage that was issued in her memory – more than for any other empress.[55] She was associated on these coins with a variety of goddesses, but particularly with those that were concerned with the afterlife. Many bore the legend *Aeternitas,* referring to Faustina's eternal life among the gods in heaven (see Figure 8.12). Remarkably, this coinage continued to be issued in unabated abundance throughout her husband's long reign.

One of the deities to appear with regularity on Faustina's coins was the Asian goddess Cybele (see Figure 8.13). She and Antoninus were particularly devoted to this goddess and seem to have taken an active role in reforming and supporting her cult.[56] The worship of Cybele was centered on the Vatican, near modern St Peter's, and included a magnificent annual procession through the city that was attended by most of the populace.[57] There is no question that the modern cult of the Virgin Mary as the Mother of God owes much of its flavor to that of her ancient predecessor, Mater Deum (Mother of the Gods).[58]

Coins of Faustina sometimes depicted Cybele with the title *Salutari* (see Figure 8.13), indicating that the empress had achieved salvation through the grace of Cybele.[59] These coins have also been interpreted as evidence that Faustina was initiated into the "mysteries" of the Great Mother. There is evidence that, during Antoninus' reign, the ritual of the *taurobolium*, or baptism with the blood of a sacrificed bull, was first given official status, possibly as an alternative to castration for priests of the cult.[60] However, it is unlikely that Faustina submitted to the ordeal of the *taurobolium* (the third-century emperor Elagabalus is the only imperial figure known to have done so[61]).

After her death, the deified Faustina was worshiped in a new cult with its own priesthood, established by decree of the senate.[62] Gold and silver statues of her were set up and an impressive temple was dedicated to her in the Roman Forum (see Figure 8.14).[63] It contained an image of the seated Faustina, holding a scepter and prepared to receive her votaries. This temple was rededicated to include Antoninus after his death, and its shell and front columns still stand as part of the Church of San Lorenzo in Miranda.[64] Antoninus celebrated special games in Faustina's name, and her statues were erected in all four of the circuses (racing arenas) in Rome.[65] The senate also voted to erect a special golden statue of Faustina, which Antoninus paid for himself.[66]

We may get an idea of the poignancy of these commemoratives from some of the sculptures of Faustina that survive today. One of the most beautiful shows her in the guise of the goddess Ceres, holding a torch in her right hand, with poppies and wheat stalks in her left.[67] She is depicted with a serene, youthful beauty and the detached expression of the gods.

Antoninus further honored his wife's memory by establishing a charitable organization for the benefit of poor Italian girls, called the Puellae Faustinianae, or "Faustina's girls." It provided financial support, free education, and perhaps even dowries for underprivileged young women.[68] Clearly, Faustina's presence in the hearts and minds of the citizens of the empire continued long after her death.

Antoninus' love for his wife and grief at her passing cannot be doubted, but public displays of devotion are perhaps less convincing than private words. It is fortunate that a letter of his survives, written to his friend Cornelius Fronto a couple of years after Faustina's death. In thanking Fronto for compliments to the emperor in a speech to the senate, Antoninus expresses his particular gratitude for remarks made in honor of "my Faustina." He writes: "In truth, I would rather live with her on Gyara (a desolate island of exile) than in the palace without her."[69]

This comment is sometimes interpreted as a reference to the younger Faustina, Antoninus' daughter.[70] However, it is the deceased empress who was more likely to have been praised in a speech to the senate at this time.

Also, the recently widowed Antoninus knew first hand the pain of living in the palace without his wife, and the comment seems awkward for a father to have made about a soon-to-be-married daughter in her teens.

Antoninus eventually consoled himself in his loneliness by taking one of his wife's former slaves, a woman named Galeria Lysistrate, as his mistress.[71] However, his coinage and public monuments made it clear than he never forgot Faustina.[72]

As it happens, our main literary source of information about the reign of Antoninus Pius is the infamous *Historia Augusta*, which is never shy about disparaging the emperors and their families. Its writer was obviously opposed to the imperial system, and nearly all of the empresses are accused of misconduct, as if to prove that even the best emperors were unable to govern their own wives, not to mention the empire.[73] Faustina did not escape the historian's poison pen: "Much was said against her unrestrained and irresponsible way of living (*nimiam libertatem et vivendi facilitatem*), which Antoninus suppressed with sadness."[74]

This statement, which is incredibly mild by *Historia Augusta* standards, has its ambiguities. Did Antoninus suppress his wife's loose living, or the complaints against it? The text does not make this clear, but his mildness and tolerance of free speech make the former interpretation more likely.[75]

Even if the charge against Faustina was based on more than thin air, it is difficult to imagine the nature of her offenses. If she was something of a free spirit and given to frivolity, this might have put her at odds with her fastidious husband. Cassius Dio reports that Antoninus took pains to investigate the fine points of "even small and commonplace matters," and states that he was called stingy and "a splitter of cumin seed" because of this tendency.[76] The fourth-century emperor Julian II echoed this charge and accused Antoninus of "fussing about trifles."[77] Julian added that he was temperate in matters of state, but not in "love affairs."[78] This may have been a reference to Faustina's alleged indiscretions, or it may point instead to amorous adventures on Antoninus' part, or to the behavior of his mistress, Galeria Lysistrate, who reportedly dabbled in influence peddling at court.[79]

In any case, the honors Faustina received from the senate and people of Rome after her death, and her husband's loyalty to her memory, are ample proofs of their affection for her and her reputation as a dignified and honorable empress. We can be certain that if there was a large body of evidence against her, the writer of the *Historia Augusta* would have explored it fully.

As Antoninus grew older, he became stooped and had to have willow boards strapped to his chest to straighten his posture.[80] His old age was enlivened by a horde of grandchildren and an exemplary relationship with Marcus Aurelius, his devoted nephew and son-in-law, who shouldered more and more of the burden of rule as the years passed. On 7 March, 161, Antoninus died at the age of 74 at Lorium, his childhood home, reportedly from overindulging in Swiss cheese.[81]

Although Antoninus' reign is known for its uneventful peace and prosperity, there were uprisings in several parts of the empire.[82] These included disturbances in Egypt, Mauretania (modern Morocco), and Dacia (modern Romania). A revolt in Britain led to serious fighting and the erection of a new fortified rampart across the island known as the Antonine Wall.[83] About 80 miles (128 km) north of Hadrian's Wall, it was built of turf rather than stone and stretched for 37 miles (59 km). It was abandoned not long after its construction, however, and Hadrian's Wall came back into use as the empire's frontier in Britain.[84]

Earthquakes also disturbed the calm in the eastern provinces in 140 and again in the 150s, and a serious famine was relieved by Antoninus' distribution of wine and grain at his own expense.[85] All of these problems were dealt with by the efficient imperial administration without requiring the emperor to set foot out of Italy.[86]

If expansion marked the reign of Trajan, and consolidation that of Hadrian, the age of Antoninus saw the onset of economic stagnation and the first, almost imperceptible, hints of decline.[87] There were several reasons for this. First, the increasing prosperity of the empire had depended to some degree on the influx of wealth in the form of spoils from conquest. With the loss of this income, the cost of sustaining a large standing army (roughly 300,000 men) had become a heavy financial burden. Also, the empire suffered from an unfavorable balance of trade, with substantial resources (especially gold) heading east to pay for silk from China, spices and gemstones from India, and aromatics from Arabia.[88]

Another reason for the lack of economic vigor was the absence of technological innovation. The tendency to conservatism and idealization of the past in Roman culture contributed to this, as did a dread of the consequences of progress, as is shown by a couple of telling anecdotes.

Suetonius records that the emperor Vespasian destroyed the blueprints of a labor-saving device that would aid in moving stone columns because he feared that it would put poor Roman laborers out of work.[89] Similarly, it was claimed that Tiberius executed a man who had discovered a way of making unbreakable glass so that he would take his secret with him. The emperor was concerned that such a substance would wreak havoc on the price of gold.[90] Whether these stories are true or not, they were believed to be true, and would certainly have discouraged potential inventors.

It is doubtful that many Romans were aware of the threats to their prosperity or the beginnings of its erosion. With the advantage of hindsight, however, the writer of the *Historia Augusta* reported a series of inauspicious signs that occurred during Antoninus' reign, supposedly warning of troubles to come. Besides the usual natural disasters like earthquakes, floods, fires, and famines, there were other calamities and prodigies. The wooden stands at the Circus Maximus in Rome collapsed, killing over a thousand people.[91] Quintuplets were born, as well as a "two-headed child," and a huge crested snake was seen to devour itself. Also observed were the sprouting of barley in the treetops and the sudden and unaccountable tameness of four wild Arabian lions.[92]

If these omens signaled the displeasure of the gods, Antoninus certainly was not held responsible for them. He had died with the empire flourishing and its borders secure. He had also done his best to preserve the financial stability of the realm, leaving the astounding sum of 675 million silver denarii (2.7 billion sesterces) in the treasury.[93]

The honors paid to the revered emperor after his death were overwhelming.[94] One of his most impressive monuments was a pink granite column erected in Rome on a marble base, topped with a bronze statue of the deified emperor (see Figure 8.23). The column has been severely damaged and the statue has been lost, but its 8-foot-high (2.4-meter) base has survived and is now in the Vatican. It is decorated with three beautiful reliefs, the largest of which is a dignified representation of the reunion in heaven of the deified Antoninus and Faustina.[95] They are identified by various symbols with the gods Jupiter and Juno and are borne aloft by a winged male figure. Below them are personifications of the city of Rome and the Campus Martius, the site of their funerals.[96] (It is uncertain whether they were cremated, as their imperial predecessors had been, or inhumed, an eastern practice that was becoming fashionable in Rome.[97])

Some modern critics dislike this exquisitely carved scene for its "extreme pomposity,"[98] but it is clearly a masterpiece of imperial art and must have evoked powerful emotions in those who admired the emperor and his wife, especially while it retained its original lifelike coloring.

The theme of the reunion of the imperial couple after death was repeated in several contexts, including an honorary column set up at Antoninus' villa at Lorium. Its capital shows Faustina rising to heaven on the back of a peacock (Juno's bird) while her husband ascends on Jupiter's eagle.[99] The idea that the benevolent emperor and empress lived on in the realm of the gods, where they were capable of interceding on behalf of their former subjects, must have given the Romans some comfort in the difficult days that lay ahead.

Figure 8.2 The emperor Hadrian, showing his age, on a bronze sestertius, minted *c.* AD 134–138. RIC II 893, BMCRE 1657, Cohen 56; courtesy Classical Numismatic Group, Inc.

Figure 8.3 Lucius Aelius Caesar, Hadrian's first choice to succeed him, who died of tuberculosis before Hadrian passed away. Bronze sestertius minted under Hadrian in AD 137. RIC II 1055, BMCRE 1917, Cohen 58; courtesy Classical Numismatic Group, Inc.

Figure 8.4 Faustina the Elder's husband Antoninus as Caesar under Hadrian on a gold aureus struck in early AD 138. RIC II 453a, BMCRE p. 371, cf. Cohen 129; courtesy Classical Numismatic Group, Inc.

Figure 8.5 A posthumous portrait of Faustina the Elder on a gold aureus minted under Antoninus Pius, *c.* AD 141–161. RIC III 348, BMCRE 359, Cohen 5; courtesy Classical Numismatic Group, Inc.

Figure 8.6 Galerius Antoninus, the son of Faustina and Antoninus Pius, who died in early childhood. Provincial bronze coin, minted in Cyprus (?) *c.* AD 140. Cohen 2; courtesy Numismatik Lanz München.

Figure 8.7 Portrait of Faustina the Younger, daughter of Faustina the Elder and Antoninus Pius on a gold aureus minted under her father, *c.* AD 149–152. RIC III 512a, BMCRE 1089 (Pius), Cohen 236; courtesy Classical Numismatic Group, Inc.

Figure 8.8 The young Marcus Aurelius, Faustina the Elder's nephew and son-in-law. Bronze dupondius, minted under Antoninus Pius in AD 139. RIC III 1207, BMCRE 1206, Hill 245; courtesy Classical Numismatic Group, Inc.

Figure 8.9 Antoninus Pius as emperor on a bronze sestertius, minted AD 144. RIC III 616, BMCRE 1265, Cohen 589; courtesy Classical Numismatic Group, Inc.

Figure 8.10 Lucius Verus (the son of Lucius Aelius Caesar) who was designated by Hadrian (with Marcus Aurelius) to succeed Antoninus Pius as emperor. Bronze sestertius, minted *c.* AD 167–168. RIC III 1466, Cohen 211; courtesy Classical Numismatic Group, Inc.

Figure 8.11 Posthumous veiled portrait of Faustina the Elder on a silver denarius, minted under Antoninus Pius, *c.* AD 141–161. RIC III 360, BMCRE 415, RSC 78a; courtesy Classical Numismatic Group, Inc.

Figure 8.12 Aeternitas, the personification of eternity, on a bronze dupondius of Faustina the Elder, minted after Faustina's death by Antoninus Pius in AD 147. RIC III 1156, BMCRE 1549, Cohen 16; courtesy Classical Numismatic Group, Inc.

Figure 8.13 Bronze sestertius of Faustina showing Cybele (Mater Deum, or Mother of the Gods) as savior (*salutari*). Minted under Antoninus Pius, *c.* AD 141–161. RIC III 1145, Cohen 229; courtesy Numismatik Lanz München.

Figure 8.14 Temple of the Divine Faustina, with her statue enthroned within. After her husband's death, his statue was placed beside hers and the temple rededicated in both their names. Bronze sestertius minted under Antoninus Pius, *c.* AD 141–161. RIC III 1115, BMCRE 1506 (variety), Cohen 65; courtesy Classical Numismatic Group, Inc.

Figure 8.15 Seated statue of the deified Faustina enthroned in a triumphal chariot drawn by two elephants. Bronze dupondius minted under Antoninus Pius, *c.* AD 141–161. RIC III 1198, BMCRE 1604, Cohen 271; courtesy Classical Numismatic Group, Inc.

Figure 8.16 Two views of the Circus Maximus, which collapsed during the reign of Antoninus Pius, killing more than 1,000 people. A statue of Faustina the Elder was erected here after her death. (Left) bronze sestertius of Trajan, minted AD 103 (RIC II 571, BMCRE 853, Cohen 545); (right) bronze sestertius of Caracalla, minted AD 213 (RIC IV 500a, BMCRE 251, Cohen 236). Both courtesy Classical Numismatic Group, Inc.

Figure 8.17 Antoninus Pius' daughter, Faustina the Younger, depicted with three of her children on a gold aureus minted under Marcus Aurelius, *c.* AD 161–180. RIC III 682; courtesy Classical Numismatic Group, Inc.

Figure 8.18 Antoninus Pius (left) seated on curule chair on a dais beside Marcus Aurelius as Caesar. Bronze sestertius minted AD 142. RIC III 627, BMCRE 1292, Cohen 761; courtesy Classical Numismatic Group, Inc.

Figure 8.19 An Indian conception of Faustina the Elder on an imitation gold aureus minted in India, *c.* mid-second to third century. Turner cf. plate III, 166; courtesy Classical Numismatic Group, Inc.

Figure 8.20 Portrait sestertius of Faustina the Elder minted in AD 142 to commemorate the dedication of the Temple of Diva Faustina in Rome. The reverse of this coin shows the temple façade (see Figure 8.14). RIC III 1148 (Antoninus Pius), Cohen 254, Hill 417; courtesy Classical Numismatic Group, Inc.

Figure 8.21 Faustina the Elder ascending to heaven on the back of an eagle. Bronze dupondius minted under Antoninus Pius, *c.* AD 141–161. RIC III 1188, BMCRE 1462, Cohen 184; courtesy Classical Numismatic Group, Inc.

Figure 8.22 Faustina holding hands with her husband Antoninus Pius. Silver denarius minted after her death in *c.* AD 141. RIC III 381a, BMCRE 466, RSC 158; courtesy Classical Numismatic Group, Inc.

Figure 8.23 Column of Antoninus Pius depicted on a bronze sestertius minted under Marcus Aurelius *c.* AD 161. RIC III 1269 (Marcus Aurelius), BMCRE 880 (Marcus Aurelius), Cohen 354; courtesy Classical Numismatic Group, Inc.

Figure 9.1 Portrait of Faustina the Younger based on a marble sculpture found at Hadrian's Villa in Tibur, now in the Museo Capitolino, Rome. The coin is a bronze sestertius minted by her father, Antoninus Pius. Behind Faustina is an Alpine view, alluding to the time she spent on the northern frontier of the empire with her husband, Marcus Aurelius.

9

FAUSTINA THE YOUNGER

A new Messalina?

As described in the previous chapter, the emperor Antoninus modified Hadrian's arrangements for his succession by adopting Marcus Aurelius as his sole heir and betrothing him to his daughter Faustina. Marcus would rule for nineteen years as the last of the "five good emperors" and Faustina would become the first woman to succeed her mother as a Roman empress. She would also go down in history as promiscuous and disloyal, a "new Messalina." However, we will explore the possibility that this impression is false, arising from the slanders of a powerful enemy and his associates after her death.

Faustina the Younger was born in the early to mid-120s, or possibly as late as 130.[1] Her many surviving portraits reveal a beautiful, seemingly light-hearted woman like her mother. She had soft, lovely features with very large gentle eyes, a prominent, somewhat pointed nose, full cheeks, and a small mouth. Her coloring is unknown, but her son Commodus reportedly had blond hair that glistened in the sun as if powdered with gold dust.[2] She wore her luxuriant tresses in a variety of styles. At least nine distinct hairdos have been recognized for Faustina, all of which are more or less variations on a theme, with soft curls or waves framing the face and a bun at the back of the head.[3] The position and size of the bun varied, as did the texture of the hair, but the effect was uniformly charming – so much so that the ladies of Napoleon's court imitated Faustina's hairstyles more than 1,600 years after her death.[4]

As the young daughter of a Roman emperor at the height of imperial power, Faustina was surrounded by pomp and circumstance on a grand scale. Her father's seriousness and devotion to duty were balanced by her mother's elegance and cheerfulness, which must have brightened the palace atmosphere considerably. However, she would lose her mother at a crucial stage of her life, when she was probably in her mid-teens.

Faustina must have been pleased when her parents broke off her engagement to the 8-year-old Lucius Verus and betrothed her instead to the noble, brilliant, and attractive Marcus Aurelius. Marcus was born on 26 April, 121, during Hadrian's fourth year on the throne. As a young boy, his excellent qualities attracted the attention of the emperor, who called him *verissimus*, or "truest."[5] He was taught by some of the most accomplished men of his time,[6] and was early and profoundly attracted to philosophy. The personal writings of his mature years, which have come down to us as his *Meditations*, reveal much about his character.

As a youth, Marcus was fond of literature, painting, and sports.[7] He learned to hunt on horseback and to fight in full armor, though he was somewhat frail and prone to ill health.[8] Even after being elevated to imperial rank, he was unassuming in his dress and demeanor.[9]

Early portraits of Marcus Aurelius reveal a handsome young man, with a tousled mass of curly hair, large, protruding, soulful eyes, and a small mouth with cupid's bow lips. We probably have a better record of his changing appearance through life than of any other person from ancient times. The surviving portraits follow him from his teens to old age and reveal the toll that his responsibilities and personal disappointments took on him. There is a marked resemblance between Marcus and Faustina; they were, after all, first cousins (Marcus' father and Faustina the Elder were brother and sister). When he reached manhood, Marcus grew a long beard, reflecting his self-identification as a philosopher.[10]

In the spring of 145, roughly four years after her mother's death, Faustina and Marcus were married.[11] This event must have caused great excitement in Rome: it was certainly the most notable wedding in an imperial family since the union of Nero and Octavia nearly a century before.[12] Faustina's father Antoninus officiated at the ceremony and coins were issued showing the bride and groom together (see Figure 9.4).[13]

Marcus Aurelius was drawn to the philosophical school known as Stoicism (founded by Zeno in Athens, Greece, in the late fourth century BC).[14] As a Stoic, Marcus believed that the divine inhabited each human being as the soul, and was also revealed in the form of the natural universe. Therefore, he held that the virtuous life consisted of reverent and dutiful service to mankind while embracing one's worldly circumstances as the gift of God. He also believed that spiritual upliftment could be obtained through wisdom and equanimity, acquired through self-control and the contemplation of truth.

Marcus believed in the gods as different aspects of the one divine principle. As he put it: "Concerning the gods, I believe they exist and I honor them because I have experienced their power so many times."[15] However, he did not necessarily believe that the actions of human beings could influence them.[16] Nevertheless, he actively supported and participated in the rituals of religion, and received initiation into the Mysteries of Demeter and Persephone at Eleusis.[17] He believed that the individual was uplifted and the cohesion of the state was enhanced through religious practices.[18]

Religion in the Roman world had much in common with that of Hindu India today.[19] There were innumerable local deities, shrines, oracles, temples, and sacred springs and groves. The empire swarmed with mendicants and holy men and women, some attached to regional deities, others to their own inspiration or philosophical school. Among the most important were the predominately female oracles and sibyls, who were believed to speak for the gods. Less prestigious, but still influential, were a myriad of soothsayers, augurs, and astrologers. Widespread cults were generally lacking in centralized or hierarchical control or dogma. This ultimately gave the highly organized Christian Church an advantage in its long battle for supremacy.

In Stoicism, feminine virtues and qualities were held in unusually high regard.[20] This respect was shown by Antoninus Pius and Marcus Aurelius, both of whom protected and broadened women's rights and freedoms.[21] Marcus was devoted to his mother, Domitia Lucilla, a widow who derived substantial wealth from her family's tile factory near Rome.[22] In his *Meditations*, Marcus praised her for teaching him piety, generosity, to avoid evil thoughts, and to live a simple life, "very different from the ways of the rich."[23] He also thanked the gods that she spent her final years living with him and his family. Marcus seems to have carried this attitude of love and respect into his relationship with his wife.

Little is known about Faustina's personal religious or philosophical beliefs, though she probably shared many of the precepts of her father and husband. Like her mother, she seems to have been particularly devoted to the goddess Cybele and was often associated with her on imperial coins (see Figure 9.5).[24] Coins bearing Faustina's image, which were first minted under Antoninus Pius, also celebrate the traditional Roman goddesses Juno, Diana, and Venus and the personifications of joy (Laetitia), concord (Concordia), happiness (Felicitas), and mirth (Hilaritas).

On 30 November, 147, Faustina gave birth to a girl named Domitia Faustina, the first of at least fourteen (and probably fifteen) children that she and Marcus would have together over the next twenty-three years.[25] (Six girls and eight boys, including two sets of twins, are recorded with reasonable certainty.) On the following day, Faustina was rewarded with the title of Augusta, and Marcus, now technically outranked by his wife, was granted new powers.[26]

Faustina's fecundity would bring both joy and sadness. Joy in the blessing of so many children in the imperial family after a long line of childless emperors; sadness in that all but six would die as children and that the only boy to reach manhood, Commodus, would prove to be among the worst of emperors.

Glimpses of the domestic life of Faustina's young family come from letters between her husband and one of his tutors, the rhetorician Marcus Cornelius Fronto. These contain intimate details about the family's health and happiness. For example, Marcus writes Fronto that "Faustina has been feverish today . . . but, thank the Gods, she makes me less anxious by being a very obedient patient."[27] In another letter, he is grateful for some hope of the recovery of an infant daughter who was suffering from diarrhea, fever, emaciation, and coughing spells.[28] Sadly, his hopes were dashed when the child died.[29] Some years later, Marcus wrote Fronto: "Our Faustina is recovering her health. Our little chick Antoninus is coughing somewhat less. The occupants of our little nest offer prayers to you, each according to his or her age."[30]

In Marcus' letter, he remarks that his little daughter's illness "has kept us plenty busy."[31] This comment and others paint the picture of a close-knit, "hands-on" family – not one in which the nursing and raising was left entirely to servants. Indeed, Marcus credited Fronto with having made him aware that members of the elite patrician order, to which both Marcus and Faustina belonged, were often "somewhat lacking in normal affection,"[32] a tendency he clearly strove to avoid.

Though Marcus was a devoted husband and father, he probably was not a great romantic. His writings frequently dwell on the brevity of life and the gross nature of the human body. He characterized sexual intercourse as "internal friction followed by the convulsive release of mucus."[33] However, he was undoubtedly loyal to Faustina. As he put it: "It would seem exceedingly unfair for a husband to insist on chastity from his wife if he does not practice it himself."[34]

According to one theory, Faustina's coin portraits revealed a new hairdo each time she gave birth.[35] There must have been much excitement among the women of the empire as each new style was revealed. The imperial coinage also celebrated Faustina's growing family (see Figures 8.17, 9.6, 9.7, 9.8). One issue shows Faustina standing and holding two small babies in her arms, with a pair of young children huddling close on either side (see Figure 9.7). The legend proclaims "Happy Days!"

Her first set of twin boys, born in 149, were depicted on the coins of their grandfather, with their heads poking out of crossed cornucopiae (see Figure 9.6).[36] On another coin reverse, Faustina's second set of twins, born in 161, are shown as infants cavorting together in a throne-like crib (see Figure 9.8).[37]

These later twins (one of whom was Commodus) were born on 31 August, 161, nearly six months after Antoninus Pius died and their father became emperor. Marcus Aurelius had established a precedent by naming the younger Lucius Verus as his co-emperor, equal to him in power in every way, except that Marcus alone held the post of chief priest (Pontifex Maximus).[38] This arrangement, which restored Hadrian's original plan, was successful because Lucius Verus deferred to his older colleague.[39]

Marcus Aurelius was as beloved as any of his predecessors among the so-called "five good emperors" (the others being Nerva, Trajan, Hadrian, and Antoninus Pius).[40] However, while they had presided over periods of success and prosperity at home and abroad, Marcus' popularity was won and maintained through a series of hardships and disasters, which began soon after his accession.

In the autumn of 161 a flood did serious damage to the city of Rome, followed by a famine that affected much of Italy.[41] Meanwhile, the king of the Parthian Empire invaded the Roman client kingdom of Armenia and placed his own man on the throne. When the Roman governor of Cappadocia marched a legion into Armenia in response, his army was massacred and he committed suicide.[42] As if on cue, hostile tribes on the frontiers of Britain and Germany took advantage of the situation and raised arms against Rome. The German tribesmen even made minor forays into Roman territory.[43]

An advantage of having two emperors was that one could take the field in a military crisis while the other remained at Rome to administer the empire. In 162, Marcus sent the more vigorous Lucius Verus to answer the Parthian challenge.[44] Hand-picked generals were also dispatched to Britain and Germany to deal with the lesser dangers there.[45] A series of Roman victories was won in the East by Lucius' generals (particularly Avidius Cassius, whom we shall meet again) and security was gradually restored.[46] The Parthian challenge was met so successfully, in fact, that the eastern border remained relatively quiet for the next thirty years. However, the situation on the northern frontier proved far more dangerous.[47]

In 164, while Lucius was still in the eastern provinces, Marcus and Faustina decided it was time for him to marry. They may have become alarmed by rumors that the pleasure-loving Lucius had fallen under the spell of a beautiful woman of low birth named Panthea.[48] Her influence over the junior emperor was said to be so great that she induced him to shave off part of his magnificent beard.[49] In any case, he was promptly married to Faustina's 14-year-old daughter, Lucilla, to whom he had been betrothed for three years.[50]

According to the historian Herodian, who was born late in Marcus' reign, Faustina and the emperor generally chose husbands for their daughters on the basis of "disciplined habits and sober lives" rather than wealth or pedigree.[51] Lucius Verus, however, was not known for these virtues and, in fact, has been compared to Nero for his sensuality and extravagant tastes.[52] Nevertheless, Marcus was extremely fond of him.[53] In his *Meditations* he praised Verus for his affection and deference, and for setting examples of how *not* to behave.[54]

Lucilla was sent east under the care of Marcus' sister Annia[55] and the wedding was celebrated at Ephesus in Asia Minor. The bride was granted the title of Augusta[56] and she became the youngest Roman empress to date. Unfortunately, neither of Lucilla's parents was able to attend the wedding. Faustina gave birth to her last son about this time – a boy named Hadrianus, who was fated to die in childhood like all but one of his brothers.[57] Perhaps Faustina's pregnancy or Hadrianus' precarious infancy prevented her from accompanying her daughter.

Though Lucius was twenty years older than his bride, their marriage seems to have been reasonably happy, producing three children.[58] In late 165, when Lucilla became pregnant, Faustina and some of her other children traveled to the East to be with her.[59] This was probably Faustina's first extended separation from her husband.

By August of 166, the Parthians had been thoroughly pacified and their two capital cities captured and sacked.[60] Therefore, Lucius was able to return to Rome, along with Faustina, Lucilla, and the rest of their party. They were received in the capital with jubilation.[61] The empire's enemies had been defeated, new territory had been acquired in the East, and the royal families were prospering. A triumph was celebrated on 12 October in Rome. The children of the imperial family rode in the procession and Lucius arranged for two of Faustina's sons, including Commodus, to be awarded the title of Caesar, marking them as heirs to the throne.[62]

The mood of celebration was short-lived, however. By the end of the year, the Germans had again crossed the northern border.[63] The Roman army repelled the invaders, but the situation had become critical. Then came a serious outbreak of plague, presumably brought into the empire by the veterans of Lucius' eastern armies as they returned from the Parthian war.[64] The exact nature of the pestilence is unknown (smallpox and bubonic plague have been suggested[65]), but it raged throughout the eastern two-thirds of the empire for the next twenty years, hitting the army and city dwellers especially hard. In Rome, perhaps as many as 2,000 people died per day at the peak of the epidemic, their bodies carried off in wagons and carts.[66]

Most Romans believed that misfortunes such as these signaled the displeasure of the gods and foretold future calamities. Accordingly, Marcus called upon the priests of the state religion to perform special religious ceremonies in order to soothe the people and mollify the gods.[67] Unfortunately, this spiritual remedy for the empire's troubles had its indirect victims. The Christians, whose numbers were still relatively small, refused to participate in the public sacrifices.[68] To Marcus and many of his subjects this was tantamount to treason.

Sacrifice to the *genius*, or spirit, of the emperor and to the gods of the Roman state was the equivalent of pledging allegiance to the empire. Refusal to do so was seen as more than religious nonconformity: it was disloyalty and the rejection of civic duty. In the prevailing atmosphere of fear and uncertainty, the non-cooperation of the Christians was viewed as an internal threat – almost a form of rebellion. The response was sporadic persecution, sanctioned but apparently not instigated by the emperor, in which numerous Christians were killed.[69]

The persecution of Christians has stained the reputation of Marcus Aurelius.[70] However, he saw them as a collection of stubborn, overly dramatic exhibitionists,[71] whose refusal to cooperate with his policies threatened Roman society at a time of extreme peril. His contempt for them may be more understandable in light of the stories he must have heard about them. For example, the sacrament of communion, in which Christians were said to drink the blood and eat the flesh of their deity, was sometimes misunderstood as a cannibalistic feast.[72] Marcus probably satisfied himself that this charge was not true, but even his teacher and close friend Fronto described the orgies that Christians were believed to indulge in:

> They gather at a regular time for a feast, bringing their entire families, including members of both sexes and all ages. After much indulgence, when they have become drunk and are overtaken with lust and impure desires, they put out the lights and have sexual orgies, making love to whomever they happen to find in the darkness. All are guilty of incest . . .[73]

The danger of a renewed barbarian attack on the northern provinces had become so acute that Marcus decided both emperors were needed at the front.[74] In the spring of 168, he and Lucius Verus left Rome to inspect and strengthen the empire's defenses.[75] Faustina may have accompanied her husband on this tour; at least she seems to have been with him on his return journey through northern Italy in January 169.[76] It was on this return trip that Lucius Verus suffered a sudden stroke in his carriage, dying three days later at the age of 39.[77] This stunning loss must have only increased the public's sense of foreboding.

In describing the death of Lucius, later historians reported the first of many calumnies against Faustina. The *Historia Augusta* cites rumors that the empress had a clandestine affair with her son-in-law, and then murdered him by sprinkling poison on his oysters because he had told his wife Lucilla about it.[78] This incredible charge is no more believable than reports that Lucius was poisoned by Marcus Aurelius or killed by his own wife.[79] As we shall see, many more vicious tales would be told about Faustina after her death.

With the passing of Lucius Verus, and his eldest son only 8 years old, Marcus needed men in high places to help him deal with the coming crisis in the north. Therefore, he decided to marry Lucilla, still only 19 and widowed for less than a year, to the experienced Claudius Pompeianus, in or around his fifties, who became his principal military adviser.[80]

Some historians claim that both Lucilla and Faustina disliked Pompeianus and opposed this marriage.[81] Lucilla had been co-empress with her mother for more than four years and may well have been reluctant to marry a much older man of modest origins (he was a provincial from Syria) whose prospects seemed to be comparatively limited.[82] On the other hand, Marcus may have intended to make Pompeianus his heir, at least until his own sons had attained maturity. In any case, Marcus insisted on the match and the wedding took place in the autumn of 169, just before the emperor headed back north.[83]

Lucilla and Pompeianus had children[84] and remained married for thirteen years until their deaths at the hands of Commodus, who killed them for attempting to overthrow him in 182. (Cassius Dio claims that Lucilla put

Pompeianus up to staging a coup because she disliked her husband and wanted to be rid of him; Herodian says that she acted on her own.[85] It seems likely that they acted together for their mutual advancement, then paid the price for failure.)

Faustina's alleged dismay over Lucilla's marriage would have been compounded at this time by grief when her 7-year-old son died from an operation on a tumor under his ear.[86] The empress often experienced the pain of losing a child: at least eight of her offspring died during her lifetime. Her affection for her children is glimpsed in a surviving inscription. When her son Commodus recovered from an illness, Faustina had a stone monument erected with the words *Salvo Commodo Felix Faustina*, or "Commodus is well again and Faustina is happy!"[87]

By 169 it was clear to Marcus Aurelius that a major war with the northern barbarians was inevitable. In preparation, he enlisted slaves, gladiators, and even semi-civilized bandits into the army – desperate measures made necessary because of the number of troops recently lost to disease and the seriousness of the threat.[88] Reluctant to increase taxes in these uneasy times, Marcus auctioned off many of his household treasures to raise money, including some of Faustina's silken, gold-embroidered robes and her jewelry.[89] The empress probably shared her husband's attitude of renunciation, so consistent with her father Antoninus' remark that, as servants of the state, they owned nothing on their own.[90] Marcus told the senate that "even the house we live in belongs to you."[91]

In 170 the Roman army launched a pre-emptive strike across the northern frontier. To the horror of Romans everywhere, it met with a shocking defeat and was answered with a barbarian invasion of the empire.[92] The dam had finally broken. German invaders streamed deep into Roman territory, even besieging the city of Aquileia in northeastern Italy, only 300 miles (480 km) from Rome itself.[93] Not since the end of the second century BC had a foreign enemy set foot on Italian soil.

In Greece, the famous shrine of Eleusis near Athens was destroyed.[94] Everywhere the invaders went the loss of life and damage to property were severe. Beyond mere looting, the German tribesmen were desperate to settle in the empire in order to escape warlike tribes that were invading their lands from the north.[95] Even German women joined their men in fighting against the Romans, this being a matter of survival.[96]

Through tremendous Roman effort, the barbarians were gradually beaten back over a period of two years and the empire's boundaries were restored.[97] However, Marcus was forced to allow large numbers of Germans to settle under supervision on Roman territory,[98] and he would spend the remainder of his life fighting wars and trying to maintain order along the northern frontier.

After their hard-won victory over the German invaders, the Roman soldiers requested a cash reward from the emperor. Demonstrating his courage and high principles, Marcus refused, saying that this money "would be squeezed from the blood of your families."[99] He also insisted that the fate of his regime did not depend on the Roman army, but on the will of heaven.[100] This rebuff of the troops involved some measure of risk on the emperor's part, but, as Cassius Dio said, "nothing could compel Marcus Aurelius to do anything that was against his principles."[101]

It was during these years, while he was stationed at his northern military outposts, that Marcus composed his famous *Meditations*.[102] These extraordinary writings, written in Greek, show the emperor to have been a wise, conscientious, and thoroughly humble and decent man. They reveal his struggle to apply philosophy to the conduct of his life, ever mindful of his mortality. Marcus was determined to do his duty and to avoid being corrupted by the temptations of power. The *Meditations* continue to instruct and inspire people to this day. A sampling, addressed by the emperor to himself, follows:

> Be careful not to become a "Caesar." Don't take on that hue, for it could happen. Remain uncomplicated, good, pure, genuine, just, devout, gracious, and affectionate – and diligent in doing what is right . . .[103]

> How have you behaved towards the gods, your parents, brothers, children, teachers, those who looked after you when you were small, your friends, relatives, and slaves? Ask yourself if you have behaved so that it can be said of you: "He has never wronged a man in word or deed."[104]

> You may choose to live with a calm and peaceful mind, even if the entire world cries out against you and wild beasts tear you limb from limb.[105]

> Always be content with your lot in life; nature intends it for you and has made you for it . . .[106]

> The man who does not tend his own thoughts will always be unhappy.[107]

> Be like a sea cliff that remains steadfast against the waves until they are tamed.[108]

> It is enough to attend to one's inner divinity and to worship it sincerely.[109]

> You may choose, whenever you wish, to retire into yourself. There is no place where a man can find greater peace and freedom from trouble than within his own soul.[110]

> Everything in the universe is connected to everything else, and the links are sacred.[111]

Pass through your life in harmony with nature, and complete the journey in peace. Let go of life like an olive that falls when it is ripe, honoring the power that produced it and the tree that it grew upon.[112]

Meet death gracefully, for the power that releases you is full of grace.[113]

In about the year 170, Faustina gave birth to the last of her children, a girl named Vibia Sabina after Hadrian's wife.[114] (It is interesting that her last two children, Hadrian and Sabina, were named for the emperor and empress who had preceded her parents on the throne.) With the end of her childbearing years, Faustina felt free to live with her husband at his fortifications on the northern frontier. She and her younger children spent long periods with him at his headquarters, enduring the relative hardships of life at the front.[115] In 174 Marcus rewarded Faustina with the unprecedented title Mater Castrorum, or "Mother of the Camp," which was celebrated on coins bearing her image (see Figure 9.14).[116]

The emperor's health was often poor, and early in 175, while he was at his base of Sirmium on the Save River (in former Yugoslavia), he became so ill that it was feared he would not recover. There are even hints that the emperor considered committing suicide, viewed as an acceptable act under certain circumstances by the Stoics.[117] Faustina was with him at the time and must have been deeply concerned, not only for the welfare of her husband but also for their family. Her son Commodus was only 13 and still too young to succeed to the throne.

It was at this inopportune moment that news came of a serious revolt within the empire. Avidius Cassius, a hero of the Parthian war under Lucius Verus and now the governor of Syria, had proclaimed himself emperor.[118] He was a close friend of Marcus Aurelius and apparently acted in the belief that the emperor was dead.[119] All of the eastern provinces south of Asia Minor joined Cassius, including Egypt.[120]

Marcus was heartbroken. Not only had his friend and one of his most capable generals deserted him, but the rebellion forced him into a hasty settlement with the Germans, just when he seemed close to a more permanent solution.[121] He summoned Commodus from Rome, had him initiated prematurely into legal manhood, and officially proclaimed his son heir to the throne.[122] This was intended to prevent Cassius from taking power should Marcus die before Cassius had been subdued. Marcus then prepared to meet the usurper's challenge, but before his army was even ready to march, word came that Cassius had been killed by his own soldiers.[123] The rebellion had lasted only a little more than three months.[124]

Amazingly, later historians claimed that Faustina had played a key role in this revolt.[125] The historian Cassius Dio, who was about 12 at the time, later reported that the empress, afraid that an outsider would take the throne if her husband died, had secretly sent a message to Avidius Cassius. She allegedly asked him to marry her and become emperor in the event of Marcus' death. When Cassius received a false report of the emperor's passing, he claimed the purple, and then failed to withdraw when he discovered that Marcus Aurelius was alive after all.[126]

It is possible that Faustina approached Avidius Cassius as a potential protector for herself and her family in the event of her husband's death. She may well have preferred him to the likeliest candidate to replace Marcus, her son-in-law Pompeianus, whom she reportedly disliked. However, she would never have supported a challenge to her husband's rule and must have been horrified when the rebellion occurred.

Even the *Historia Augusta* argues for Faustina's innocence in this matter.[127] It presents a series of letters, purportedly between Marcus and Faustina, in which she begs her husband to protect his family and to be severe with Cassius and the other rebels.[128] These letters have numerous geographical and personal details that seem to prove their authenticity, but which contain inaccuracies that prove exactly the opposite. Nevertheless, it is interesting that someone went to the trouble of inventing letters that portray Faustina as vehemently opposed to Cassius and his cause.

After the death of Cassius, Marcus decided to visit the eastern provinces, taking Faustina, Commodus, and other family members with him.[129] The party left Sirmium by the end of July 175, sailed to the Danube, crossed the Balkans into Thrace, and traveled across what is now northern Turkey.[130] The journey continued southeast during the winter to the foothills of Mount Taurus and the village of Halala in the province of Cappadocia, where Faustina sickened and died in late 175.[131]

The cause of Faustina's death is a mystery. The empress was in her late forties or early fifties and the difficult winter journey through rough terrain could not have been easy for her. Cassius Dio says that she either died from gout or killed herself to avoid the penalty for conspiring with Avidius Cassius.[132]

The latter scenario is very unlikely. Besides Faustina's probable innocence, Marcus was so lenient in dealing with the rebels that he even regretted the death of Avidius Cassius.[133] In view of this, he would certainly not have severely punished his own wife. The *Historia Augusta* says that Faustina died from a sudden illness.[134] It is probable that the rumors of her complicity with Cassius arose because of the timing of her death, so soon after the uprising.

The village in which Faustina passed away was renamed Faustinopolis and a temple was erected there in her honor.[135] A vast memorial coinage was issued, more extensive than for any previous empress other than her mother (see Figures 9.17, 9.18).[136] The Roman senate set up silver images of Faustina and Marcus Aurelius in the Temple of Venus and Rome in the capital, and an altar was erected in their honor where all Roman newlyweds would offer sacrifice.[137] The senate ordered that a golden statue of the empress would be carried into the theater whenever Marcus was in attendance and placed in the special section where Faustina formerly sat, surrounded by the influential women of Rome.[138]

Marcus Aurelius honored his wife of thirty years in a eulogy[139] and established a new order of underprivileged girls to be supported by the state as a tribute to her. This order, like the similar institution dedicated to her mother, was called the Puellae Faustinianae ("Faustina's girls").[140] Cassius Dio states that Marcus wrote the senate immediately after his wife's death, begging them not to execute any senators implicated in Cassius' rebellion, "as if through this he might be consoled for losing her."[141] He may also have sought comfort in the Mysteries of Eleusis, into which Marcus and Commodus were initiated in September, 176, only months after Faustina's death.[142]

Marcus never remarried after his wife's passing, preferring eventually to take the daughter of her steward as his mistress.[143] The emperor said that to marry again would unfairly burden his children with a stepmother.[144]

Throughout the remaining five years of his reign, he continued to pay homage to his wife. In fact, his grief over her loss became legendary. Nearly two hundred years after her death, the emperor Julian II, who idolized Marcus Aurelius, commented that he had mourned her excessively, even though she was *"not a virtuous woman."*[145] Julian also criticized Marcus for enrolling Faustina among the gods.[146]

As Julian's comments suggest, Faustina has gone down in history as a model of misconduct.[147] Many ancient writers charged her with adultery, treason, and even murder. She was believed to have had innumerable lovers from all levels of society. The historian Sextus Aurelius Victor wrote that she shamelessly cruised for sexual partners among the sailors who worked naked on the beaches of Campania in Italy.[148] The empress supposedly seduced senators as well as gladiators and pantomime actors.[149] Many believed that Commodus, who fought publicly as a gladiator when emperor, was fathered by a gladiator rather than by the dignified Marcus Aurelius.[150] We have already encountered the rumors of Faustina's liaison with and subsequent murder of her son-in-law, Lucius Verus, and the charges of her conspiracy with Avidius Cassius.

According to Cassius Dio and the author of the *Historia Augusta*, Marcus was anything but ignorant of his wife's scandalous behavior.[151] The latter claims that, during an illness, Faustina confessed to her husband that she had had an affair with a particular gladiator, the supposed father of Commodus. Marcus consulted his soothsayers about what should be done to remove his wife's passion, and they advised him to execute the gladiator and have Faustina wash her lower body in his blood just before lying with her husband.[152] This abomination (strangely reminiscent of the spiritual cleansing in bull's blood in the *taurobolium*) would certainly have cooled Faustina's ardor, but it would have horrified the gentle Marcus as much as his wife.

The *Historia Augusta* also reports that Marcus once caught Faustina breakfasting with one of her high-ranking lovers, and yet promoted him and others like him to high positions.[153] Paradoxically, this historian says that Marcus was either ignorant or pretended to be ignorant of Faustina's affairs and even actively defended his wife in his letters.[154] He states that when Marcus was told about her misdeeds, and urged to divorce or even kill her, he replied: "If I send her away, I will also have to return her dowry," which, of course, was the Roman Empire.[155]

What are we to make of all this? Surely, where there is so much smoke there must be some fire? If we consider the case in support of Faustina, we find that it rests on very meager literary evidence. However, the primary witness on her behalf is the man who knew her best and to whom she was married for thirty years. In the first book of his *Meditations*, in which he expresses his gratitude for the good things in his life, Marcus Aurelius gives thanks that he was "blessed with a wife so obedient, loving, and unaffected."[156] This testimony should not be dismissed lightly; it was not written for anyone but Marcus Aurelius himself to read.

There are other arguments in favor of Faustina, including the abundant and often distinctive honors paid to her by her husband and by the senate and Roman people. There is no hint that she was denied the public credit due to an empress who fulfilled her role with energy and dignity.

The stories of her adulteries could easily have arisen after her death in response to the outrageous behavior of her unpopular son Commodus. Also, if the stories of Faustina's debauchery were true, we might wonder how she ever found the time and opportunity to carry on such a frantic sex life while bearing and raising fourteen (or fifteen) children. She was rarely parted from her husband, even choosing to share his hardships on the frontier when she did not have to. Furthermore, Fronto's letters to Marcus belie the stories that the emperor's children were not his own. He comments repeatedly about Marcus' remarkable resemblance to them: "They are exactly like you in appearance; nothing could be more similar," and, regarding their infant daughter, "so much that is good from both of your faces is mixed together in hers."[157]

So how did the gossip against Faustina gain such force and credibility? It seems as if the empress had some very powerful enemies. As a matter of fact, there *is* ample evidence of animosity between her and perhaps the richest, most influential private citizen of the time: the gifted Athenian orator Herodes Atticus.[158]

In an age when orators and philosophers were like pop stars, able to attract crowds of people eager to marvel at their verbal and intellectual gymnastics, Herodes Atticus was a superstar.[159] As a sophist, he was part teacher, part lawyer, and part entertainer. His students, many of whom became celebrities in their own right after his death, included the young Marcus Aurelius and Lucius Verus.[160]

Herodes Atticus was as famous for his prodigious wealth and magnificent gifts to the cities of Greece as for his academic prowess. Nevertheless, he was a controversial figure with at least as many enemies as friends.[161] He had a reputation for treating his slaves and freedmen harshly.[162] He berated and mocked his mentally retarded son and didn't hesitate to humiliate his rivals and students with his razor-sharp wit.[163]

In about 160 Atticus was charged with murdering his own wife, Annia Regilla.[164] It was claimed that he had a servant beat Regilla for some minor offense when she was eight months pregnant. Atticus proclaimed his innocence and tried to prove it by an ostentatious display of mourning.[165] To some, these gestures proved his innocence; to others they proved his guilt.[166] He was acquitted for lack of evidence, but the suspicions lived on.[167]

As the richest man in the eastern half of the empire, Atticus behaved in a high-handed way and was often accused of playing the tyrant.[168] Opposition to him in Athens grew until, in 174, he formally accused three city officials of conspiring against him.[169] Rather than stand trial in Athens, where Atticus' influence was strong, the three men went to Marcus Aurelius' headquarters at Sirmium to plead their case before the emperor.[170] Faustina and her youngest child Sabina, aged 3, were with Marcus and urged him to provide for the needs of the defendants. They also let him know that they were firmly opposed to Herodes Atticus in this matter. Little Sabina supposedly even fell at her father's knees, begging him in her baby talk to save her Athenians.[171]

Faustina had ample reason to dislike Atticus. When she was about 10 years old, her father Antoninus had been involved in a quarrel with him on Mount Ida in Asia Minor. The two men and their parties had met on a narrow road, and, when neither side would give way, a shoving match ensued.[172] Some even said that Atticus struck the future emperor during this incident.[173] Furthermore, the unfortunate Regilla was related to Faustina and about her age.[174] It is very possible that the two were girlhood friends in Rome, where Regilla's family had a villa on the Appian Way.[175] Faustina would not have forgotten the accounts of Atticus' cruelty towards her.

Atticus, whose portraits show as a bearded and somewhat gaunt-looking man, arrived in Sirmium accompanied by the servant who had allegedly beaten Regilla. This servant brought with him his beautiful twin daughters, whom Atticus cherished as if they were his own.[176] The night before the case was to be heard by the emperor, lightning struck the building in which the girls were staying and both were killed.[177]

The next day, the grief-stricken Atticus forgot his usual eloquence and complained bitterly to Marcus that he had been *sacrificed to the whims of a mere woman and her three year-old child.*[178] He abused Marcus for ingratitude and, when warned by the praetorian prefect that he was courting death by speaking so bluntly to an emperor, the aged orator replied that "an old man does not have many fears" and stormed out of the proceedings.[179] Marcus wept when he heard the charges brought against his former tutor, and was forced to punish Atticus' servants for their roles in the crimes.[180] Atticus himself lived away from Athens for about a year in what may or may not have been a voluntary exile.[181]

Certainly, Faustina would not have appreciated Atticus' crack about the "whim of a mere woman," and she may have had a role in his removal from Athens. It is interesting that the orator waited until shortly after Faustina's death to write to Marcus Aurelius in a successful attempt to renew their friendship.[182] The emperor, who always treated his former teachers with profound respect,[183] replied in a friendly manner, even mentioning his own grief over the loss of Faustina.[184] The emperor also wrote a letter to the people of Athens, urging them to forgive Atticus for his excesses and welcome him home.[185]

Marcus' attitude toward people who had injured him, expressed in his *Meditations*, may have been applied in the case of Atticus, or, if the rumors were true, in the case of Faustina herself:

> How strange it may seem for a man to love those who have done him wrong. However, this can happen if he remembers that they are his kinsmen and that the injury was done unintentionally or through ignorance – and that both of them will soon be dead. Besides, he has been done no real harm, for the injury has not made his mind worse than it was before.[186]

Atticus outlived Faustina by a few years, dying in his 70s in the late 170s.[187] To the end of his life he was surrounded by adoring pupils, many of whom became famous writers and sophists in their own right (e.g. Aelius Aristides, Aristocles, Hadrianus of Tyre).[188] As we shall see, some of these men and their students would rise to positions where they could determine how their teacher's enemies would be remembered. We may wonder if the image of Faustina as a latter-day Messalina was the creation of Herodes Atticus and his followers. If so, then his revenge for the humiliation at Sirmium would have been complete.

Marcus Aurelius, aged 58, passed away on 17 March, 180, probably at his northern base of Vindobona (modern Vienna, Austria).[189] His 19-year-old son Commodus, who had been a co-emperor since 177, now became sole emperor and ruled the empire badly.[190] The historians record numerous cases of cruelty, incompetent rule, and personal extravagance on the part of Commodus, culminating in his murder on the last day of 192.[191] Besides his execution of Lucilla and her husband, referred to on p. 161, Commodus exiled and then killed his own wife, Bruttia Crispina, for adultery.[192]

Marcus Aurelius has been blamed for abandoning the tradition established by his four predecessors of selecting the best available man to succeed him. It has been charged that he let his paternal affection for Commodus over-rule his better judgment.[193] This is nonsense: Marcus was the first emperor since Vespasian even to have a son who *could* succeed him. Any other choice would almost certainly have led to civil war, especially as Commodus had served as co-emperor for five years before Marcus died.[194]

The contempt in which later writers held Commodus was due in large part to his enthusiastic participation in gladiatorial contests.[195] This was considered thoroughly inappropriate behavior for an emperor by the Roman upper class.[196] Previous rulers (Caligula and Hadrian, for example) had dabbled in the sport,[197] but no emperor had ever showed his passion for the games so openly. Commodus fought in the arena himself and claimed to have bested 12,000 opponents.[198]

The historian Cassius Dio was an eyewitness to some of Commodus' performances. He tells us that his public battles were mere exhibitions, without steel weapons or the shedding of blood.[199] However, he also says that Commodus sometimes killed or maimed his opponents in private contests held within the palace.[200] Dio adds the delicious comment that when he and his fellow senators watched the emperor's antics in the arena they would chew laurel leaves so that they would not burst out laughing.[201]

Faustina had passed away before Commodus became emperor, and prob-ably before he began his public exhibitions (365 of his appearances in the arena came while Marcus Aurelius was still alive[202]). Certainly, she was aware of her son's fascination with the games and may have urged him to focus on more constructive and appropriate interests for a prince.

The assassination of Commodus after nearly thirteen years on the throne (perhaps fittingly, he was strangled in his bath by a wrestler[203]) precipitated a series of civil wars that were reminiscent of the struggles for power following the death of Nero. The eventual winner was an African by the name of Septimius Severus.

Severus had great admiration for Marcus Aurelius.[204] Cassius Dio tells us that before he married the future empress Julia Domna in 187 Severus had a dream in which the empress Faustina herself made ready their nuptial bed in the Temple of Venus, perhaps signifying his imperial destiny.[205] He claimed to model his reign on that of Marcus Aurelius, even renaming his older son for the deified emperor.[206]

However, when that son, better known as Caracalla, assumed the throne, he showed a peculiar dislike for Faustina, though he was born thirteen years after her death. He revoked her deification and de-consecrated the temple in Cappadocia that Marcus Aurelius had erected for her.[207] Significantly, Caracalla's teacher, Antipater the Syrian, was the student of Herodes Atticus' leading disciple, Hadrianus of Tyre.[208] Furthermore, two of Faustina's accusers, the historians Cassius Dio and Marius Maximus, as well as Atticus' admiring biographer and Antipater's student, the sophist Philostratus, were all closely associated with Caracalla's court. Certainly, these men influenced the young emperor's attitude toward Faustina. It is also interesting that Antipater, Hadrianus, and Caracalla's mother's family all hailed from the Syrian provinces, where support for Avidius Cassius (also a Syrian) had been enthusiastic.[209]

In 212 Caracalla ordered the death of Faustina's daughter, Cornificia, then in her fifties. The manner of her death, recorded by Cassius Dio, reflects the dignity of her upbringing: "Her last words were 'My poor, unhappy soul, trapped in an unworthy body, go forth, be free, show them that you are the daughter of Marcus Aurelius!' Then she took off her ornaments, composed herself, opened her veins, and died."[210]

The happy promise of Faustina's large family did not bear the expected fruit. Of her six children that survived to adulthood, at least three (Cornificia, Lucilla, and Commodus) came to sticky ends. Her fourth daughter, Fadilla, is said to have warned Commodus of a plot during the latter part of his reign before disappearing from history.[211] The two remaining daughters, Faustina III and Sabina, grew up to marry, and then died under unknown circumstances.[212]

The reign and death of her son Commodus came to symbolize the end of the golden age of Rome and the beginning of troubled times. As Cassius Dio put it, "the kingdom of gold gave way to one of iron and rust."[213] Indirectly, some of the blame for Rome's decline was laid at Faustina's door. The stories of Commodus having been the offspring of her gladiator lover hinted that had she remained loyal to her husband his virtues might have surfaced in his heir, and the "kingdom of gold" might have been prolonged.

The crucial role of women in the decline and fall of Roman imperial dynasties was a common theme in Roman history, though seldom stated unequivocally. Nero, who brought about the end of the Julio-Claudians, was portrayed as the creation of his mother Agrippina and unduly influenced in his evil actions by his second wife Poppaea. Though she was honored by the succeeding dynasty, Domitia was held responsible for the fall of the Flavians through her complicity in the murder of her husband Domitian. As we shall see, the next dynasty, the Severan, was said to have met its demise because of the avarice and presumption of a woman, the empress Julia Mamaea.

The dynasty of Antoninus Pius, Marcus Aurelius, and the Faustinas, known as the Antonine, came to an end because of the faults of Commodus, who was believed by later Romans to have been the fruit of Faustina's indiscriminate lusts. Most modern historians believe that the attacks on Faustina's character and stories of her infidelity were unjust, and that Faustina was, as her husband put it, "obedient, loving, and unaffected."[214] In any case, the difficulties that the Roman Empire now confronted were caused by many factors, and, as the great Marcus Aurelius had discovered, could not easily be solved, even by the best of rulers.

Addendum: Commodus and the gladiatorial tradition

Something about the way of the gladiator had an irresistible appeal to Commodus. Perhaps his staged victories gave him a way to emulate his brilliant and accomplished father, who was clearly a man of very different gifts. While Marcus achieved his victories on the field of battle and in the realms of scholarship, administration, and philosophy, Commodus basked in the glory of the arena. Or perhaps he was drawn to the games for the same reasons as the multitude. The gladiators provided high drama and excitement while surrendering themselves to the horrors and uncertainties of life and death. The spectacle of the arena was an awe-inspiring one, for princes as well as the mob.

The phenomenon of the gladiators (from *gladius*, the Roman word for sword) is a feature of Roman culture that is appalling to modern sensibilities. The idea of a crowd of spectators clamoring to see men (and sometimes women) fight to the death for entertainment seems barbaric, sadistic, and cruel.[215] The writer and philosopher Seneca agreed with this assessment. He wrote about his own horrifying experience as a spectator at the games and commented on the evil effects of witnessing such atrocities.[216]

"Man is a thing which is sacred to mankind," he said, "but nowadays he is killed in play, for fun!"[217] But Seneca's was almost a solitary voice against the practice, though Marcus Aurelius was so averse to bloodshed that he severely limited gladiatorial contests and even required gladiators to fight with blunt weapons so that no one would be killed.[218] When popular demand forced him to allow a specially trained man-eating lion to appear in the arena, he refused to even look at it.[219]

Indeed, there were other forms of carnage for amusement besides gladiatorial combat. Condemned criminals and prisoners were routinely thrown to wild beasts in the arena, which must have been a powerful disincentive to crime. Spectacles of punishment and mortal combat were believed to be morally instructive, teaching audiences about courage and honor and hardening them for the challenges of war.[220]

It should be remembered that, like most people before the twentieth century, ancient Romans were accustomed to public executions and punishments and regularly witnessed or participated in the slaughter of animals for food. Hence, they were undoubtedly less squeamish about bloodshed than most people are today.

The extreme popularity of gladiators is beyond question: children imitated them, men argued over their merits, and women adored them.[221] A gladiator's sweat was collected and sold as a prime aphrodisiac and his blood was believed to have curative powers.[222] Women would throw themselves at famous fighters in the streets or bribe guards to give them access to a gladiator's quarters at night.[223]

There can be no understanding of the gladiatorial tradition without an appreciation of its cultural context and meaning to Romans in general.

Gladiatorial combats seem to have been introduced by the Etruscans, who ruled Rome until the late sixth century BC.[224] Initially, they were part of the funerary observances in honor of dead noblemen.[225] As time went on, contests were incorporated into festivals and as entertainment at dinner parties, though they continued to be staged in memory of deceased individuals, sometimes years after their passing. Wealthy and ambitious Romans discovered that sponsoring public contests could be an important way to gain popularity.

The custom spread to cities throughout the empire, as evidenced by numerous ruined amphitheaters today.[226] In some cases, the combatants were condemned criminals or foreign deserters and prisoners of war, but the most popular gladiators formed a class of professional, carefully trained fighters. Julius Caesar won popularity by exhibiting 320 pairs of gladiators in one event, while the emperor Trajan matched 10,000 men against each other in games that went on for a period of four months.[227]

Many gladiators were slaves – in fact, a common punishment for a slave was to be sold to a troupe of gladiators.[228] However, under the emperors, an increasing number of Romans of free and even noble birth endured social disgrace by enlisting as gladiators in search of excitement, money, and a glorious end.[229] It has been estimated that, by the end of the first century BC, more than half of all gladiators were volunteers.[230]

Gladiators were more than entertainers or athletes – they were in a vague but historical sense sacrificial victims, not only to the enjoyment of their masters and the audience but also to the shades of the dead and, in an abstract sense, to the Roman order of things.[231] The Romans were a profoundly spiritual people who believed that the will of the gods (who were understood by most ancients to be different aspects or manifestations of a single divine power[232]) was reflected in external symbols. These included astrological signs, freaks of nature, the entrails of sacrificial animals, and the worldly circumstances of human beings. If a person was conquered by his enemies, or reduced to crime or slavery, it was not because of economic conditions, psychological disorders, or social injustices; it was due to the will of heaven. Therefore, the miserable condition of a gladiator or criminal was divinely ordained.

The attitude of the gladiators was reflected in their famous salute to Claudius before a mock sea battle: "Hail Emperor; we who are about to die salute you!"[233] Similarly, the *sacramentum gladiatorium*, or gladiators' sacred oath, expressed the fighter's submission. He agreed to allow himself to be "burnt with fire, bound with chains, beaten with rods, and killed with steel."[234]

The gladiator surrendered himself utterly to his master, dedicating his body and soul to him. Some measure of salvation was believed to come from meeting one's destiny with dignity and aplomb. The gladiator's oath made him a co-conspirator in his own destruction. He renounced both fear and hope and welcomed death, which made him in a sense unconquerable. If the crowd and one's betters were entertained or inspired by a noble struggle and a valiant death, so much the better; the gladiator had transformed his degradation into glory.[235]

The Romans admired this fearless resignation, which echoed the pledge of obedience given by a Roman soldier to his general or the emperor and thus symbolized one of the keys to Roman success.[236] Cicero, writing in the first century BC, celebrated the gladiator's courage and dignity:

> Gladiators, either ruined men or foreigners – what blows they endure! How those who are well disciplined prefer to accept the blow rather than to avoid it in a disgraceful way! How often it becomes clear that they would rather do nothing else than satisfy either their master or the people! Even when weakened by their wounds, they ask the master's wishes and indicate that, if they have done enough for the master, they wish to fall. What gladiator, even a mediocre one, has ever groaned or changed the expression on his face? Who has acted disgracefully, not only while he stood but also when he fell? Who, having fallen, when ordered to receive the death blow, has pulled his neck back? Such is the power of practice, contemplation, and custom.[237]

Despite his willingness to die, the professional gladiator did have some chance of survival. It is estimated that, in the first century AD, he stood one chance in seven of surviving a career in the arena, though the odds were much worse for untrained gladiators and grew worse for all combatants later in Roman history.[238]

9.2   9.3   9.4

9.5

9.6   9.7   9.8

Figure 9.2 Portrait of a young Faustina the Younger on a gold aureus minted by Antoninus Pius, *c.* AD 147–149. RIC III 506b, BMCRE 1046, Cohen 154 (variety); courtesy Classical Numismatic Group, Inc.

Figure 9.3 Marcus Aurelius as Caesar on a bronze sestertius, minted under Antoninus Pius, AD 144. RIC III 1231 (Antoninus Pius), Cohen 237.

Figure 9.4 A gold aureus marking the marriage of Marcus Aurelius and Faustina the Younger (shown with Concordia, the personification of harmony, between them). Struck under Antoninus Pius, *c.* AD 145–147. RIC III 434, BMCRE 611, Cohen 1021; courtesy Classical Numismatic Group, Inc.

Figure 9.5 Bronze sestertius of Faustina with Cybele, "the Great Mother," on the reverse. Minted under Marcus Aurelius, *c.* AD 161–175. RIC III 1663, BMCRE 933, Cohen 169; courtesy Freeman and Sear.

Figure 9.6 Bronze sestertius of Antoninus Pius showing the first of two pairs of twin sons born to his daughter Faustina and Marcus Aurelius. The infants' heads are depicted emerging from cornucopiae ("horns of plenty"). Coin minted under Antoninus Pius, *c.* AD 148–149. RIC III 857, BMCRE 1827; courtesy Edward J. Waddell, Ltd.

Figure 9.7 Faustina with six of her fourteen or fifteen children on a bronze sestertius minted by Marcus Aurelius, *c.* AD 161–180. RIC III 1674, BMCRE 952, Cohen 224; courtesy Classical Numismatic Group, Inc.

Figure 9.8 The twin sons of Faustina and Marcus Aurelius, Commodus and Antoninus, born in AD 161, in a throne-like crib. Bronze sestertius of Faustina, minted *c.* AD 161. RIC III 1665, BMCRE 936, Cohen 193; courtesy Classical Numismatic Group, Inc.

Figure 9.9 Marcus Aurelius (left) shaking hands with his junior co-emperor, Lucius Verus. Bronze sestertius of Lucius Verus, minted March–December AD 161. RIC III 1285, BMCRE 860, Cohen 29; courtesy Freeman and Sear.

Figure 9.10 Lucius Verus, co-emperor with Marcus Aurelius and the husband of Lucilla, Faustina's daughter. Bronze sestertius minted *c.* AD 163–164. RIC III 1396, Cohen 249; courtesy Classical Numismatic Group, Inc.

Figure 9.11 Annia Lucilla, Faustina's daughter, in the guise of Fecunditas (the personification of fertility), with her three children by Lucius Verus. Bronze sestertius minted *c.* AD 164–180. RIC III 1736 (Marcus Aurelius), BMCRE 1197ff. (Marcus Aurelius), Cohen 21; courtesy Classical Numismatic Group, Inc.

Figure 9.12 Lucilla, the wife of Lucius Verus and daughter of Faustina the Younger. The reverse shows Pietas, the personification of piety and devotion, probably in the form of Lucilla, who mourns the death of her husband in AD 169 when she was 20. Gold aureus minted under Marcus Aurelius, *c.* AD 169–180. RIC III 774, BMCRE 316, Cohen 49; courtesy Classical Numismatic Group, Inc.

Figure 9.13 Portrait of Marcus Aurelius as emperor on a bronze sestertius minted *c.* AD 163–164. RIC III 891, BMCRE 1092, Cohen 985; courtesy Classical Numismatic Group, Inc.

Figure 9.14 Faustina as MATRI CASTRORUM, or "Mother of the Camp." The reverse shows the empress making a sacrifice over an altar, with three legionary standards to her right. Bronze sestertius struck *c.* AD 175–176. RIC III 1659, Cohen 164; courtesy Classical Numismatic Group, Inc.

Figure 9.15 Provincial portrait of the young Commodus as Caesar on a silver tetradrachm minted in Antioch, Syria *c.* AD 175–177. Unpublished; courtesy Freeman and Sear.

Figure 9.16 Provincial portrait of Faustina the Younger on a copper drachm minted in Alexandria, Egypt, under Antoninius Pius, *c.* AD 153–154. Dattari 3291, Demetrio 2126; courtesy Classical Numismatic Group, Inc.

Figure 9.17 Bronze sestertius minted in honor of Faustina after her death and deification. The obverse shows her veiled portrait; the reverse an enthroned statue of the empress being drawn in a triumphal chariot by two elephants. RIC III 1698 (Marcus Aurelius), BMCRE 1569, Cohen 11; courtesy Freeman and Sear.

Figure 9.18 The deified Faustina borne aloft to heaven on a peacock. Bronze sestertius, minted after AD 175. RIC III 1702 (Marcus Aurelius), BMCRE 1570, Cohen 69; courtesy Classical Numismatic Group, Inc.

Figure 9.19 A bronze sestertius minted by Commodus in honor of the deified Marcus Aurelius. The reverse shows Marcus being carried to heaven by an eagle on a thunderbolt. RIC III 659 (Commodus), BMCRE 394 (Commodus); courtesy Classical Numismatic Group, Inc.

9.20   9.21

                                                       9.22

Figure 9.20 Bronze medallion (diameter 40 mm) showing Commodus as emperor wearing a cuirass, struck AD 189. Gnecchi, p. 58, 56 and plate 82, number 3; courtesy Freeman and Sear.

Figure 9.21 Portrait coin of Bruttia Crispina, the wife of Commodus. Gold aureus, struck *c.* AD 177–182. RIC III 287, BMCRE 47–49, Cohen 39; courtesy Classical Numismatic Group, Inc.

Figure 9.22 The emperor Commodus as the Roman Hercules, wearing the lion skin and with the club (reverse) associated with that hero. Bronze sestertius minted AD 191–192. RIC III 637, BMCRE 711–712, Cohen 192; courtesy Classical Numismatic Group, Inc.

Figure 10.1 Portrait of Julia Domna based on a sculpture from Gabii, Italy, now in the Musée du Louvre, Paris. The coin is a bronze sestertius. Behind Julia is the Orontes River valley in her native Syria. To the left and center are examples of the famous cedars of Lebanon, and a statue of Aphrodite/Venus with whom she was often identified.

10

JULIA DOMNA

The philosopher

When Septimius Severus became emperor in 193, he pretended that his reign was a continuation of the preceding Antonine dynasty. He even announced his retroactive "adoption" as the son of his idol Marcus Aurelius and astonished the Roman senate by deifying his "brother," the despised Commodus.[1] However, Severus and the dynasty that he founded heralded a significant change in the empire's power structure. For the first time, a family without Italian ancestry ruled the Roman world.

Severus was an African who spoke Latin with an accent,[2] and his wife, Julia Domna, was a native of Syria. She would reign as empress for twenty-four years (AD 193–217), first with her husband and then with her unmarried son. Arguably, Julia would make a deeper impression on her times than any other woman in Roman history.

According to one historian, Julia's father was Julius Bassianus, the hereditary high priest of the sun god Elagabal at his prestigious temple in the city of Emesa (modern Homs, Syria) on the Orontes River.[3] Her family was probably descended from a dynasty of petty kings who had ruled Emesa before its incorporation into the Roman Empire in the late first century AD.[4]

The date of Julia's birth is not known, but coins of her younger sister Julia Maesa, minted about 220, show a woman nearing 60 (see Figures 11.2, 11.17).[5] Thus, Julia Domna was probably born around 160. Domna and Maesa are Semitic names, possibly Arabic, and Emesa is believed to have been founded by an Arab tribe.[6] It had strong cultural and economic ties to the Phoenician coastal cities of Aradus, Byblos, and Berytus (modern Beirut), as well as to Palmyra, the important desert trading post to the east.[7] Emesa was a cultural crossroads, marked by a seething cross-fertilization of Greek, Persian, Phoenician, Arab, and Roman influences.[8] It must have been a stimulating place for a young girl to grow up.

Julia Domna's adult interests in religion, philosophy, and literature must reflect an excellent education as a child. She probably learned three languages: Greek, the language of culture and local government; Aramaic, Emesa's native tongue; and Latin, the language of the Roman rulers.[9] Her father's high position in the temple of Elagabal brought the family wealth and social prominence. Neighboring potentates sent annual tribute to the shrine, and pilgrims came to Emesa from far and wide to worship the conical black stone (probably a meteorite) that symbolized the spiritual power of the god.[10]

The later Roman poet Avienus described the temple of Emesa and its environs:

> The lofty temple of Emesa glistens in the rays of the rising sun. The city spreads over the broad fields, its towers reaching into the sky. The citizens of Emesa live busy, disciplined lives and worship the radiant sun god. Their towering temple, with its high triangular top, rivals the peaks of Lebanon, green with their cedars.[11]

We can imagine Julia's pride and awe when she watched her father conduct the ceremonies of worship. He wore gold and purple trousers, an ankle length, gold-embroidered purple tunic, and a jeweled diadem.[12] Animal sacrifices were performed, with the burning of incense and spilling of wine, while crowds of people displayed their religious emotions in ecstatic music and dancing.[13]

The temple of Elagabal (called Heliogabalus by the Greeks) was but one of several important centers of religious pilgrimage in Syria. Other famous shrines included those of Baal at Baalbek (Heliopolis), also on the Orontes, 50 miles (80 km) south of Emesa, and of the Syrian goddess Atargatis and her consort Hadad at Hierapolis (Bambyce), 130 miles (208 km) to the north. Julia must have visited both of these holy places, so important in the religious life of her native land.

We are fortunate to have an eyewitness account of the temple at Hierapolis by the Syrian writer Lucian, who hailed from the city of Samosata, about 90 miles (144 km) to the north. He visited Hierapolis in the mid to late second century AD and left a vivid account of the temple and its customs as they existed in Julia's time.[14]

Lucian tells us that the temple at Hierapolis faced east, toward the rising sun. Its entrance hall was a breathtaking sight, the doors covered with gold. The roof and interior of the temple also gleamed with gold. Fragrances from Arabia emanated from the temple, lingering in the visitors' clothes and memories for a long time.

He wrote that the inside of the temple was divided into two parts – a larger area for the public and a smaller chamber for selected priests. There were golden statues of a seated goddess named Atargatis, or "the Syrian goddess," supported by carved lions. Beside her was a statue of her consort, the god Hadad, supported by bulls.

Atargatis held a scepter in one hand and a spindle in the other. On her head was a crown consisting of rays and a tower. She was clothed in gold and gems, one of which was placed on her head and seemed to fill the temple with a ruby light that was especially bright at night. Lucian claimed that the goddess' gaze seemed to follow him as he moved – no matter where he stood, she seemed to be looking directly at him.

A large bronze altar stood outside the temple, as well as bronze statues of kings and priests. There was a courtyard filled with sacred animals: bulls, eagles, bears, horses, and lions – all of them tame. There was also a lake with a variety of sacred fish, some of them very large. The fish had names, and Lucian says that they would answer when called. One of them even wore jewelry.

There were sacrifices twice each day (involving bulls, cows, sheep, or goats), which were attended by all. The sacrifices to Hadad were made in silence, but those to Atargatis were accompanied by singing, flute-playing, and the shaking of rattles.

Pilgrims to this temple always shaved their heads and eyebrows. Each one sacrificed and then ate a sheep, spreading its fleece on the ground and kneeling on it for prayer. The worshiper placed the animal's feet and head on his own head and asked that his sacrifice be accepted. Then he set off for home, bathing only with cold water and sleeping on the ground until he had arrived there.

Though the idea of animal sacrifice may be distasteful to modern readers, it should be remembered that the animals were eaten after being consecrated to the gods. Indeed, the practice compares very favorably with its modern counterpart, the slaughterhouse, where many more animals are killed with much less reverence.

Julia was probably in her late teens in about the year 180 when a rising soldier named Septimius Severus was posted to Syria.[15] Severus was a deeply religious man and he certainly visited the noted shrines in this province, including that of Elagabal in Emesa, where he probably met Julia.[16] He was 35 years old (born 11 April, 145) and married to a woman named Paccia Marciana, with whom he may have had two daughters.[17] However, Julia Domna must have made an impression on Severus, for several years later, after his wife had died and he had become governor of a province in Gaul nearly 2,000 miles (3,200 km) away, he remembered her and made a proposal of marriage. The offer was accepted by Julia's family and the two were married sometime between 185 and 187.[18]

Julia's apprehension as she traveled half way across the known world to begin her life with the much older Severus can only be imagined. It is interesting that, when he wrote his autobiography (now lost), there was no mention of his first wife, to whom he had been married for ten years.[19] However, he did erect statues in her memory when he became emperor.[20]

There is a romantic story about the reason for Severus' interest in Julia. The *Historia Augusta* claims that, when in Gaul, Severus heard that her horoscope predicted she would marry a king.[21] Being ambitious and a great believer in astrology, he resolved to marry Julia and enlisted his friends in Syria to arrange the match.[22] This story, true or not, may have been spread as propaganda after Severus came to the throne as evidence of divine sanction for his rule.[23] However, it certainly would not have been wise to broadcast it while Commodus was still in power.

Julia Domna was, by most accounts, a woman of stunning beauty[24] and rare intellectual gifts. Her numerous portraits show that she had an oval face, attractive aquiline features, large, widely spaced brown eyes, luxurious arching eyebrows that met in the middle, a prominent nose, and a somewhat small mouth with dimples in each corner. The best portraits evoke her intelligence and sensitive, inquisitive nature. Julia was said to be skilled in the interpretation of dreams, and Cassius Dio counts craftiness among her qualities, which he says she passed on to her son Caracalla. However, Dio, who was from Bithynia in Asia Minor, apparently believed that *all* Syrians possessed this trait.[25]

Julia's portraits seem to have evolved subtly over time, with a gradual increase in "ethnicity" as her aquiline features were ever more sharply and realistically portrayed. This may reflect a lessening of the need to show Severus and his family as the literal descendants of Marcus Aurelius and the Antonines. Signs of advancing age remained muted, however, even in her last portraits. The contrast in apparent age between the last coin portraits of Julia Domna (see Figure 10.31) and more realistic ones of her younger sister, stuck just a couple of years later (see Figure 11.2), is quite striking.

Julia Domna's brown hair was worn in a consistent style, parted in the middle and crimped into a series of deep, symmetrical waves over her ears and almost to her shoulders, with a large, plaited bun covering the back of her head. In later years, this style was modified somewhat, with the bun gradually diminishing in size and the tightly waved hair covering more of her head like a helmet, with braided or twisted loops brought forward from the nape of the neck to her temples.

Many portraits make it clear that Julia wore wigs, saving herself countless hours with her hairdressers.[26] No empress is more easily recognized from her hairdo than Julia Domna. Though derived from earlier styles similar to those worn by Faustina the Younger, Julia's coiffure became distinctive and influenced women's fashions for much of the third century.[27]

When Julia joined Septimius Severus in Gaul, they probably spoke to each other in Greek rather than in Latin.[28] Perhaps their conversation was spiced with expressions in the related, Phoenician-based languages of their homelands.[29]

Severus was from a prominent family in the harbor city of Lepcis Magna (or Leptis Magna in Latin) on the Mediterranean coast of what is now Libya. It had been founded by Phoenicians from the city of Tyre and was later used as a trading post by the Carthaginians.[30] He was a small, sturdily built man,[31] with rounded features, a furrowed brow, large eyes, a dark complexion, curly hair, and a long beard (which had probably turned gray by the time he became emperor). He was ambitious, energetic, decisive, competent, and passionately interested in religion and the occult, avidly seeking out oracles and secret lore wherever he went.[32] He also appears to have had some interest in literature and philosophy,[33] though not to the same degree as his wife.

His military career was definitely on the fast track. After serving in Gaul, he governed Sicily and then the important frontier province of Upper Pannonia (modern Austria and Hungary). His appointment to Pannonia in 191, which put Severus in command of three legions (the nearest large army to Rome), showed that he had joined the highest circle of Commodus' government.[34]

Meanwhile, Julia had begun to raise a small family. On 4 April, 188, at Lugdunum (modern Lyons, France), she gave birth to her first child, a boy named Septimius Bassianus.[35] He would later be renamed Marcus Aurelius Antoninus, but is best known as the emperor Caracalla. On 7 March, 189, a little less than one year later, she gave birth in Mediolanum (Milan), Italy, to a second boy, named Septimius Geta for Severus' father.[36] These are Julia's only known children. She had succeeded in giving her husband two male heirs, which, as time would show, was more than enough.

Severus' rapid rise was largely due to the friendship and patronage of Helvidius Pertinax, the praetorian prefect under Commodus.[37] Therefore, when Commodus was murdered on the last day of 192 and Pertinax was declared the new emperor, Severus must have anticipated an important role in the new government. However, on 28 March, 193, after a reign of less than three months, Pertinax was assassinated by the praetorians, who proceeded to offer the empire to the highest bidder.[38] A wealthy senator named Didius Julianus won the auction by promising each guardsman 25,000 sesterces, or about two years' pay.[39]

We can imagine how Julia and Severus reacted to the news of these events. The Praetorian Guard, which had not seen combat in more than a decade, was an army of only 10,000 men. Severus had 30,000 troops under his personal command and could count on 20,000 more, who were serving under his brother Geta, the governor of the nearby province of Lower Moesia.[40] They may well have reasoned that, if the emperor was going to be chosen by an armed force, it might as well be Severus' army, as large as any in the empire. Accordingly, Severus arranged to be hailed as Augustus by his troops on 9 April, 193, at Carnuntum, nearly 500 miles (800 km) from Rome.[41]

But Septimius Severus wasn't the only general to seize this opportunity.[42] The governor of Syria, Pescennius Niger, was also proclaimed emperor by his legions and quickly won the support of the eastern provinces.[43] Severus gained the advantage over Niger by acting quickly. He neutralized a potential western rival, Clodius Albinus, the governor of Britain, by persuading him to accept the title of Caesar and making him heir apparent to the throne.[44] Severus then seized Rome, where Didius Julianus, the man who had purchased the empire, was killed on 1 June, 193, after a reign of only sixty-six days.[45]

Severus dismissed the praetorians, replaced them with a new guard of his own hand-picked troops, and compelled the senate to recognize him as the legitimate ruler.[46] Julia Domna was promptly acclaimed Augusta,[47] and she and Severus turned east to deal with the challenge from Pescennius Niger. However, by May of 194, before Severus had even arrived on the scene, Niger's forces had been defeated and he was dead.[48] Septimius Severus was the sole ruler of the Roman Empire.

Soon after Niger's demise, Julia made a triumphant visit to her home town of Emesa.[49] She bestowed honors and riches on the city and arranged for it to be exempted from paying taxes to Rome.[50] It is not known if her parents were still living at this time, but her sister Julia Maesa was probably with her. In fact, the sisters would remain together for the duration of Domna's reign.[51] Severus rapidly advanced Maesa's soldier husband, Julius Avitus Alexianus, making him first a senator and then a consul.[52]

The empress stayed with her husband during his extended eastern campaigns, which included punitive expeditions against some of the king-doms outside the empire that had sided with Pescennius Niger.[53] She must have endured numerous hardships while traveling with the army through the difficult terrain of the Middle East. Accordingly, she was rewarded on 14 April, 195, with the title Mater Castrorum, or "Mother of the Camp," an honor first bestowed on Marcus Aurelius' wife Faustina twenty years before.[54]

When all serious resistance in the East had been crushed, Severus felt secure enough to cancel his arrangement with Clodius Albinus and make his elder son Caesar and heir to the throne instead.[55] Betrayed by the wily emperor, Albinus had himself proclaimed Augustus by his troops and crossed the English Channel to fight for his interests.[56] Severus marched his army west and, on 19 February, 197, fought a decisive battle near Lugdunum (Lyons) in Gaul.[57] The action was fierce and the outcome long in doubt, but Albinus was finally defeated and driven to suicide.[58]

According to the *Historia Augusta*, Severus rode his horse over the naked corpse of his rival, cut off his head and sent it to Rome, and tossed Albinus' body – as well as those of his wife and son – into the Rhône River.[59] This savage behavior is in startling contrast to the mildness of Marcus Aurelius after the death of the usurper Avidius Cassius only twenty-two years before. (Ironically, Clodius Albinus had been one of only two eastern governors to remain loyal to Marcus in that uprising.[60]) Many of the supporters of Albinus were also executed, including twenty-nine senators.[61]

At last, nearly four years after claiming the throne, Severus had removed all of his rivals. It was said that Julia had been the driving force behind his relentless pursuit of absolute power.[62] However, Severus seems to have had sufficient ambition and ruthlessness to accomplish the deed without pressure from his wife.

The civil wars that followed the death of Commodus had brought almost a century of political stability to a shocking end. The loss of life and property was enormous, reminiscent of the similar internecine conflict that had followed the death of Nero in AD 68. The economic consequences were particularly severe in the western provinces – especially in Gaul and Spain, where the ancient wine business never recovered.[63]

And there was an even heavier cost: the struggles for power marked the beginning of the so-called age of the soldier-emperors, when the army and the men who controlled it determined the empire's course. More and more wealth was diverted to the soldiers, who received dramatic raises in pay.[64] (Severus and Caracalla doubled the military budget between them.[65]) The Roman Empire gradually took on the character of a military dictatorship in which taxes were high and individual liberties were in decline.[66]

It might seem that, with the last of his challengers removed, Severus would settle down to enjoy the fruits of his victories. Instead, he sent his army east once again, taking sail from Italy to join them in Syria. His objective this time was the destruction of Rome's old enemy, the Parthian Empire, which had exploited the war with Clodius Albinus to invade Roman territory.[67] Julia and her two sons went with the emperor, as did Severus' closest friend, Fulvius Plautianus, the new prefect of the Praetorian Guard.[68] Plautianus was from the emperor's home town of Lepcis Magna, was probably related to him, and was even rumored to have been his lover as a boy.[69] As we shall see, he would become a thorn in Julia's side.

Once again, Severus was victorious. In two campaigning seasons – 198 and 199 – he thoroughly defeated the Parthians, capturing their major cities and allowing his army to plunder their capital.[70] Only one fortress was able to withstand his attack – the desert stronghold of Hatra, which had also eluded the emperor Trajan. It was twice besieged by Severus' army, but never taken.[71] The second attempt on the citadel was nearing success after twenty days when Severus broke off the siege.[72]

It is reported that Julia Domna had persuaded her husband to spare Hatra because her religious sensibilities would not allow her to condone the desecration of a holy shrine to the sun god.[73] However, this story is unlikely to be true – if the empress had these qualms, why did she wait until twenty days into the second siege to express them? Still, the story does reflect Julia's deep interest in religious matters and suggests an influence over her husband's decisions.

Religion was also a major reason for an imperial visit to Egypt in 199.[74] Severus was devoted to the Egyptian god Serapis, as Julia was to the god's consort, the goddess Isis.[75] They worshiped at important shrines in Memphis and in Alexandria, where Severus viewed the embalmed body of the deified hero Alexander the Great.[76]

The party also played tourist by visiting the Pyramids and Sphinx and the Colossi of Memnon at Thebes in southern Egypt.[77] They may even have had their portraits painted. A round wooden picture of the emperor, empress, and their two boys, found in Egypt and dating to about this time, is the only surviving contemporary painting of a Roman royal family.[78] Julia is shown looking confidently at the viewer, wearing a necklace and earrings of large pearls and a golden tiara.

In 202, the imperial family returned to Rome after five years' absence and showered the enthusiastic population with gifts.[79] Julia finally had the opportunity to settle into the imperial palace, which was considerably enlarged under her rule.[80] A fire had severely damaged the capital in 191 or 192, and she and Severus took advantage of the opportunity to leave their mark on the appearance of the great city.[81] A magnificent arch was erected in honor of the Parthian victories (see Figure 10.17), 75 feet tall and 82 feet wide, with an internal staircase. The arch was topped by gilded bronze statues, including images of Severus and his sons in a chariot, pulled by six horses.[82]

Other notable constructions in Rome included the Septizonium (or Septizodium), a fanciful, decorative building at least three stories high, dedicated to the seven known planets.[83] Possibly begun by Severus were the gigantic Baths of Caracalla, which would be dedicated in 216.[84]

For her part, Julia took personal responsibility for restoring the Temple of Vesta, which had been destroyed in the fire.[85] This graceful round building, depicted on Julia's coins (see Figure 10.18), housed the sacred fire of the goddess.[86] It had been damaged and rebuilt several times before Julia's structure, which survives in ruins today.[87]

Severus' home town of Lepcis Magna, which the royal family visited in 203, was also embellished with lavish buildings, rivaling those of Rome in size and magnificence.[88] It was given a new harbor and a vast forum, 1,000 by 600 feet (305 by 183 meters) in size and surrounded by colonnades.[89] An arch was erected, with reliefs showing the emperor and his family engaged in religious rites and triumphal processions.[90]

Severus and his family must have visited his relatives in Lepcis, including his sister Septimia Octavilla. The *Historia Augusta* tells us that Septimia once visited her brother in Rome, but that her almost complete ignorance of Latin embarrassed him so much that he sent her home.[91]

In the frenetic early years of Severus' reign, Julia's power and influence rivaled or exceeded those of any previous empress.[92] She seems to have accompanied the emperor on most or all of his travels and to have enjoyed a pivotal role in policy-making.[93] Her prominence on the coinage and on official inscriptions and monuments was unprecedented. More provincial coins would be minted in her name than for any other person in Roman history, other than her husband and her elder son.[94]

Julia's influence on her husband's policies might explain Severus' decision to break tradition and allow legionary soldiers to marry and live with their wives and children.[95] Previously, the soldiers' women were considered concubines and neither they nor their children had legal status. Also, Severus' prohibition in 200 of the increasingly popular gladiatorial combats between women may reflect Julia's concern for the welfare of her sex.[96]

Despite Julia's early prominence, she was soon eclipsed by her husband's closest advisor, Fulvius Plautianus. What probably began as an uneasy rivalry between the emperor's wife and his best friend eventually erupted into a bitter struggle for power. Plautianus often criticized Julia to her husband and treated her with contempt.[97] The historian Cassius Dio, who was an eyewitness to the life of Julia's court, says that Plautianus conducted investigations into her conduct, even torturing noblewomen to get evidence against her.[98] He eventually won the upper hand by accusing the empress of adultery and of plotting against her husband.[99]

Although Julia was never convicted of these crimes (under Augustus' laws, infidelity on the part of an empress was treason and was punishable by death[100]), she was forced into the background. The extent of Plautianus' ascendancy was demonstrated in 200 when his daughter, Fulvia Plautilla, was betrothed to Julia's 12-year-old son Caracalla.[101] The empress must have been deeply distressed by this development, and disgusted when their opulent wedding was celebrated in 202 as part of the observance of Severus' tenth anniversary as emperor.[102] Plautilla's dowry was described as being sufficient for fifty princesses.[103]

Perhaps from loyalty to his mother, Caracalla despised his bride, refusing to eat or sleep with her.[104] However, the union had the emperor's sanction and Plautilla was given the title of Augusta, making her co-empress with Julia.[105]

We can only speculate on the nature of the relationship between Severus and Plautianus. The possibility that they were relatives or even lovers has been mentioned.[106] Plautianus' power allowed him to acquire prodigious wealth, an overbearing manner, and an extravagant lifestyle.[107] At one point, he went so far in his ostentation that Severus censured him for erecting too many statues of himself, though he soon recovered the emperor's favor.[108] Severus even wrote, "I love Plautianus so much that I pray I will die before he does!"[109]

Cassius Dio tells us that Julia sought distraction from these misfortunes in the study of philosophy, passing her time in conversation with sophists and other learned men.[110] This has given rise to the legend that a circle of writers, poets, and philosophers gathered around the empress in a sort of intellectual *salon*.[111] Proposed members of Julia's group include the brilliant physician Galen (doctor to Marcus Aurelius); the historians Cassius Dio and Marius Maximus (though Dio detested Caracalla and would criticize Julia for her "low birth" and crafty nature[112]); the poet and future emperor Gordian I; the writer Diogenes Laertius (who apparently wrote his history of Greek philosophy for Julia, citing her interest in Plato); the sophist Antipater the Syrian (who tutored Julia's sons); the poet Oppian (who dedicated a work to Julia and Caracalla and compared the empress to the goddess of love); and, among others, the writer and historian Aelian.[113]

Modern scholars have questioned the idea that she was the center of such an illustrious group.[114] In fact, the direct evidence for its membership is quite sparse. The philosopher Philostratus, who wrote biographies of the sophists, tells us specifically that he was a member of Julia's circle of "philosophers and astrologers."[115] He described her as "the philosophic Julia" and "a devoted admirer of all rhetorical exercises."[116] Philostratus mentions a second sophist, Philiscus the Thessalian, as being a member of Julia's group, and credits her with obtaining the professorship of rhetoric at Athens for this man.[117] This must have been but one of many times that she advanced the career of a protégé.

The popularity of sophists was at its height in Julia's time. It was customary for them to display their skill and learning in extempore responses to questions (such as "Should a man marry?"), or to speak on a given historical theme.[118] One wonders what sort of questions and challenges Julia posed to the men she encountered.

Whether or not she presided over a formal "circle," it is obvious that Julia could satisfy her urge for intellectual stimulation by summoning whomever she pleased. Her husband also liked to gather talented people around him, who would certainly have been engaged in conversation by the inquisitive empress.[119] There can be no doubt that Julia associated with many of the most gifted and accomplished people of her day.

One of these was an anonymous sculptor known to modern scholars as "the Caracalla Master," so named because of his unforgettable, often ferocious-looking portraits of Julia's son.[120] His works, which are distinguished by their psychological insight, clearly inspired many of the triumphs of portraiture that would be created during the next half century. The "Caracalla Master" produced highly individualized portraits of members of the royal family (not including Severus himself), and it seems likely that the empress took a personal interest in his career.[121]

Julia's involvement with the visual arts is also inferred from the increase in eastern influence on imperial art and architecture.[122] This is especially seen in sculpture, where Greco-Roman realism was blended with the more abstract spiritualism of oriental art. Frontality in portraiture, a distinctive feature of Syrian art in particular, became more common in other parts of the empire at this time.[123]

Julia's interest in literature is attested by Philostratus.[124] This was a time of great popularity for romantic and humorous novels by Greek writers such as Iamblichus (*Babylonian Story*), who was from Julia's own Emesa, Achilles Tatius (*Leucippe and Clitophon*), and Longus (*Daphnis and Chloe*), as well as the Latin author Lucius Apuleius (*Metamorphoses, or The Golden Ass*).[125] Their stories were often much more than fanciful yarns; many could also be read as sophisticated allegories of human life, philosophy, and the spiritual journey.[126]

One of the most celebrated novelists of the time was Heliodorus. His *Aethiopica* (Ethiopian Story), one of the finest surviving examples of Roman literature, may have been written during or shortly after Julia's lifetime.[127] Like Iamblichus, he was a native of Emesa and it is possible that he associated with the empress.[128]

The *Aethiopica* describes the thrilling odyssey of a pair of star-crossed lovers, Chariclea and Theagenes, as they journey from Delphi in Greece to Chariclea's home in Meroe, the capital of Ethiopia. Their wanderings, which are complicated by encounters with brigands and numerous other obstacles, take them through a succession of seven different locations, each more welcoming and civilized than the last. When they finally reach Meroe, they are recognized by their royal parents, married to each other, and celebrated as priests.[129]

In a reflection of the times, the heroine of the *Aethiopica* (Chariclea) is, like the Severan empresses beginning with Julia Domna, courageous and resourceful, often excelling her lover Theagenes in initiative and understanding.[130] One modern scholar has remarked that "feminine psychology" was in fashion in the late second century and the early third,[131] perhaps accounting for the prominence of and sympathy for female protagonists in literature. Julia Domna may have been too busy and serious-minded to be a devotee of romance novels, but it is possible that she enjoyed them for their hidden philosophical meanings and references.

The empress' fascination with religion and philosophy was shown by her interest in the sage Apollonius of Tyana (a town in Cappadocia, east-central Turkey), whose biography she commissioned Philostratus to write. Apollonius died at an advanced age in the late first century AD. One of his disciples kept a written account of his exploits, which was given to Julia Domna. She turned the document over to Philostratus and ordered him to edit the memoirs, with special attention to "style and diction."[132] Philostratus also consulted other sources in preparing his "Life of Apollonius of Tyana," which, unfortunately, was not published until after Julia's death.[133] This work is a travelogue and adventure story, as well as the biography of a saint, chronicling his journeys and escapades in Babylon, India, Spain, Ethiopia, Rome, and numerous points in between.

Apollonius professed to follow in the philosophical footsteps of Pythagoras (sixth century BC). Like his predecessor, Apollonius was a celibate vegetarian who lived simply and believed in reincarnation.[134] He opposed gladiatorial contests and cruelty to animals, and was credited with the ability to foretell the future and, possibly, to resurrect the dead.[135] He is also described as a devoted worshiper of the sun, which certainly would have endeared him to Julia and her family.[136]

Philostratus claimed that Apollonius came into direct contact with the emperors Vespasian, Titus, Domitian, and Nerva.[137] He was also imprisoned by Nero's henchman Tigellinus, and by Domitian, whom he confronted in person.[138] The Hindu brahmins of India profoundly influenced Apollonius, telling him that they knew all things because they started with knowing themselves.[139] He received initiation from them, and reported that "he saw Indian brahmins living upon the earth and yet not on it, protected without fortifications, and owning nothing, yet having the wealth of all men."[140]

Saying that he was inspired "to teach men how to pray and make sacrifice to the gods," Apollonius attracted disciples during his lifetime and was widely venerated after his death.[141] When he became emperor, Julia's son Caracalla built a temple in his honor, and numerous other temples to Apollonius were erected in Asia Minor.[142] As Julia Domna took a special interest in his life and teachings, we may get some idea of her beliefs from the sayings attributed to him:

> The sage who has self-knowledge and always remains in touch with his conscience never shrinks from what terrifies others.[143]

> The soul that ponders how it is that God cares for all people and delights in their worship, and that considers carefully what is good and just and temperate, will soar through the heavens.[144]

> Oh gods, grant that I may have little and want nothing.[145]

> How wonderful it would be if people cared less for wealth and there was more equality . . . Then men would be in harmony with each other and the whole earth would be like one family.[146]

> The gods do not need our sacrifices. So what should we do to win their favor? In my opinion, we should acquire wisdom, and do as much good as we can to the men who deserve it.[147]

> I don't care much about constitutions, for I know that my life is governed by the gods.[148]

> In truth, there is no death and there is no birth; they only seem to exist.[149]

Philostratus records the story that Apollonius came back to life after death, appeared before his disciples, and continued to teach them before ascending to heaven.[150] This tale seems like a response to the claims of Christ's resurrection from the dead. It has even been suggested that pagan Romans encouraged the legend of Apollonius, or even invented it, as a counterbalance to the growing cult of Christianity.[151] However, other scholars reject this idea.[152] Eusebius, the fourth-century Christian writer, who attacked Apollonius as an unworthy rival of Christ, admitted that no one had suggested a comparison between the two before the late third century, more than sixty years after Philostratus wrote his biography.[153]

On the whole, Christians were tolerated under Septimius Severus, though he prohibited evangelism and conversion to the faith.[154] This policy resulted in some instances of persecution, including the famous case of Perpetua, a North African upper-class woman whose conversion led to her execution in 203.[155]

As a Syrian who would spend much time in Antioch, where Christians were especially prominent, Julia Domna was certainly familiar with their precepts.[156] It is likely that her interests embraced a wide range of philosophies and religions, including those of both Christ and Apollonius. There was even a tale that Julia had the Christian philosopher Origen brought to her by an armed guard so that she could hear his teaching.[157] Her niece, Julia Mamaea, who also reportedly met with Origen, exhibited a strong interest in the cult of Christ.[158]

Besides her promotion of Apollonius, and her possible curiosity about Christianity, Julia Domna's spiritual interests were documented by innovations on her coins and her patronage of non-European cults. An example is the Phoenician goddess Tanit, who was worshiped in Rome as the Celestial Goddess (Dea Caelestis).[159] Julia's coins celebrated Tanit (see Figure 10.20), as well as Isis and Cybele, both of whom she was often identified with (see Figure 10.21).[160] Her coins also honored the traditional Roman goddesses Venus, Juno, and Ceres.[161] Julia encouraged the growing spirit of syncretism, in which all gods were perceived to be the manifestations of a single divine creative energy, perhaps most commonly symbolized as the sun, the principal deity of her homeland.[162]

The change in religious emphasis at this time is evident in imperial portraiture. While Marcus Aurelius and other Antonines were typically shown with half-closed eyes, suggesting the introspection of Stoicism, the Severans are often portrayed looking upward, as if gazing toward the sun and the heavens.[163] Even the movement toward frontality in portraiture, associated with eastern art, probably echoed the conventions of solar imagery.

Whatever her intellectual diversions may have been, Julia was not the sort to endure her loss of prestige at the hands of Fulvius Plautianus for long. By 204 there were signs that she was returning to her husband's favor.[164] In June of that year, Severus celebrated the "Saecular Games" in Rome. These were a lavish series of contests, rituals, and festivities that marked the passing of a *saeculum*, or sacred interval of time equal to 110 years – the approximate maximum length of one human life.[165] Julia was given a prominent role in these observances, leading 109 other married women (including her sister's elder daughter, named Julia Soaemias) onto the Capitol to conduct banquets in honor of the goddesses Juno and Diana.[166]

The empress' cause also received a boost in 204 when Severus' brother Geta, with his dying breaths, told the emperor the truth about Plautianus.[167] Others warned Severus that his prefect was plotting to take the throne.[168] Alarmed, he stripped Plautianus of most of his power.[169] Julia's most formidable ally in her struggle for power was her son Caracalla.[170] He had been made Augustus and joint-emperor with his father in 198, and he deeply resented Plautianus' power and arrogance.[171] On 22 January, 205, the 16-year-old Caracalla made his move.[172]

There are two versions of Plautianus' downfall, both of which end with his murder in Severus' presence at Caracalla's command.[173] Cassius Dio relates that after Plautianus was dead someone plucked a few hairs from his beard and took them to Julia and her daughter-in-law Plautilla. His words "Behold your Plautianus!" must have inspired opposite but equally powerful emotions in the two women.[174]

Plautilla was promptly banished, along with her brother, to the island of Lipara, off the coast of Italy, where she was executed six years later at Caracalla's orders.[175] Two men replaced Plautianus as prefects of the Guard, serving as joint commanders. One of these was a lawyer named Papinian (Aemilius Papinianus), probably a Syrian and possibly related to Julia Domna, who became the most respected jurist in Roman history.[176]

The system of law that was developed under the Roman Empire is perhaps its most lasting contribution to civilization.[177] Modern legal systems have been built on its principles, which were largely established during and immediately after Julia Domna's reign. Papinian was particularly responsible for these advances. He and his two students, Ulpian (also a Syrian) and Paulus, wrote so brilliantly and extensively that, when the sixth-century Byzantine emperor Justinian I ordered that Roman law be codified, the writings of these three men comprised more than half of the documentation.[178]

Two centuries after his death, Papinan's writings were still consulted as the final word whenever legal experts reached an impasse regarding a judgment.[179] His opinions were valued for their originality, precision, fairness, and humanity.[180] Whether she was related to Papinian or not, Julia must have been overjoyed to see such an enlightened man replace her nemesis.

With the fall of Plautianus, the empress was restored to her position of supreme influence with her husband. However, she and the 60-year-old emperor had new worries. Caracalla and his younger brother Geta, who had been named Caesar in 198, did not get along.[181] It seemed clear that Caracalla, now co-emperor with his father, was being groomed to succeed him, but Geta's future role was uncertain. The teenaged boys engaged in a bitter rivalry, even competing over who could behave more outrageously.[182] Cassius Dio writes that they consorted with gladiators and charioteers, abused women and boys, embezzled money, and quarreled violently.[183] Caracalla even broke his leg in a hotly contested chariot race with Geta.[184] Though coins were issued that celebrated the "harmony" of the pair, exactly the opposite was true.[185]

Geta, who closely resembled his father physically, seems to have had somewhat less violent tastes than his brother.[186] He was reportedly more devoted to Julia than Caracalla was and followed in his mother's footsteps by including men of learning in his circle.[187] Herodian claims that he was more popular with the people than Caracalla because of his generosity and moderation.[188] Nevertheless, he seems to have competed for power just as furiously, and Cassius Dio accuses him of equally extreme behavior.[189]

Severus believed that his sons' excesses were partly the result of living in Rome.[190] The city was full of temptations, and each prince attracted his own band of followers, who encouraged the brothers in their competition.[191] So when a military crisis arose in Britain in 208 he decided to take his whole family with him to deal with it.[192] The emperor reasoned that the austerity and discipline of military life would teach his sons responsibility and keep them too busy to quarrel with each other.[193]

Julia accompanied her husband and sons to Britain, spending much of her time with Geta in Londinium (London) and Eboracum (York), the capitals of the two British provinces.[194] She and her younger son handled the administrative affairs of the empire while Severus and Caracalla campaigned successfully against the Caledonian tribesmen in what is now Scotland.[195]

Cassius Dio records an interesting encounter between Julia Domna and the wife of an enemy chieftain. Curious about local customs, the empress had noticed that the Caledonian women were surprisingly free with their sexual favors. When she chided the woman about this, her response was to the point: "We satisfy our desires in a better way than you Roman women do. We have intercourse openly with the best men while you are seduced in secret by the worst."[196]

Despite Severus' hopes, the sojourn in Britain did nothing to improve relations between his sons.[197] Now in his mid-sixties, Severus was suffering from either gout or arthritis, plus the effects of smallpox, which he had contracted in Egypt some years before.[198] His feet were so crippled that it was difficult for him to stand and he had to be carried in a litter.[199] In 210, perhaps in an effort to protect Geta from his brother after he was gone, Severus elevated his younger son to the rank of Augustus.[200] This meant that both of his sons would succeed as co-emperors.

Such an arrangement was not unprecedented: Severus had already shared rule with Caracalla for twelve years, and Marcus Aurelius was joint-emperor with Lucius Verus and, later, with his son Commodus. However, these had been amicable pairings, with one partner much older and clearly in charge.

Caracalla's disappointment must have been acute. There were stories that he tried to do away with both Severus and Geta.[201] Cassius Dio charges that he tried to kill his father with his sword, in full view of the Roman and barbarian armies.[202] Julia's attitude toward the joint succession is unknown. In any case, once made, the plan could not easily be broken.

The following year, on 4 February, 211, Severus died in Eboracum at the age of 65.[203] Julia was present and must have heard his last words to his sons, now aged 23 and 22: "Get along with each other, pay the soldiers well, and don't bother about anyone else!"[204] There are reports that Caracalla immediately tried to induce the army to kill Geta and recognize him as sole emperor, but that the soldiers refused out of respect for Severus' wishes.[205]

Julia persuaded the brothers to agree to a partial reconciliation, and the imperial family left for Rome, carrying Severus' ashes with them.[206] The emperors'
refusal to eat together on the journey for fear of being poisoned showed that
things were far from right.[207]

Herodian gives a full and fascinating account of Severus' funeral in
Rome.[208] A wax model of the emperor was placed on a huge ivory couch covered with golden drapes at the entrance to the palace.[209] This effigy was
attended for a full seven days, as if it were the dying emperor himself. The
entire senate, dressed in black, was in attendance, as were the most illustrious
women of Rome, wearing white dresses (the color of mourning) and no jewelry.[210] Each day, the doctors inspected the wax model, announced the deteri-
orating condition of the emperor, and ultimately declared him to be dead.[211]

At this juncture, the noblest Roman knights carried the couch and effigy
to the Forum where hymns and chants were sung by choirs of high-born
children and women of impeccable reputation.[212] The image was placed on
the second tier of a richly decorated wooden pyre five stories high (see Figure
10.25).[213] Incense, spices, fruits, and perfumes were heaped on the structure
– parting gifts from cities and important people throughout the empire. A
procession of knights on horseback and people in chariots, wearing masks of
famous Roman generals and emperors, rode around the pyre in formation
and in time to a rhythmic dance.[214]

Caracalla and Geta then set the funeral pyre ablaze. The flames consumed
it rapidly, releasing the fragrances of incense, spices, and perfumes.[215] An
eagle, set loose from the very top of the structure, was believed to carry the
soul of the emperor to heaven.[216] (A peacock was believed to convey the soul
of a deceased empress, who was honored with similar multi-story funeral
pyres and elaborate rites.[217]) With this ceremony, which Julia must have
witnessed with profound emotion, the deification of Septimius Severus
became official.

After her husband's apotheosis, Julia preserved the continuity of government while her sons jockeyed for position.[218] They divided the palace, even
walling up the hallways that connected the two halves of the complex.[219]
There was talk of dividing the empire as well, giving Caracalla the western
provinces and Geta the eastern, with Alexandria as his capital.[220] Julia's
response to this was: "You can divide the empire, but how will you divide
your mother?" She then burst into tears and drew the brothers into her
arms.[221] The idea was dropped, but the feud continued.

In early 212, after several months of uneasy joint rule, Caracalla approached
Julia and asked her to arrange a conciliatory meeting in her chambers.[222] After
Geta had arrived in his mother's room, a band of Caracalla's soldiers, or, alternatively, Caracalla himself, rushed in and stabbed the younger emperor to
death, wounding Julia Domna's hand in the process.[223] Geta reportedly
threw himself on his mother's bosom and pleaded, "Mother, mother who bore
me! Help! I am being murdered!"[224]

The aftermath of the assassination was horrible.[225] Perhaps as many as 20,000 of Geta's supporters and Caracalla's enemies were massacred, including Papinian for refusing to sanction the murder.[226] Geta's portraits were removed from public monuments and paintings – even individual coins (see Figure 10.28).[227] Cassius Dio claims that Julia was forbidden to mourn for her son or to show any sorrow, even in private. In fact, she was required to rejoice and laugh openly, as if in celebration.[228] Cornificia, the daughter of Marcus Aurelius, was killed two days after the murder for weeping with the empress over her loss.[229]

All of this makes a heart-wrenching story, but the possibility exists that Julia Domna had approved or even instigated Geta's removal. The stability of the empire and the fate of the royal family were obviously in jeopardy. Julia must have realized that joint rule was impossible and that neither of her sons would survive the sole rule of the other. When faced with a similar problem ten years later, her sister Julia Maesa would sacrifice a daughter and a grandson (Julia Soaemias and Elagabalus) for the security of the empire, and so that another daughter and grandson (Julia Mamaea and Severus Alexander) could live to rule (see Chapter 11).[230] Perhaps Julia Domna made the same kind of choice: difficult for a mother, but mandatory for an empress and stateswoman. However, Julia could never have condoned the extent of her son's vengeance, which claimed the lives of many of her friends and allies, such as Papinian.

Caracalla was not particularly interested in civil administration. His heart was with the soldiers, with whom he spent most of his time, living, dressing, and eating as a common legionary.[231] Therefore the burden of rule fell largely on Julia.[232] As her son remained unmarried, she continued as empress and first lady of the empire, with more power than ever before.[233]

The titles that she was now awarded were unprecedented: *Julia Pia Felix Augusta, Mater Augusti Nostri et Castrorum et Senatus et Patriae* ("Julia, the pious and happy Augusta, mother of our Augustus and the camp and the senate and the fatherland").[234] She was even given her own detachment of the Praetorian Guard.[235] While the emperor pursued military glory in Germany, and later in Armenia and Parthia, Julia received embassies and petitions and presided over the day-to-day running of the government.[236]

There were religious innovations under Caracalla that were probably encouraged by his mother. The family interest in the cults of Isis and Serapis led to the consecration of their worship within the sacred district of Rome for the first time. Despite the fact that many previous emperors (including Septimius Severus) had honored these deities, none had officially installed them at the center of Roman religious life.[237] Caracalla even built a magnificent temple to Serapis in the capital, with a façade of twelve columns 60 feet (18.3 meters) high.[238]

Julia Domna undoubtedly had a role in the most famous administrative act of Caracalla's reign.[239] Shortly after the death of Geta, the Constitutio

Antoniniana was announced, giving Roman citizenship to virtually every free male inhabitant of the empire.[240] (The exceptions were probably barbarians who had recently been settled within its borders.[241]) This privilege had previously been limited to Italians and the provincial elite. Though the act has been criticized as a way to broaden the base for certain "citizens-only" forms of taxation,[242] it was a revolutionary move, reminiscent of Apollonius of Tyana's egalitarian teachings and consistent with Severus' policy of improving the position of his provincial subjects.[243] It may also have been intended to distract the people from the scandal of Geta's murder.

In 213, Caracalla waged war against the German tribes.[244] He won the loyalty of the troops by sharing their hardships – and by increasing their pay by 50 percent or more.[245] Caracalla was greatly impressed by the ways of the German and Celtic "barbarians." He took to wearing German clothes and derived his famous nickname from the *caracallus*, a Gallic or German hooded cloak that he favored.[246] He even sported a blond wig styled in the German fashion.[247] For this, and perhaps for financial subsidies made to secure peace, Caracalla was loved by many of the Germans, on both sides of the frontier.[248]

His German campaigns were successful, leading to twenty years of peace in the North.[249] However, the emperor had begun to suffer from a mysterious disease with both physical and mental symptoms.[250] Cassius Dio even describes him as "out of his mind."[251] He was tortured by frightening visions and was rumored to have become impotent.[252] His sickness was supposedly caused by spells cast by the Germans; some members of the Alamanni tribe even claimed responsibility.[253] Caracalla made repeated prayers and sacrifices to the gods, especially Serapis and the healing god Aesculapius, but without relief.[254] He even appealed unsuccessfully to Grannus, a Celtic deity identified with Apollo, who was worshiped by the Germans and Dacians.[255]

The historians Cassius Dio and Herodian have much to say about the crimes committed by Caracalla after this sickness had taken hold.[256] He reportedly became obsessed with black magic and massacred large numbers of innocent people in several places that he visited (e.g. Germany, Pergamon, Alexandria, and Parthia).[257] These horrors were perpetrated under circumstances that suggest the emperor was engaging in human sacrifice.[258]

It is not known if Julia was present for any of her son's atrocities, nor what she thought of them. However, it is clearly impossible to reconcile her refined spiritual and philosophical inclinations with Caracalla's deeds. Apollonius of Tyana, whom the empress admired, vehemently opposed sacrificing animals, not to mention human beings.[259] Cassius Dio wrote that Caracalla consistently ignored his mother's "excellent" advice while "covering himself with blood, committing crimes, and spending money recklessly."[260] Her dismay and sense of foreboding about the future are reflected in Dio's remark that she increasingly devoted herself to the study of philosophy at this time.[261]

Caracalla's massacres certainly made him hated and feared, which apparently pleased him. He supposedly relished being called "the beast"[262] and had himself portrayed on coins and in sculptures with a menacing scowl (see Figure 10.26). (One stone likeness from Egypt is positively monstrous.[263]) Herodian tells us that Caracalla had a violent temper, and he reportedly rewarded a jester for remarking that he always had a savage expression.[264]

Cassius Dio, who knew Caracalla personally, wrote that, unlike his mother, he had no regard for learning or philosophy and even held the well educated in contempt.[265] However, Dio detested Caracalla, who he said "devastated the earth and the sea and left absolutely nothing unharmed."[266] This hyperbole cautions us to take his other claims with a grain of salt. Dio did concede that, though Caracalla was obstinate and cruel, he was also physically strong, shrewd, eloquent, and possessed sound judgment.[267] Herodian echoed this praise, complimenting the emperor on his legal decisions, and the fourth-century historian Aurelius Victor effused about Caracalla's patience, accessibility, and, surprisingly, his "calm nature."[268]

By the spring of 214, despite his illness, Caracalla had assembled a large army at the Danube camps for an invasion of the Parthian Empire.[269] The young emperor was thoroughly obsessed with Alexander the Great, whom he identified with so strongly that he informed the Roman senate he was the Macedonian conqueror come to life again.[270] It became his ambition to emulate Alexander's conquest of the Persians by subduing their successors, the Parthians.[271]

When the "new Alexander" marched east, he followed almost exactly in the footsteps of his hero.[272] He visited the supposed tomb of Achilles at Troy (as Alexander had done) and "took the cure," without much effect, at the shrine of Aesculapius in Pergamon (modern Bergama, Turkey).[273] Obviously, Caracalla was in no hurry. A full year after he and his army had begun their march, they finally arrived at Antioch in northern Syria, where Julia established the imperial court and continued to conduct the administration of the empire.[274] Antioch had a population of as many as 500,000 people, the third largest city in the empire after Rome and Alexandria.[275] It was also the logical place from which to launch an invasion of Parthia.

Herodian claims that Caracalla proposed marriage to the Parthian princess at this point, perhaps in an effort to avoid war.[276] He says that the two sides assembled for the nuptials, but that Caracalla suddenly ordered his troops to attack the unarmed Parthians, thereby beginning the war with a shameful victory.

This story is unlikely to be true, but it may reflect an attempted strategy on the part of Julia Domna and her son. A union between the royal houses of Parthia and Rome would have been a diplomatic and political triumph. Roman defensive strategy was perennially complicated by the presence of serious threats on two fronts, the northern and eastern. The neutralization of the Parthians through an alliance by marriage at the highest level would have been very much in Roman interests. Instead, the Roman army would inflict such crippling defeats on their enemy in the coming war that the Parthians soon fell to the more bellicose Sassanian Persians. This new power in the East would beleaguer the Romans almost as relentlessly as the Germans for centuries to come.[277]

Julia's official duties while her son pursued his military agenda included the handling of the imperial correspondence.[278] This arrangement is blamed for Caracalla's downfall in April, 217. Cassius Dio tells us that a letter warning the emperor of a prophecy that his praetorian prefect Opellius Macrinus would succeed him was diverted to Julia in Antioch.[279] Because of this delay, Macrinus, who was with the emperor in Mesopotamia, learned of the prediction before Caracalla did.[280]

Realizing how the superstitious emperor would respond to this news, Macrinus reportedly took preemptive action. On April 8, 217, when Caracalla was riding with an escort to visit a temple of the moon god near the city of Carrhae, he stopped to relieve himself. As his bodyguards turned away in respect for his privacy, a soldier or soldiers, supposedly acting under instructions from Macrinus, stabbed the emperor to death.[281] He was only 29 years old. The prefect claimed innocence of the crime and bided his time. Three days later, he arranged for the army to declare him the new emperor.[282]

Ironically, Macrinus had been a protégé of Plautianus.[283] He was a Moor of humble birth and the first emperor who was not of the senatorial class.[284] Macrinus continued to insist that he was innocent of his predecessor's death, knowing that the army loved Caracalla and would never accept his murderer as their new emperor.[285] It is possible, of course, that he was telling the truth.

When news of the assassination reached Antioch, Julia was staggered. She reportedly struck herself so violently on the breast that she aggravated a cancer that had been in remission.[286] Cassius Dio says that she resolved to starve herself to death. However, he insists that this was not because of grief over Caracalla's death but because she could not face losing her power and retiring into private life.[287] According to Dio, Julia hated Caracalla for having murdered Geta and for his many other evil deeds.[288] Obviously, a mother's emotions were not so simple, but it appears unlikely that Julia was close to a son who shared so few of her tastes.

Julia was in an awkward position regarding the new emperor. Macrinus had received reports that she was being critical of him. However, realizing that he needed her support, he wrote respectfully to her, offering to let her keep her titles and royal retinue, including her detachment of praetorian guardsmen.[289] He also sent Caracalla's remains to her for proper burial and arranged for his deification.[290]

Macrinus' deference to Julia came to an abrupt end, however, when he intercepted a letter revealing her plans to have him murdered and to seize the throne.[291] He ordered her to leave Antioch, but Julia died before she could obey.[292]

The cause of death is reported as either breast cancer or suicide by star-vation.[293] Cancer seems the more likely explanation. Julia had shown in earlier crises, such as the Plautianus affair, that she was no quitter, and the emaciation and inability to take food that her cancer may have caused could have been misinterpreted. Also, her sister Julia Maesa was probably with her and unlikely to have allowed her to give up without a fight. Indeed, it is tempting to imagine the sisters remembering the words of the novelist Heliodorus: "Please recall that you are a human being, subject to change and rapid reversals of fortune. So why be in a rush to destroy yourself when a brighter future may await you?"[294]

Indeed, Maesa would lead the family back to political dominance within fourteen months of Caracalla's death. The restored Severan dynasty presided over the deification of Julia Domna, and her remains were buried with those of Severus and their sons in the tomb of the Antonines in Rome.[295]

Though she exercised unprecedented power as empress during her final years, they were probably unpleasant times for Julia Domna. She was appar-ently battling breast cancer, and the burden of her official duties must have been heavy, especially as her son's actions were out of her control and so diametrically opposed to her principles.

As was usual with Roman empresses, rumors of Julia's sexual promiscuity persisted and grew after her death.[296] Even in her lifetime, there was gossip that she and her unmarried son Caracalla were lovers.[297] Later historians claimed that she had seduced him, as Agrippina the Younger had suppos-edly done to Nero, and even become his wife.[298] Stories of her affairs with other men may have been inspired by her unusual intimacy with the artists and intellectuals with whom she associated. In any case, the criticism was balanced by the legend of her remarkable beauty, intellectual attainments, and competent rule.

Evidence of Julia's continuing popularity exists in the form of a beautiful statue of her as the goddess Ceres from the port of Ostia near Rome. It has survived partly because it was buried with great care – indeed reverence – presumably in order to protect it from marauding Christians long after the empress had passed away.[299]

The legacy of Julia Domna's life and reign was profound. More than any previous Roman empress, she managed to combine beauty and brains with real political power.[300] Her example laid the groundwork for the political dominance of her sister and two nieces. Though Julia Maesa's grandsons remained officially in charge, it was she and her daughters who were the true powers behind the throne for the next seventeen years.

More lasting than her political significance was Julia Domna's influence on the cultural life of the empire. The infusion of eastern religious and artistic ideas that she encouraged had a lasting impact.[301] Provincial had ceased to mean inferior, either politically or culturally, and the dominance of the western part of the Roman Empire had been broken for good.

Figure 10.2 Busts of Septimius Severus and Julia Domna on a provincial bronze coin (diameter 39 mm), minted in Stratonikeia, Caria, *c.* AD 193–211. SNG von Aulock 2668, Howgego 536; courtesy Classical Numismatic Group, Inc.

Figure 10.3 An impression of the temple of Elagabal in Emesa, Syria, showing the conical stone (relative size exaggerated) sacred to that god, emblazoned with the image of an eagle. Bronze coin (diameter 32 mm) minted under the usurper Uranius Antoninus, *c.* AD 253–254. BMC Galatia etc. p. 241, 24; courtesy Classical Numismatic Group, Inc.

Figure 10.4 Two views of the temple of Baal (Jupiter Heliopolitanus) at Heliopolis (Baalbek) in Syria. (Left) Bronze coin (diameter 30 mm) struck in Heliopolis under Philip I, *c.* AD 244–249 (BMC 16 (variety), Price and Trell pp. 162 and 171, fig. 284); courtesy Freeman and Sear. (Right) Bronze coin (diameter 30 mm), struck in Heliopolis under Philip I, *c.* AD 244–249 (BMC Galatia, etc. p. 292, 15 (variety)); courtesy Classical Numismatic Group, Inc.

Figure 10.5 Sensitive portrait of Septimius Severus as emperor on a bronze sestertius, minted *c.* AD 194–195. RIC IV 676, BMCRE 516–517, Cohen 29; courtesy Classical Numismatic Group, Inc.

Figure 10.6 Appealing early portrait of Julia Domna on a bronze sestertius, minted *c.* AD 195. (Compare features to portrait on Figure 10.29.) RIC IV 867, BMCRE 778, Cohen 224; courtesy Freeman and Sear.

Figure 10.7 Julia Domna (facing) with her sons, Caracalla (left) and Geta (right), on a gold aureus of Septimius Severus, minted AD 202. RIC IV 181b; courtesy Italo Vecchi.

Figure 10.8 Helvidius Pertinax, the successor to Commodus as emperor and the patron of Septimius Severus. Bronze sestertius minted AD 193. RIC IV 20, BMCRE 42, Cohen 34; courtesy Freeman and Sear.

Figure 10.9 Didius Julianus, a Roman emperor for sixty-six days after the murder of Pertinax. Bronze sestertius minted in AD 193. RIC IV 16, BMCRE 28, Cohen 17; courtesy Classical Numismatic Group, Inc.

Figure 10.10 Bronze sestertii of (left) Manlia Scantilla and (right) Didia Clara, the wife and daughter, respectively, of Didius Julianus. He was deposed by Septimius Severus. (Left) RIC IV 18a, Cohen 6. (Right) RIC IV 20, BMCRE 38, Cohen 4. Both pictures courtesy Classical Numismatic Group, Inc.

Figure 10.11 Pescennius Niger, a pretender to the throne after the murder of Commodus, on a silver denarius minted AD 193 in Antioch, Syria. BMCRE 317 (variety), RSC 80a (variety); courtesy Classical Numismatic Group, Inc.

Figure 10.12 Clodius Albinus, governor of Britain and Caesar under Septimius Severus. Bronze sestertius minted *c.* AD 194–195. He rebelled against Severus after Caracalla replaced him as Caesar. RIC IV 54a, BMCRE 535, Cohen 49; courtesy Classical Numismatic Group, Inc.

Figure 10.13 The young Caracalla as Caesar on a gold aureus, minted AD 199. RIC IV 27b, BMCRE 152, Cohen 405; courtesy Classical Numismatic Group, Inc.

Figure 10.14 Portrait of Julia Domna on a silver denarius struck in Laodicea, Syria, under Septimius Severus, *c.* AD 193–211. Unpublished; courtesy Classical Numismatic Group, Inc.

Figure 10.15 Septimius Severus on horseback, holding a spear. Gold aureus minted AD 200. RIC IV 165c, BMCRE p. 193 note, Hill 429; courtesy Classical Numismatic Group, Inc.

Figure 10.16 The god Serapis, to whom Septimus Severus was devoted, depicted on a bronze coin (diameter 28 mm) minted in Marcianopolis, Moesia Inferior, under Caracalla, *c.* AD 211–217. Pick 656; courtesy Classical Numismatic Group, Inc.

Figure 10.17 The Triumphal Arch of Septimius Severus, which still stands in Rome today. It was erected in honor of his victories in Parthia. Silver denarius minted AD 206. RIC IV 259, BMCRE 320, RSC 104; courtesy Classical Numismatic Group, Inc.

Figure 10.18 Copper as of Julia Domna showing the domed Temple of Vesta in Rome, which she restored. The scene depicts four Vestal Virgins (or perhaps the empress with three Vestals) and two small children attending a sacrifice in front of the domed temple. Minted under Caracalla in AD 215. RIC IV 607, BMCRE 232, Cohen 234; courtesy Classical Numismatic Group, Inc.

Figure 10.19 Two very different portraits of Plautilla, the wife of Caracalla. She was the daughter of Plautianus, the boyhood friend and advisor of Septimius Severus. (Left) Silver denarius minted AD 203. RIC IV 367 (Caracalla), BMCRE 422 (Septimius Severus), RSC 16. (Right) Bronze coin (diameter 33 mm) struck in Germe, Lydia, *c.* AD 202–205. Lindgren and Kovacs 729. Both courtesy Classical Numismatic Group, Inc.

Figure 10.20 The Dea Caelestis, or Celestial Goddess, riding a lion and holding a scepter and thunderbolt. Silver denarius of Septimius Severus, minted AD 204. RIC IV 266, BMCRE 335, RSC 222; courtesy Classical Numismatic Group, Inc.

Figure 10.21 Julia Domna as the goddess Cybele, enthroned in a carriage drawn by four lions. The legend MATER AVGG refers to her status as "Mother of the (two) Augusti" (the two Gs indicating her two sons), making her the counterpart of the goddess, who as MATER DEVM is the "Mother of the Gods." Gold aureus minted under Septimius Severus *c.* AD 210–211. RIC IV 562, BMCRE 47, Cohen 116; courtesy Classical Numismatic Group, Inc.

Figure 10.22 A provincial bronze coin (diameter 30 mm), struck in Byzantium, Thrace, *c.* AD 198–209, which seems to show the animosity between Caracalla (left) and his younger brother Geta. Mionnet Supplement II p. 260, 339; courtesy Classical Numismatic Group, Inc.

Figure 10.23 Septimius Severus (center) on horseback with his two sons, Caracalla and Geta. Gold aureus minted AD 201. RIC IV 305, BMCRE 374, Cohen 770; courtesy Classical Numismatic Group, Inc.

Figure 10.24 Late portrait of Septimius Severus on a bronze sestertius, minted AD 210. RIC IV 796, BMCRE 185, Cohen 547; courtesy Freeman and Sear.

Figure 10.25 Five-story funeral pyre of Septimius Severus, topped by a *quadriga* (chariot drawn by four horses) and an eagle carrying off the soul of the emperor. Silver denarius minted AD 211. RIC IV 191f, RSC 89; courtesy Classical Numismatic Group, Inc.

Figure 10.26 Portrait sestertius of Caracalla as emperor, minted AD 213. RIC IV 511a; courtesy Classical Numismatic Group, Inc.

Figure 10.27 Geta as emperor on a bronze sestertius, minted AD 211. RIC IV 171a, BMCRE 45, Cohen 199; courtesy Classical Numismatic Group, Inc.

Figure 10.28 This coin presents the confronted busts of Caracalla and Geta, but with Geta and his name having been intentionally erased after his murder. Bronze coin (diameter 39 mm) of Stratonikeia, Caria, minted AD 211–212. SNG von Aulock 2682, cf. 2685, Howgego 84; courtesy Classical Numismatic Group, Inc.

Figure 10.29 Portrait of Julia Domna on a bronze sestertius, minted under Caracalla *c.* AD 213. RIC IV 590, BMCRE 215, Cohen 178; courtesy Classical Numismatic Group, Inc.

Figure 10.30 Caracalla with a shield on a silver tetradrachm, minted AD 215–217 in Edessa, Mesopotamia. Prieur 847, Bellinger 140; courtesy Classical Numismatic Group, Inc.

Figure 10.31 The deified Julia Domna on a bronze sestertius struck by one of her great-nephews, Elagabalus or Severus Alexander. RIC IV 609, cf. RIC IV 716 (Severus Alexander), Banti 6, BMCRE p. 589 (Elagabalus), Cohen 25; courtesy Classical Numismatic Group, Inc.

Figure 11.1 Portrait of Julia Mamaea, adapted from a marble bust in the Museo Capitolino, Rome. The coin is a bronze sestertius (see Figure 11.15 for a similar example). Behind Julia is a statue of her son, Severus Alexander, which is now in the Museo Nazionale, Naples. The architectural setting is imaginary, based on the reconstructed Severan theater at Sabratha, Libya, and on sculptures from Roman sarcophagi.

11

JULIA MAMAEA

A woman in charge

During Julia Domna's quarter century on the throne, the members of her extended family amassed stupendous wealth[1] and rose to prominent positions in the imperial government. Her sister Julia Maesa's husband, Julius Avitus Alexianus, had served as consul and provincial governor.[2] Maesa's two daughters, Julia Soaemias and Julia Avita Mamaea, assumed prominent positions at court, and their Syrian husbands held important posts under both Septimius Severus and Caracalla.[3]

When Julia Domna died in 217, after Caracalla had been murdered and replaced by Macrinus, it seemed that Julia Maesa and her family were bound to lose both their wealth and prestige. Instead, they quickly regained control of the throne and held it for another seventeen years. During this period, Julia Maesa and her younger daughter Julia Mamaea were, in effect, the rulers of the Roman Empire.

Macrinus was in a difficult position after Caracalla's assassination. Whether he had been responsible for the emperor's death or not, he had to proclaim his innocence or face reprisals from an army that adored his predecessor. Though Julia Maesa and her powerful relations represented a clear threat to his rule, any action against them would seem disloyal to Caracalla's memory. Therefore, he merely ordered Julia Maesa to leave Antioch after Julia Domna's death and to return to her family home in Emesa, Syria.[4] Macrinus made the crucial mistake of leaving her family's fortune intact.[5]

Julia Maesa must have been encouraged by this arrangement: Emesa was an excellent base for mounting a *coup*, close to military bases where many soldiers still held her family in high esteem.[6] She gathered her family around her and, with the assistance of a high-ranking soldier named Eutychianus,[7] planned a return to power.

The first step was to choose a male candidate from within the family to replace Macrinus. Maesa's own husband had died in Cyprus shortly before Caracalla, and the husband of her older daughter Julia Soaemias had also recently passed away.[8] However, Soaemias had a 14-year-old son named Varius Avitus Bassianus, better known to history as Elagabalus. He was destined to be the hereditary priest of the Emesan sun god,[9] but his grandmother Maesa had a different post in mind for him – emperor of Rome.

Maesa's younger daughter, Julia Mamaea, was also in Emesa by the summer of 218 with her 9-year-old son Alexander (Gessius Alexianus Bassianus).[10] Mamaea was probably born no later than the mid-to-late 180s, and was therefore in her thirties at this time. She was married to her second husband, a Roman knight named Gessius Marcianus from the nearby Syrian cult center of Arca Caesarea, where their son was born on 1 October, 208.[11]

Mamaea's first husband, whose name is unknown, had been a senator and consul.[12] Gessius was a knight and of lower status, but Julia had been allowed to keep her senatorial rank after she married him.[13] Besides Alexander, Julia had two daughters, one of whom was married, and there are hints of another son who had died young.[14]

The *Historia Augusta* claims that Julia Mamaea gave birth to Alexander in a temple dedicated to Alexander the Great in Arca Caesarea. According to this account, she and her husband were attending the annual festival in honor of the Macedonian hero and named their son Alexianus after him to mark the occasion of his birth.[15] However, Julia's father also bore the name Alexianus, suggesting another explanation.

The *Historia Augusta* also recorded other, even less believable stories about Alexander's birth. In one tale, for example, a bright star appeared in the heavens the day after he was born; in another, Julia Mamaea dreamed of giving birth to a purple snake (signifying royalty) the night before her son came into the world.[16]

No identified portraits of Julia Mamaea's husbands survive, but her likeness may be seen on numerous coins and a few marble busts. Her features seem to convey character more than classical beauty. She is depicted as a serious, intelligent woman with a broad, oval face, strong, slightly pointed chin, and an aquiline nose. Her mouth was small and rounded, with a protruding lower lip and jaw that gave her an air of strength and determination. Julia's almond-shaped eyes were framed by arching brows that nearly met in the middle.

Julia Mamaea's unchanging hairstyle was a more severe version of her aunt Julia Domna's – somewhat shorter and with the hair tucked behind her ears, but with the same tightly crimped waves and small braided bun at the back. This modification of Julia Domna's "helmet" became standard for imperial women in the third century, with the small coiled bun sometimes replaced by a straight braid brought up to the crown of the head at the back. Unfortunately, very little is reliably recorded about Julia Mamaea's personality, so our impressions must be formed from the events that bore her mark.

Her mother Julia Maesa was not long settled in Emesa before she made her play for power. The new emperor Macrinus was occupied with ending the Parthian war that he had inherited from Caracalla. After suffering a defeat in battle, he arranged to buy peace from the Parthian king for the enormous sum of 200 million sesterces.[17] This arrangement offended the Roman troops, who became even more disenchanted when he tried to roll back some of the pay raises they had received under Caracalla.[18]

Meanwhile, Julia Maesa offered to distribute her wealth among the soldiers in northern Syria in exchange for their support.[19] The province was crawling with troops, assembled by Caracalla for his eastern war, and most of them still revered the former emperor.[20] Maesa showed her genius for political strategy by spreading the word that her oldest grandchild, Julia Soaemias' teenaged son Elagabalus, was actually the illegitimate son of Caracalla.[21] (As it happens, Julia Soaemias and Caracalla had both been in Rome when Elagabalus was conceived, so the claim could not easily be refuted.[22]) Elagabalus was given Caracalla's official name, Marcus Aurelius Antoninus, and presented as the true heir to the throne.[23]

Word of Elagabalus' parentage and of Maesa's willingness to reward his supporters spread quickly among the soldiers.[24] During the night of 15 May, 218, the young candidate and his mother Julia Soaemias, as well as Julia Maesa, Julia Mamaea, and her son Alexander, were brought secretly to the fortified camp of the Roman legion at Raphanea, near Emesa.[25] The next day, Elagabalus was dressed in a purple robe and hailed by the troops as their new emperor.[26]

Macrinus' reaction came swiftly. In an effort to secure the loyalty of his troops, he canceled their pay cuts and promised them huge bonuses instead.[27] Macrinus also induced the senate in Rome to declare war, not only on Julia Maesa, Elagabalus, and his mother, but also on Julia Mamaea and her son Alexander.[28] He also sent Julianus, his praetorian prefect, to attack Raphanea and kill Elagabalus.[29]

Julianus' first response to the rebellion must have devastated Julia Mamaea. He executed her husband Gessius and her daughter and son-in-law.[30] This tragedy certainly drew Julia and her young son Alexander closer to each other, and to their surviving relatives.

When Macrinus' forces reached Raphanea, the besieged soldiers displayed Elagabalus and bags of money from the ramparts, calling on the attacking soldiers to change sides and support the "son of Caracalla."[31] The boy's family resemblance to the former emperor (see Figure 11.6) supported their claims, and many of Macrinus' troops defected on the spot.[32] Their commander Julianus was killed and his head was sent to Macrinus.[33] More and more of the soldiers in the area deserted to support Elagabalus, including another legion at the Syrian city of Apamea.[34] On 8 June, 218, the issue was decided in a conclusive battle 24 miles (38 km) from Antioch.[35]

A man named Gannys, who had been raised in Julia Maesa's household and was reputed to be Julia Soaemias' lover, commanded Elagabalus' army.[36] Though inexperienced in military matters, Gannys' preparations for battle were reasonably sound.[37] Even so, the day might have been lost if not for the surprising heroism of Julia Maesa, Julia Soaemias, and Elagabalus.

At a crucial moment, the two women, who were witnessing the struggle from their chariots, jumped into the fray and exhorted their fleeing troops to stand and fight.[38] This, plus Elagabalus' timely appearance on horseback with his sword drawn and Macrinus' sudden withdrawal from the scene, ensured the victory.[39]

Macrinus fled north, even shaving off his hair and beard to avoid being recognized, but was eventually captured and executed.[40] Julia Maesa's *coup* had been successful – she was named Augusta and Mater Castrorum ("Mother of the Camp"[41]), and her family was back on top of the Roman world.

Julia Mamaea's head must have been spinning by this point. In the space of a couple of years at most, she had endured the loss of a father, husband, daughter, aunt, and son-in-law. She had seen her first cousin (Caracalla) toppled from the throne, replaced by Macrinus, and then succeeded by her nephew, Elagabalus. And, suddenly, her mother was the most powerful person in the Roman Empire.

Clearly, Julia Maesa was a remarkable woman. She had lived with her older sister Julia Domna throughout her long reign and learned much about politics and how to govern the empire.[42] Her response to the events following Caracalla's death was calculated and effective. Though she had lost both her husband and her sister in very short order, she did not hesitate to do what was necessary to protect her family's interests.

Maesa's coin portraits are unusual among those of the empresses for their unflinching realism (see Figures 11.2, 11.17). While the portraits of imperial women were invariably individualized and realistic, they generally failed to portray the ravages of age. (The portraits of Domitia, Trajan's wife Plotina, and his sister Marciana are notable exceptions.) Julia Maesa, however, was depicted with sagging jowls and bags under her eyes. With a child as emperor (Elagabalus was only 14, born in March, 204[43]), she may have wanted to emphasize the fact that there was age and experience behind the throne. Maesa wore her hair in a simple style, eschewing the rigid waves that were affected by nearly all empresses in the late second century and the early third.

Despite the excellence of his grandmother, Elagabalus was not a fortunate choice for emperor. He had already immersed himself in his role as high priest of the sun god Elagabal, from whom he derived his popular (though unofficial) nickname.[44] This job seems to have interested him far more than that of Roman emperor, though he took full and creative advantage of the opportunity imperial power and wealth gave him to live extravagantly.[45]

The ancient historians Cassius Dio, Herodian, and others wrote much about Elagabalus' unusual sexuality and bizarre behavior. It is said that he often dressed as a woman, wearing make-up, jewelry, and false breasts, and asked his doctors to surgically change him into a female.[46] He engaged in numerous homosexual relationships, marrying a man named Hierocles and selling himself as a female prostitute.[47] However, Elagabalus also reportedly slept with countless women and married as many as six times.[48]

Elagabalus' religious zeal and foreign dress may have inspired some of the stories of his unconventional sexual behavior. The Romans considered his normal priestly costume and oriental finery, consisting of silk robes and abundant jewelry, as effeminate, possibly giving rise to rumors of the emperor's transvestism.[49] Also, rumors of his desire for castration may have arisen from his circumcision, which Cassius Dio tells us was performed as part of his priestly discipline while he was emperor.[50]

On the other hand, his apparent feminine identification may have been connected with his religious mood. His deity, Elagabal, was represented by a conical black stone, possibly with phallic symbolism. It has been suggested that, as the male priest of a phallic god, the young emperor was encouraged to assume a female persona in his worship.[51] The emperor was also devoted to the Mother of the Gods, whom he envisioned as a consort to his deity.[52] He sometimes imitated the feminine appearance and behavior of the *galli*, Cybele's castrated priests, and even participated in the *taurobolium*, bathing himself in bull's blood.[53] Perhaps in ritual identification with the female consort of Elagabal, he harnessed lions to his chariot, dressed as a woman, and called himself Cybele, the Great Mother of the Gods.[54]

If Elagabalus had remained in Syria, he probably would have been admired as a flamboyant but dedicated holy man. As emperor, he became a scandal. Elagabalus' first serious excesses occurred on the way to Rome. Accompanied by his mother and grandmother, as well as by Julia Mamaea, Alexander, and Gannys, he spent the winter of 218/219 in Nicomedia, the capital of Bithynia (northwestern Turkey).[55] He performed his priestly duties there, in full exotic regalia, and Julia Maesa and Gannys warned him that such behavior would not be accepted in the capital.[56] Gannys even tried to discipline the teenaged emperor and make him behave more moderately.[57] Elagabalus, who probably saw this as an attempt to interfere with his religious duties, killed Gannys, possibly with his own hand.[58] His response to his grandmother's warnings was to have a painting of himself in priestly attire sent to Rome for display in the senate building. This, he hoped, would allow the senators to become accustomed to his appearance before he arrived.[59]

The Romans do seem to have adjusted fairly well to their new ruler's looks, and they even tolerated and participated in his worship of Elagabal.[60] However, they had greater difficulty adjusting to his habit of appointing low-born, often unqualified or corrupt favorites to important positions in the government.[61] The soldiers of the Praetorian Guard resented serving under a prefect who had once been a dancing clown[62] and an effeminate emperor who was so unwarlike that he despised an emperor's usual military titles because they "came from the shedding of blood."[63]

The young emperor's marital adventures seem to have unfolded in this way. First, he married the noble Julia Cornelia Paula so that he "might become a father."[64] However, he soon divorced her because of a blemish on her body, stripped her of her titles, and told her to return to private life.[65]

Then he broke one of Rome's most sacred laws by marrying a Vestal Virgin, Julia Aquilia Severa, and professed the hope that this marriage between a priest and priestess would produce "god-like children."[66]

After discarding Severa, there followed a succession of four wives,[67] including Annia Aurelia Faustina, whose husband had recently been killed on Elagabalus' orders.[68] A granddaughter of Marcus Aurelius, Annia was chosen for her beauty as well as for her pedigree, but the emperor soon sent her packing as well.[69] Eventually, he remarried Aquilia Severa, the ex-Vestal.[70] However, none of these unions produced any offspring. All three of his wives who are known by name were depicted on coins and received the title of Augusta (see Figures 11.11–13).[71]

Elagabalus continued to practice his religious duties in Rome. He had the *baetyl*, or sacred stone, of Elagabal brought to the capital and erected a splendid temple in its honor: the Elagabalium on the Palatine Hill.[72]

Herodian describes the unforgettable scene as the emperor brought the symbol of his deity to its magnificent new shrine.[73] The stone was placed in a gem-studded golden chariot (see Figure 11.10) drawn by four white horses, whose reins were attached to the stone as if it were driving. Elagabalus ran backwards in front of the chariot, holding the horses' bridles and gazing adoringly at his idol. Attendants on either side of the emperor kept him from tripping and falling, and gold-colored sand was scattered on the road to ease his progress.

A throng of fascinated spectators watched the procession, which included contingents of the cavalry and infantry as well as images of other gods and precious gifts for the temple.[74] Members of the crowd held torches and showered Elagabalus with wreaths and flowers as he passed. When the stone had been installed for worship, the emperor gave the people a festival. He climbed a high tower and distributed prizes, including gold and silver cups, clothing, and tokens to be exchanged for domestic animals. Many people were killed during the scramble for these gifts.[75]

The administration of the empire, largely in the hands of Julia Maesa, ran smoothly while Elagabalus pursued his various sexual and religious fantasies.[76] By 221, however, Maesa knew that patience for her grandson's exploits was wearing thin.[77] When he expressed a desire to have his "husband" Hierocles named Caesar, she opposed him. Elagabalus responded by threatening Maesa, even though she was supported in her views by many of the soldiers.[78]

Julia Maesa resolved to remove her grandson from the throne. Her new choice for emperor was Julia Mamaea's son Alexander, now entering his teens. Maesa persuaded the unsuspecting Elagabalus to adopt his younger cousin and name him Caesar by convincing him that Alexander could attend to the tedious official duties while he pursued his religious practices.[79] Elagabalus announced the adoption to the senate, probably in June, 221.[80] He boasted that at last he had a son, and a rather large one at that.[81] Coins were issued in Alexander's name (see Figure 11.7), and perhaps for Julia Mamaea as well.[82]

It is ironic that Julia Mamaea, who is almost alone among Roman empresses in not being accused of adultery by the ancient historians, was pronounced guilty of just that – by her own mother. In order to promote Alexander as a candidate for the purple, Julia Maesa broadcast the claim that he, like Elagabalus, was the product of an adulterous relationship with Caracalla.[83] Mamaea's pride in her chastity was not equal to her ambition, and she confirmed her mother's story.[84]

Alexander, now given the name Marcus Aurelius Alexander Caesar, seems to have been agreeable and mild-mannered throughout his life, and thoroughly devoted to his mother.[85] Her dominance over him was so complete that even as a grown man he was derisively called Alexander Mamaeae: "Mamaea's son."[86] His portraits reveal a strong resemblance to her, with the same small mouth and prominent lower lip, long nose, oval face, and protruding ear lobes. His portraits often present a somewhat blank, naive-looking expression, even when he was in his twenties. The ancient historians are unanimous in praising his purity and good intentions, but fault him for remaining so abjectly under his mother's thumb.[87]

Mamaea carefully insulated her son from the corrupting influence of Elagabalus' court and kept him busy with a rigorous routine of study and exercise. She obtained distinguished tutors to further his education in Greek and Latin, while discouraging excessive study of philosophy and music, subjects that she deemed inappropriate for a prince.[88] Nevertheless, Alexander is said to have become an accomplished musician and singer.[89] Besides history and rhetoric, he was trained in wrestling, sword fighting, and other "manly arts."[90] However, to Elagabalus' displeasure, Julia did not allow her son to be schooled in his cousin's exotic religious practices or to participate in his extravagant lifestyle.[91]

The contrast between the emperor's and Alexander's manners of living is shown by their eating habits, as described by the *Historia Augusta*. Elagabalus was a gourmet of the first order, enjoying a wide variety of rare and exotic delicacies. He gave summer banquets with different food color themes, such as green, blue, and iridescent, and served wine with a variety of novel flavorings, including mastic, pennyroyal, pinecone, and roses.[92] He savored exotic foods such as camels' heels, peacock and nightingale tongues, and mullet beards (barbels). Even his servants dined on thrush and flamingo brains, partridge eggs, parrots' heads, and peacocks, and his dogs were served goose livers.[93]

Alexander, on the other hand, dined simply on bread, greens, vegetables, hares and other game, and only indulged in a goose on feast days or a pheasant on the major holidays. Dessert consisted of fruits, of which he was especially fond, and he drank cold water, mead, and wine in moderation. His one imitation of his cousin was to drink rose-flavored wine in summer.[94]

Elagabalus' contempt for his well-behaved cousin was increased by Alexander's growing popularity.[95] The soldiers in particular appreciated his simple virtues and moderate behavior, so different from the emperor's.[96] The historian Herodian claims this so incensed Elagabalus that he banished Alexander's teachers from court, even executing some of them, and bitterly regretted having adopted the boy he now saw as a dangerous rival.[97]

Fearful that Elagabalus would try to poison Alexander, Julia Mamaea forbade him from tasting any food or drink that had not been prepared by her own hand-picked servants.[98] With Maesa's help, she took whatever steps were necessary to protect her son, including the distribution of money to the soldiers in order to win their support.[99]

The imperial family was now divided into two camps, with the emperor and his mother Julia Soaemias on one side, and Julia Mamaea, Julia Maesa, and Alexander on the other.[100] There is evidence that Julia Soaemias was locked in a struggle with her mother to be the dominant force behind the throne.[101] When Elagabalus announced his adoption of Alexander, both women appeared in the senate house (unprecedented for females), and they possibly attended senate meetings on other occasions as well.[102] Julia Soaemias also claimed titles that rivaled those of Julia Maesa, including Mater Senatus ("Mother of the Senate").[103]

Cassius Dio adds that Julia Mamaea and her sister had begun to squabble openly, each attempting to inflame the soldiers against the other.[104] One suspects that there was little love lost between them, even before their sons had come to crossed purposes. Their characters seem to have been quite different. Mamaea was admired for her chastity (despite Caracalla), religious piety, and intellectual gifts, which were very much in the mold of her aunt Julia Domna.[105] She was prudent, frugal, and sober in her lifestyle.[106]

In contrast, Julia Soaemias is said to have gloried in the profligacy of her son's court.[107] She was beautiful, sensuous, and frivolous in her tastes and pursuits. Elagabalus put her at the head of a women's senate, called the *senaculum*, which was charged with determining the intricacies of female social protocol. It decided who could wear what in public; who could ride in a chariot, a carriage, or a litter; who could wear gold or jewels on her shoes and who could not – hardly the sort of business that would have appealed to the serious-minded Mamaea.[108]

By the beginning of 222, Elagabalus and Alexander were so estranged that they no longer appeared together in public.[109] The emperor even tried to have his rival killed.[110] The Praetorian Guard was so outraged at this attempted assassination that it rebelled and forced Elagabalus to guarantee Alexander's safety and to dismiss some of his most unpopular officials.[111] When Elagabalus broke his promise and formed yet another plot against his cousin, the guardsmen responded by murdering the emperor, reportedly in a latrine.[112] They also killed Julia Soaemias before proclaiming Alexander the successor to the throne.[113] The victims' heads were cut off and their bodies dragged through the streets before being cast aside. Elagabalus' headless corpse was tossed into the Tiber River, earning him the derisive nickname "Tiberinus."[114]

It is probable that Julia Maesa was responsible for the murders of her daughter and grandson, and that the Guard had acted on her orders.[115] This must have been a painful sacrifice for her to make, but necessary for the empire's stability and to preserve her family's grip on power.

Elagabalus, born in 204, was still in his teens when he was assassinated in early March 222.[116] Perhaps many of the excesses for which he is remembered may be chalked up to the exuberance of youth and the extremes of his religious passions and sexual curiosity. Indeed, some of his antics, such as seating dinner guests on deflatable cushions and startling sleeping friends by putting tame lions, leopards, and bears in their bedrooms, are what might be expected from an unusually imaginative teenager with unlimited power.[117]

Alexander ascended the throne at the tender age of 13, but whatever youthful passions or impulses he may have had were kept in check by his mother and grandmother.[118] Maesa and Mamaea were determined to erase the negative impression of Elagabalus and present Alexander as a very different sort of ruler. He was given the name Marcus Aurelius Severus Alexander to emphasize his relationship to Septimius Severus, Julia Domna's husband and the founder of the Severan dynasty, as well as to the venerated Marcus Aurelius.[119] Alexander was shown on coins and official portraits with the crewcut and armor of a military man. He abandoned the richly decorated garb of his cousin and always wore plain clothing, with no jewelry. The luxurious ostentation of the court was replaced by simplicity, even austerity.[120]

The sacred stone of Elagabal was apparently returned to Emesa and his vast temple in Rome rededicated to the thoroughly Roman god Jupiter the Avenger.[121] The senate, infuriated when Elagabalus had broken custom by bringing his mother and grandmother into their chamber, was appeased by a declaration that any man who brought a woman there would be condemned to Hades.[122]

Julia Mamaea was promptly made an Augusta and, as Cassius Dio put it, "took control of affairs."[123] Alexander's subordinate status was revealed in one of his titles: *Juliae Mamaeae Augustae filio Juliae Maesae Augustae nepote*, "the son of Julia Mamaea and the grandson of Julia Maesa."[124]

To ensure the best possible government, the two Julias immediately selected a council of sixteen of the most dignified senators to guide the new emperor.[125] Later, a committee of seventy learned and respected senators, jurists, and civil servants was created to approve all imperial actions and edicts.[126] Taxes were reduced, and measures were taken to assist beleaguered landowners.[127] Unqualified officials appointed by Elagabalus were dismissed and replaced by men of good character and appropriate experience.[128]

Steps were also taken to fight government corruption, which had been rampant under Elagabalus, and the cost of the imperial court was drastically curtailed.[129]

The changes introduced by Julia Mamaea and her mother were almost revolutionary. The senators selected for the council of sixteen, chosen for their moderation and long experience, seem to have been given real power.[130] Herodian claims that "[n]o official statements or actions were made without the approval of this council. Rather than an arbitrary tyranny, this was an aristocratic form of government, which was welcomed by the people and the army as well as the senate."[131]

This might appear to have been a concession forced on the imperial family as the price for their survival after the debacle of Elagabalus. However, the real beneficiaries of the new arrangement were the senators, who were not directly responsible for Elagabalus' fall. Also, Herodian's statement comes on the heels of his claim that "the imperial administration and policy-making were controlled by Julia Maesa and Julia Mamaea, who tried to restore a moderate and dignified form of government."[132]

The most distinguished legal men of the age, Ulpian (Domitius Ulpianus) and Paulus, held high positions under the new system, the former serving as prefect of the Praetorian Guard.[133] Ulpian, said to be the only man permitted to confer alone with the emperor, possessed high ideals and an encyclopedic knowledge of Roman law.[134] He held the opinion that all human beings were "born free" and that slavery was unnatural.[135] Though the emancipation of slaves was not going to happen, Ulpian did have a humanizing and egalitarian effect on Roman jurisprudence.[136] Indeed, the reign of Severus Alexander was noted for its leniency and lack of political bloodshed, and for its abundance of new laws.[137]

The *Historia Augusta* records an interesting anecdote involving both slavery and justice. It claims that Alexander once punished a soldier for mistreating an old woman by making him her slave so that he could support her. When other soldiers grumbled at this, the emperor stood firm.[138]

It was during Alexander's reign that the stupendous Baths of Caracalla were completed in Rome.[139] The buildings were filled with works of art and covered nearly 120,000 square meters – the various pools could accommodate 16,000 bathers at one time.[140] Also, the Baths of Nero were refurbished and renamed for Alexander,[141] who arranged for all public baths in Rome to be lit with oil lamps for night bathing.[142]

In 217 the Colosseum had been struck by lightning and severely damaged by the resulting fire. The repairs took several years, during which gladiatorial contests were held elsewhere.[143] When the work was completed, it was commemorated on Alexander's coins (see Figure 11.16).[144] He also added some apartments to the palace in Rome and built a villa and pool at Baiae, all of which were named for his mother.[145]

Despite Maesa's and Mamaea's best efforts to rule the empire in a just and orderly manner, they couldn't control the Praetorian Guard. Perhaps as early as 223 (or, alternatively, in 228), the praetorians became embroiled in street fighting with the people of Rome.[146] For three days the violence continued before the embattled soldiers brought the mob to terms by threatening to set the capital on fire.[147]

Ulpian seems to have been one of the many victims of this disturbance. He was killed by the praetorians, apparently because they resented his strictness. Cassius Dio tells us that the prefect fled to the palace and sought the emperor's protection, but was cut down, despite Alexander's and Julia Mamaea's protests.[148]

Sometime between 223 and 226 Julia Maesa also died, probably in her early to mid-sixties, and was promptly deified.[149] Julia Mamaea was deprived not only of a mother but also of her political mentor and colleague. With Alexander still in his teens, she was now in charge of the imperial government.

Her power and responsibilities were matched by her titles; besides her status as Augusta and "mother of the Augustus, camp, senate, and fatherland," she was named *mater universi generis humanis*, "the mother of the whole human race."[150] Herodian claims that Julia took extreme measures to maintain her control of her son, even after he had grown into manhood. She supposedly posted a guard to keep persons who might be corrupting influences away from Alexander and kept him occupied with judicial work.[151]

Although her position seemed secure, Julia must have had the feeling that she was riding a wild beast. The praetorians were always unpredictable, and there was turmoil in various places within and outside of the empire. In the East, Rome's age-old enemies the Parthians had been conquered by the much more aggressive Sassanid Persians, who were preparing to invade Rome's eastern provinces.[152] In the north, barbarian tribes were threatening both the Rhine and Danube borders.[153]

Meanwhile, many uprisings had to be dealt with inside the empire.[154] In 228, mutinous troops in Mesopotamia killed their commander and some even defected to the Persians.[155] A whole series of usurpers seems to have challenged unsuccessfully for the throne.[156]

Despite the difficulties she faced alone, Julia Mamaea never remarried after the death of Gessius Marcianus in 218. She had relied heavily on Ulpian as her partner in government,[157] but she does not seem to have had a lover. Obviously, a husband of Julia's would automatically become an important figure, possibly even a rival to her son, which may explain her decision to remain single. The danger of outsiders marrying into the royal family was forcefully brought home to her when she arranged a marriage for Alexander – his father-in-law soon attempted to take over the government.[158]

According to Herodian, when it came time for Alexander to marry, Julia supplied him with a wife from a suitably noble family.[159] There is some confusion about the number of Alexander's wives (there may have been as many as three[160]) and which of them had the overly ambitious father. The only woman whose name is known for certain is Sallustia Orbiana (full name Cnaea Seia Herennia Sallustia Barbia Orbiana[161]), who married the emperor in 225 or 226 and was made an Augusta.[162] Her coin portraits show a pretty woman with large eyes, full cheeks, a small mouth, and a weak chin (see Figure 11.18). Presumably it was her father, named Sallustius Macrinus, who fell foul of Julia Mamaea in about 227 or 228.[163]

The story goes that Sallustius, who seems to have won a military victory in the North at some point, was adopted, or about to be adopted, by Alexander and made Caesar.[164] Julia Mamaea, either suspicious of Sallustius' power, or, as Herodian tells us, jealous of Orbiana, insulted the young empress and banished her from the palace.[165] Sallustius made the audacious move of going to the praetorian camp and asking the soldiers to support his daughter's cause, which was tantamount to attempting a *coup d'état*.[166] Fortunately, the praetorians remained loyal and obeyed Julia's order to put Sallustius to death.[167] Orbiana was exiled to Libya, against Alexander's will according to Herodian – eloquent proof of Julia's control over him.[168]

Another story, told in the *Historia Augusta*, might reflect Julia's influence. When an official made a gift of two enormous pearls to Alexander's wife, the emperor tried to sell them, not wanting her to set an example of unseemly extravagance. When a buyer could not be found, the pearls were dedicated to Venus and used as earrings on her statue.[169]

Despite their obedience to Julia Mamaea in the Sallustius affair, the praetorians were still something of a law unto themselves. In 229 Alexander's colleague in the consulship was none other than Cassius Dio, the historian.[170] Dio was unpopular with the praetorians because, he claims, he had earned a reputation as a disciplinarian during his military command in Pannonia.[171] So tenuous was Alexander's control over the Guard that he suggested that Dio spend his tenure as consul away from Rome, to be on the safe side.[172]

The emperor and his mother soon faced a much greater threat than a fractious Praetorian Guard. In 230 the Persians overran Roman Mesopotamia and raided other parts of the empire, possibly including Julia's home province of Syria.[173] The Persian king, Artaxerxes (or Ardashir), announced his intention to reclaim all of the Achaemenid Persian territories that had been conquered by Alexander the Great more than five hundred years before.[174] These included Egypt, the Middle East, and Asia Minor: the wealthiest and most populous part of the Roman Empire.

Julia Mamaea and Alexander left Rome by the spring of 231 to meet the Persian challenge.[175] Their route east to Antioch took them through the northern provinces, where they gathered troops to reinforce the eastern legions.[176] (A milestone, found in Thrace and apparently erected during this journey, bears the name of Julia Mamaea – the first recorded case of an empress being honored in this way.[177])

After an unsuccessful series of diplomatic efforts to avert war, the Roman army attacked.[178] The contemporary historian Herodian describes a complicated Roman strategy in which their forces were divided into three columns, intended to invade the northern, central, and southern Persian territories. The northern offensive was successful, but Herodian claims that Alexander, who was with the central column, failed to advance, resulting in the complete annihilation of the southern army.[179] The emperor seems to have been ill at this time, but the historian blames his inaction on cowardice, or on Julia Mamaea's "womanly timidity" and over-protectiveness of her son.[180]

Despite Herodian's gloomy account of the war, the Romans managed to recover the province of Mesopotamia from the Persians, who remained quiet for the rest of Alexander's reign; other historians claimed that the Persians had been routed.[181] The *Historia Augusta* even praises the emperor for his courage in battle.[182] Probably the war, which was very costly for both sides, ended in stalemate.[183] It was the first of a series of conflicts between the two powers that would continue for 400 years.[184]

Whatever actually happened, Julia and Alexander returned to Rome in 233 and celebrated a triumph for their Persian "victories."[185] Games and largess were given to the people, and Alexander received the title of Persicus Maximus.[186] Julia was rewarded for her part in the victory with the formation of two new, state-supported orders of underprivileged children, called the Mamaeanae (girls) and Mamaeani (boys) in her honor.[187]

In the winter of 231/232, while Julia Mamaea was still in Antioch, she arranged to meet with and be instructed by Origen, the famous Christian writer and teacher.[188] According to the fourth-century Church historian Eusebius, the empress was anxious to test Origen and had him brought to her by military escort. Eusebius claims that Origen conferred with Julia for some time, "revealing to her the glory of the Lord."[189]

Origen was born about 185 into a Christian family in Alexandria and lost both his father and family fortune in about 201 in the persecution of his faith under Septimius Severus.[190] Origen's austere lifestyle would probably have appealed to the self-controlled Julia. He is even said to have guaranteed his chastity by having himself castrated. His biographer, Eusebius, wrote that he took this step to avoid gossip about his ministry with women and to comply with the words of Christ in Matthew 19:12: "There are eunuchs who have been eunuchs from birth, and there are eunuchs who have been made eunuchs by others, and there are eunuchs who have made themselves eunuchs for the sake of the kingdom of heaven. He who can receive this, let him receive it."[191]

It seems likely that Origen hoped to eliminate the distractions of sexuality so that he could concentrate his energies on spiritual contemplation. It was commonly believed that sexual intercourse robbed a man of his strength and spiritual vigor. Pythagoras was supposed to have told a man that he could consort with a woman "[w]hen you want to lose all your strength."[192]

Ideas such as these eventually led to the celibacy of Christian priests and monastics. Origen apparently came to regret his castration, however, commenting on its negative effects and rejecting a literal interpretation of the passage in Matthew.[193]

Origen's writings may give some insight into the teachings that Julia Mamaea received from him. He was one of the most prolific writers of ancient times and his works have been called the first serious attempt to give Christianity a systematic theology.[194] They also present advice on how to pray, closely reasoned interpretations of scriptures, and concise statements of opinion and faith:

> How can a mind that has contemplated the everlasting kingdom of Christ find value in the kingdoms of the world?[195]

> A mind that can perceive light is necessarily of the same nature as every other mind that can perceive light. Similarly, if wisdom and holiness can be perceived by both the divine power and the human soul, then they are also of one substance. And if the divine is immortal, then so is the human soul.[196]

> The outer man can smell good and bad odors with his nostrils. Similarly, the inner man has spiritual nostrils which can detect the good odor of righteousness and the bad odor of sin.[197]

> Once Jesus has convinced us to abandon idols and the worship of many gods, our enemy cannot persuade us to commit idolatry, however he may try.[198]

There was much misogyny to be found in the works of ancient writers, both pagan and Christian. "Womanish" was an often-used derogatory term and womanly qualities were generally considered inferior. For example, when Origen wrote to some fellow Christians, he began: "to Tatiana, who is honest and manly. Womanish characteristics have left her, as also happened with Sarah."[199]

With the ascendancy of Christianity, such attitudes began to acquire theological support, based on the ancient traditions of Judaism (which barred women from some of the holiest rites and places) and on the teachings of early Christian evangelists. The most influential of these was Paul of Tarsus (died *c.* 65), who made his views quite clear in I Timothy, 2:11–15:

> A woman should learn silently and submissively. I allow no woman to teach or have authority over men. She should remain silent. Adam was created first, then Eve; and Adam was not deceived, but Eve was, and she became a sinner. However, woman shall be saved by bearing children, if she behaves modestly, in faith, love, and sanctity.

One might wonder what Julia Mamaea, who ruled the Roman world, would have thought of these instructions. In any event, she appears to have had a genuine curiosity about the new religion. Origen held the Greek philosopher Plato in high esteem and sought to interpret Christ's teachings in the light of Greek philosophy.[200] His theology also had a strong solar element,[201] which may have attracted the empress, whose family had long been associated with the solar priesthood. Christ was sometimes identified at this time with the sun god Sol Invictus (the "Unconquered Sun"),[202] a deity who often appeared on Alexander's coins (see Figure 11.21).[203]

Besides Origen, Julia may also have consulted with a Christian teacher from Rome named Hippolytus, who dedicated his treatise on the resurrection to her.[204] Later Christians were emboldened by her interest to claim that the empress had been a convert to Christianity.[205] However, her exclusive adherence to any one religion is unlikely.[206]

Julia Mamaea's personal religious beliefs may be reflected in her son's practices. Alexander is said to have admired the Golden Rule, which he heard from a Jew or a Christian, and to have had it inscribed in the palace and on public buildings.[207] In Alexandria and Antioch, he was even sarcastically called the "chief rabbi."[208] However, he also worshiped Apollonius of Tyana, was devoted to the sun god, and richly endowed the temples of Isis and Serapis.[209] According to the *Historia Augusta*, Alexander kept two chapels for his private worship: one contained images of Christ, Abraham, Apollonius, Orpheus, Alexander the Great, and the best of the deified emperors; the other was dedicated to great men and heroes such as Cicero, Virgil, and Achilles.[210]

Julia's respect for a variety of deities is implied by a medallion struck during her reign (see Figure 11.22), which depicts her with the attributes of no less than five goddesses, including Ceres, Diana, and Isis.[211] This was an age of syncretism and religious tolerance, and Julia was clearly an open-minded woman.[212] Both pagans and Christians acknowledged her piety and high-mindedness.[213] The leniency toward Christianity that characterized her reign was not continued by her successors, however, and both Origen and Hippolytus died in the 250s as the result of religious persecution.[214]

Even before Julia and Alexander had left the East, they received word that German barbarians had crossed the northern frontier and were ravaging Roman territory.[215] Though the Persian problem had not been satisfactorily settled, they had no choice but to turn their attentions west. Many of the troops that had been assembled to fight the Persians were now dispatched to the northern provinces, where Julia Mamaea and Alexander would rejoin them after spending the winter of 233/234 in Rome.[216]

By this time, many of the Roman soldiers were in a rebellious mood. There had been mutinies during the eastern campaign, involving Roman troops from Egypt and Syria, and officers from Mesopotamia.[217] There was a general dissatisfaction with the outcome of the eastern war and the lack of booty from it.[218] Though Julia and Alexander strove mightily to keep the army well paid and well fed, they were forced to cut down somewhat on military expenditures, and they tried to limit the soldiers' pay and bonuses.[219] These measures were not appreciated.

Many troops had been brought from the northern frontier by Alexander to fight against the Persians. These men suffered from the harsh desert climate and diseases they encountered in the Middle East, and many became disgruntled by what they perceived as preferential treatment for the eastern soldiers.[220] When news came of the barbarian invasion of their home territory they were understandably anxious to return home to protect their compatriots and to take out their frustrations on the German tribesmen.[221] Because of this, feelings were high when the German campaign began in 234 on the Rhine frontier.[222]

A bridge was constructed to allow the Roman army to cross the Rhine and invade enemy territory. A medallion was issued showing Alexander crossing this bridge on horseback.[223] The soldiers were eager for a clear-cut victory and the financial rewards this would bring. However, Julia and Alexander now made a fatal error. Fearing that they would become overextended by engaging in a full-scale war in the North while the Persian threat was far from removed in the East, they decided to purchase a settlement from the barbarians. They must have recalled how Caracalla's payments to the Germans in 213 had helped bring twenty years of comparative peace.[224]

The soldiers were furious, scandalized that large sums of money would be going to the enemy rather than to themselves, and humiliated by the emperor's reluctance to engage the Germans in battle.[225] Also, those soldiers who came from the northern provinces would be deprived of their chance to avenge the recent devastation of their homeland.[226]

To make matters much worse, there were rumors that Julia and Alexander were planning to march them to the East once again after a truce with the Germans had been assured.[227] Not surprisingly, the northern legions rebelled.[228] For them, the time of refined, peace-loving philosopher boy-emperors who were ruled by their mothers was over; they wanted a man's man and a fearless warrior to lead them against the barbarians.[229]

Their choice couldn't have been more different from the gentle Alexander. Julius Verus Maximinus was a virtually illiterate soldier of peasant stock, probably from the western part of Thrace.[230] He was supposedly 8 feet 6 inches tall, strong enough to break a horse's leg with his fist, and had thumbs so thick that his wife's bracelets fit them like rings.[231] These details sound like gross exaggerations, but his portraits do show an enormously powerful-looking man with a lantern jaw, massive, jutting chin, beetling brow, large, hooked nose, and, perhaps surprisingly, a rather thoughtful expression.

Despite his terrifying appearance and humble origins, Maximinus was a competent and experienced general.[232] He had gained recognition under Septimius Severus for his superhuman feats of strength,[233] but had subsequently proven that he also had gifts as a military leader, even serving as

222

Alexander's governor of the crucial province of Mesopotamia after the Persian war.[234] Most recently, he had been put in charge of training new recruits for the anticipated attack on the German tribes.[235]

In early March, 235, Maximinus was hailed as the new emperor by the northern legions at Moguntiacum (modern Mainz, Germany) on the Rhine.[236] His army marched on Julia's and Alexander's camp in the nearby village and military headquarters of Vicus Britannicus (modern Bretzenheim).[237]

Herodian claims that Alexander reacted to news of the rebellion by going into a panic, raging against the ungrateful usurper and begging his troops to protect him.[238] At first, the eastern troops seem to have remained loyal, but their resolve began to fade when they witnessed the noise and dust raised by Maximinus' approaching army.[239] Those who still hesitated were won over by Maximinus when he promised huge cash rewards for their support.[240]

Terrified, the 26-year-old Alexander supposedly rushed back into his tent and threw himself into his mother's arms, weeping and blaming her for his misfortunes.[241] Maximinus dispatched a tribune and some centurions to kill Alexander and Julia Mamaea and their loyal courtiers.[242] The *Historia Augusta* tells us that Alexander was stabbed by many soldiers before he died on 21 March, 235.[243] Presumably, Julia died in the same way; one account has her clutching her son to her breast as the blows were struck.[244] She was probably about 50 years of age.

Maximinus fulfilled the expectations of the soldiers by paying them a hefty bonus and campaigning successfully across both the Rhine and Danube rivers.[245] The formidable new emperor fought in person and exhibited remarkable bravery in the heat of battle.[246] He even had paintings of his exploits displayed in the senate chamber in Rome – a stark but telling contrast to the painting of Elagabalus in his priestly finery that had been exhibited there less than twenty years before.[247]

Despite Maximinus' successes, the tumultuous times caught up with him in 238 (a year that would see no fewer than six emperors[248]). He was killed in his tent by his own troops, or, alternatively, committed suicide to avoid a "womanish" display of grief over the murder of his son.[249]

The *Historia Augusta* states that Julia Mamaea was revered by her subjects and that she and her son were sincerely mourned.[250] A feast day in their honor was still being celebrated more than a century and a half after their deaths, and Alexander was deified and buried in a magnificent tomb.[251]

However, several writers criticized Julia Mamaea for her tireless acquisition of gold and silver, which, some said, was responsible for her son's downfall.[252] Julia answered the criticism of her hoarding by insisting that she was saving the money for the soldiers, and this was certainly true.[253] Subsequent events showed that her alleged avarice was actually prudence. The German invasion of 233 had long been anticipated by the imperial government,[254] and the Persian challenge was extremely serious. She must have seen that enormous resources would be needed to deal with major threats on two fronts. Maximinus, who inherited a full treasury because of Julia's foresight, still had to impose burdensome taxes in order to meet his military expenses.[255]

The death of Julia Mamaea and her son was more than the end of the Severan dynasty, which had been founded forty-two years before. It also signaled the end of peace, political stability, and economic prosperity for half a century. Given the turmoil of the times, Alexander's reign of almost exactly thirteen years was a remarkable achievement, due largely to Julia's efforts to involve the best senators, lawyers, and civil servants in governing the empire. Not one of the ten emperors who followed Alexander lasted even half as long. In the end, however, it was the army that decided who would rule.

While Julia Mamaea's career represented the pinnacle of feminine influence on the administration of the Roman Empire,[256] her death virtually signaled its end. There followed a succession of beleaguered soldier-emperors who had to face invasions, economic collapse, and a series of rebellions and civil wars.[257] The changes brought on by these disasters limited the role of empresses in government and diminished the people's prosperity and individual liberties, especially for women.

It is probably no coincidence that the potent eastern "women's goddesses" Cybele and Isis disappeared from the official coinage at this time,[258] and that the personification of feminine modesty and chastity (Pudicitia – see Figure 6.11) became more prominent. When order was finally restored fifty years after Julia Mamaea's assassination, the Roman Empire had become a very different place.

Figure 11.2 Portrait of Julia Maesa, the younger sister of Julia Domna and mother of Julia Mamaea, on a silver denarius, minted *c.* AD 218–226. RIC IV 268, BMCRE 76, RSC 36; courtesy Classical Numismatic Group, Inc.

Figure 11.3 Julia Soaemias, the older sister of Julia Mamaea and the daughter of Julia Maesa. Silver denarius minted under Elagabalus, *c.* AD 218–222. RIC IV 243, BMCRE 55; courtesy Classical Numismatic Group, Inc.

Figure 11.4 Portrait of Julia Mamaea on a silver denarius, minted under Severus Alexander, *c.* AD 222–235. RIC IV 358, BMCRE 713, RSC 76; courtesy Classical Numismatic Group, Inc.

Figure 11.5 Marcus Opellius Severus Macrinus, Caracalla's successor as emperor, reigned AD 217–218. Bronze sestertius minted January–June AD 218. RIC IV 160, BMCRE p. 522 (note), Cohen 105; courtesy Italo Vecchi.

Figure 11.6 A family resemblance emphasized: (Left) The deified Caracalla on a silver denarius, minted by his cousin Elagabalus, *c.* AD 218–219. RIC IV 717 (Severus Alexander), BMCRE 7 (Elagabalus), RSC 32. (Right) Elagabalus on a bronze sestertius, minted *c.* AD 218–222, RIC IV 369, Cohen 253. Both courtesy Classical Numismatic Group, Inc.

Figure 11.7 Julia Mamaea's son, later the emperor Severus Alexander, as Caesar under his cousin Elagabalus. Silver denarius minted *c.* AD 221–222. RIC IV 3, RSC 198; courtesy Classical Numismatic Group, Inc.

Figure 11.8 The youth of Elagabalus at the time of his accession (aged 14) is emphasized by the portrait on this silver denarius, minted in Antioch, Syria, *c.* AD 218. RIC IV 187, BMCRE 274; courtesy Heather Howard.

Figure 11.9 Elagabalus in his priestly robes, holding a *patera* (offering bowl) over a lighted altar, with a cypress branch in his left hand. RIC 326, Cohen 200; courtesy Heather Howard.

Figure 11.10 Reverse of a gold aureus of Elagabalus showing the sacred stone of the god Elagabal (see Figure 10.3) being drawn by a team of four horses (*quadriga*). Minted in Antioch, Syria *c.* AD 218–219. RIC IV 196a (variety), BMCRE 273 (note); courtesy Classical Numismatic Group, Inc.

Figure 11.11 Julia Paula, Elagabalus' first wife, on a bronze sestertius minted *c.* AD 219–220. RIC IV 381, BMCRE 415, Cohen 8; courtesy Classical Numismatic Group, Inc.

Figure 11.12 Aquilia Severa, a one-time Vestal Virgin and twice married to Elagabalus. Silver denarius minted *c.* AD 220–222. RIC IV 227, BMCRE 184 (note), RSC 2b; courtesy Classical Numismatic Group, Inc.

Figure 11.13 Annia Faustina, one of Elagabalus' wives and the granddaughter of Faustina the Younger and Marcus Aurelius. Bronze coin of Side, Pamphylia, minted *c.* AD 221–222. Apparently unpublished; courtesy Numismatik Lanz München.

Figure 11.14 Severus Alexander as emperor on a bronze sestertius, minted *c.* AD 230. RIC IV 500, BMCRE 625, Cohen 390; courtesy Classical Numismatic Group, Inc.

Figure 11.15 Portrait of Julia Mamaea on a bronze sestertius, minted *c.* AD 222–235. RIC IV 701 (Severus Alexander), Cohen 69.

Figure 11.16 Bi-metallic medallion of Severus Alexander, showing the Colosseum (compare to Figure 5.19) in Rome, damaged by fire in AD 217 and repaired by Elagabalus and Severus Alexander. Struck AD 224. Gnecchi III p. 42, BMCRE 156/7; courtesy Italo Vecchi.

11.17   11.18   11.19

11.22

11.20   11.21   11.23

Figure 11.17 Portrait of Julia Maesa on a bronze sestertius, minted *c.* AD 222–223. RIC IV 420, Cohen 42; courtesy Freeman and Sear.

Figure 11.18 Sallustia Orbiana, the wife of Severus Alexander, on a bronze sestertius minted in AD 225. RIC IV 655, BMCRE 293, Cohen 4; courtesy Classical Numismatic Group, Inc.

Figure 11.19 Severus Alexander with his wife, Sallustia Orbiana, on the reverse of a bronze sestertius minted in Orbiana's name, AD 225. RIC IV 657, BMCRE 293, Cohen 6; courtesy Classical Numismatic Group, Inc.

Figure 11.20 The Sassanid Persian king Artaxerxes (Ardashir) I, reigned AD 224–241, who invaded eastern parts of the Roman Empire in AD 230. Silver drachm. Göbl V/2, 16; courtesy Classical Numismatic Group, Inc.

Figure 11.21 Reverse of bronze sestertius of Severus Alexander honoring the sun god Sol, who holds a whip (for driving his chariot across the sky) and wears a radiate crown. Struck in AD 231. RIC IV 511, BMCRE 742, Cohen 413; courtesy Classical Numismatic Group, Inc.

Figure 11.22 Bi-metallic medallion of Julia Mamaea, minted AD 228. The empress is shown with the attributes of Ceres, Diana, Abundance, Isis, and Victory. The reverse shows her as Felicitas (happiness and prosperity), surrounded by goddesses. Gnecchi II, S. 83, 2; courtesy Numismatik Lanz München.

Figure 11.23 Severus Alexander, seated on a curule chair on a raised dais, distributing largess, with Liberalitas (the personification of liberality) beside him. Gold aureus minted AD 226. Unpublished; courtesy Classical Numismatic Group, Inc.

11.24

11.25

11.27

11.26

11.28

Figure 11.24 Severus Alexander on horseback, preceded by Victory, on a bronze sestertius minted *c.* AD 222–231. RIC IV 596, Cohen 492; courtesy Classical Numismatic Group, Inc.

Figure 11.25 Portrait of the emperor Maximinus I, who violently succeeded Severus Alexander in AD 235. Bronze sestertius minted *c.* AD 235–238. RIC IV 81, Cohen 38, BMCRE 148.

Figure 11.26 Sensitive portrait of Severus Alexander on a gold aureus, minted AD 229. RIC IV 204, BMCRE 557, Cohen 132; courtesy Classical Numismatic Group, Inc.

Figure 11.27 Unusual left-facing portrait of Julia Mamaea on a copper as, minted *c.* AD 222–235. RIC IV 696 (Severus Alexander), BMCRE 196, Cohen 64; courtesy Freeman and Sear.

Figure 11.28 Provincial portrait of Julia Mamaea on a potin tetradrachm, minted in Alexandria, Egypt, *c.* AD 230–231. Köln 2512, Dattari 4534, BMC 1762, Milne 3037; courtesy Classical Numismatic Group, Inc.

Figure 12.1 Portrait of Helena, the mother of Constantine I, based on a marble head in the Museo Capitolino, Rome. The coin is a gold medallion of two solidi. The first openly Christian empress, Helena stands within the Via Latina Catacomb in Rome, with a depiction of the raising of Lazarus from the dead on the left.

12

EPILOGUE

The later Roman empresses

A case could be made that the classical Roman Empire fell in the quarter century after Julia Mamaea's death in 235. By the 260s, after devastating invasions, epidemics, and political and economic chaos, the empire had split into three separate states. Barbarians, who were pillaging Roman territory almost at will, had killed one emperor in battle (Trajan Decius, reigned 249–251) and another had been captured by a Persian king (Valerian, reigned 253–260). The empire's population had declined and large areas of farmland had been abandoned.[1] It was in many ways a new empire that was established within the traditional boundaries during the late third century by emperors like Claudius II Gothicus, Aurelian, Probus, and Diocletian (reigns from 268–305).

Unfortunately, the century's two best historians, Cassius Dio and Herodian, had ceased writing by 238, leaving us largely at the mercy of unreliable, late fourth-century sources such as the *Historia Augusta*. As a result, the Roman empresses of this period are shadowy figures at best. Many of them are completely lost to history, some are known by name and little more, others only from their coins or portraits – the identity of their husbands being a matter for conjecture. With a couple of exceptions, these women seem to have had little role in governing the empire. Their husbands mostly performed this task while leading armies in the field, where they faced an endless series of enemy invasions and challenges for the throne.

The post-Severan empresses

Maximinus' wife, Caecilia Paulina, seems to have died before or just after his accession as all of her coins were issued posthumously.[2] She was therefore spared the murders of her husband and son in 238, after only three years of rule. Her portraits show a woman with large but pleasant features that suggest strength equal to her prodigious husband's (see Figure 12.2).

The next Augusta to emerge from the mists of this troubled time is Furia Sabinia Tranquillina, the young wife of the emperor Gordian III (reigned 238–244). She was the daughter of his praetorian prefect Timesitheus, an experienced, capable man known for his eloquence and culture.[3] The marriage took place in 241 when the emperor was only 16.[4] Gordian relied heavily on his father-in-law, especially after war broke out with the Persians in 241,[5] so his position was considerably weakened when Timesitheus fell ill and died in 243.[6] Within a year, his new prefect Philip the Arab had deposed and executed Gordian,[7] and Tranquillina disappeared from history.

Philip (reigned 244–249) bought peace from the Persians for no less than 10,000 pounds of gold and turned west to consolidate his power.[8] His wife, Marcia Otacilia Severa, is best known from the multitude of coins issued in her name. These, plus a number of marble busts, show a woman with a round, pleasant face and rather blunt features. A later tradition sprang up that both Philip and Otacilia were Christians. Eusebius states that the theologian Origen wrote to each of them.[9] While their regime does seem to have been tolerant of Christianity, modern scholars doubt that they ever converted to that faith.[10]

In April, 248, Philip celebrated the thousandth anniversary of the founding of Rome with lavish games, featuring gladiatorial contests and a host of exotic animals.[11] Coins were issued in Otacilia's name with a depiction of a hippopotamus on the reverse (see Figure 12.6).[12] (One wonders what the plumpish empress thought of this.) Philip's coins bear images of an antelope and a stag, and there is an elk (moose) on those of his son, Philip II.

Despite this display of pomp and optimism, Philip's turn to be deposed came in 249 after a reign of less than five years. He was killed in Macedonia in a battle against the army of Trajan Decius, one of his provincial governors.[13] Philip's son and wife may have lived on in Rome for a while, before the Praetorian Guard put them to death.[14]

Decius (249–251) earned the lasting enmity of Christians by demanding that they perform a sacrifice to the pagan gods as a declaration of loyalty to the state.[15] Those Christians who refused to comply became martyrs.[16] His empress, Herennia Etruscilla, is believed, because of her name, to have been descended from an ancient Etruscan family.[17] Her coins show an agreeable-looking woman with a cheerful expression (see Figure 12.8) that belies the desperation of her husband's reign. His rise to the purple had resulted from military successes against the barbarian Goths.[18] However, they killed Decius and his older son in an ambush in 251 after a reign of less than two years.[19] His successor, Trebonianus Gallus (reigned 251–253), agreed to share the throne with Decius' younger son Hostilian and, in deference to the widowed Herennia, Gallus did not elevate his wife Baebiana to the rank of Augusta.[20] To continue Herennia's misfortunes, however, Hostilian soon died from the plague.[21]

The next two empresses to leave a mark on history are Cornelia Supera, who was unknown before her coins surfaced in the eighteenth century (see Figure 12.14),[22] and Egnatia Mariniana. They are believed to have been the wives of the two immediate successors of Trebonianus Gallus: Aemilian, who rebelled against Gallus and ruled for less than three months,[23] and Valerian I (reigned 253–260), who remained loyal to Gallus and toppled Aemilian.[24]

Valerian's presumed wife Mariniana (some have suggested that she was his sister[25]) is only represented on commemorative coins (see Figure 12.16). Therefore she must have died before or shortly after Valerian assumed the throne.[26] In 260, after a reign of nearly seven years, he was captured by the Persian ruler Shapur I.[27] According to some accounts, the emperor was humiliated by his captors, even made to serve as a human footstool whenever Shapur mounted his horse.[28] Valerian reportedly died in captivity and was stuffed, dyed vermilion, and put on display by the Persians.[29]

Salonina: begotten of gold

The monotonous train of hard-bitten, worried-looking soldier-emperors was relieved somewhat by the reign of Gallienus, Valerian's son and co-emperor from 253. Gallienus (reigned 253–268) remained in power after his father's capture, but immediately faced catastrophes in both the East and the West. The governor of Lower Germany, Postumus, took advantage of the confusion to set up an independent kingdom in Britain, Gaul, and Spain.[30] Meanwhile, after a Persian offensive in the East was stopped by Odenathus, a Roman client and the king of the Syrian city of Palmyra, Gallienus had no choice but to grant him semi-independence and authority over the eastern Roman armies.[31]

Gallienus seems to have been a rather flamboyant personality, somewhat in the mode of Nero, or even Elagabalus. He is said to have indulged his extravagant tastes for high living, artistic expression, and even cross-dressing.[32] However, he also fought bravely to protect and reunite the empire throughout his fifteen-year reign (miraculous longevity for the times), only to be murdered by his officers in 268.[33]

In light of Gallienus' troubles, it is somewhat surprising that he presided over a sort of artistic and intellectual renaissance. With his wife, Cornelia Salonina (also called "Chrysogone" or "born of gold"[34]), he pursued his enthusiasms for poetry, literature, philosophy, and classical sculpture.[35] The couple befriended the great Neoplatonic philosopher Plotinus, and Gallienus was initiated into the Eleusinian Mysteries.[36] Despite his enthusiasm for paganism, Gallienus was tolerant of the Christians, whom his father had persecuted.[37] He was acknowledged to be a first-class poet and rhetorician.[38] A poem of his that survives in the *Historia Augusta* is remarkable for its romantic beauty:

> Go and carry on, young ones, and sweat as one with all the inner feelings that you share.

> Let not your murmurs be outdone by doves, nor your circling arms by ivy, nor your kisses by clinging seashells.

Have your play: but don't put out the watchful lamps.

They see all in the night, yet remember nothing on the morrow.[39]

Gallienus' empress Salonina was given the titles of Augusta and Mater Castrorum (Mother of the Camp) in 254.[40] Her portraits on coins, and on a marble bust believed to be of her, show a beautiful, meditative woman with an oval face, large rounded nose, strong chin, full lips, straight brow, and almond-shaped eyes (see Figure 12.19).[41] Gallienus reportedly loved her to distraction,[42] though he is also said to have been enamored of a German princess by the name of Pipa (or Pipara), whom he may have accepted into his court under the terms of an alliance with her father's tribe.[43]

There is a tradition that Salonina enjoyed a profound, even scandalous, influence over her husband.[44] She reportedly persuaded him to found an idyllic "philosopher's state" in the Italian countryside, but it is not known whether this dream was ever realized.[45] She also took an interest in government, evaluating and sometimes disapproving of her husband's appointments.[46] It has been argued that she was a Christian, based on the evidence of coins inscribed *Salonina in Pace* (Salonina in Peace), which may be an allusion to that faith.[47] However, this theory does not seem to be supportable, though Gallienus' tolerance of Christianity does suggest imperial sympathy for the sect.[48]

There is a humorous story in the *Historia Augusta* about Salonina being duped by a salesman into buying glass gems, thinking they were real. When she discovered the ruse and complained to her husband, he had the man arrested and prepared to expose him to a lion as punishment. When the lion's cage was opened – a chicken emerged. Gallienus said, "He deceived, and then was himself deceived." The man was released, no doubt thoroughly shaken by the experience.[49]

Despite Gallienus' reported infidelities and his attachment to Pipa, the evidence is that he loved and remained devoted to Salonina. She was with him at his military headquarters shortly before his assassination and probably died with him.[50]

Zenobia: queen of Palmyra

In 267 Odenathus, the Palmyrene king who had protected the eastern provinces from the Persians, was assassinated.[51] His successor was Vabalathus, a son by his second wife, Bat-Zabbai, better known in history by her Roman name, Septimia Zenobia.[52] Zenobia served as regent for her teenaged son and promptly offended Gallienus by showing too much independence from Rome.[53] Her armies defeated Gallienus' attempts to bring her back in line, and Zenobia extended Palmyra's sphere of influence to include Egypt, all of Syria and Palestine, and much of Asia Minor.[54]

Zenobia was one of the most remarkable women of ancient times. Admired for her chastity, dark beauty, and keen intelligence, she was an expert horse-woman who loved to hunt.[55] Her portraits on coins tell us little about her actual appearance (see Figure 12.24) because she is represented as a garden-variety Augusta in the mold of Julia Mamaea. Zenobia claimed to be descended from the Ptolemaic queen Cleopatra,[56] with whom she shared a gift for languages, speaking Greek, Egyptian, Aramaic, and Latin.[57] Palmyra had strong ties to the city of Emesa, only about 90 miles (144 km) to the west, and she probably also modeled herself after the recent Julias of Emesa: Domna, Maesa, and Mamaea.[58]

Palmyra's empire existed in part because the Roman army was too preoc-cupied with barbarian invasions to suppress it. However, after 270, when the brilliant general Aurelian ascended the throne, Roman order was grad-ually restored. In 272, after Vabalathus had been declared emperor in the East and Zenobia named Augusta, their forces were defeated in battle by Aurelian.[59] The queen tried to escape on camelback, but was overtaken and captured by the Roman cavalry.[60]

According to the *Historia Augusta*, Zenobia was taken to Rome and, along with Tetricus, the last ruler of the western rebel state established by Postumus, exhibited in Aurelian's triumphal procession.[61] After this humil-iation, however, she definitely seems to have landed on her feet. Aurelian reportedly gave her a splendid villa at Tibur (modern Tivoli, Italy), where she spent the rest of her life in dignity and comfort, possibly even marrying a Roman senator.[62]

Ironically, Aurelian's empress Ulpia Severina is as obscure as Zenobia is famous. She was named Augusta in 274, about the time of her husband's triumph.[63] Her stylized coin portraits (see Figure 12.27) do not tell us much about her actual appearance. She is usually given a rather worried look, often with a furrowed brow. Indeed, her husband was a tough customer; his nick-name *manu ad ferrum* means "sword in hand."[64]

The *Historia Augusta* relates an incident in which Aurelian dismissed Severina's request to keep a valuable roll of purple silk. His answer: "Fabrics should not be worth their weight in gold."[65] On the other hand, he report-edly intended to restore the *senaculum*, or women's senate, which had existed under Elagabalus, provided that its priestess leaders were approved by the men's senate.[66]

Aurelian's officers murdered him in 275. It may be that Severina stayed in power for a time after her husband's death, cooperating with the Roman senate during an interregnum, or interval between rulers, until a new emperor was chosen. This man, named Tacitus, was a senator and suppos-edly a descendant of the first-century historian of the same name. His reign was to be very brief (late 275 to July 276).[67]

Diocletian and Roman recovery

The reconstruction of the Roman Empire, achieved through the superb generalship of men like Aurelian, was confirmed by the organizational genius of Diocletian, who became emperor in 284. His reforms helped to inaugurate an era of relative prosperity and security that would last until the second half of the fourth century. Diocletian named a co-emperor, Maximian, to rule the western provinces while he held sway in the East. In 293, he appointed two Caesars, Constantius in the West and Galerius in the East, to help with the task of government. Then, in 305, Diocletian astonished the Roman world by abdicating and retiring to his fortress/palace at Spalato (modern Split) in Dalmatia on the Adriatic coast.[68]

Despite her husband's success, Diocletian's wife Prisca is little known. Her portrait appears with his on a mausoleum frieze in Spalato,[69] but there were no coins minted in her honor. Their daughter Galeria Valeria was married in 293 to Galerius, the Caesar of the East. Galeria's coin portraits, with some exceptions (see Figure 12.32), are engraved in the unflattering style of the period and show the squared features and block-shaped head of her father.

Prisca was with her daughter in Thessalonica, Greece, in 311 when her son-in-law Galerius died of a horrible disease. His successor in the East, Maximinus II, proposed to the widowed Galeria, but she refused him. Despite the retired Diocletian's request to have his wife and daughter returned to him, they were mistreated by the enraged Maximinus and exiled to a remote village in Syria. They managed to escape by disguising themselves as ordinary women, but their fifteen-month journey to rejoin Diocletian in Spalato ended when they learned of his death in December, 311. In 314 they were recognized in Greece, publicly beheaded, and their bodies were thrown into the sea.[70]

Prisca and Galeria may have been Christians, or at least Christian sympathizers.[71] This would have put them at odds with their husbands as both Diocletian and Galerius were determined enemies of that faith. Ironically, the end of official opposition to Christianity came at the same time as their deaths. Maximinus II was deposed by Licinius, who favored Christianity and ironically may have had Prisca and Galeria executed because they were the wives of former persecutors of their own religion.[72]

Helena: mother of Constantine

The new emperor of the West, who had persuaded Licinius to look favorably on Christianity,[73] was none other than Constantine the Great. He was the son of Constantius I and Flavia Julia Helena, a barmaid from Bithynia. Constantius had discarded Helena in 293 when he became Caesar, but summoned the grown Constantine to his court before he died in 306. Constantine became Caesar of the West, married the princess Fausta, and brought his mother Helena to live with him at court.[74]

There followed a long power struggle that would end Diocletian's division of the empire into East and West and establish Constantine as the sole Roman emperor in 324. During these civil wars, Constantine allegedly had an experience that led to his acceptance of Christianity. In 312, before his battle with a rival at the Milvian Bridge in Rome, he saw a vision of the cross and received a message that his army would be victorious under this symbol.[75] His subsequent success reportedly convinced Constantine of the potency of the Christian god, and in 324 he named Christianity the official state religion.[76]

Despite nearly three centuries of growth in numbers, Christians still comprised only 20 percent of the empire's population at this time,[77] which is roughly equivalent to the proportion of non-Hindus in modern India.[78] However, the Christians were highly organized and concentrated in the major cities (the term "pagan" means "country dweller"), so their influence was disproportionate to their numbers.[79]

One can imagine Helena's pride at her son's incredible rise. Whether she was a Christian before Constantine's vision or not, she became the first empress to avow the faith openly. Her son treated her with respect and affection, awarding her the title *nobilissima femina* ("most noble woman") in 318.[80] She was also named Augusta in 326, and in that year her influence with Constantine was demonstrated in dramatic fashion.

The story goes that Constantine had a son from his first marriage named Crispus. The empress Fausta was jealous of this rival to her three sons by Constantine and arranged to have him executed by telling the emperor that Crispus had tried to seduce her, which was tantamount to treason. Helena knew that her grandson was innocent of the charge and managed to convince Constantine that he had made a dreadful error. Fausta's punishment was being boiled alive in her own bath.[81]

Helena's portraits, on coins and on marble busts, were made during her later years. She was probably born about 250, so she would have been in her seventies when most of her coins were issued.[82] Nevertheless, she is depicted as a relatively young woman, with a broad, unlined face, large nose, small mouth, a serene and somewhat pious expression, and a marked resemblance to her son (see Figures 12.1, 12.34).

The empress Helena's greatest imprint on history came when she was nearing 80. She conducted a pilgrimage to Jerusalem in search of artifacts associated with the life of Jesus Christ. Tales of her miraculous discoveries, which supposedly included the true cross, were probably exaggerations or inventions. Nevertheless, they did much to publicize and promote public interest in the Christian faith. One modern writer (Michael Grant) even described Helena as "the most popular and successful archeologist" of all time.[83] She used her great wealth to patronize Christianity and had two churches built in Jerusalem before her death in around 330. The Roman Catholic Church later rewarded Helena for her services to Christianity by proclaiming her "Saint Helena."[84]

The curtain closes

The late fourth century and the early fifth witnessed a series of events that would confirm the end of the old Roman world. In 378, the Visigoths and Ostrogoths annihilated the eastern emperor Valens and his army near the city of Hadrianopolis in Thrace (modern Edirne, Turkey).[85] The magnitude of this disaster ended any Roman pretensions to military supremacy over their barbarian foes.[86] From then on, survival would depend on diplomatic strategy, an area in which the women of the period would prove to excel.

The next two events that helped to seal the fate of the old empire came during the reign of the emperor Theodosius I. In 391 he outlawed all religions other than the officially approved version of Christianity.[87] This signaled the death knell for the pagan traditions on which classical Roman civilization was based, though their demise would take centuries.[88] There is evidence of an exodus of pagan artists and thinkers from the empire at this time, some of whom went as far as India to escape religious persecution. Indeed, this led to a flowering of art and culture under the Guptas in India that had unmistakable signs of Greco-Roman influence.[89]

Theodosius decided to leave the empire to both of his sons, Arcadius and Honorius, so his death in 395 led to the permanent division of the Roman Empire into two halves, East and West.[90] The two new Roman worlds were dominated by a remarkable series of empresses for much of the next century.

In the East, Eudoxia, the wife of Arcadius and mother of Theodosius II, was a strong, capable administrator who ran the government for some years before her death in 404. From 414, her daughter Pulcheria carried on her mother's work by ruling the eastern empire with her sister-in-law, Theodosius II's wife Eudocia. When Eudocia retired to Jerusalem in 441, Pulcheria continued to run the government, choosing the virtuous general Marcian to be her husband and the new emperor after Theodosius' death in 450.[91]

The eastern empire enjoyed relative peace and prosperity during this period – despite an attack by Attila the Hun. This was in marked contrast to the situation in the West. Galla Placidia, the daughter of Theodosius I and half-sister of the current western emperor Honorius, was actually carried off by the Goths when they sacked Rome in 410. She was married to a barbarian king in 414, then sold back to the Romans for 600,000 measures of corn when her husband died. Galla Placidia survived these experiences to rule the West on behalf of her son, Valentinian III, from 425 until 437, then dedicated the rest of her life to building churches and other sacred buildings in Ravenna, Italy. She died in Rome in 450 at the age of 68.[92]

Galla Placidia's daughter-in-law, Licinia Eudoxia, had a similarly eventful life as empress. Her husband, Valentinian III, was assassinated in 455. She was forced to marry his murderer and successor, only to be carried off to Carthage by the Vandals, who sacked Rome later in the same year. In 462 she was released and spent the rest of her life in Constantinople, the capital of the eastern Roman Empire.[93]

By 476, the barbarians had deposed the last western emperor. The eastern state persisted through the centuries, known today as the Byzantine Empire, and was not finally extinguished until 1453. However, the glory and true character of the empire of Augustus and Marcus Aurelius, Agrippina and Julia Mamaea had long since become a faint memory.

Many of the achievements of the empresses of the Roman Empire's golden age have been obscured, and not only by the ravages of time. Their contributions were underestimated or distorted by historians, both contemporary and from later periods. The senatorial prejudice against absolute rulers, the Christian prejudice against pagan women who were worshiped like goddesses, and the chauvinism of male authors – all inspired various writers to treat these women unfairly. Stories of their sexual exploits and political intrigues were exaggerated, or even fabricated.

Thus, the dignified Livia became a scheming poisoner, the noble Faustinas became brainless adulterers, and the brilliant Syrian Julias, wanton, ruthless, or avaricious. Even modern historians have often been unable to resist the sensational tales of debauchery and crime, perpetuating the myths of the Roman empresses as personifications of evil and excess. However, a balanced look at the evidence inevitably leads to different conclusions.

On the whole, the empresses were admirable and accomplished women who fulfilled important roles in society, encouraging its religious, artistic, and charitable institutions. They symbolized some of the most potent and benevolent ideals of Roman culture and were worshiped as living symbols of the gods. They used their influence to promote favored causes and individuals, and, occasionally, to choose the ruler of the empire – or even to rule it themselves. The empresses of Rome were indispensable architects of one of the greatest societies in human history, and their deeds bear fruit to this day.

Figure 12.2 Silver denarius of Caecilia Paulina, the deified wife of the emperor Maximinus I, reigned AD 235–238. RIC IV 2, BMCRE 127, RSC 2; courtesy Classical Numismatic Group, Inc.

Figure 12.3 Bronze sestertius of Maximinus I, reigned AD 235–238, the husband of Caecilia Paulina. RIC IV 90, BMCRE 191, Cohen 109; courtesy Classical Numismatic Group, Inc.

Figure 12.4 Silver antoninianus of Sabinia Tranquillina, the wife of Gordianus III (reigned AD 238–244) and daughter of his Praetorian Prefect, Timesitheus. The reverse shows Tranquillina clasping hands with her husband. RIC IV 250, RSC 4; courtesy Classical Numismatic Group, Inc.

Figure 12.5 Bronze sestertius of Gordianus III, reigned AD 238–244. RIC IV 274a, Cohen 1; courtesy Classical Numismatic Group, Inc.

Figure 12.6 Bronze sestertius of Otacilia Severa, the wife of Philip I, with a hippopotamus (featured in the celebration of Rome's 1,000th anniversary) on the reverse. Minted *c.* AD 248–249. RIC IV 200a, Cohen 65; courtesy Harlan J. Berk, Ltd.

Figure 12.7 Bronze sestertius of Philip I (reigned AD 244–249), minted AD 245. RIC IV190, Cohen 216.

Figure 12.8 Bronze dupondius of Herennia Etruscilla, wife of Trajan Decius, reigned AD 249–251. RIC IV 136d, Cohen 24; courtesy Classical Numismatic Group, Inc.

Figure 12.9 Bronze double-sestertius of Trajan Decius, minted *c.* AD 249–251. RIC IV 115c, Cohen 40; courtesy Classical Numismatic Group, Inc.

Figure 12.10 Bronze sestertius of Herennius Etruscus, the elder son of Herennia Etruscilla and Trajan Decius, reigned AD 249–251. He was Caesar AD 250–251, Augustus (co-emperor) AD 251. RIC IV 167a, Cohen 12 (variety); courtesy Freeman and Sear.

Figure 12.11 Bronze sestertius of Hostilian, the younger son of Herennia Etruscilla and Trajan Decius, reigned AD 249–251. RIC IV 215a, Cohen 31; courtesy Freeman and Sear.

Figure 12.12 Bronze sestertius of Trebonianus Gallus, emperor from AD 251–253. RIC IV 112, Cohen 54; courtesy Freeman and Sear.

Figure 12.13 Gold binio of Volusian, the son of Trebonianus Gallus (reigned 251–253) and his wife Baebiana. RIC IV 151, cf. Cohen 82; courtesy Classical Numismatic Group, Inc.

Figure 12.14 Silver antoninianus of Cornelia Supera, presumed to be the wife of the short-lived emperor Aemilian, who reigned in AD 253. RIC IV 30, RSC 5; courtesy Classical Numismatic Group, Inc.

Figure 12.15 Bronze dupondius of Aemilian struck in AD 253. RIC IV 54b, Cohen 68; courtesy Classical Numismatic Group, Inc.

Figure 12.16 Bronze sestertius of the deified Egnatia Mariniana, wife (?) of Valerian I, who reigned AD 253–260. RIC V part 1, 9 (variety); courtesy Classical Numismatic Group, Inc.

12.17   12.18   12.19

12.20   12.21   12.22

12.23   12.24   12.25

Figure 12.17 Bronze sestertius of Valerian I, minted *c.* AD 249–251. He was taken prisoner by Shapur I of Persia in AD 260. RIC V 155, Cohen 40; courtesy Freeman and Sear.

Figure 12.18 Shapur I, king of Sassanian Persia and captor of the Roman emperor Valerian I. Silver drachm, minted *c.* AD 241–272. Göbl III 1, MACW 811ff.; courtesy Classical Numismatic Group, Inc.

Figure 12.19 Cornelia Salonina, wife of Gallienus, reigned AD 253–268. Bronze sestertius, minted *c.* AD 254–255. RIC V 46, Cohen 62.

Figure 12.20 Bronze sestertius of Gallienus (reigned AD 253–268), son of Valerian I and husband of Salonina, minted *c.* AD 254–255. RIC V part 1, 209, Cohen 132; courtesy Classical Numismatic Group, Inc.

Figure 12.21 Silver medallion (diameter 33 mm) of Valerian II, the elder son of Salonina and Gallienus. Valerian II was Caesar AD 256–258. RIC V part 1, 12, RSC 36a; courtesy Classical Numismatic Group, Inc.

Figure 12.22 Antoninianus of Saloninus, the younger son of Salonina and Gallienus. Saloninus was Caesar AD 258–260 and became co-emperor (Augustus) with his father in 260, but was soon put to death by Postumus. RIC V 35, RSC 21; courtesy Classical Numismatic Group, Inc.

Figure 12.23 Bronze sestertius of Postumus, ruler of a breakaway state consisting of Britain, Gaul, and Spain, *c.* AD 259–268. RIC V part 1, 180, Cohen 423; courtesy Classical Numismatic Group, Inc.

Figure 12.24 Portrait of Septimia Zenobia (Bat-Zabbai) on an antoninianus (double denarius) minted in Antioch, Syria *c.* AD 271–272. RIC V part 2, 2; courtesy Classical Numismatic Group, Inc.

Figure 12.25 Reverse of an antoninianus of Aurelian with a portrait of Vabalathus, son of Zenobia, minted in Antioch, Syria *c.* AD 271–272. RIC V part 1, 381, Cohen 1; courtesy Classical Numismatic Group, Inc.

Figure 12.26 Gold medallion (8 aurei) of Claudius II Gothicus, who succeeded Gallienus on the throne and reigned AD 268–270. RIC V part 1, 1 (Rome), Gnecchi 1, plate 3, 8; courtesy Classical Numismatic Group, Inc.

Figure 12.27 Copper as of Severina, the wife of Aurelian, reigned AD 270–275. RIC V 7, Cohen 9; courtesy Freeman and Sear.

Figure 12.28 Gold aureus of Aurelian, reigned AD 270–275. RIC V part 1, 14 (variety); courtesy Classical Numismatic Group, Inc.

Figure 12.29 Gold aureus of Probus, reigned AD 276–282. RIC V part 2, 587 (variety), Cohen 1; courtesy Classical Numismatic Group, Inc.

Figure 12.30 Copper follis of Diocletian (ruled AD 284–305) as senior Augustus, minted in Trier *c.* AD 305. RIC VI 676a; courtesy Classical Numismatic Group, Inc.

Figure 12.31 Copper follis of Maximianus (ruled AD 286–305, and again in 306–308) as junior Augustus, minted in Alexandria *c.* AD 304–305. RIC VI 38 (variety); courtesy Classical Numismatic Group, Inc.

Figure 12.32 Copper follis of Galeria Valeria, daughter of Diocletian and wife of Galerius (Caesar in AD 293–305, Augustus in AD 305–311), minted in Alexandria AD 308. RIC VI 74; courtesy Classical Numismatic Group, Inc.

Figure 12.33 Bronze medallion (diameter 36 mm) of Galerius as Caesar, minted in Rome *c.* AD 293–294. Gnecchi II p. 132, 3 and plate 129, 1, Cohen 137; courtesy Classical Numismatic Group, Inc.

Figure 12.34 Flavia Julia Helena, mother of Constantine I ("the Great"), mistress of Constantius I Chlorus. Bronze follis, minted *c.* AD 324–325. RIC VII 187; courtesy Classical Numismatic Group, Inc.

Figure 12.35 Gold solidus of Constantius I Chlorus as Caesar, minted in Antioch, AD 293. Constantius I, the father of Constantine I the Great, served as a Caesar AD 293–305 and as an Augustus AD 305–306. RIC VI 7; courtesy Classical Numismatic Group, Inc.

Figure 12.36 Flavia Maxima Fausta, daughter of Maximianus and wife of Constantine I (ruled AD 307–337). Bronze follis, minted in Siscia AD 326. RIC VII 205; courtesy Numismatik Lanz München.

Figure 12.37 Gold solidus of Constantine I, "the Great," struck AD 335. RIC VII 243; courtesy Classical Numismatic Group, Inc.

Figure 12.38 Aelia Eudoxia, wife of Arcadius (reigned AD 383–408). Gold solidus, minted in Constantinople, *c.* AD 402–403. RIC X 28; courtesy Classical Numismatic Group, Inc.

Figure 12.39 Gold solidus of Arcadius, struck in Constantinople *c.* AD 387–402. RIC X 7; courtesy Numismatik Lanz München.

Figure 12.40 Aelia Eudocia, wife of Theodosius II (reigned AD 402–450). Gold solidus, minted in Constantinople, *c.* AD 423–429. RIC X 228; courtesy Classical Numismatic Group, Inc.

Figure 12.41 Gold medallion (2 solidi) of Theodosius II, struck in Constantinople in *c.* AD 430 or 435. RIC X 216; courtesy Freeman and Sear.

Figure 12.42 Aelia Pulcheria (Augusta from AD 414), sister of Theodosius II and wife of Marcian (reigned AD 450–457). Gold solidus, minted in Constantinople, *c.* AD 423–425. RIC X 226; courtesy Classical Numismatic Group, Inc.

Figure 12.43 Gold solidus of Marcian, struck in Constantinople *c.* AD 450–457. RIC X 510; courtesy Classical Numismatic Group, Inc.

12.44

12.45

12.46

12.47

Figure 12.44 Galla Placidia, daughter of Theodosius I, mother of Valentinian III, and half-sister of Honorius and Arcadius. She was carried off by the Goths and married for a time to a barbarian king. Gold solidus, minted in Aquileia, Italy, in AD 425. RIC X 1808; courtesy Freeman and Sear.

Figure 12.45 Gold solidus of Honorius (reigned AD 393–423), struck in Constantinople, *c.* AD 397–402. RIC X 8; courtesy Classical Numismatic Group, Inc.

Figure 12.46 Licinia Eudoxia, wife of Valentinian III (reigned AD 425–455). Gold solidus, minted in Ravenna, Italy, *c.* AD 439. RIC X 2023; courtesy Classical Numismatic Group, Inc.

Figure 12.47 Gold solidus of Valentinian III, minted in Ravenna, Italy, *c.* AD 426–430. RIC X 2011; courtesy Classical Numismatic Group, Inc.

APPENDIX

Chronology of the Roman Empire

Dates	Roman emperors, ROYAL MALES, other males	Roman empresses, ROYAL FEMALES, other females	Significant events
44 BC	Julius Caesar		15 March (Ides) Julius Caesar assassinated
43 BC			Death of Cicero
42 BC	Octavian (born 23 September 63 BC, later *Augustus*) Mark Antony (Marcus Antonius) Livius Drusus Calidianus (father of *Livia*)	Hortensia *Livia* (born 58 BC)	Protest against taxation of women led by Hortensia Battle of Philippi, defeat of assassins of Julius Caesar, suicide of Livius Drusus Calidianus Birth (16 November) of *Tiberius* Deification of Julius Caesar by senate
40 BC	Lucius Antonius (brother of Mark Antony) Tiberius Claudius Nero (first husband of *Livia*)	Fulvia (wife of Mark Antony) – her heroism at Perusia OCTAVIA, sister of Octavian	Perusine War between forces of Octavian and Mark Antony – siege of Perusia Death of Fulvia Marriage of OCTAVIA and Mark Antony
39 BC		Scribonia (wife of Octavian)	Truce between Octavian and Mark Antony Birth of JULIA, daughter of Octavian and Scribonia
38 BC			Marriage (17 January) of *Livia* and Octavian Birth of DRUSUS I, son of *Livia*
37 BC			OCTAVIA reconciles her husband (Mark Antony) and her brother (Octavian)
36 BC			Birth (31 January) of *Antonia* (the Younger), daughter of OCTAVIA and Mark Antony, mother of CLAUDIUS

Dates	Roman emperors, ROYAL MALES, other males	Roman empresses, ROYAL FEMALES, other females	Significant events
35 BC		CLEOPATRA, Queen of Egypt, consort of Julius Caesar and Mark Antony	OCTAVIA and *Livia* granted sacrosanct status
32 BC			Mark Antony divorces OCTAVIA
31 BC	MARCUS AGRIPPA		Defeat of Mark Antony's and CLEOPATRA's forces at the Battle of Actium
30 BC			Suicides of Mark Antony and CLEOPATRA
27 BC	*Augustus* (reigned *c.* 31 BC–AD 14)		Octavian becomes *Augustus*, the first Roman emperor
25 BC	MARCELLUS, son of OCTAVIA, nephew of *Augustus*	JULIA, daughter of *Augustus*	Marriage of JULIA and MARCELLUS
23 BC			Death of MARCELLUS Near fatal illness of *Augustus*
21 BC			Marriage of JULIA and MARCUS AGRIPPA
20 BC			Birth of GAIUS CAESAR, son of JULIA and MARCUS AGRIPPA
19 BC			Birth of JULIA II, daughter of JULIA and MARCUS AGRIPPA
18 BC	Crinagoras, Greek poet, described *Antonia*'s wedding		Marriage of *Antonia* and DRUSUS I
17 BC			Birth of LUCIUS CAESAR, son of JULIA and MARCUS AGRIPPA
15 BC			Birth of GERMANICUS German campaigns of DRUSUS I commence Conquest of Alps by DRUSUS I and *Tiberius*
14 BC			Birth of AGRIPPINA I (approximate date)
13 BC			Birth of LIVILLA (approximate date), daughter of *Antonia*
12 BC			Death of MARCUS AGRIPPA Birth of AGRIPPA POSTUMUS, son of JULIA and MARCUS AGRIPPA
11 BC			Marriage of JULIA and *Tiberius* Death of OCTAVIA, mother of *Antonia*

Dates	Roman emperors, ROYAL MALES, other males	Roman empresses, ROYAL FEMALES, other females	Significant events
10 BC			Birth (1 August) of *Claudius*
9 BC			Death of DRUSUS I, husband of *Antonia*, father of *Claudius*
6 BC			*Tiberius* goes to Rhodes in self-imposed exile
4 BC			Birth of Seneca (or in 5 BC)
2 BC			JULIA banished from Rome *Augustus* named *Pater Patriae*
2			Death of LUCIUS CAESAR
4			Death of GAIUS CAESAR, son of JULIA and husband of LIVILLA Adoption of AGRIPPA POSTUMUS and *Tiberius* by *Augustus*
5			Marriage of AGRIPPINA I and GERMANICUS
9	Publius Quinctilius Varus		Massacre of three Roman legions under Varus by the Germans Birth of *Vespasian*
12			Birth (31 August) of *Caligula*
14	*Tiberius* (reigned 14–37) GERMANICUS DRUSUS II	AGRIPPINA I	Death (19 August) of *Augustus* Accession (19 August) of *Tiberius* Revolt of Roman troops on German frontier quelled by GERMANICUS, AGRIPPINA I, and DRUSUS II, son of *Tiberius*
15			Birth (6 November) of *Agrippina II*
17			GERMANICUS celebrates triumph in Rome GERMANICUS and family tour eastern provinces
19	Gnaeus Calpurnius Piso, enemy of GERMANICUS and AGRIPPINA I	Plancina, wife of Piso and protégé of *Livia* LIVILLA	Death (10 October) of GERMANICUS at Antioch, Syria LIVILLA, wife of DRUSUS II, gives birth to twin sons
22	Valerius Maximus, Roman moralist, wrote under *Tiberius*		Near fatal illness of *Livia*
23			Death of DRUSUS II, son of *Tiberius*

Dates	Roman emperors, ROYAL MALES, other males	Roman empresses, ROYAL FEMALES, other females	Significant events
26	Lucius Aelius Sejanus, Praetorian Prefect, *Tiberius'* henchman		*Tiberius* leaves Rome for Capri, never returns to capital Sejanus consolidates his power
28	Gnaeus Domitius Ahenobarbus, father of *Nero*		Marriage of *Agrippina II* to Ahenobarbus
29		*Antonia*	Death of *Livia* *Antonia* becomes highest-ranking royal woman DRUSUS CAESAR, son of AGRIPPINA I, turns against her AGRIPPINA I exiled to Pandateria
31			*Antonia* reveals Sejanus' plot against *Tiberius* Death (18 October) of Sejanus
33			Death (18 October) of AGRIPPINA I
35			Birth (8 November) of *Nerva*
36	Herod Agrippa, Jewish prince, friend of *Claudius* and *Caligula*		Herod Agrippa imprisoned by *Tiberius*, aided by *Antonia*
37	*Caligula* (reigned 37–41)	*Livia Orestilla*	Death (16 March) of *Tiberius* Accession (18 March) of *Caligula* (*Gaius*) Death (1 May) of *Antonia* Birth (15 December) of *Nero* Marriage of *Caligula* and *Livia Orestilla*, his second wife
38		*Lollia Paulina*	Death of DRUSILLA, *Caligula's* favorite sister Marriage of *Caligula* and *Lollia Paulina*, *Caligula's* third wife
39	Marcus Aemilius Lepidus, widower of DRUSILLA	*Caesonia*	Marriage of *Caligula* and *Caesonia* Lepidus and *Caligula's* sisters, *Agrippina II* and JULIA LIVILLA, accused of planning a coup Exile of *Agrippina II* and JULIA LIVILLA to Ponza Birth (30 December) of *Titus*

249

Dates	Roman emperors, ROYAL MALES, other males	Roman empresses, ROYAL FEMALES, other females	Significant events
41	*Claudius* (reigned 41–54) Passienus Crispus, husband of *Agrippina II*	*Messalina*, wife of *Claudius*	Assassination (24 January) of *Caligula* Murder of *Caesonia, Caligula's* wife Death of *Nero's* father, Ahenobarbus Marriage (date approximate) of *Agrippina II* to Passienus Crispus
42	Lucius Annaeus Seneca, writer, tutor to *Nero*	JULIA LIVILLA	Deification of *Livia* JULIA LIVILLA, sister of *Agrippina II,* executed, Seneca banished Conquest of Britain begins
48	Gaius Silius "marries" *Messalina* in mock ceremony		*Messalina* executed
49	Pallas, former slave of *Antonia's,* advisor to *Claudius*	*Lollia Paulina*	Marriage (January 1) of *Claudius* and *Agrippina II* Recall of Seneca Death of *Lollia Paulina,* former wife of *Caligula*
50			*Nero* adopted by *Claudius*
51	Burrus, Praetorian Prefect under *Claudius* and *Nero*		*Nero* effectively named heir to throne by *Claudius* Birth (24 October) of *Domitian*
52	Narcissus, freedman advisor to *Claudius*		Draining of the Fucine Lake, Narcissus blamed for chaos Illness of *Claudius*
53		*Octavia* DOMITIA LEPIDA	Marriage of *Nero* and *Octavia,* daughter of *Claudius* and *Messalina* Death of DOMITIA LEPIDA, *Nero's* Aunt Illness of *Claudius*
54	*Nero* (reigned 54–68)	Locusta, accused of helping *Agrippina II* poison *Claudius*	Death (13 October) of *Claudius* Deification of *Claudius* Death of Narcissus
55	BRITANNICUS	Acte, freedwoman	Murder of BRITANNICUS, son of *Claudius* Liaison between *Nero* and Acte Birth (approximate date) of the historian Tacitus
56			Birth (18 September) of *Trajan* (alternatively, in 53)

Dates	Roman emperors, ROYAL MALES, other males	Roman empresses, ROYAL FEMALES, other females	Significant events
59	Anicetus, tutor of Nero, naval commander, instrumental in murder of Agrippina II		Murder (March) of Agrippina II by Nero's troops
60		BOUDICCA	Revolt in Britain, led by BOUDICCA, queen of the Celtic Iceni tribe Birth (approximate date) of Juvenal, satirist
61			Death of BOUDICCA, British rebellion suppressed Birth of Pliny the Younger (alternatively 62)
62	Ofonius Tigellinus, Praetorian Prefect under Nero	Poppaea Sabina	Death of Octavia Marriage of Nero and Poppaea Sabina, his second wife Death of Burrus, replaced by Tigellinus Retirement of Seneca
63			Birth (approximate date) of Plotina, wife of Trajan
64			Great Fire of Rome (July)
65	Paul of Tarsus, Christian evangelist	BERENICE, Jewish queen loved by Titus	Pisonian conspiracy against Nero put down Suicide of Seneca Death of Paul of Tarsus (approximate date)
66	Gnaeus Domitius Corbulo, Nero's foremost general and father of Domitia Longina Petronius, author of Satyricon	Statilia Messalina	Marriage of Nero and Statilia Messalina, his third and final wife Revolt of Annius Vinicianus Death of Corbulo (or in 67) Death of Petronius Beginning of First Jewish Revolt in Judaea
68	Galba (reigns 8 June 68–15 January, 69)		Revolt of Julius Vindex (March) Galba joins revolt Death (9 June) of Nero
69	Otho (reigned 15 January–16 April) Vitellius (reigned 2 January–20 December)	DOMITILLA, wife of Vespasian, died before his accession	Year of the four emperors – civil war rages in the empire T. Flavius Sabinus, Vespasian's brother executed Vespasian's forces take Rome (20 December)

Dates	Roman emperors, ROYAL MALES, other males	Roman empresses, ROYAL FEMALES, other females	Significant events
	Vespasian (reigned 1 July, 69–79) Titus Flavius Sabinus, brother of Vespasian Caius Licinius Mucianus, Vespasian's ally		Birth (approximate date) of the historian Suetonius
70			Domitian represents his father Vespasian in Rome Vespasian enters Rome Marriage of Domitia Longina and Domitian Destruction of Jerusalem by Titus
71			Triumph of Vespasian and his son Titus
73			Fall of Masada, end of Jewish revolt
75			Construction of the Flavian Amphitheater (Colosseum) begins in Rome
76			Birth (24 January) of Hadrian
77	Josephus Pliny the Elder		Jewish writer Josephus publishes his account of the Jewish War (approximate date) Roman writer Pliny the Elder publishes his Natural History
78			Marriage of Trajan and Plotina (approximate date)
79	Titus (reigned 79–81)	Julia Titi (Flavia Julia), daughter of Titus	Death (23 June) of Vespasian Deification of Vespasian Eruption of Vesuvius Death of Pliny the Elder
81	Domitian (reigned 81–96)	Domitia Longina	Death (13 September) of Titus Accession (14 September) of Domitian
83			War against the German Chatti tribe Separation or divorce and reunion of Domitian and Domitia Longina
85			Dacian war begins Birth (approximate date) of Sabina, wife of Hadrian

Dates	Roman emperors, ROYAL MALES, other males	Roman empresses, ROYAL FEMALES, other females	Significant events
86			Birth (19 September) of *Antoninus Pius*
87			Death of *Julia Titi* (approximate date)
89	Saturninus, usurper		Revolt of Saturninus War on the Danube frontier Philosophers banned from Italy
90	Apollonius of Tyana, pagan saint		Death (approximate date) of Apollonius of Tyana
95	TITUS FLAVIUS CLEMENS, cousin of *Domitian* Lucius Aelius Lamia Plautius Aelianus, first husband of *Domitia Longina*	FLAVIA DOMITILLA, niece of *Domitian*	TITUS FLAVIUS CLEMENS executed and FLAVIA DOMITILLA exiled for "atheism" Lucius Aelius Lamia Plautius Aelianus executed
96	*Nerva* (reigned 96–98)		Assassination (18 September) of *Domitian* Accession of *Nerva* *Domitia Longina* (died *c.* 126–140) retains Augusta title
97	Tacitus, historian		Revolt of the Praetorian Guard against *Nerva* Adoption (25 October) of *Trajan* by *Nerva* Consulship of Tacitus, the historian
98	*Trajan* (reigned 98–117)	*Plotina*	Death (28 January) of *Nerva* Accession of *Trajan* Birth (approximate date) of *Faustina I*, wife of *Antoninus Pius*
99			*Trajan* enters Rome as emperor
100	Pliny the Younger, Roman politician and advisor to *Trajan* Juvenal, satirist	*Sabina*	Consulship awarded to Pliny the Younger, who delivers Panegyricus in *Trajan*'s honor Marriage of *Hadrian* and *Sabina* Death (approximate date) of Juvenal, satirist Birth (approximate date) of Marcus Cornelius Fronto, rhetorician and tutor to *Marcus Aurelius*

Dates	Roman emperors, ROYAL MALES, other males	Roman empresses, ROYAL FEMALES, other females	Significant events
101	DECEBALUS, king of Dacia		Trajan's first war with Dacia
102			Trajan returns to Rome (December), celebrates triumph for victories in Dacia
105			Trajan departs Rome (4 June) for his second war with Dacia
106			Death of DECEBALUS, annexation of Dacia
107			Return (June) of Trajan to Rome
108			Hadrian becomes consul for the first time
110			Birth of Antinoos (approximate date)
			Marriage (approximate date) of Faustina I and Antoninus Pius
112		Marciana	Death (29 August) of Marciana, Trajan's sister
113			Dedication of Trajan's Column
			Trajan leaves (autumn) for Parthian war
115			Trajan injured (13 December) by a serious earthquake in Antioch, Syria
116			Trajan enters the Parthian capital of Ctesiphon
117	Hadrian (reigned 117–138)	Sabina	Death (c. 9 August) of Trajan at Selinus
			Accession (12 August) of Hadrian
119		Matidia I MATIDIA II, sister of Sabina	Death of Matidia I, Sabina's mother
121			Hadrian begins first imperial tour
			Birth (26 April) of Marcus Aurelius
122	Suetonius, historian and politician Septicius Clarus, advisor to Hadrian		Construction of Hadrian's Wall begun
			Septicius Clarus and Suetonius banished (approximate date) for disrespect to Sabina
123			Death of Plotina (approximate date)

Dates	Roman emperors, ROYAL MALES, other males	Roman empresses, ROYAL FEMALES, other females	Significant events
125			Work begins on Hadrian's Villa at Tibur
			Birth (approximate date) of Faustina II, wife of Marcus Aurelius
			Birth (approximate date) of Lucius Apuleius, African novelist
126			Birth (1 August) of Pertinax
128		Julia Balbilla	Imperial party in Greece, Julia Balbilla joins Sabina
130	Antinoos, Bithynian boyfriend of Hadrian	PAULINA	Death of PAULINA, sister of Hadrian
			Death of Antinoos in Egypt
132			So-called Second Jewish Revolt begins
135			Second Jewish Revolt suppressed
136	AELIUS CAESAR	Sabina	Death (alternatively 137) of Sabina
			Adoption of AELIUS CAESAR by Hadrian
138	Antoninus Pius (reigned 138–161)	Faustina I	Death (1 January) of AELIUS CAESAR
			Antoninus Pius accepts (25 February) adoption by Hadrian
			Death (10 July) of Hadrian
			Accession of Antoninus Pius
139			Betrothal of Faustina II and Marcus Aurelius
140			Death (approximate date) of Faustina I
			Death (approximate date) of the historian Suetonius
142			Antonine Wall begun in Britain
145			War in Mauretania
			Marriage (spring) of Faustina II and Marcus Aurelius
			Birth (11 April) of Septimius Severus
147			900th anniversary of the founding of Rome
			Birth (30 November) of DOMITIA FAUSTINA, first of the children of Faustina II and Marcus Aurelius

Dates	Roman emperors, ROYAL MALES, other males	Roman empresses, ROYAL FEMALES, other females	Significant events
150			Birth of Cassius Dio, Bithynian historian
152			Rebellion in Egypt
160	Herodes Atticus, sophist from Athens		Herodes Atticus accused of having his wife Annia Regilla murdered Birth (approximate date) of *Julia Domna*
161	*Marcus Aurelius* (reigned 161–180) *Lucius Verus* (co-emperor 161–169)	*Faustina II*	Death (7 March) of *Antoninus Pius* Accession of *Marcus Aurelius* and *Lucius Verus* Betrothal of *Lucius Verus* and *Lucilla*, daughter of *Marcus Aurelius* Birth (31 August) of *Commodus* Flood ravages Rome (autumn) Famine in Italy Parthia invades Armenia, war with Rome begins
162		Panthea, mistress of *Lucius Verus*	*Lucius Verus* travels to Parthia
164		*Lucilla*	Marriage of *Lucilla* and *Lucius Verus* Birth of *Macrinus*
165	Iamblichus, Syrian novelist		*Faustina II* joins her daughter *Lucilla* in the East Iamblichus writes *A Babylonian Story* (very approximate date)
166			Parthia defeated, triumph celebrated (12 October) in Rome Plague spreads in Roman Empire
168			*Marcus Aurelius* and *Lucius Verus* inspect northern defenses
169	Claudius Pompeianus, military advisor to *Marcus Aurelius*		Death (January or February) of *Lucius Verus* Marriage (autumn) of *Lucilla* and Claudius Pompeianus
170	Lucius Apuleius, African novelist		Defeat of Roman expedition, Germans invade empire *Faustina II* gives birth to VIBIA SABINA, the last of her 14 (or 15) children Lucius Apuleius writes *Metamorphoses, or The Golden Ass* (very approximate date)

Dates	Roman emperors, ROYAL MALES, other males	Roman empresses, ROYAL FEMALES, other females	Significant events
172			Birth (approximate date) of Philostratus, philosopher and biographer, associate of *Julia Domna*
174			*Faustina II* awarded the title *Mater Castrorum* Herodes Atticus appears before *Marcus Aurelius* in Sirmium
175	Avidius Cassius, governor of Syria		Revolt in East and death of Avidius Cassius Imperial party leaves (July) Sirmium to tour eastern provinces Death of *Faustina II* at Halala (Faustinopolis)
176	Marcus Cornelius Fronto, Roman rhetorician, tutor of *Marcus Aurelius*		*Marcus Aurelius* and *Commodus* initiated in Eleusinian Mysteries, celebrate triumph in Rome Death of Marcus Cornelius Fronto
177	*Commodus* (reigned 177–192)		*Commodus* made co-emperor
178		*Bruttia Crispina*	Death (approximate date) of Herodes Atticus Marriage of *Commodus* and *Bruttia Crispina* Birth (approximate date) of Herodian, historian
179			Roman armies defeat German tribes
180			Death (17 March) of *Marcus Aurelius* Posting (approximate date) of *Septimius Severus* to Syria
182			Deaths of *Lucilla* and Claudius Pompeianus for plotting against *Commodus*
187			Marriage (approximate date) of *Julia Domna* and *Septimius Severus* Birth (approximate date) of *Julia Mamaea*
188			Birth (4 April) of *Caracalla*
189			Birth (7 March) of *Geta*

Dates	Roman emperors, ROYAL MALES, other males	Roman empresses, ROYAL FEMALES, other females	Significant events
190	Lucian of Samosata, Syrian writer Achilles Tatius, Greek novelist		Death (approximate date) of Lucian of Samosata (born c. 120) Achilles Tatius writes *Leucippe and Clitophon* (very approximate date)
191			*Septimius Severus* made governor of Upper Pannonia Serious fire in Rome (alternatively in 192)
192			Assassination (31 January) of *Commodus*
193	*Pertinax* (reigned 1 January– 28 March, 93) *Didius Julianus* (reigned 28 March–1 June, 93) *Septimius Severus* (reigned 9 April, 193–211)	*Manlia Scantilla*, *Didia Clara*, wife and daughter of *Didius Julianus* *Julia Domna*	Accession and murder of *Pertinax* Auction of the empire by the Praetorian Guard Accession and murder of *Didius Julianus* Pescennius Niger claims throne (April) *Septimius Severus* claims throne (9 April) CLODIUS ALBINUS named Caesar *Septimius Severus* enters Rome
194			Death (by May) of Pescennius Niger
195	CLODIUS ALBINUS		*Julia Domna* awarded title *Mater Castrorum* *Caracalla* named Caesar CLODIUS ALBINUS rebels *Septimius Severus*' first Parthian War
197			Defeat and death (19 February) of CLODIUS ALBINUS
198	*Caracalla* (reigned 198–217)		*Septimius Severus*' second Parthian War, ending in Roman victory and annexations *Caracalla* becomes co-emperor *Geta* named Caesar
199			Imperial family visits Egypt
200	Plautianus, friend and advisor to *Septimius Severus* Longus, Greek novelist	*Plautilla*	Prohibition of gladiatorial combats between women *Julia Domna* eclipsed by Plautianus Betrothal of *Caracalla* and *Plautilla* Longus writes *Daphnis and Chloe* (very approximate date)

Dates	Roman emperors, ROYAL MALES, other males	Roman empresses, ROYAL FEMALES, other females	Significant events
202			Imperial family returns to Rome Marriage of *Plautilla* and *Caracalla*
203	Philostratos, Greek philosoper and biographer Origen, Christian philosopher	Perpetua, Christian martyr	Imperial family visits *Septimius Severus'* home town of Lepcis Magna *Julia Domna* concentrates on studies and discussions with learned men Philostratos commissioned by *Julia Domna* to write *Life of Apollonius of Tyana* Execution of Perpetua for conversion to Christianity *Julia Domna* reportedly meets with Origen (approximate date)
204			Saecular Games celebrated in Rome, *Julia Domna* returning to prominence Death of SEPTIMIUS GETA, brother of *Septimius Severus* Birth (March) of *Elagabalus*
205	Papinian, Syrian jurist		Murder of Plautianus Exile of *Plautilla* Papinian made Praetorian Prefect
208	*Geta* (reigned 210–211)		War in Britain against the Caledonians, entire imperial family goes there Birth of *Diadumenian*, son of *Macrinus* Birth (1 October) of *Severus Alexander*
210			*Geta* named Augustus, giving him equal rank with *Caracalla*
211			Death (4 February) of *Septimius Severus* Accession of *Caracalla* and *Geta* as co-emperors Execution of *Plautilla*
212			Murder (or December, 211) of *Geta* Death of Papinian Constitutio Antoniniana released, making most free males citizens of Rome

Dates	Roman emperors, ROYAL MALES, other males	Roman empresses, ROYAL FEMALES, other females	Significant events
213			War against the German tribes Birth of *Gallienus* (approximate date)
214			Birth (9 September) of *Claudius II Gothicus*
215	Heliodorus, Syrian novelist		*Caracalla* goes to Egypt, conducts massacre there Heliodorus writes *Aethiopica* (very approximate date)
216			*Caracalla* attacks Parthians Baths of Caracalla dedicated
217	*Macrinus* (reigned 217–218) *Diadumenian*, son of *Macrinus*		Murder (8 April) of *Caracalla* Accession (11 April) of *Macrinus* Death of *Julia Domna* *Diadumenian* named Caesar Philostratus publishes *Life of Apollonius of Tyana* (approximate date)
218	*Elagabalus* (reigned 218–222) Gannys, general for *Elagabalus*	*Julia Maesa*, sister of *Julia Domna* *Julia Soaemias*, mother of *Elagabalus*	*Elagabalus* declared emperor by his troops (16 May) *Diadumenian* named Augustus Defeat (8 June) of *Macrinus* near Antioch Accession of *Elagabalus* *Julia Maesa* named Augusta and *Mater Castrorum* Deaths of *Diadumenian* and *Macrinus*
219		*Julia Paula*	*Elagabalus* (early) winters in Nicomedia, Bithynia, on way to Rome, murders Gannys Marriage of *Julia Paula* and *Elagabalus*
220		*Aquilia Severa*	Marriage of *Aquilia Severa* and *Elagabalus*
221		*Annia Faustina*	*Elagabalus* adopts *Severus Alexander* and names him Caesar Marriage of *Annia Faustina* and *Elagabalus*
222	*Severus Alexander* (reigned 222–235)	*Julia Mamaea*	Assassination (11 March) of *Elagabalus* and *Julia Soaemias* Accession (13 March) of *Severus Alexander*

Dates	Roman emperors, ROYAL MALES, other males	Roman empresses, ROYAL FEMALES, other females	Significant events
223	Ulpian, jurist and prefect of the Praetorian Guard		Revolt of Praetorian Guard (alternatively in 228) Ulpian murdered by praetorians Death (between 223 and 226) of *Julia Maesa*
225		*Sallustia Orbiana*	Marriage (alternatively in 226) of *Sallustia Orbiana* and *Severus Alexander* Birth (20 January) of *Gordian III*
226			Parthian Empire overthrown by Sassanid Persians
227	Sallustius Macrinus		Sallustius Macrinus, father of *Sallustia Orbiana*, attempts coup (alternatively in 228), executed *Sallustia Orbiana* exiled
228			Revolt of Roman troops in Mesopotamia
229	Cassius Dio, historian		Consulship of Cassius Dio
230	ARTAXERXES, Persian king		Sassanid Persians under ARTAXERXES (ARDASHIR I) invade Roman territory
231			*Julia Mamaea* and *Severus Alexander* leave Rome to meet the Persian challenge *Julia Mamaea* meets with Origen in Antioch (alternatively in 232)
233			*Julia Mamaea* and *Severus Alexander* celebrate triumph in Rome Germans invade Roman territory
234			German campaign begins
235	*Maximinus I* (reigned 235–238) *Maximus Caesar*, son of *Maximinus I*	*Caecilia Paulina*, wife of *Maximinus I*	Death (21 March) of *Severus Alexander* and *Julia Mamaea* Accession of *Maximinus I* Death of Cassius Dio, Bithynian historian
238	*Gordian I* (reigned in January) *Gordian II* (reigned in January) *Balbinus* (reigned February–May) *Pupienus* (reigned February–May)		Deaths (24 June) of *Maximinus I* and his son, *Maximus* Series of unsuccessful usurpers, culminating in accession of *Gordian III* Herodian, historian, ends his history

261

Dates	Roman emperors, ROYAL MALES, other males	Roman empresses, ROYAL FEMALES, other females	Significant events
	Gordian III (reigned May, 238– February, 244) Herodian, historian		
241	Timesitheus, prefect of Praetorian Guard for *Gordian III* SHAPUR I, king of Persia	*Tranquillina*	Marriage of *Gordian III* and *Tranquillina*, daughter of Timesitheus Invasion of Roman Empire by Persians
243			Death of Timesitheus
244	*Philip I* (reigned 244–249) *Philip II*, son of *Philip I*	*Otacilia Severa*	Death (February) of *Gordian III* Accession of *Philip I*, who buys peace from the Persians
245			Birth (22 December) of *Diocletian*
248			Celebration of the 1,000th anniversary of the founding of Rome
249	*Trajan II Decius* (reigned 249–251)	*Herennia Etruscilla*	Deaths of *Philip I* and *Philip II*
250	*Herennius Etruscus*		*Herennius Etruscus*, son of *Trajan II Decius*, named Caesar Birth (approximate date) of *Helena*, mother of *Constantine I*
251	*Trebonianus Gallus* (reigned 251–253) *Hostilian* *Volusian*		*Herennius Etruscus*, son of *Trajan II Decius*, named co-emperor *Hostilian*, son of *Trajan II Decius*, named Caesar *Trajan II Decius* and *Herennius Etruscus* killed (June) in battle by the Goths Accession of *Trebonianus Gallus* *Hostilian*, son of *Trajan II Decius*, made co-emperor, dies from plague
253	*Aemilian* (reigned August–October) *Valerian I* (reigned 253–260) *Gallienus* (reigned 253–268)	*Cornelia Supera*, presumed wife of *Aemilian* *Egnatia Mariniana*, presumed wife of *Valerian I* *Salonina*, wife of *Gallienus*	Deaths (August) of *Trebonianus Gallus* and *Volusian* Usurpation and death of *Aemilian* Accession (October) of *Valerian I* and his son *Gallienus* as co-emperors

Dates	Roman emperors, ROYAL MALES, other males	Roman empresses, ROYAL FEMALES, other females	Significant events
260	POSTUMUS, governor of Lower Germany, rules breakaway state ODENATHUS, client king of Palmyra Plotinus, philosopher	PIPA (or PIPARA), German princess, mistress of *Gallienus*	Capture (June) of *Valerian I* by the Persians under SHAPUR I Revolt of POSTUMUS in the West ODENATHUS repels Persians *Gallienus* and *Salonina* befriend Plotinus (approximate date), preside over artistic renaissance
267	VABALATHUS, king of Palmyra	ZENOBIA	Assassination of ODENATHUS ZENOBIA, queen and effective ruler of Palmyra, declares independence from Rome and establishes independent state in East
268	*Claudius II Gothicus* (reigned 268–270)		Assassination (September) of *Gallienus*
270	*Quintillus* (reigned for 17 days to 2 months) *Aurelian* (reigned 270–275)	*Severina*, wife of *Aurelian*	*Claudius II Gothicus* dies of plague (August) *Quintillus*, brother of *Claudius II Gothicus*, rules briefly Accession (August) of *Aurelian*
272			Defeat of ZENOBIA and VABALATHUS by *Aurelian* Eastern and western breakaway states returned to empire Birth (27 February) of *Constantine I* (alternatively 273)
274			*Severina* named Augusta
275	*Tacitus* (reigned 275–276)		Assassination (September or October) of *Aurelian* Possible interregnum after death of *Aurelian* Accession of *Tacitus*
276	*Florianus* (reigned July–September) *Probus* (reigned 276–282)		Murder (July) of *Tacitus* Accession and murder of *Florianus* Accession of *Probus*
282	*Carus* (reigned 282–283)		Murder (September) of *Probus*
283	*Carinus* (reigned 283–285) *Numerian* (reigned July/August–November)		*Carus* (July or August) killed by lightning Accession and death of *Numerian* Accession of *Carinus*

Dates	Roman emperors, ROYAL MALES, other males	Roman empresses, ROYAL FEMALES, other females	Significant events
284	Diocletian (reigned 284–305)	Prisca, wife of Diocletian	Accession of Diocletian (20 November) Murder of Numerian
285			Murder of Carinus
286	Maximian (reigned 285–305, 306–308)		Diocletian names Maximian co-emperor for the West Revolt of Carausius in Britain
293		Galeria Valeria Helena	Diocletian appoints Caesars for East (Constantius I) and West (Galerius) Helena, mother of Constantine I, discarded by Constantius I Marriage of Galeria Valeria, daughter of Diocletian, to Galerius
300			Birth of CRISPUS, son of Constantine I
303			Beginning of major persecution of Christians
305	Constantius I (reigned 305–306) Galerius (reigned 305–311)		Abdication of Diocletian and Maximian Accession of Constantius I (West) and Galerius (East)
306	Severus II (reigned 306–307) Maxentius (reigned 306–312)		Death of Constantius I, father of Constantine I Accession of Severus II Rebellion of Maxentius
307	Constantine I ("the Great") (reigned 307–337)	Fausta, second wife of Constantine I	Death of Severus II Maxentius controls Italy and Africa Constantine I becomes western emperor Marriage of Fausta, daughter of Maximian, and Constantine I
308	Licinius I (reigned 308–324)		
310			Death (3 December) of Maximian
311	Maximinus II Daia (reigned 310–313)		Death of Galerius Accession of Maximinus II Daia in East
312			Constantine I defeats (28 October) Maxentius at the Milvian Bridge

264

Dates	Roman emperors, ROYAL MALES, other males	Roman empresses, ROYAL FEMALES, other females	Significant events
313		Constantia	Suicide of Maximinus II Daia Joint rule of Constantine I and Licinius I Marriage of Licinius I and Constantia, half-sister of Constantine I Edict of Mediolanum (Milan) announcing tolerance of Christianity
314			Murder of Prisca and Galeria Valeria
318			Helena named Nobilissima Femina
324	Constantine I		Abdication of Licinius I Sole rule of Constantine I begins
325			Execution of Licinius I
326			Helena named Augusta Execution of Crispus Death of Fausta
330			Death of Helena (approximate date) Dedication of Constantinople
331			Birth (alternatively 332) of Julian II "the Apostate"
337	Constantius II (reigned 337–361)		Death of Constantine I
360	Julian II (reigned 360–363)		Revolt of Julian II against Constantius II Temporary restoration of paganism
361			Death of Contantius II
363	Jovian (reigned 363–364)		Death of Julian II in battle against the Persians
364	Valens (reigned 364–378) Valentinian I (reigned 364–375)		Death of Jovian Accession of Valens in the East Accession of Valentinian I in the West
367	Gratian (reigned 367–383)		Accession of Gratian, shared throne with his father, Valentinian I, and then with his brother, Valentinian II
375	Valentinian II (reigned 375–392)		Death of Valentinian I Accession of Valentinian II and Gratian in West

Dates	Roman emperors, ROYAL MALES, other males	Roman empresses, ROYAL FEMALES, other females	Significant events
378	*Theodosius I* (reigned 379–395)		Catastrophic defeat of eastern emperor *Valens* by Ostrogoths and Visigoths at Hadrianopolis Appointment of *Theodosius I* as eastern emperor by *Gratian*, the western emperor
388			Birth (approximate date) of *Galla Placidia*
391			*Theodosius I* outlaws all religions save official Christianity
395	*Arcadius* (reigned 395–408) *Honorius* (reigned 395–423)	*Eudoxia*, wife of *Arcadius*, mother of *Theodosius II*	Death of *Theodosius I*, leaves the eastern empire to his son *Arcadius*, the western empire to his son *Honorius*
404			Death of *Eudoxia* Ravenna becomes western capital
408	*Theodosius II* (reigned 408–450)	*Eudocia*, wife of *Theodosius II*	Death of *Arcadius* *Theodosius II* becomes eastern emperor
410		*Galla Placidia*, daughter of *Theodosius I*, mother of *Valentinian III*	Sack of Rome by Goths, *Galla Placidia* carried off by them
414		*Pulcheria*, sister of *Theodosius II*	*Eudocia* and *Pulcheria* effective rulers of eastern empire Marriage of *Galla Placidia* to a barbarian king
423	*Johannes* (reigned 423–425)		Death of *Honorius* *Johannes* usurps power in West
425	*Valentinian III* (reigned 425–455)		Death of *Johannes* Accession of *Valentinian III* as western emperor, *Galla Placidia* effective ruler
437			Retirement of *Galla Placidia*
441			*Eudocia* retires to Jerusalem
450	*Marcian* (reigned 450–457)		Death of *Theodosius II* Death of *Galla Placidia* Marriage of *Pulcheria* and *Marcian*
453			Death of *Pulcheria*
455		*Licinia Eudoxia*, wife of *Valentinian III*	Assassination of *Valentinian III*

Dates	Roman emperors, ROYAL MALES, other males	Roman empresses, ROYAL FEMALES, other females	Significant events
462			*Licinia Eudoxia* released by Vandals
476			*Romulus Augustulus*, last puppet emperor of the western empire, deposed by barbarians
1453			Final fall of the eastern empire at the hands of the Ottoman Turks

NUMISMATIC REFERENCES

AC   Y. T. Nercessian, *Armenian Coins and Their Values*, Los Angeles, 1995.

Bellinger   A. Bellinger, *The Syrian Tetradrachms of Caracalla and Macrinus*, New York, 1940.

BMC   Various Authors, *Catalog of Greek Coins in the British Museum*, 29 vols, London, 1873–1927 (reprinted).

BMCRE   H. Mattingly *et al.*, *Coins of the Roman Empire in the British Museum*, London, 1932–1962.

Burgos   A. Burgos, *La Moneda Hispanica desde sus Origenes Hasta el Siglo V*, Vol. 1, Madrid, 1987.

Cohen   H. Cohen, *Description Historique des Monnaies Frappées sous l'Empire Romain*, 8 vols, Paris, 1880–1892 (reprint).

Crawford   M. Crawford, *Roman Republican Coinage*, 2 vols, Cambridge, 1974.

Curtis   Col. J. Curtis, *The Tetradrachms of Roman Egypt*, Chicago, 1957 (reprinted).

Dattari   G. Dattari, *Numi Augg. Alexandrini*, Cairo, 1901 (reprinted).

Demetrio   F. Feuerdant, Collections Giovanni di Demetrio, *Numismatique, Egypte Ancienne*, Paris, 1872.

Dewing   L. Mildenberg and S. Hurter, *The Dewing Collection of Greek Coins*, ACNAC 6, New York, 1985.

Gnecchi   F. Gnecchi, *I Medaglioni Romani*, 3 vols, Milan, 1912 (reprinted).

Göbl   R. Göbl, *Sasanian Numismatics*, Braunschweig, 1971.

Hendin   D. Hendin, *Guide to Biblical Coins*, 3rd edition, New York, 1996.

Hill   P. V. Hill, *The Coinage of Septimius Severus and His Family*, London, 1977.

Howgego   C. J. Howgego, *Greek Imperial Countermarks*, London, 1985.

Jameson   R. Jameson, *Monnaies Grecques Antiques*, 4 vols, Paris, 1913–1932 (reprinted).

Köln   A. Geissen, *Katalog Alexandrinischer Kaisermünzen Köln*, 5 vols, Cologne, 1974–1983.

Lindgren   H. Lindgren, *Ancient Greek Bronze Coins*, Quarryville, 1993.

Lindgren and Kovacs H. Lindgren and F. Kovacs, *Ancient Bronze Coinage of Asia Minor and the Levant*, San Mateo, 1985.

MACW	M. Mitchiner, *Oriental Coins and Their Values: The Ancient and Classical World*, London, 1978.
Mazard	J. Mazard, *Corpus Nummorum Numidiae Mauretaniaeque*, Paris, 1955–1958.
Milne	J. G. Milne, *Catalogue of Alexandrian Coins in the Ashmolean Museum*, Oxford, 1927 (reprinted).
Mionnet	T. Mionnet, *Description des Médailles Antiques, Grecques et Romaines*, 7+9 vols, Paris, 1806–1837 (reprinted).
Pick	B. Pick and K. Regling, Die Antiken Münzen von Dacien und Moesien, *AMNG* vol. 2, Berlin, 1912.
Price and Trell	M. J. Price and B. Trell, *Coins and Their Cities*, London, 1977.
Prieur	M. Prieur, *A Type Corpus of the Syro-Phoenician Tetradrachms and Their Fractions from 57 BC to AD 253*, Lancaster, 2000.
RIC	H. Mattingly *et al.*, *The Roman Imperial Coinage*, 10 vols, London, 1923–1994.
RPC	A. Burnett, M. Amandry, and P. Ripollès, *Roman Provincial Coinage*, Vol. 1, London and Paris, 1992.
RSC	D. Sear *et al.*, *Roman Silver Coins*, 5 vols, London, 1978–1987.
Sear	D. Sear, *The History and Coinage of the Roman Imperators, 49–27 BC*, London, 1998.
SNG ANS	*Sylloge Nummorum Graecorum*, American Numismatic Society, New York, 1969–.
SNG Copenhagen	*Sylloge Nummorum Graecorum*, Danish National Museum, Copenhagen, 1942– (reprinted).
SNG Levante	*Sylloge Nummorum Graecorum*, Switzerland: East Levante–Cilicia, Bern 1986.
SNG Lloyd	*Sylloge Nummorum Graecorum*, Lloyd Collection. London, 1933–1937.
SNG Lockett	*Sylloge Nummorum Graecorum*, Lockett Collection, London, 1938–1949.
SNG von Aulock	*Sylloge Nummorum Graecorum*, Sammlung Hans von Aulock, Berlin, 1957–1968 (reprinted).
Svoronos	J. Svoronos, *Ta Nomismata tou Kratous ton Ptolemaion*, Athens, 1904–1908.
Sydenham	E. Sydenham, *The Coinage of Caesarea in Cappadocia*, London, 1933 (reprinted and revised).
Sydenham	E. Sydenham, *The Coinage of the Roman Republic*, London, 1952 (reprinted).
Thompson	M. Thompson, The Mints of Lysimachos, in *Essays Robinson*, pp. 163–182, Oxford, 1968.
Turner	P. J. Turner, *Roman Coins from India*, Royal Numismatic Society Special Publication 22, London, 1989.
Waddington	W. Waddington, W. Babelon, and T. Reinach, *Recueil Général des Monnaies Grecques d' Asie Mineure*, Paris, 1904–1925.
Wruck	W. Wruck, *Die Syrische Provinzialprägung von Augustus bis Traian*, Stuttgart, 1931.
Youroukova	Y. Youroukova, *The Coins of the Ancient Thracians*, Oxford, 1976.

NOTES

INTRODUCTION

1 Lefkowitz and Fant, pp. 115–116.
2 Ibid., p. 112.
3 Harl, p. 117; Grant, *History of Rome*, p. 247.
4 Kleiner *et al.*, *I Claudia*, p. 28; Kleiner *et al.*, *I Claudia II*, p. 4; Fantham *et al.*, pp. 376–382.
5 Livy, *History of Rome*, 34.1; Lefkowitz and Fant, p. 143.
6 Appian, *Civil Wars*, 4.32–4; Valerius Maximus, 8.3.3; Lefkowitz and Fant, pp. 149–151.
7 Balsdon, *Roman Women*, p. 272.
8 Kleiner *et al.*, *I Claudia*, p. 30.

1 LIVIA: FIRST LADY OF THE EMPIRE

1 Graves, *I Claudius*.
2 Dio, 48.44.1.
3 Tacitus, *Annals*, 5.1.
4 Dio, 47.15.3–4.
5 Suetonius, *Tiberius*, 6.
6 Ibid.
7 Barrett, *Livia*, p. 21.
8 Suetonius, *Claudius*, 1; Dio, 48.34.3.
9 Hanfmann, pp. 91–92.
10 Ovid, *Ex Ponto*, 3.1.117.
11 Barrett, *Caligula*, p. 2.
12 Suetonius, *Augustus*, 84.
13 Barrett, *Livia*, p. 130.
14 Dio, 48.34.3; Suetonius, *Augustus*, 63.
15 Dio, 48.44; Suetonius, *Tiberius*, 4; Tacitus, *Annals*, 5.1.
16 Suetonius, *Augustus*, 79.
17 Ibid., 53, 74, 83, 87.
18 Orator and writer (ibid., 85, 86); gambling (ibid., 19); dinner parties (ibid., 20); light drinker (ibid., 77).
19 Fishing (ibid., 22); coins (ibid., 23); fossils (ibid., 72; Mayo, pp. 142–144).
20 Galinsky, p. 146; see Barrett, *Livia*, p. 309 for a discussion of the possibility that Livia was born in 59 BC rather than 58.
21 Dio, 48.44.3.
22 Ibid., 48.44.3–4.

23 Ibid., 48.44.5.
24 Suetonius, *Claudius*, 1; never claimed paternity (*Gaius*, 23); date of conception (Barrett, *Livia*, p. 27).
25 Suetonius, *Augustus*, 63.
26 Dio, 48.44.4.
27 Suetonius, *Tiberius*, 4; Balsdon, *Roman Women*, p. 71.
28 Grant, *The Twelve Caesars*, pp. 56, 71.
29 Ibid., p. 61; Grant, *History of Rome*, p. 256; Scarre, p. 25; Shuckburgh, p. 191.
30 City of marble (Dio, 56.30.3; Suetonius, *Augustus*, 28); Livia and Agrippa (Kleiner *et al.*, *I Claudia*, p. 30; Wright, *Marcus Agrippa*, pp. 128f.).
31 Galinsky, pp. 128–140, 369.
32 Fantham *et al.*, p. 304; Balsdon, *Roman Women*, p. 75.
33 Fantham *et al.*, p. 299.
34 Ibid., pp. 307–313; Balsdon, *Roman Women*, pp. 75–79.
35 Fantham *et al.*, pp. 302–366; Balsdon, *Roman Women*, pp. 77–78.
36 Balsdon, *Roman Women*, pp. 76, 202.
37 Galinsky, p. 130; Balsdon, *Roman Women*, pp. 71–77, 185, 208.
38 Suetonius, *Augustus*, 73.
39 Dio, 55.12.6; Balsdon, *Roman Women*, pp. 92–93; Kleiner *et al.*, *I Claudia*, pp. 29–35; Scarre, p. 19; Hanfmann, p. 226; Lanciani, pp. 138–144.
40 Lanciani, p. 140.
41 Augustus may have had as many as four wives: Servilia, Claudia, Scribonia, and Livia, but marriage to the first two women is uncertain. Womanizing (Suetonius, *Augustus*, 69, 71; Dio, 54.19.3).
42 Suetonius, *Augustus*, 71; Dio, 58.2.5.
43 Suetonius, *Augustus*, 71.
44 Ibid., 62.
45 Barrett, *Livia*, p. 120.
46 Coins, gems, statues (Spaeth, pp. 23, 169–173); temple (Tacitus, *Annals*, 2.49).
47 Venus (Kleiner, *Roman Sculpture*, p. 77); Cybele (Roller, p. 313; Turcan, p. 43).
48 Kleiner *et al.*, *I Claudia*, p. 37.
49 Dio, 49.38.1–2; Kleiner *et al.*, *I Claudia*, p. 28.
50 Kleiner *et al.*, *I Claudia*, p. 28.
51 Ibid., p. 33.
52 Barrett, *Livia*, pp. 35–38.
53 Ibid., p. 37.
54 Ibid., p. 106.
55 Ibid., p. 38.
56 Ibid., p. 37.
57 Ibid., p. 35.
58 Suetonius, *Augustus*, 80–81.
59 Dio, 53.30.1–3; Balsdon, *Roman Women*, p. 91.
60 Suetonius, *Augustus*, 63–65.
61 Suetonius, *Tiberius*, 7.
62 Literature and art (Macrobius, *Saturnalia*, 2.5.2); lifestyle (Suetonius, *Augustus*, 65–66).
63 Macrobius, *Saturnalia*, 2.5.8.
64 Ibid., 2.5.6.
65 Suetonius, *Augustus*, 65.
66 Macrobius, *Saturnalia*, 2.5.7.
67 Suetonius, *Augustus*, 65.
68 Dio, 55.10.12; Seneca, *On Benefits*, 6.32.1.
69 Tacitus, *Annals*, 62; Suetonius, *Augustus*, 65.

70 Dio, 55.10.14; Suetonius, *Augustus*, 65.
71 Dio, 57.18.1; Tacitus, *Annals*, 53.
72 Galinsky, p. 29.
73 See Grant and Mulas.
74 Barrett, *Livia*, p. 139.
75 Dio, 55.1–2.
76 Livy, *Epitome*, 140; Levick, *Claudius*, pp. 11–12.
77 Dio, 55.2.5.
78 Seneca, *To Marcia on Consolation*, 3.1–2.
79 Tacitus, *Annals*, 1.33; Suetonius, *Tiberius*, 50.
80 "Ovid," *Consolatia ad Liviam*, 1–12 (once attributed to Ovid, true author unknown).
81 Seneca, *To Marcia on Consolation*, 4.1.2.
82 Barrett, *Livia*, p. 108.
83 Seneca, *To Marcia on Consolation*, 3.2.
84 Suetonius, *Tiberius*, 16.
85 Ibid., 12–14.
86 Suetonius, *Julius Caesar*, 84–88.
87 Ibid., 85; Lanciani, pp. 267–268.
88 Grant, *The Twelve Caesars*, p. 55.
89 Kiefer, p. 111.
90 Lyttleton and Forman, pp. 84–85.
91 Ibid., p. 77.
92 Return from exile (Suetonius, *Tiberius*, 13); adoption (ibid., 21).
93 Marcellus (Dio, 53.33.4); Gaius and Lucius (Dio, 55.10.10); Agrippa Postumus (Tacitus, *Annals*, 1.3, 1.6; Dio, 57.3.6; Suetonius, *Tiberius*, 22).
94 Tacitus, *Annals*, 2.77.
95 Dio, 55.22.2, 56.30.2; Tacitus, *Annals*, 5.1.1.
96 Suetonius, *Gaius*, 23.
97 Levick, *Tiberius*, pp. 271f.; Balsdon, *Roman Women*, pp. 90f.
98 Tacitus, *Annals*, 5.10.
99 Hopkins, "Probable Age Structure," pp. 245–264; Hopkins, "Death and Renewal."
100 Lyttleton and Forman, pp. 96, 98.
101 Dio, 53.33.4–5.
102 Seneca, *On Mercy*, 1.9.6.
103 Dio, VI, 55.16.5, 19.3, 19.5, 20.2.
104 Ibid., 55.14–22.
105 Vellius Paterculus, 2.130.
106 Balsdon, *Roman Women*, pp. 93, 270, 276.
107 Kokkinos, p. 72, note 12, p. 198, note 11; Balsdon, *Roman Women*, p. 93.
108 Dio, 55.8.2.
109 Kleiner *et al.*, *I Claudia*, pp. 28–34.
110 Dio, 58.2.3.
111 Barrett, *Livia*, pp. 143f.
112 Plutarch, *Numa*, 10; Fantham *et al.*, pp. 234–237.
113 Tacitus, *Annals*, 4.16.4.
114 Dio, 58.2.4.
115 Valerius Maximus, 6.1 pref.
116 Vellius Paterculus, 2.130.
117 Kleiner, *Roman Sculpture*, p. 76.
118 Ovid, *Ex Ponto*, 3.1.142.
119 Barrett, *Livia*, p. 105.

120 Ibid., p. 107.
121 Seneca, *To Marcia on Consolation*, 4.3.
122 Ibid., 4.4.
123 Tacitus, *Annals*, 5.1.
124 Balsdon, *Roman Women*, p. 91.
125 Julia the Younger (Tacitus, *Annals*, 4.71); Julia the Elder (Barrett, *Livia*, p. 51).
126 Suetonius, *Gaius*, 7.
127 Suetonius, *Claudius*, 3.
128 Tacitus, *Annals*, 2.34.
129 Ibid., 3.15.3.
130 Kokkinos, pp. 16, 148.
131 Suetonius, *Augustus*, 99.
132 Ibid., 100.
133 Dio, 56.42.2–4.
134 Ibid., 56.46.5.
135 Tacitus, *Annals*, 1.11; Suetonius, *Augustus*, 100.
136 Dio, 56.46.2–5.
137 Ibid.; Suetonius, *Augustus*, 100.
138 Dio, 56.32.1; Tacitus, *Annals*, 1.8; Suetonius, *Augustus*, 101.
139 Suetonius, *Tiberius*, 51; Dio, 57.12.6.
140 Dio, 57.12.
141 Tacitus, *Annals*, 1.14; Dio, 57.12.
142 Tacitus, *Annals*, 1.14.
143 Suetonius, *Tiberius*, 50–51.
144 Ibid., 50; Dio, 57.16.2.
145 Dio, 57.12.4, 58.2.3.
146 RIC I 23.
147 Kleiner *et al.*, *I Claudia*, pp. 59–60.
148 Tacitus, *Annals*, 3.71.
149 Ibid., 3.64.
150 Kleiner *et al.*, *I Claudia*, p. 35.
151 Ibid.; Kleiner, *Roman Sculpture*, pp. 63–66; Hanfmann, pp. 80, 160; Strong, p. 86.
152 Kleiner *et al.*, *I Claudia*, p. 31.
153 Barrett, *Livia*, p. 113.
154 Ibid.
155 Ibid., p. 29.
156 Ibid., p. 110.
157 Ibid., p. 109.
158 Pliny the Elder, *Natural History*, 7.16.75.
159 Exceptions to the rule (Kleiner *et al.*, *I Claudia II*, pp. 131–132).
160 Tacitus, *Annals*, 5.1; Dio, 58.2.1.
161 Dio, 58.2.2.
162 Ibid., 58.2.3.
163 Ibid., 58.2.6.
164 Suetonius, *Tiberius*, 51; Dio, 58.2.3; Tacitus, *Annals*, 5.2.
165 Reinstatement (Suetonius, *Gaius*, 16.3; Dio, 59.2.4); funeral oration (Tacitus, *Annals*, 6.1).
166 Dio, 60.5.2–3.
167 Ibid., 60.5.3.
168 Kleiner *et al.*, *I Claudia*, p. 37.
169 Dio, 49.38.1–2; Kleiner *et al.*, *I Claudia*, pp. 28, 37.
170 Grant, *The Twelve Caesars*, p. 61.

2 ANTONIA: "SUPREME IN BEAUTY AND MIND"

1 Plutarch, *Antony*, 31.4; Suetonius, *Augustus*, 61.
2 Plutarch, *Antony*, 31.2–3.
3 Huzar, p. 142.
4 Giacosa, p. 107, No. II.
5 Plutarch, *Antony*, 1.3–4, 3.4–6, 4.1–4; Huzar, p. 23.
6 Courage, affability, and generosity (Plutarch, *Antony*, 8, 23.1, 51.2); arts (Grant, *Cleopatra*, pp. 112–114; Plutarch, *Antony*, 1.4–5, 23.2–3; Huzar, pp. 253–257).
7 Plutarch, *Antony*, 5.2–4, 57.1; Huzar, pp. 63f.
8 Huzar, p. 82; Plutarch, *Antony*, 14.1–2.
9 Plutarch, *Antony*, 53–54.
10 Dio, 50.3.2, 50.26.1–3.
11 Balsdon, *Roman Women*, pp. 71, 201.
12 Ibid., p. 71.
13 Education (Livy, 34.2.11–34.3.2).
14 Kokkinos, p. 11.
15 Valerius Maximus, 4.3.3.
16 Tacitus, *Annals*, 1.3; Suetonius, *Augustus*, 63; Dio, 53.30–31.
17 Seneca, *To Marcia on Consolation*, 2.3–4.
18 Shuckburgh, p. 162.
19 Crinagoras, 9.239; Kokkinos, p. 119.
20 Plutarch, *Antony*, 87.3; Josephus, *Antiquities of the Jews*, 18.6.6.
21 Pliny the Elder, *Natural History*, 7.80; Valerius Maximus, 4.3.3.
22 Kleiner *et al.*, *I Claudia II*, p. 134, the Nomentum portrait, Museo Nazionale Romano 125713.
23 Levick, *Claudius*, p.12; Kokkinos, p. 33.
24 Valerius Maximus, 4.3.3.
25 Crinagoras, 6.345, cf. 9.239.
26 Suetonius, *Claudius*, 1.6.
27 Ibid., 2.
28 Ibid., 1.
29 Ibid.
30 Suetonius, *Claudius*, 1; Dio, 54.32.2.
31 Suetonius, *Claudius*, 1; Tacitus, *Annals*, 1.33.
32 Suetonius, *Claudius*, 1.
33 Suetonius, *Tiberius*, 50.
34 Suetonius, *Claudius*, 1.
35 Ibid.; Dio 55.5.2.
36 Suetonius, *Claudius*, 2.
37 Livy, *Epitome*, 140.
38 Valerius Maximus, 5.5.3; Pliny the Elder, *Natural History*, 7.84.
39 Suetonius, *Tiberius*, 7.3.
40 Campus Martius (Suetonius, *Claudius*, 1); interment (Dio, 55.2.3; Suetonius, *Claudius*, 1).
41 Dio, 55.1.3–5.
42 Griffin, p. 145.
43 Dio, 57.18.9; Tacitus, *Annals*, 2.69.
44 Tiberius (Dio 55.2.2); Augustus (Livy, *Epitome*, 140).
45 Suetonius, *Claudius*, 1.
46 "Ovid," *Consolatia ad Liviam*, 299–342; Kokkinos, p. 15.
47 Josephus, *Antiquities of the Jews*, 18.6.6; Valerius Maximus, 4.3.3.
48 Kokkinos, p. 16; Valerius Maximus, 4.3.3.

49 Kokkinos, p. 164.
50 Dio, 51.13.7.
51 Levick, *Claudius*, p. 12; Kokkinos, p. 11.
52 Kokkinos, pp. 11, 71f., 84.
53 Pliny the Elder, *Natural History*, 9.172.
54 Barrett, *Agrippina*, p. 186.
55 Ibid.
56 Tacitus, *Annals*, 1.
57 Ibid., 4.3.
58 Ibid., 2.84; RIC I (Tiberius) 28.
59 Suetonius, *Claudius*, 30–31.
60 Ibid., 3.
61 Ibid.
62 Levick, *Claudius*, p. 19.
63 Alexandria (Barrett, *Caligula*, p. 24); Palestine (Griffin, p. 213); Mauretania (Barrett, *Caligula*, p. 24).
64 Levick, *Claudius*, p. 165; Kokkinos, p. 25.
65 Ferrill, p.154.
66 Kokkinos, p. 25.
67 Tacitus, *Annals*, 11.1.
68 Suetonius, *Vitellius*, 2.
69 Kokkinos, pp. 17, 43–45.
70 Tacitus, *Annals*, 2.53.
71 Griffin, p. 214; Barrett, *Caligula*, p. 13.
72 Kokkinos, pp. 18, 20.
73 Tacitus, *Annals*, 2.69; Suetonius, *Gaius*, 1.
74 Suetonius, *Gaius*, 2.
75 Tacitus, *Annals*, 3.2.
76 Friendly terms (Josephus, *Antiquities of the Jews*, 18.6.6).
77 Tacitus, *Annals*, 3.3.
78 Kokkinos, pp. 24, 38, 39.
79 Tacitus, *Annals*, 4–5.
80 Barrett, *Agrippina*, pp. 38–39.
81 Suetonius, *Gaius*, 10.
82 Tacitus, *Annals*, 6.39.
83 Josephus, *Antiquities of the Jews*, 18.6.6.
84 Tacitus, *Annals*, 4.2.
85 Caenis (Dio, 65.14.1–5); Pallas (Josephus, *Antiquities of the Jews*, 18.6.6).
86 Dio, 58.9–10.
87 Josephus, *Antiquities of the Jews*, 18.6.6.
88 Caenis (Suetonius, *Vespasian*, 3).
89 Suetonius, *Tiberius*, 62; Tacitus, *Annals*, 4; Dio, 57.22.2.
90 Dio, 58.11.6–7.
91 Kokkinos, pp. 25, 164.
92 Dio, 58.11.7.
93 Veyne, pp. 27–29.
94 Barrett, *Caligula*, p. 36; Josephus, *Antiquities of the Jews*, 18.6.1.
95 Josephus, *Antiquities of the Jews*, 18.6.1.
96 Ibid., 18.6.4.
97 Ibid., 18.6.6–7.
98 Barrett, *Caligula*, pp. 221–222.
99 Suetonius, *Gaius*, 15.
100 Suetonius, *Claudius*, 11; Dio 59.3.4.

101 Dio, 59.3.4.
102 Suetonius, *Gaius*, 23.
103 Ibid.
104 Ibid., 29.
105 Barrett, *Caligula*, p. 24.
106 Suetonius, *Gaius*, 24; Barrett, *Agrippina*, p. 54.
107 Kokkinos, p. 28.
108 Ibid., p. 37; Barrett, *Caligula*, p. 62.
109 Kokkinos, p. 28; Barrett, *Caligula*, p. 219.
110 Suetonius, *Claudius*, 1; Barrett, *Caligula*, p. 203.
111 Kokkinos, p. 28.
112 Dio, 60.5.1–2.
113 Suetonius, *Claudius*, 11.
114 Spaeth, p. 30; BMCRE 109, 111 (Claudius).
115 Kokkinos, pp. 116–120.
116 Suetonius, *Claudius*, 1.
117 Kokkinos, pp. 31, 57, 146, 161.

3 AGRIPPINA THE ELDER: HEROINE OF THE RHINE BRIDGE

1 Suetonius, *Augustus*, 65.
2 Tacitus, *Annals*, 1.33.
3 Ibid.: 4.52 (fierce); 2.71 (harsh); 4.12 (arrogant); 6.25 (power hungry).
4 Suetonius, *Augustus*, 86.
5 Tacitus, *Annals*, 4.52.
6 Ibid., 6.25.
7 Dio, 54.28–30; Seneca, *Epistulae Morales*, 14.46.
8 Suetonius, *Augustus*, 29, 42.
9 Dio, 54.29.4.
10 Suetonius, *Gaius*, 7; Suetonius, *Augustus*, 64; Tacitus, *Annals*, 1.32.
11 Dio, 57.18.6–8.
12 Comedies (Suetonius, *Claudius*, 11; Suetonius, *Gaius*, 3); law (Dio, 56.24.7; 26.1).
13 Josephus, *Antiquities of the Jews*, 18.6.8.
14 Mazzolani, p. 184.
15 Tacitus, *Annals*, 1.35, 2.24.
16 Suetonius, *Gaius*, 7.
17 Barrett, *Caligula*, p. 6.
18 Suetonius, *Augustus*, 34.
19 Ibid., 23; Dio, 56.19–23.
20 Tacitus, *Annals*, 1.3.
21 Dio, 56.23.1–4, 57.5.4.
22 Suetonius, *Gaius*, 8.4.
23 Tacitus, *Annals*, 1.41.
24 Suetonius, *Tiberius*, 15; Suetonius, *Gaius*, 1; Dio, 55.13.3.
25 Tacitus, *Annals*, 1.30–2.36.
26 Ibid., 1.34.
27 Ibid., 1.31–32.
28 Ibid., 1.34–35.
29 Ibid., 1.35.
30 Suetonius, *Tiberius*, 25; Suetonius, *Gaius*, 1; Dio, 57.5.1–2.
31 Tacitus, *Annals*, 1.35; Dio, 57.5.
32 Tacitus, *Annals*, 1.35–36.

33 Dio, 57.5.3.
34 Tacitus, *Annals*, 1.37.
35 Ibid., 1.39.
36 Ibid., 1.40.
37 Ibid., 1.41.
38 Dio, 57.5.5–7.
39 Suetonius, *Gaius*, 48.
40 Ibid., 1; Tacitus, *Annals*, 1.49.
41 Tacitus, *Annals*, 1.50–51.
42 Agrippa Postumus (ibid., 1.53; Dio, 57.18.1a); Julia (Dio, 57.3.5–6).
43 Tacitus, *Annals*, 1.60.
44 Ibid., 1.60–62.
45 Ibid., 1.64–68.
46 Ibid., 1.69.
47 Barrett, *Agrippina*, p. 27.
48 Tacitus, *Annals*, 1.69.
49 Ibid.
50 Ibid.
51 Ibid., 1.14, 1.44; Barrett, *Agrippina*, p. 231.
52 Tacitus, *Annals*, 1.69.
53 Ibid., 2.24.
54 Ibid., 2.25, 2.41; Dio, 57.18.1, 60.8.7.
55 Barrett, *Agrippina*, pp. 26–27.
56 Tacitus, *Annals*, 2.43.
57 Ibid., 1.33, 2.43.
58 Ibid., 2.41–42.
59 Ibid., 2.41.
60 Ibid., 2.47.
61 Ibid., 1.42; Suetonius, *Gaius*, 1.
62 Antonia (Kokkinos, pp. 17, 43–45); places visited (Tacitus, *Annals*, 2.55).
63 Griffin, p. 214; Barrett, *Caligula*, p. 13.
64 Dio, 53.32.1; Suetonius, *Augustus*, 66.
65 Tacitus, *Annals*, 2.55.
66 Ibid., 2.43; Seneca, *On Anger*, 1.18.3.
67 Tacitus, *Annals*, 2.57.
68 Ibid., 2.55.
69 Ibid.
70 Ibid., 2.59–60.
71 Ibid., 2.59.
72 Ibid.
73 Suetonius, *Tiberius*, 52.
74 Tacitus, *Annals*, 2.59.
75 Ibid., 2.59–60.
76 Ibid., 2.59; Suetonius, *Tiberius*, 52.
77 Tacitus, *Annals*, 2.69.
78 Renunciation of friendship (Suetonius, *Gaius*, 3); orders to Piso (Tacitus, *Annals*, 2.70).
79 Tacitus, *Annals*, 2.70.
80 Harsh manner (Barrett, *Agrippina*, p. 30).
81 Tacitus, *Annals*, 2.72.
82 Suetonius, *Gaius*, 1; Dio, 57.18.9; Tacitus, *Annals*, 2.73; Dio, 57.18.9.
83 Tacitus, *Annals*, 2.69.
84 Suetonius, *Gaius*, 5.

85 Tacitus, *Annals*, 2.82; Josephus, *Antiquities of the Jews*, 18.6.8.
86 Suetonius, *Tiberius*, 52; Suetonius, *Gaius*, 2; Dio, 57.18.6.
87 Tacitus, *Annals*, 2.75.
88 Ibid., 3.1.
89 Ibid.
90 Ibid.
91 Ibid., 3.2.
92 Ibid., 3.4.
93 Ibid., 3.6–7.
94 Ibid., 3.10–18.
95 Ibid., 3.16; Suetonius, *Tiberius*, 52.
96 Tacitus, *Annals*, 3.17.
97 Ibid., 4.12.
98 Ibid., 1.69, 4.12.
99 Ibid., 4.12.
100 Ibid., 4.17.
101 Ibid., 4.19.
102 Ibid., 4.52.
103 Ibid.
104 Ibid.
105 Ibid.; Suetonius, *Tiberius*, 53.
106 Tacitus, *Annals*, 4.52.
107 Ibid., 4.53.
108 Suetonius, *Tiberius*, 53.
109 Ibid., 51.1.
110 Tacitus, *Annals*, 4.54.
111 Ibid., 4.60.5–6.
112 Ibid., 4.71.
113 Ibid., 5.3.
114 Ibid., 5.4.
115 Suetonius, *Tiberius*, 53.
116 Ibid., 64.
117 Ibid., 53.
118 Tacitus, *Annals*, 6.25.
119 Ibid., 6.23.
120 Ibid., 6.25.
121 Augustus on Gallus (ibid., 1.13); Gallus and Tiberius (ibid., 1.12, 2.36; Dio, 58.3).
122 Vipsania, the mother of Drusus the Younger, was restored to the Julio-Claudian clan after her death in AD 20 and was honored with statues and inscriptions and possibly even with her portraits on coins issued in Drusus' name (RIC I 43 (Tiberius)). See Burns, "Vipsania on Roman Coins?".
123 Gallus and Sosia (Tacitus, *Annals*, 4.20); Gallus and Piso (ibid., 3.11).
124 Gallus and Sejanus (Dio, 58.3.1; Gallus *re* Agrippina (Tacitus, *Annals*, 4.70).
125 Tacitus, *Annals*, 6.25.
126 Ibid., 1–6.
127 Suetonius, *Tiberius*, 56–68.
128 Dio, 57.1.1–4.
129 Eutropius, 7.11.
130 Julian, *The Caesars*, 310.
131 Grant, *Roman Emperors*, pp. 16–24; Levick, *Tiberius*, pp. 121, 127–128.
132 Suetonius, *Tiberius*, 54.
133 Suetonius, *Gaius*, 15; Dio, 59.3.5; Kokkinos, p. 29.

134 Suetonius, *Gaius*, 15; RIC (Caligula) 42.
135 Dio, 59.3.6, 4.3.
136 Kleiner, *Roman Sculpture*, p. 152, fig. 127, Kunsthistorisches Museum, Vienna.
137 RIC (Titus) 231.

4 AGRIPPINA THE YOUNGER: SISTER OF CALIGULA, MOTHER OF NERO

 1 Suetonius, *Gaius*, 24.
 2 Dio, 59.3.4.
 3 Suetonius, *Gaius*, 15; Dio, 59.3.4, 59.9.2.
 4 RIC (Caligula) 26.
 5 Tacitus, *Annals*, 6.15.
 6 Ibid., 4.73; Suetonius, *Nero*, 5.
 7 Marriage (Tacitus, *Annals*, 4.75); consulship (Dio, 58.20.1).
 8 Suetonius, *Nero*, 5.
 9 Ibid.
10 Ibid.
11 Tacitus, *Annals*, 12.7.
12 Dio, 61.31.5–6.
13 Pliny the Elder, *Natural History*, 7.71; Barrett, *Agrippina*, p. 41.
14 Tacitus, *Annals*, 12.7.
15 RIC (Caligula), 26.
16 Dio, 59.9.4–7; Suetonius, *Gaius*, 13–18.
17 Suetonius, *Gaius*, 15.
18 Ibid.; RIC (Caligula), 42, 43, 47.
19 Philo, 11, 14; Grant, *The Twelve Caesars*, p. 124; Suetonius, *Gaius*, 14.2; Dio, 59.8.1–2; Barrett, *Caligula*, pp.73ff.
20 Dio, 59.2.6; Suetonius, *Gaius*, 37.
21 Suetonius, *Gaius*, 37, 52, 55; Seneca, *On Firmness*, 18.3.
22 Suetonius, *Gaius*, 25; Dio, 59.3.3.
23 Suetonius, *Gaius*, 27, 28, 30, 49; Seneca, *On Anger*, 33.1–4; Josephus, *Antiquities of the Jews*, 19.2.4.
24 Gemellus (Suetonius, *Gaius*, 23; Dio, 59.8).
25 Seneca, *On Firmness*, 18.1–6.
26 Suetonius, *Gaius*, 29.
27 Entertainments (ibid., 18–19); gods and goddesses (ibid., 52; Dio, 59.26.6).
28 Dio, 59.10.1; Suetonius, *Gaius*, 18.
29 Suetonius, *Gaius*, 54.
30 Ibid., 55.
31 Ibid., 24.
32 Suetonius, *Nero*, 34; Tacitus, *Annals*, 12.7; Barrett, *Agrippina*, p. 41.
33 Suetonius, *Gaius*, 24.
34 Adultery (Tacitus, *Annals*, 14.2.4; Suetonius, *Gaius*, 24; Dio, 59.2.6–8, 59.22.6); banishment (Dio, 59.22.8).
35 Dio, 59.22.8; Barrett, *Agrippina*, p. 67.
36 Suetonius, *Nero*, 6.
37 Suetonius, *Gaius*, 29.2.
38 Ibid., 58; Dio, 59.29.
39 Josephus, *Antiquities of the Jews*, 19.2.4; Suetonius, *Gaius*, 59.
40 Suetonius, *Claudius*, 10; Dio, 60.1.
41 Dio, 60.4.1–2.

42 Burial by Agrippina and Julia Livilla (Suetonius, *Gaius*, 59); mausoleum of Augustus (Barrett, *Caligula*, p. 167).
43 Tacitus, *Annals*, 11.1–2, 12.7; Suetonius, *Claudius*, 26; Dio, 60.14.3–4, 60.18.1–4.
44 Dio, 60.8.5.
45 Ibid.
46 Suetonius, *Claudius*, 29; Dio, 60.8.5.
47 Tacitus, *Annals*, 11.12.
48 Holland, *Nero*, p. 232.
49 Suetonius, *Galba*, 5.
50 Tacitus, *Annals*, 6.20.
51 Barrett, *Agrippina*, p. 85.
52 Seneca, *On Benefits*, 1.15.5.
53 Barrett, *Agrippina*, p. 85.
54 Ibid.
55 Ibid.
56 Juvenal, *Satires*, 4.81, Scholiast.
57 Suetonius, *Nero*, 6; Tacitus, *Annals*, 11.11.
58 Tacitus, *Annals*, 11.12; Suetonius, *Claudius*, 26, 29.
59 Tacitus, *Annals*, 11.26–27; Suetonius, *Claudius*, 29; Dio, 60.31.
60 Suetonius, *Claudius*, 26; Tacitus, *Annals*, 11. 37–38.
61 Suetonius, *Claudius*, 26.
62 Tacitus, *Annals*, 12.1.
63 Ibid., 10.1; Suetonius, *Gaius*, 25.
64 Josephus, *Antiquities of the Jews*, 18.6.6.
65 Tacitus, *Annals*, 12.2.
66 Ibid.
67 Tacitus, *Annals*, 12.6–7; Suetonius, *Claudius*, 26.
68 Tacitus, *Annals*, 12.7; Dio, 60.31.8.
69 Tacitus, *Annals*, 12.8; Suetonius, *Nero*, 7.
70 Tacitus, *Annals*, 12.8; Suetonius, *Nero*, 7.
71 RIC (Claudius), 102, 105–6.
72 Carriage (Tacitus, *Annals*, 12.42; Dio, 60.33.1); jewelry and clothes (Tacitus, *Annals*, 12.56).
73 Tacitus, *Germania*, 28.
74 Dio, 60.33.7.
75 Tacitus, *Annals*, 12.37.
76 Ibid.
77 Ibid., 12.42.
78 Barrett, *Agrippina*, p. 120.
79 Levick, *Claudius*, p. 25.
80 Suetonius, *Claudius*, 32; Tacitus, *Annals*, 12.56–57; Dio, 60.33.3.
81 Tacitus, *Annals*, 12.57; Dio, 60.33.5.
82 Tacitus, *Annals*, 13.1.
83 Ibid., 12.59.
84 Ibid., 12.22.
85 Ibid.
86 Ibid.
87 Dio, 60.32.3–4.
88 Tacitus, *Annals*, 12.64.
89 Ibid., 12.65.
90 Suetonius, *Nero*, 7.
91 Tacitus, *Annals*, 12.64–65.

92 Ibid., 12.64, 12.22.
93 Suetonius, *Claudius*, 30–31.
94 Ibid., 2–4.
95 Ibid., 7.
96 Ibid., 13.
97 Ibid., 29.
98 35 and 221 (Seneca, *Apocolocyntosis*, 13); 35 and 300 (Suetonius, *Claudius*, 29).
99 Barrett, *Agrippina*, p. 105.
100 Tacitus, *Annals*, 12.41.
101 Griffin, pp. 29–30; Levick, *Claudius*, p. 73.
102 Suetonius, *Nero*, 7.
103 Burns, "Was Nero the Natural Son of Claudius?," pp. 6f.
104 Pallas (Tacitus, *Annals*, 12.65); Seneca (Dio, 61.10.1; Tacitus, *Annals*, 13.42); praetorian prefects (Tacitus, *Annals*, 15.50; Dio, 59.23.9); her son, Nero (Suetonius, *Nero*, 28; Tacitus, *Annals*, 14.2).
105 Dio, 59.22.6.
106 Suetonius, *Nero*, 5.
107 Ibid.
108 Ibid., 6.
109 Griffin, p. 20.
110 Suetonius, *Nero*, 6.
111 Ibid.
112 Griffin, p. 23.
113 Suetonius, *Nero*, 6.
114 Tacitus, *Annals*, 11.11.
115 Levick, *Claudius*, pp. 56–58.
116 Suetonius, *Claudius*, 26; Tacitus, *Annals*, 12.3; Dio, 60.31.6, 61.11.3–4.
117 Tacitus, *Annals*, 12.5.
118 Suetonius, *Claudius*, 39.
119 Ibid., 26; Tacitus, *Annals*, 12.7 (Tacitus says it was only one marriage).
120 Suetonius, *Claudius*, 26.
121 Ibid., 39.
122 Tacitus, *Annals*, 12.26.
123 Ibid., 12.3.
124 Ibid., 12.3–4.
125 Suetonius, *Claudius*, 43.
126 Tacitus, *Annals*, 12.66; Dio, 60.34.2.
127 Tacitus, *Annals*, 12.66; Dio, 60.34.2.
128 Tacitus, *Annals*, 12.67.
129 Ibid., 12.68–69; Suetonius, *Claudius*, 45.
130 Dio, 60.35.4.
131 Suetonius, *Nero*, 45; Griffin, p. 32.
132 Levick, *Claudius*, p. 77.
133 Tacitus, *Annals*, 12.69.
134 Levick, *Claudius*, p. 78.
135 Ibid.
136 Ibid., 12.69.
137 Suetonius, *Vespasian*, 9.
138 Dio, 61.3.2.
139 Suetonius, *Nero*, 9.
140 Griffin, p. 39.
141 RIC 9; but see Barrett, *Agrippina*, p. 167.

142 Victor, 5 (p. 7).
143 Suetonius, *Nero*, 39.
144 Barton, pp. 145–146.
145 Ibid., pp. 107–108, 140f.
146 Suetonius, *Nero*, 6.
147 Ibid., 7; Tacitus, *Annals*, 13.2.
148 Seneca, Loeb Vol. I, Basore, Intro. p. x.
149 Seneca, *Epistulae Morales*, 31.11.
150 Ibid., 51.1–2.
151 Ibid., 23.6.
152 Roller, p. 315.
153 Suetonius, *Nero*, 56.
154 Ibid.
155 Ibid., 21; Dio, 62.10.2–3.
156 Dio, 62.6.3–5.
157 Suetonius, *Nero*, 28; Dio, 62.13.1.
158 Dio, 62.13.2; Tacitus, *Annals*, 15.37; Suetonius, *Nero*, 29.
159 Suetonius, *Nero*, 29.
160 Seneca, Loeb Vol. I, pp. 357–447.
161 Suetonius, *Nero*, 52, 53; Tacitus, *Annals*, 13.3, 14.14–16.
162 Athletics (Tacitus, *Annals*, 13.3, 14.14; Dio, 61.6.1–3); philosophy (Tacitus, *Annals*, 14.16).
163 Suetonius, *Nero*, 52.
164 RIC 10; but see Barrett, *Agrippina*, p. 167.
165 Tacitus, *Annals*, 13.5.
166 Ibid.; Dio, 61.3.3–4.
167 Tacitus, *Annals*, 13.12.
168 Dio, 61.7.
169 Tacitus, *Annals*, 14.2.
170 Suetonius, *Nero*, 28; Dio, 62.1.
171 Tacitus, *Annals*, 13.13.
172 Ibid., 13.14.
173 Ibid.; Zonoras, in Dio, Loeb Vol. VIII, p. 49.
174 Tacitus, *Annals*, 13.15–17; Suetonius, *Nero*, 33.
175 Tacitus, *Annals*, 13.18.
176 Loss of bodyguard (Dio, 61.8.5–6); removal from palace (Suetonius, *Nero*, 34).
177 Tacitus, *Annals*, 13.18.
178 Ibid., 13.19.
179 Ibid.
180 Ibid., 13.20.
181 Ibid.
182 Ibid., 13.21.
183 Ibid.
184 Ibid., 13.21–22.
185 Suetonius, *Nero*, 34.
186 Dio, 61.9.
187 Tacitus, *Annals*, 11.2.
188 Ibid., 14.1; Dio, 61.12.1.
189 Tacitus, *Annals*, 14.3.
190 Ibid.; Suetonius, *Nero*, 34.
191 Tacitus, *Annals*, 14.4–5.
192 Ibid., 14.5.
193 Ibid.

194 Ibid.,14.8.
195 Suetonius, *Nero*, 34; Tacitus, *Annals*, 14.7.
196 Tacitus, *Annals*, 14.8.
197 Ibid., 14.8–9; Dio, 61.12–13.
198 Suetonius, *Nero*, 34; Tacitus, *Annals*, 14.9; Dio, 61.14.2–3.
199 Tacitus, *Annals*, 14.9.
200 Barrett, *Agrippina*, p. xx.
201 Suetonius, *Nero*, 34.
202 Ibid., 39.
203 Tacitus, *Annals*, 14.12.
204 Dio, 62.16.2.
205 Tacitus, *Annals*, 14.12.
206 Ibid., 14.10.
207 Seneca, *On Providence*, 2.12, translation by James R. Burns.
208 Tacitus, *Annals*, 15.60–64; Suetonius, *Nero*, 35.
209 Tacitus, *Annals*, 14.9; Dio, 61.2.1–2.

5 DOMITIA LONGINA: THE SURVIVOR

1 Date of birth (Syme, pp. 810–811); orator (Tacitus, *Annals*, 13.8, 15.26); graciousness (Tacitus, *Annals*, 15.30; Syme, p. 820); ostrich comment (Seneca, *On Tranquillity of Mind*, 17.1); success under Claudius (Tacitus, *Annals*, 11.16; Dio, 61.30.4–6); success under Nero (Tacitus, *Annals*, 13.8–9, 34f., 14.23f., 15.24f.; Dio, 62.20f).
2 Strength (Dio, 62.19.2); "even Corbulo" (Juvenal, *Satires*, 3.251); memoirs (Grant, *Nero*, p. 70).
3 Tacitus, *Annals*, 14.51.57; Dio, 61.13, 62.12–13.
4 Tacitus, *Annals*, 15.38–39.
5 Ibid., 15.39, 43; Suetonius, *Nero*, 38.
6 Tacitus, *Annals*, 15.39; Suetonius, *Nero*, 38.
7 Suetonius, *Nero*, 31, 38; Tacitus, *Annals*, 15.38.
8 Syme, p. 822; Griffin, pp. 177–181.
9 Dio, 62.19.2–4, 26.5–6.
10 Assignment for Corbulo (Griffin, p. 117); death of Corbulo ordered by Nero (Dio, 62.17.5).
11 Dio, 62.17.6.
12 Ibid., 62.17.4–6.
13 Griffin, pp. 178–179; Levick, *Vespasian*, pp. 24–25.
14 McDermott and Orentzel, p. 69.
15 Ibid.; Syme, pp. 820f.
16 Tacitus, *Annals*, 3.31.4.
17 Dio, 59.15.3–5.
18 Pliny the Elder, *Natural History*, 7.39; Syme, p. 805.
19 Syme, p. 811.
20 McDermott and Orentzel, p. 78.
21 Ibid., p. 70.
22 Suetonius, *Nero*, 49.
23 See Tacitus, *Histories*.
24 Suetonius, *Vitellius*, 3–5.
25 Ibid., 4, 10, 13–14.
26 Ibid., 8.
27 Suetonius, *Vespasian*, 3.
28 Tacitus, *Histories*, 3.59.

29 Josephus, *Wars of the Jews*, 4.11.4.
30 Tacitus, *Histories*, 3.74.
31 Suetonius, *Domitian*, 1; Philostratos, *Life of Apollonius*, 5.30.
32 Suetonius, *Domitian*, 1; Tacitus, *Histories*, 3.74.
33 Domitian hailed as Caesar (Tacitus, *Histories*, 3.86, 4.2); escorted to his father's house (ibid., 3.86).
34 Ibid., 4.1; Dio, 64.22.2, 65.2.1.
35 Domitian's complexion (Tacitus, *Agricola*, 45; Pliny, *Panegyricus*, 48.5); modesty (Suetonius, *Domitian*, 18); quick temper (Suetonius, *Domitian*, 12).
36 Deep voice of Domitian (Philostratos, *Life of Apollonius*, 7.28); poetry of Domitian (Suetonius, *Domitian*, 2; Statius, *Achilleid*, 1.17.18).
37 Suetonius, *Domitian*, 20.
38 Ibid., 22; Victor, 11.
39 Powers of seduction (Tacitus, *Agricola*, 7); affairs (Suetonius, *Domitian*, 1).
40 McDermott and Orentzel, p. 78.
41 Ibid., p. 71.
42 Suetonius, *Domitian*, 1; Dio, 65.3.4.
43 Suetonius, *Domitian*, 1; Dio, 65.3.4.
44 Suetonius, *Titus*, 10.
45 Procopius, *Secret History*, 8.15–16.
46 Dio, 67.3.2.
47 Tacitus, *Histories*, 2.76; Levick, *Vespasian*, p. 191.
48 Tacitus, *Histories*, 4.51; Dio, 65.2.2–3; Suetonius, *Domitian*, 1.3.
49 Suetonius, *Domitian*, 2.
50 Ibid.
51 Tacitus, *Annals*, 3.55.
52 Suetonius, *Vespasian*, 8.5; Dio, 65.10.2.
53 Suetonius, *Titus*, 2.
54 Suetonius, *Vespasian*, 4; Levick, *Vespasian*, p.25.
55 Philostratos, *Life of Apollonius*, 5.29.
56 Suetonius, *Vespasian*, 8.
57 Ibid., 22.
58 Ibid., 23; Dio, 65.14.5.
59 Suetonius, *Vespasian*, 23; Dio, 65.14.5.
60 Suetonius, *Vespasian*, 20.
61 Dio, 65.11.1–3.
62 Suetonius, *Vespasian*, 13.
63 Artistic interests (Tacitus, *Histories*, 4.86); beginning a family (ibid.; Dio, 65.3.4, 65.9.3–5).
64 Jones, p. 38.
65 Southern, p. 28; Levick, *Vespasian*, p. 191.
66 Suetonius, *Domitian*, 30.
67 Martial, *Epigrams*, 6.3.
68 Jones, p. 37; Southern, p. 29.
69 BMCRE, 2.312, no. 65, plate 61.19.
70 D'Ambra, p. 42, figs 28, 29.
71 Deification (Silius Italicus, *Punica*, 3.626–629); sprinkling of snow (Martial, *Epigrams*, 4.3).
72 Suetonius, *Vespasian*, 23.4.
73 Ibid., 22; McDermott and Orentzel, p. 88.
74 Suetonius, *Domitian*, 22.
75 Ibid., 20.
76 Jones, p. 39.

77 Kindhearted (Suetonius, *Titus*, 3, 8); Titus mourned (ibid., 7).
78 Ibid., 6.
79 Titus' divorce (Grant, *The Twelve Caesars*, p. 232); love for Berenice (Suetonius, *Titus*, 7; Tacitus, *Histories*, 2.2, 2.81).
80 Suetonius, *Titus*, 7; Dio, 65.15.3, 66.8.1.
81 Suetonius, *Titus*, 10; Dio, 66.26.3–4.
82 Suetonius, *Domitian*, 2.
83 Dio, 66.26.4.
84 Jones, p. 38.
85 Suetonius, *Domitian*, 3.
86 Balsdon, *Roman Women*, pp. 256–257.
87 Lefkowitz and Fant, p. 222, no. 334, inscription 8959.
88 Juvenal, *Satires*, 6.503–4, translation by James R. Burns.
89 Ibid., 6.617.
90 Suetonius, *Domitian*, 9.
91 Killing of flies (Suetonius, *Domitian*, 9); cruel actions of Domitian (Suetonius, *Domitian*, 9, 10; Pliny, *Letters*, 4.11.6, and *Panegyricus*, 48.3, 52.7; Tacitus, *Agricola*, 47); enthusiasm for gladiatorial contests (Suetonius, *Domitian*, 4).
92 Pairing of cripples, dwarfs, and women (Suetonius, *Domitian*, 4); castration prohibited (ibid., 7; Ammianus Marcellinus, 18.4.5; Dio, 67.2.3; Philostratos, *Life of Apollonius*, 6.42; Martial, *Epigrams*, 9.6, 8); Domitian devoted to eunuchs (Dio, 67.2.3; Jones, p. 31; Southern, p. 39); Earinus (Statius, *Silvae*, 3.4, *The Tresses of Flavius Earinus*).
93 Jones, pp. 31–32; Southern, pp. 119–125; Statius, *Silvae*, 4.2.
94 Dio, 67.9.
95 Suetonius, *Domitian*, 3.
96 Divorce of Domitia (Suetonius, *Domitian*, 3.6); Paris murdered (Dio, 67.3.1).
97 Suetonius, *Domitian*, 10.
98 Dio, 67.3.1; Jones, pp. 39–42.
99 Suetonius, *Domitian*, 10.
100 Dio, 67.3.2.
101 Suetonius, *Domitian*, 3; Dio, 67.3.2.
102 Suetonius, *Domitian*, 13.
103 Pliny, *Letters*, 4.11.7; Dio, 67.3.2; Philostratos, *Life of Apollonius*, 7.7.
104 Affair continues after Domitia's return (Dio, 67.3.2); abortion (Suetonius, *Domitian*, 22; Pliny, *Letters*, 4.11.7; Juvenal, *Satires*, 2.28–33).
105 Abortions performed skillfully (Juvenal, *Satires*, 6.595f.); abortions legal (Veyne *et al.*, p. 164; Fantham *et al.*, pp. 301–2).
106 Southern, p. 41; Jones, pp. 34–36.
107 Suetonius, *Domitian*, 8.
108 D'Ambra, p. 9.
109 Suetonius, *Titus*, 10.
110 Ibid.
111 Jones, p. 36.
112 Southern, p. 109; D'Ambra, p. 11.
113 Martial, *Epigrams*, 6.3.
114 Jones, p. 39.
115 Ibid., p. 37.
116 Pliny, *Panegyricus*, 95.3; Tacitus, *Histories*, 1.1.
117 Pliny, *Letters*, 7.27.14.
118 Pliny, *Panegyricus*, 76.3–7.
119 See Southern; also Jones.
120 Suetonius, *Domitian*, 8.

121 Adultery (Juvenal, *Satires*, 2.28–35); religious practices encouraged (Suetonius, *Domitian*, 8).
122 Pliny, *Letters*, 4.11.6; Dio, 67.3.3–5; Philostratos, *Life of Apollonius*, 7.6.
123 Suetonius, *Domitian*, 8; Pliny, *Letters*, 4.11.6–11.
124 Scantinian Law (Suetonius, *Domitian*, 8); castration outlawed (ibid., 7); restricted mimes and farces (Pliny, *Panegyricus*, 46.1); censored satirical poets (Veyne *et al.*, p. 164); exiled senator (Suetonius, *Domitian*, 8).
125 Jones, pp. 126–141.
126 Suetonius, *Domitian*, 4, 15; Philostratos, *Life of Apollonius*, 7.24,32; Dio, 67.1.2; D'Ambra, pp. 10–11.
127 Minerva's son (Southern, p. 121); bedroom shrine (Dio, 67.16.1).
128 Temple restored with grandeur (Suetonius, *Domitian*, 5); gilding of temple (Jones, p. 74).
129 Pliny, *Panegyricus*, 49.8, Loeb pp. 432–433, note 1.
130 Valerius Maximus, 7.3.8.
131 Pliny, *Panegyricus*, 76.3, Book VIII 14.8.
132 Southern, pp. 48–50.
133 Ibid., pp. 50f.
134 Connolly and Dodge, pp. 220–223; Jones, pp. 95–96.
135 Suetonius, *Domitian*, 18.
136 Ibid.
137 Juvenal, *Satires*, 4.38.
138 Suetonius, *Domitian*, 13; Dio, 67.4.4.
139 Suetonius, *Domitian*, 4; Dio, 67.8.1.
140 Gold coins (Suetonius, *Domitian*, 4); clay balls (Dio, 67.4.4–5).
141 Suetonius, *Domitian*, 13; Dio, 67.5.7.
142 Pliny, *Letters*, 3.11.3; Dio, 67.11.2–3.
143 Pliny, *Letters*, 3.11.1; Philostratos, *Life of Apollonius*, 6.1; Suetonius, *Domitian*, 10.
144 Levick, *Vespasian*, p. 199.
145 Suetonius, *Domitian*, 15.
146 Dio, 67.14.2–3; Bennett, p. 32; Southern, pp. 115–116; Jones, pp. 114–115.
147 Suetonius, *Domitian*, 10.
148 Ibid.
149 Ibid.
150 Southern, pp. 55–58.
151 Suetonius, *Domitian*, 7.
152 Ibid., 21; Marcus Aurelius, Misc. letters of, in Loeb, *Fronto*, Vol. 2, p. 311.
153 Suetonius, *Domitian*, 17.
154 Ibid.; Philostratos, *Life of Apollonius*, 8.25.
155 Suetonius, *Domitian*, 17.
156 Ibid.; Dio, 67.18.2.
157 Suetonius, *Domitian*, 23.
158 Dio, 68.3.3–4.
159 Suetonius, *Domitian*, 14; Dio 67.15.2; Victor, 11.
160 Dio, 67.15.2–5.
161 Syme, p. 824; Jones, p. 37.
162 Josephus, *Life of Flavius Josephus*, 76.
163 Jones, p. 37; McDermott and Orentzel, p. 83; Southern, p. 118.
164 Jones, p. 37; Bennett, p. 33; Southern, p. 121.
165 Pliny, *Panegyricus*, 52.3–5; Dio, 68.1.1.
166 Jones, p. 37.
167 Suetonius, *Domitian*, 17.
168 Jones, p. 37; McDermott and Orentzel, pp. 83–85.

169 Procopius, *Secret History*, 8.15–16.
170 Ibid., 8.16–18.
171 Ibid., 8.19–20.
172 Ibid., Loeb, Comparetti, Appendix III, pp. 364–369.

6 PLOTINA: THE NEW LIVIA

1 Bennett, p. 24.
2 Dio, 68.13.3, 68.23.1.
3 Balsdon, *Roman Women*, pp. 133–134; Giacosa, p. 44.
4 Bennett, p. 24; Lambert, pp. 38–39.
5 King, p. 70.
6 Grant, *A Guide to the Ancient World*, p. 426.
7 Von Hagen and Tomeucci, p. 206 (gates and towers); King, p. 75.
8 King, p. 81.
9 Veyne *et al.*, p. 317.
10 Birley, *Lives of the Later Caesars*, p. 38; Bennett, pp. viii, 13.
11 Balsdon, *Romans and Aliens*, p. 121.
12 Curchin, p. 80; Birley, *Lives of the Later Caesars*, p. 38.
13 Curchin, p. 64.
14 Bennett, p. 11.
15 Julius Caesar (Grant, *The Roman Emperors*, p. 71); service in Syria (Pliny, *Panegyricus*, 14.1, 15.1–3).
16 Bennett, p. ix.
17 Kleiner *et al.*, *I Claudia*, p. 50, note 7.
18 Balsdon, *Roman Women*, p. 1.33; Henig, p. 88.
19 Tall and well-built (Pliny, *Panegyricus*, 22.2); affable (Pliny, *Letters*, 6.31.13–14; Dio, 68.31.3).
20 Dio, 68.31.3.
21 Balsdon, *Romans and Aliens*, p. 243.
22 Turcan, p. 155.
23 Vermaseren, p. 179.
24 Dio, 68.7.3; Philostratos, *Lives of the Sophists*, 488; Bennett, p. 131; Balsdon, *Roman Women,* p. 135.
25 Dio, 68.10.2.
26 Wine to excess (Julian, *The Caesars*, 318; Historia Augusta, *Hadrian,* 3.5; Fronto, Loeb Vol. II, *Fronto to Marcus*, p. 9, section 4; Dio, 68.7.4; Victor, 13.10); instructions to servants (Victor, 13).
27 Dio, 68.7.4.
28 Bennett, p. 58.
29 Julian, *The Caesars*, 311.
30 Pliny, *Panegyricus*, 83.2–3; Dio, 68.7.4.
31 Pliny, *Panegyricus*, 83.
32 Birley, *Lives of the Later Caesars*, p. 39.
33 Bennett, pp. 101f.
34 Pliny, *Panegyricus*, 14.2–5.
35 Birley, *Lives of the Later Caesars*, p. 39.
36 Bennett, pp. 45–46.
37 Ibid., pp. 45–46, 49.
38 Dio, 69.3.3–4.
39 Grant, *The Roman Emperors*, p. 70.
40 Birley, *Lives of the Later Caesars*, p. 36.
41 Bennett, p. 49.

NOTES

42 Grant, *The Roman Emperors*, p. 74.
43 Pliny, *Panegyricus*, 12f.
44 Fronto, to Lucius Verus, Loeb Vol. II, p. 205, section 9.
45 Pliny, *Panegyricus*, 47.4–5; Pliny, *Letters*, 6.31.13–14; Eutropius, 8.4.
46 Dio, 68.15.4–6; Eutropius, 8.4; Victor, 13.
47 Guests in carriage (Dio, 68.7.3); preferred to walk (Pliny, *Panegyricus*, 83.8).
48 Pliny, *Panegyricus*, 83.8.
49 Dio, 68.7.3; Pliny, *Panegyricus*, 49.
50 Eutropius, 8.5.
51 Grant, *The Roman Emperors*, p. 71.
52 Dio, 68.16.1; Victor, 13.9; Pliny, *Panegyricus*, 67.8.
53 Dio, 68.5.5.
54 Ibid.
55 Pliny, *Panegyricus*, 83.7–8.
56 Epitome, 42.21.
57 Bennett, p. 77.
58 Justinian, Balsdon, *Roman Women*, pp. 138, 306, note 33.
59 *Digest*, 37.12.5; Birley, *Lives of the Later Caesars*, p. 46.
60 Pliny, *Letters*, 10.66.
61 Bennett, pp. 81–84; Potter, p. 59.
62 Suetonius, 4.4; Philostratus, *Apollonius*, 5.7.
63 Pliny, *Panegyricus*, 84.
64 Ibid.
65 Ibid., 84.6–8.
66 Tameanko, "Evolution of the Empresses' Hairdos," p. 40.
67 Kleiner *et al.*, *I Claudia*, p. 42.
68 Julian, *The Caesars*, 327–328.
69 Pliny, *Panegyricus*, 83.4.
70 Ibid., 83.5.
71 Ibid., 83.1–3, 5–8, 84.1.
72 Marciana (ibid., 84.1–2); Plotina's training (ibid., 83.8).
73 Bennett, p. 24; Birley, *Marcus Aurelius*, p. 242.
74 Pliny, *Letters*, 9.28.1.
75 Ibid., 10.97, translation by James R. Burns.
76 Ibid., 6.31.15–17.
77 Ibid., 6.31.2, translation by James R. Burns.
78 Ibid., 6.31.13–14.
79 Ibid., 2.17.
80 Lyttleton and Forman, p. 43.
81 Ibid., p. 51.
82 Potter, p. 59.
83 Dio, 68.15.1.
84 Balsdon, *Romans and Aliens*, p. 42 (designed by Apollodorus); Strong, p. 141.
85 Dio, 68.16.3; Strong, p. 144.
86 Kleiner, *Roman Sculpture*, p. 214.
87 Dio, 68.7.1–2, 68.16.3; Eutropius, 8.4; Potter, pp. 90, 187.
88 Potter, p. 90.
89 Kleiner, *Roman Sculpture*, p. 229.
90 Epitome, 41.13.
91 Bennett, pp. 150, 183.
92 BMCRE, 529.
93 Dio, 68.14.5.

94 Marcianopolis (Kleiner *et al.*, *I Claudia*, p. 67); Matidia as Augusta (Birley, *Lives of the Later Caesars*, p. 47, note 89).
95 Birley, *Hadrian*, p. 65; Balsdon, *Roman Women*, pp. 134, 136.
96 Dio, 68.25.12.
97 Ibid., 68.24.1.
98 Ibid., 68.29.1; Julian, *The Caesars*, 327.
99 Dio, 68.29.4, 68.30.1–3.
100 Ibid., 68.32.
101 Ibid., 68.32.2.
102 Ibid., 68.31.
103 Ibid., 68.31.4.
104 Ibid., 68.33.1.
105 Ibid., 68.33.
106 Ibid., 68.33.2.
107 Birley, *Hadrian*, p. 75.
108 Dio, 68.33.2.
109 Ibid., 68.3.3.
110 Cremation (Historia Augusta, *Hadrian*, 5.10; Bennett, p. 204); ashes carried in a golden urn to Rome (Historia Augusta, *Hadrian*, 5.10); ashes placed in the base of Trajan's Column (Dio, 69.2.3).
111 Trajan's letter signed by Plotina (Dio, 69.1.4); Hadrian Plotina's choice (Victor, 13).
112 Dio, 69.1.3–4; Historia Augusta, *Hadrian*, 4.10.
113 Birley, *Lives of the Later Caesars*, p. 52, note 117.
114 Birley, *Hadrian*, pp. 4, 87.
115 Historia Augusta, *Hadrian*, 7.1–3.
116 Dio, 69.2.4–6; Historia Augusta, *Hadrian*, 7.
117 Historia Augusta, *Hadrian*, 1.4.
118 Plotina and Hadrian's marriage to Sabina (ibid., 2.10); marriage (Balsdon, *Roman Women*, p. 135).
119 Historia Augusta, *Hadrian*, 2.10.
120 Ibid., 3.10.
121 Dio, 68.33.1, 69.1.2.
122 Historia Augusta, *Hadrian*, 3.7–8.
123 Ibid., 4.1.
124 Dio, 68.7.3; Balsdon, *Roman Women*, p. 135.
125 Dio, 69.1.2.
126 Birley, *Hadrian*, p. 109.
127 Lambert, p. 91.
128 Balsdon, *Roman Women*, p. 135; Birley, *Hadrian*, p. 109
129 Fantham *et al.*, p. 353.
130 Alexander, *Scriptiones Latinae Liberae Rei Publicae*, II.7784.4–17.
131 Birley, *Hadrian*, p. 109, translation by Anthony R. Birley; used by permission.
132 Ibid.
133 Ibid.
134 Ibid., p. 110, from *Sententiae of Hadrian*, 12, translation by Anthony R. Birley; used by permission.
135 Ibid., p. 14.
136 Dio, 56.30.3.
137 Birley, *Hadrian*, p. 145.
138 Dio, 69.10.3.
139 Ibid.

140 Historia Augusta, *Hadrian*, 12.3; Dio, 69.10.3.
141 Temple rededication (Birley, *Hadrian*, p. 191; Kleiner, *Roman Sculpture*, p. 229); Plotina's ashes placed in base of Trajan's Column (Kleiner, *Roman Sculpture*, p. 214).
142 Birley, *Hadrian*, p. 289; BMCRE III 318, no. 603.
143 Kleiner *et al.*, *I Claudia*, p. 67.

7 SABINA: WIFE OF THE "GREEKLING"

1 Birley, *Hadrian*, p.16.
2 Ibid., p. 42.
3 Ibid., p. 45; Bennett, p. 55.
4 Historia Augusta, *Hadrian*, 2.10.
5 Ripe old age (Birley, *Hadrian*, pp. 16, 110; Bennett, p. 55); never married (Bennett, p. 183).
6 Kleiner, *Roman Sculpture*, p. 242.
7 Woodford, pp. 16–17.
8 Simple hairstyles of Sabina (Balsdon, *Roman Women*, p. 257); hairstyles copied (Kleiner, *Roman Sculpture*, p. 277).
9 Sour expression and grim hairdo (Grant, *The Twelve Caesars*, p. 2; Perowne, p. 35); mouth (Lambert, p. 39).
10 Lefkovitz and Fant, p. 10, no. 26.
11 Date of birth (Historia Augusta, *Hadrian*, 1.3); dress and grooming (ibid., 26.1); skin and eyes (Birley, *Hadrian*, pp. 166, 314 note 14; Lambert, p. 24; Adamantius, *Scriptores Physiognomici*, 2.51f.).
12 Historia Augusta, *Hadrian*, 26.1.
13 Kleiner, *Roman Sculpture*, p. 237.
14 Historia Augusta, *Hadrian*, 22.4–5; Kleiner, *Roman Sculpture*, p. 238.
15 Walker, back cover.
16 Historia Augusta, *Hadrian*, 14.8–11; Dio, 69.3.1–2; Julian, *The Caesars*, 311.
17 Prodigious memory (Historia Augusta, *Hadrian*, 20.7–13); names of soldiers (ibid., 9.8, 20.10).
18 Mountain climbing (ibid., 13.3; Birley, *Hadrian*, p. 159); hunting (Historia Augusta, *Hadrian*, 2.1–2, 20.13, 26.3; Dio, 69.7.3, 69.10.2–3).
19 Historia Augusta, *Hadrian*, 10.11, 14.10–11, 26.2.
20 Ibid., 14.9–11; Lambert, p. 37; Birley, *Hadrian*, p. 302.
21 Historia Augusta, *Hadrian*, 9.8–9, 20.1; Dio, 69.2.6.
22 Jealousy and intolerance of rivals (Historia Augusta, *Hadrian*, 15.10–13; Dio, 69.3); humiliation of rivals (Historia Augusta, *Hadrian*, 15.10–12; Philostratus, *Lives of the Sophists*, 530; Birley, *Hadrian*, p. 195).
23 Historia Augusta, *Hadrian*, 15.13.
24 Epictetus (Birley, *Hadrian*, pp. 60, 187); Plutarch (ibid., pp. 60, 62, 186; Lambert, p. 45); Arrian (MacDonald and Pinto, p. 16); Polemo (Birley, *Hadrian*, p. 159).
25 Dio, 69.4.
26 Birley, *Hadrian*, p. 283.
27 Historia Augusta, *Hadrian*, 15.11; Dio, 69.5.1.
28 Historia Augusta, *Hadrian*, 16.7; Historia Augusta, *Aelius*, 3.9; Julian, *The Caesars*, 311; Dio, 69.11.2–3; Birley, *Hadrian*, p. 104.
29 Historia Augusta, *Hadrian*, 14.6; Dio, 69.11.4; Lambert, p. 89.
30 Historia Augusta, *Hadrian*, 10.2–5.
31 Lambert, pp. 37–38.

32 Hadrian and dinner parties (Fronto, Loeb Vol. II, p. 9; Dio 69.7.4; Victor, 14); performances (Historia Augusta, *Hadrian*, 26.4–5).

33 Pliny, *Letters*, 1.15, translation by James R. Burns.

34 Petronius, *Satyricon*, 31–36.

35 Ibid., 36–41.

36 James, pp. 44–47.

37 Historia Augusta, *Hadrian*, 1.5.

38 Lambert, p. 73.

39 Birley, *Hadrian*, pp. 178, 215, 246.

40 Historia Augusta, *Aelius*, 5.11.

41 Birley, *Hadrian*, p. 42.

42 Ibid., pp. 52, 58, 80.

43 Ibid., p. 1; Lambert, p. 42.

44 Lambert, p. 42.

45 Corpus Inscriptionum Graecorum, Berlin, 1825–1877, nos. 4725–4730; Kleiner *et al.*, *I Claudia*, p. 69; Lambert, p. 54; Birley, *Hadrian*, pp. 115, 170, 203, 215, 231; Kleiner *et al.*, *I Claudia II*, 18.

46 Birley, *Hadrian*, p. 221; Lambert, p. 43.

47 Matidia (Lambert, p. 100); Domitia Paulina (Birley, *Hadrian*, p. 247).

48 Age of Servianus (Historia Augusta, *Hadrian*, 15.8).

49 Dio, 69.11.4; Birley, *Hadrian*, pp. 255–257.

50 Architects, builders, and stonemasons with Hadrian (Birley, *Hadrian*, p. 158); restoration and construction (Historia Augusta, *Hadrian*, 19.2; Dio, 69.5.2–3; Eutropius 7; Birley, *Hadrian*, p. 305).

51 Lambert, p. 43.

52 Pausanias, 1.5.5.

53 Historia Augusta, *Hadrian*, 10–11; Dio, 69.5.2, 69.9.1–3.

54 Birley, *Hadrian*, pp. 210–212; Lambert, p. 72.

55 Historia Augusta, *Hadrian*, 12.6–7.

56 German palisade (Birley, *Hadrian*, p. 116); Africa (ibid., p. 209).

57 Historia Augusta, *Hadrian*, 11.2; Burke, p. 111; Salway, pp. 126–134; also see Embleton and Graham.

58 Birley, *Hadrian*, p. 238.

59 Ibid., pp. 170, 178, 261.

60 Lefkovitz and Fant, p. 156, no. 186.

61 Perowne, p. 122.

62 Kleiner, *Roman Sculpture*, pp. 253–254.

63 Support of poor children (Historia Augusta, *Hadrian*, 7.8–9); age of eligibility (Birley, *Hadrian*, p. 99).

64 Dio, 69.8.2; Historia Augusta, *Hadrian*, 18.10–11.

65 Dio, 66.25, 52.18, 69.8.2.

66 Ibid., 69.8.2.

67 Historia Augusta, *Hadrian*, 7.11.

68 Birley, *Hadrian*, p. 109.

69 Dio, 69.6.3.

70 Aulus Gellius, *Attic Nights*, 3.16.12.

71 Fantham *et al.*, pp. 302–306.

72 Alexander, "Letters and Speeches of the Emperor Hadrian," p. 155; Lambert, p. 42.

73 Historia Augusta, *Hadrian*, 18.7–8.

74 Sweatshops banned (ibid., 18.9–10); sale of slaves (ibid., 18.8–9).

75 Dio, 69.14.9; Birley, *Hadrian*, pp. 228, 268; Lambert, p. 113.

76 Historia Augusta, *Hadrian*, 19.1,10–13.
77 Lambert, p. 39.
78 Historia Augusta, *Hadrian*, 26.5; Birley, *Hadrian*, pp. 192–193.
79 Lambert, p. 40.
80 Ibid.
81 Grant, *Cities of Vesuvius*, p. 141; Grant, *Art in the Roman Empire*, pp. xv–xxii; Deiss, pp. 126, 156–158; Veyne *et al.*, pp. 316–317; Brion, pp. 197–198.
82 Deiss, p. 126; Veyne *et al.*, pp. 316–317; Brion, pp. 197–198.
83 Grant, *Cities of Vesuvius*, p. 141.
84 Lambert, p. 71.
85 MacDonald and Pinto, p. 187.
86 Equal space (ibid.); decoration (Fantham *et al.*, pp. 103–104; Rutland, p. 12).
87 Lambert, pp. 44f., 107.
88 Birley, *Hadrian*, p. 283.
89 Ibid., p. 219; Lambert, p. 163.
90 Birley, *Hadrian*, pp. 178, 215; Lambert, pp. 38, 44f., 102; MacDonald and Pinto, pp. 132–133.
91 Bray, pp. 220–221.
92 Lambert, p. 105.
93 Birley, *Hadrian*, p. 178; Mylonas, pp. 155, 178.
94 Victor, 14; Birley, *Hadrian*, p. 283.
95 Birley, *Hadrian*, p. 217; Lambert, p. 100.
96 Birley, *Hadrian*, p. 63.
97 Ibid., p. 228; Lambert, p. 101; Levick, *Vespasian*, p. 165.
98 Birley, *Hadrian*, p. 250.
99 Pausanias, 1.42.3.
100 Philostratus, *Imagines*, 1.7.20–25.
101 Birley, *Hadrian*, p. 250; Lambert, p. 151.
102 Birley, *Hadrian*, p. 349, note 33.
103 Ibid., p. 250, translation by Anthony R. Birley; used by permission.
104 Ibid., p. 251.
105 Balbilla's poem (ibid.); Sappho (Lucian, *Affairs of the Heart*, 28).
106 Birley, *Hadrian*, p. 251.
107 Lambert, p. 19.
108 Ibid., p. 65.
109 Historia Augusta, *Hadrian*, 14.5–7; Dio, 69.11.2–4.
110 Dio, 69.11.2.
111 Historia Augusta, *Hadrian*, 14.6–7; Dio, 69.11.3; Victor, 14.
112 Historia Augusta, *Hadrian*, 14.7.
113 Lambert, pp. 192–193.
114 Historia Augusta, *Hadrian*, 14.6.
115 Lambert, p. 92.
116 Ibid., p. 154.
117 Birley, *Hadrian*, p. 255, translation by Anthony R. Birley; used by permission.
118 Lambert, p. 39; Birley, *Hadrian*, p. 85.
119 Lambert, p. 39.
120 Historia Augusta, *Hadrian*, 11.7.
121 Origen, *Contra Celsum*, 3.36.
122 Historia Augusta, *Hadrian*, 11.3.
123 Epitome, 14.
124 Ibid.
125 Historia Augusta, *Hadrian*, 23.9; Lambert, p. 173.
126 Birley, *Hadrian*, p. 97.

127 Historia Augusta, *Firmus, Saturninus, Proculus and Bonsus*, 1.2.
128 Sear, p. 118.
129 Augusta (Lambert, p. 73); deification (Birley, *Hadrian*, p. 294; Kleiner, *Roman Sculpture*, p. 255; Lambert, p. 173).
130 Kleiner, *Roman Sculpture*, p. 255.
131 Birley, *Hadrian*, p. 125.
132 Lambert, pp. 73, 110; Birley, *Hadrian*, p. 238.
133 Historia Augusta, *Hadrian*, 11.3.
134 Birley, *Hadrian*, p. 139.
135 Suetonius described (Pliny, *Letters*, 1.24, 3.8, 10.94); Clarus described (ibid., 1.15).
136 Birley, *Hadrian*, pp. 93, 107.
137 Ibid., p.107.
138 Temple (ibid., p. 110; Lambert, p. 39); spices (Historia Augusta, *Hadrian*, 9.9, 19.5).
139 Birley, *Hadrian*, p. 107.
140 Sabina's division (ibid., pp. 254–255; Lambert, pp. 73, 154); Matidia's division (Birley, *Hadrian*, p. 254).
141 Lambert, p. 173; Birley, *Hadrian*, p. 294.
142 Lambert, p. 173.
143 Perowne, p. 117.
144 Lambert, p. 222.

8 FAUSTINA THE ELDER: THE ETERNAL EMPRESS

1 Historia Augusta, *Antoninus Pius*, 1.1, Loeb Vol. I, see note p. 100.
2 Ibid., 4.4–5; Dio, 69.20.5; Birley, *Hadrian*, p. 294.
3 Date of birth (Historia Augusta, *Antoninus Pius*, 10.1); place of birth, ties to families of Trajan and Hadrian (Birley, *Hadrian*, p. 201).
4 Birley, *Hadrian*, p. 201.
5 Quiet and steady (ibid., p. 114); wealth (ibid., p. 201).
6 Birley, *Marcus Aurelius*, p. 29.
7 Birley, *Hadrian*, p. 201.
8 Birley, *Marcus Aurelius*, pp. 34, 236, 243.
9 Kleiner, *Roman Sculpture*, p. 278.
10 See Grant, *The Antonines*, p. 136.
11 Tameanko, "Evolution of the Empresses' Hairdos," p. 30.
12 Ibid.
13 Lucian, *Affairs of the Heart*, 40; see Loeb Edition, Vol. VIII, pp. 148–149 for discussion of authorship.
14 Historia Augusta, *Antoninus Pius*, 2, 6.4, 12, 13.1–2.
15 Date of birth (ibid., 1.8); childhood at Lorium (Historia Augusta, Loeb Vol. I, p. 102, note 1); palace at Lorium (Historia Augusta, *Antoninus Pius*, 1.8).
16 Wealthy parents (Eutropius, 8.8); from Nemausus (Historia Augusta, *Antoninus Pius*, 1.1).
17 Historia Augusta, *Antoninus Pius*, 2.1–3, 3.8, 13.3–4; Dio, 69.20.4, 69.15.3; Victor, 15; Eutropius, 8.8.
18 Curiosity (Dio, 69.3.3, Loeb Vol. VIII, p. 471); pastimes (Historia Augusta, *Antoninus Pius*, 11.2; Fronto, Loeb Vol. II, p. 9).
19 Historia Augusta, *Antoninus Pius*, 6.4–6, 12.
20 Ibid., 11.3.
21 Ibid., 10.2–3.
22 Ibid., 10.8–9.
23 Ibid., 10.4, also Loeb Vol. I, p. 124, note 3.

24 See Scarre, p. 108.
25 Historia Augusta, *Antoninus Pius*, 10.5.
26 Ibid., 9.10.
27 Scarre, p. 108; Veyne, p. 67.
28 Fronto, *to Marcus*, Loeb Vol. II, p. 9.
29 Ibid., 6.30.
30 Pollitt, p. 167.
31 Ammianus Marcellinus, 30.8.12.
32 Year of marriage (Birley, *Marcus Aurelius*, p. 34; Grant, *The Roman Emperors*, p. 82); children (Historia Augusta, *Antoninus Pius*, 1.7).
33 Marriage to Lamia Silanus (ibid.); death of Lamia (Birley, *Marcus Aurelius*, p. 34).
34 Historia Augusta, *Antoninus Pius*, 1.7, Loeb Vol. I, p. 100, note 6; Bryant, p. 14.
35 Lambert, pp. 84, 93; Marcus Aurelius, *Meditations*, 1.16.12–13, Loeb p. 13, note 5.
36 Scarre, p. 107; Grant, *The Roman Emperors*, p. 82; Historia Augusta, *Antoninus Pius*, 3.2–3.
37 De Serviez, Vol. II, p. 13.
38 Historia Augusta, *Antoninus Pius*, 3.6.
39 Philostratus, *Lives of the Sophists*, 535.
40 Ibid., 534; Birley, *Hadrian*, p. 282.
41 Philostratus, *Lives of the Sophists*, 554–555.
42 Ibid., 534–535.
43 Dio, 70.1; Victor, 14; Eutropius, 8.7.
44 Dio, 70.1.
45 Grant, *The Antonines*, p. 12; Perowne, p. 180; Historia Augusta, *Antoninus Pius*, 2.3–8; 5.1–2.
46 Historia Augusta, *Antoninus Pius*, 4.5–6; Dio, 69.21.1–2.
47 Historia Augusta, *Antoninus Pius*, 1.7, Loeb Vol. I, p. 100, note 6.
48 Historia Augusta, *Marcus Aurelius*, 6.2.
49 Birley, *Marcus Aurelius*, p. 53.
50 Historia Augusta, *Antoninus Pius*, 4.8–9.
51 Ibid., 10.1–3; Fronto, *Faustina to Marcus*, Loeb Vol. II, p. 317.
52 Condolences to Nerva (Epitome, 12.2–3; Birley, *Lives of the Later Caesars*, p. 31); Antoninus' delay (Historia Augusta, *Antoninus Pius*, 4.4–5; Dio, 69.20.5).
53 Historia Augusta, *Antoninus Pius*, 5.2.
54 Cause of death unknown (ibid., 6.7); date of death (Birley, *Marcus Aurelius*, p. 77; Scarre, p. 110).
55 Grant, *The Roman Emperors*, p. 86.
56 Vermaseren, pp. 53, 62, 75; Turcan, pp. 51–52; Grant, *The Antonines*, p. 116.
57 Ovid, *Fasti*, 4.185, 345–346; Lucretius, *De Rerum Natura*, 2.618–628.
58 Campbell, *Masks: Occidental*, p. 42; Kinsley, pp. 233, 235.
59 Vermaseren, p. 180; Turcan, pp. 51–42; Grant, *The Antonines*, p. 16; RIC 1145.
60 Turcan, p. 52; MacMullen, p. 103; Vermaseren, p. 179.
61 Historia Augusta, *Antoninus Elagabalus*, 7.1.
62 Historia Augusta, *Antoninus Pius*, 6.7.
63 Ibid.
64 Historia Augusta, *Antoninus Pius*, Loeb Vol I, pp. 114–115, note 3.
65 Tameanko, *Monumental Coins*, p. 11; Historia Augusta, *Antoninus Pius*, 6.7–9.
66 Historia Augusta, *Antoninus Pius*, 6.8–9.
67 Spaeth, p. 29, fig. 25, Louvre.
68 Historia Augusta, *Antoninus Pius*, 8.1–2; Grant, *The Antonines*, p. 15.
69 Fronto, *Antoninus Pius to Fronto*, Loeb Vol. I, p. 129; see Balsdon, *Roman Women*, p. 144.

70 Fronto, *Antoninus Pius to Fronto*, Loeb Vol. I, p. 128, note 1.
71 Birley, *Lives of the Later Caesars*, p. 103, note 14.
72 Birley, *Marcus Aurelius*, p. 77.
73 Fantham *et al.*, pp. 355–356.
74 Historia Augusta, *Antoninus Pius*, 3.7–8, translation James R. Burns.
75 For example, Lucian, *The Passing of Peregrinus*, 16; Historia Augusta, *Antoninus Pius*, 11.8; Marcus Aurelius, *Meditations*, 6.30; Grant, *The Antonines*, p. 27.
76 Historia Augusta, *Antoninus Pius*, 7.7–8; Grant, *The Antonines*, p. 174; Dio, 69.3.3, Loeb Vol. VIII, p. 471.
77 Julian, *The Caesars*, Loeb, p. 357.
78 Ibid.
79 Historia Augusta, *Antoninus Pius*, 8.9.
80 Ibid., 13.1–2.
81 Ibid., 12.4–5; Victor, 16; Eutropius 8.8.
82 Peace and prosperity (see Aelius Aristides, *Orations, To Rome*; Potter, p. 61); uprisings (Grant, *The Roman Emperors*, p. 86).
83 Historia Augusta, *Antoninus Pius*, 5.3–5.
84 Scarre, p. 108.
85 Earthquakes (Historia Augusta, *Antoninus Pius*, 9.1, Loeb Vol. I, p. 121, note 7; Dio, 69.4.1–2); famine relief (Historia Augusta, *Antoninus Pius*, 8.11).
86 Historia Augusta, *Antoninus Pius*, 7.11.
87 Grant, *The Antonines*, p. 23; Carson, p. 238.
88 Harl, pp. 297f.; Pliny the Elder, *Natural History*, 6.26.100, 12.41.84.
89 Suetonius, *Vespasian*, 18.
90 Pliny the Elder, *Natural History*, 36.195; Dio, 57.21.7; Petronius, *Satyricon*, 51.
91 Grant, *Gladiators*, p. 81; Historia Augusta, Loeb Vol. I, p. 120, note 6.
92 Historia Augusta, *Antoninus Pius*, 9.1–5.
93 Eutropius, 8.8; Harl, p. 78; Grant, *The Antonines*, p. 174.
94 Historia Augusta, *Antoninus Pius*, 13.3–4.
95 Kleiner, *Roman Sculpture*, p. 287.
96 Boardman *et al.*, p. 801; Grant, *The Antonines*, p. 139.
97 Scarre, p. 111; Kleiner *et al.*, *I Claudia*, p. 76; Grant, *The Antonines*, p. 139; Marcus Aurelius, *Meditations*, 5.33.
98 Strong, p. 197; see also Henig, p. 79; Kähler, p. 164.
99 Kleiner *et al.*, *I Claudia*, p. 76.

9 FAUSTINA THE YOUNGER: A NEW MESSALINA?

1 Kleiner, *Roman Sculpture*, pp. 268, 277; Birley, *Marcus Aurelius*, pp. 34–35, 45.
2 Herodian, 1.7.5.
3 Kleiner, *Roman Sculpture*, p. 278.
4 Grant, "High Art of Portraiture," p. 39.
5 Historia Augusta, *Marcus Aurelius*, 1.10.
6 Ibid., 2–3.
7 Herodian, 1.2.3; Historia Augusta, *Marcus Aurelius*, 4.8–10.
8 Hunting on horseback (Historia Augusta, *Marcus Aurelius*, 4.8; Fronto, Loeb Vol. 1, p. 179); fighting in full armor (Dio, 72.36.2); frail health (Dio, 71.1.2, 71.6.3–4, 72.36.3; Fronto, Loeb Vol. I, p. 181).
9 Dio, 72.35.3–6, 72.34.5.
10 Historia Augusta, *Marcus Aurelius*, 2.6.
11 Historia Augusta, *Antoninus Pius*,10.2–3; Historia Augusta, *Marcus Aurelius*, 6.6; Birley, *Marcus Aurelius*, p. 44.
12 Historia Augusta, *Antoninus Pius*, 10.2–3; Balsdon, *Roman Women*, p. 142.

13 Birley, *Marcus Aurelius*, p. 90; Historia Augusta, *Marcus Aurelius*, Loeb Vol. I, p. 147, note 5; also see Cohen, ii, p. 127, nos. 3–4.
14 Dio, 71.1.2; Historia Augusta, *Marcus Aurelius*, 2.7–3.3–4, 16.5; Eutropius, 8.11.
15 Marcus Aurelius, *Meditations*, 12.8.
16 Grant, *The Climax of Rome*, p. 134.
17 Support for religion (Dio, 72.34.2); initiation (Historia Augusta, *Marcus Aurelius*, 27.1–2; Birley, *Marcus Aurelius*, p. 194).
18 Grant, *The Climax of Rome*, p. 134.
19 Campbell, *Transformations of Myth*, pp. 122–127; Campbell, *Masks: Oriental*, pp. 326–327.
20 Musonius Rufus, in Lefkowitz and Fant, pp. 50–53; da Costa.
21 da Costa, The Consecration Phenomena of Faustina the Elder, *The Celator: Journal of Ancient Art and Artifacts*, February, 1994.
22 Grant, *The Antonines*, p. 25.
23 Marcus Aurelius, *Meditations*, 1.3.
24 Cybele (Grant, *The Climax of Rome*, p. 187); coins (e.g. RIC 1663).
25 Kleiner *et al.*, *I Claudia*, p. 44; Birley, *Marcus Aurelius*, pp. 247–248.
26 Faustina made Augusta (Kleiner *et al.*, *I Claudia*, pp. 44, 243); new powers (Historia Augusta, *Marcus Aurelius*, 6.6).
27 Fronto, Loeb Vol. I, pp. 194–195.
28 Ibid., pp. 202–203.
29 Ibid., note 1.
30 Fronto, Loeb Vol. II, p. 33.
31 Fronto, Loeb Vol. I, p. 203.
32 Marcus Aurelius, *Meditations*, 1.11.
33 Ibid., 6.13.
34 Fronto, cf. Loeb Vol. II, p. 290.
35 Kleiner, *Roman Sculpture*, p. 280; Kleiner *et al.*, *I Claudia*, pp. 44, 71, 79.
36 BMCRE, 1827–1829; Birley, *Marcus Aurelius*, p. 106.
37 RIC 1665; see also Rohrman, "Mater Castrorum."
38 Historia Augusta, *Marcus Aurelius*, 7.5–6; Grant, *The Roman Emperors*, p. 93.
39 Marcus Aurelius, *Meditations*, 1.17.
40 Herodian, 1.4.7–8.
41 Historia Augusta, *Marcus Aurelius*, 8.4, 8.5.
42 Dio, 71.2.1; Historia Augusta, *Marcus Aurelius*, 8.6.
43 Historia Augusta, *Marcus Aurelius*, 8.7–8.
44 Dio, 71.1.3; Historia Augusta, *Marcus Aurelius*, 8.9–10.
45 Birley, *Marcus Aurelius*, p. 123.
46 Dio, 71.2.
47 Historia Augusta, *Marcus Aurelius*, 12.13–14.
48 Birley, *Marcus Aurelius*, p. 129; Grant, *The Antonines*, p. 29; Marcus Aurelius, *Meditations*, 8.37.
49 Scarre, p. 115.
50 Dio, 71.1.3; Historia Augusta, *Marcus Aurelius*, 7.7–9.
51 Herodian, 1.2.2.
52 Historia Augusta, *Lucius Verus*, 10.8–9; Birley, *Marcus Aurelius*, p. 126.
53 Fronto, *Ad Ver.*, 2.1, Loeb Vol. II, p. 133; Fronto, *Ad M. Caes.*, 2.17, Loeb Vol. II, p. 97; Marcus Aurelius, *Meditations*, 1.17.4.
54 Marcus Aurelius, *Meditations*, 1.17.4.
55 Historia Augusta, *Marcus Aurelius*, 9.2–4.
56 Birley, *Marcus Aurelius*, p. 129.
57 Ibid., p. 162.
58 Ibid., pp. 129, 247.

59 Ibid., p. 143; Fronto, Loeb Vol. II, p. 237.
60 Dio, 71.2.3.
61 Historia Augusta, *Marcus Aurelius*, 12.7; Birley, *Marcus Aurelius*, p. 145.
62 Historia Augusta, *Marcus Aurelius*, 12.8–11.
63 Ibid., 12.13.
64 Ibid., 13.3–6, Loeb Vol. I, p. 67, note 4.
65 Von Hagen and Tomeucci, p. 174.
66 Historia Augusta, *Marcus Aurelius*, 13.3–4; Eutropius, 8.12; Potter, p. 61.
67 Historia Augusta, *Marcus Aurelius*, 13.1–3.
68 Birley, *Marcus Aurelius*, p. 152.
69 Fronto, Loeb Vol. II, p. 282, note 1; Birley, *Marcus Aurelius*, p. 202–204.
70 Marcus Aurelius, *Meditations*, Loeb edition, p. 383.
71 Marcus Aurelius, *Meditations*, 11.3; Loeb edition, p. 385.
72 Burkert, p. 111; Birley, *Marcus Aurelius*, p. 202.
73 Fronto, *Ex Octavio Minucii felicis*, ix, 8.
74 Historia Augusta, *Marcus Aurelius*, 12.14.
75 Historia Augusta, *Lucius Verus*, 9.7.
76 Ibid., 10.1–2.
77 Stroke of Verus (Eutropius, 8.10); death of Verus (Historia Augusta, *Marcus Aurelius*, 14.8; Historia Augusta, *Lucius Verus*, 9.11).
78 Historia Augusta, *Lucius Verus*, 10.1–2.
79 Verus poisoned by Marcus Aurelius (ibid., 10.2–3; Historia Augusta, *Marcus Aurelius*, 14.4–6); Verus killed by Lucilla (Historia Augusta, *Lucius Verus*, 10.3–4).
80 Birley, *Marcus Aurelius*, p. 179.
81 Historia Augusta, *Marcus Aurelius*, 20.6–7; Dio, 73.4.5, Loeb. p. 79.
82 Historia Augusta, *Marcus Aurelius*, 20.6–7; Birley, *Marcus Aurelius*, pp. 161–162; Balsdon, *Roman Women*, p. 148.
83 Historia Augusta, *Marcus Aurelius*, 20.6.
84 Birley, *Marcus Aurelius*, p. 247.
85 Dio, 73.4.5–6; Herodian, 1.8.3–5.
86 Historia Augusta, *Marcus Aurelius*, 21.3–4.
87 Balsdon, *Roman Women*, p. 145.
88 Historia Augusta, *Marcus Aurelius*, 21.6–8; Grant, *Gladiators*, p. 93.
89 Historia Augusta, *Marcus Aurelius*, 17.4–5, 21.9–10; Eutropius, 8.13.
90 Historia Augusta, *Antoninus Pius*, 4.8–9.
91 Dio, 72.33.2.
92 Birley, *Marcus Aurelius*, p. 163.
93 Ammianus Marcellinus, 29.6.1; Dio, 72.1.2, Loeb Vol. IX, p. 11.
94 Birley, *Marcus Aurelius*, p. 164.
95 Grant, *The Roman Emperors*, p. 89.
96 Dio, 72.1.3, Loeb, pp. 12–13.
97 Ibid., 72.10; Potter, p. 61.
98 Dio, 72.11.4–5; Historia Augusta, *Marcus Aurelius*, 24.3–4.
99 Dio, 72.10.3.
100 Ibid.
101 Ibid., 72.30.2.
102 Marcus Aurelius, *Meditations*, Loeb edition, p. xi.
103 Marcus Aurelius, *Meditations*, 6.30.
104 Ibid., 5.31.
105 Ibid., 7.68.
106 Ibid., 12.1.
107 Ibid., 2.8.
108 Ibid., 4.49.

109 Ibid., 2.13.
110 Ibid., 4.3.
111 Ibid., 7.9.
112 Ibid., 4.48.
113 Ibid., 12.36.
114 Marcus Aurelius, *Meditations*, Loeb edition, p. 367.
115 Ibid., p. 23, note 6.
116 *Mater Castrorum* (Dio, 72.10.5, Loeb p. 33; Historia Augusta, *Marcus Aurelius*, 26.8–9; Birley, *Marcus Aurelius*, p. 178); coin (RIC (Marcus Aurelius) 1714).
117 Marcus Aurelius considers suicide (Birley, *Marcus Aurelius*, p. 185); Stoicism and suicide (Seneca, *Epistle*, 58.32–36, Loeb Vol. IV).
118 Historia Augusta, *Avidius Cassius*, 6–7.
119 Ibid., 7.1–3.
120 Grant, *The Roman Emperors*, p. 90.
121 Dio, 72.21.17; Historia Augusta, *Marcus Aurelius*, 24.5–6, 25.1.
122 Dio, 72.22.2; Historia Augusta, *Marcus Aurelius*, 22.11–12.
123 Dio, 72.27, Loeb Vol. IX, p. 47.
124 Ibid., p. 46.
125 Historia Augusta, *Marcus Aurelius*, 24.5–6; Historia Augusta, *Avidius Cassius*, 7.1, 9.9.
126 Dio, 72.22–23, Loeb Vol. IX, pp. 36ff.
127 Historia Augusta, *Avidius Cassius*, 9.6–11.1.
128 Ibid., 9.7–11.8.
129 Historia Augusta, *Marcus Aurelius*, 25.11–12, Loeb Vol. I, p. 194, note 3.
130 Birley, *Marcus Aurelius*, p. 191.
131 Historia Augusta, *Marcus Aurelius*, 26.4–5.
132 Dio, 72.29.1.
133 Ibid., 72.27–28, 72.31.3–4; Historia Augusta, *Avidius Cassius*, 7.8–9.
134 Historia Augusta, *Marcus Aurelius*, 26.4–5.
135 Ibid., 26.6–7, 9; Birley, *Marcus Aurelius*, p. 19
136 Grant, *The Climax of Rome*, p. 168
137 Temple (Dio, 72.31.1); altar (ibid., 72.31.1–2).
138 Ibid., 72.31.3.
139 Historia Augusta, *Marcus Aurelius*, 26.5; Birley, *Lives of the Later Caesars*, p. 134.
140 Historia Augusta, *Marcus Aurelius*, 26.6–7.
141 Dio, 72.30.1.
142 Historia Augusta, *Marcus Aurelius*, 27.1–2.
143 Ibid., 29.10.
144 Ibid.
145 Julian II idolized Marcus Aurelius (Ammianus Marcellinus, 16.1.4); Marcus criticized (Julian, *The Caesars*, p. 359).
146 Julian, *The Caesars*, p. 409.
147 Historia Augusta, *Marcus Aurelius*, 26.5.
148 Victor, 16
149 Historia Augusta, *Marcus Aurelius*, 19.8, 23.7; Historia Augusta, *Commodus*, 8.1.
150 Historia Augusta, *Marcus Aurelius*, 19.4–6.
151 Dio, 72.34.3–4; Historia Augusta, *Marcus Aurelius*, 19.8–9.
152 Historia Augusta, *Marcus Aurelius*, 19.1–5, translation by James R. Burns.
153 Ibid., 29.1–3.
154 Historia Augusta, *Marcus Aurelius*, 23.7, 26.5–6; Birley, *Marcus Aurelius*, p. 191.
155 Historia Augusta, *Marcus Aurelius*, 19.9.
156 Marcus Aurelius, *Meditations*, 1.17.7.
157 Fronto, Loeb edition, Vol. II, p. 119; Fronto, Loeb edition, Vol. I, p. 251.

158 Birley, *Marcus Aurelius*, p. 63.
159 Ibid., p. 62; Boardman *et al.*, p. 658; Philostratus, *Lives of the Sophists*, Loeb Vol. I, p. xxxiii; Aulus Gellius, 12.1.
160 Historia Augusta, *Marcus Aurelius*, 2.4.
161 Grant, *The Antonines*, p. 102; Lambert, p. 28.
162 Philostratus, *Lives of the Sophists*, 549; Birley, *Marcus Aurelius*, pp. 77f.
163 Atticus mocked his mentally retarded son (Philostratus, *Lives of the Sophists*, 558); humiliation of rivals and students (Aulus Gellius, 1.2.6–13, 9.2).
164 Philostratus, *Lives of the Sophists*, 555–556; Birley, *Marcus Aurelius*, p. 113; Grant, *The Antonines*, pp. 102–187.
165 Philostratus, *Lives of the Sophists*, 551, 556, 557.
166 Tobin, p. 34.
167 Philostratus, *Lives of the Sophists*, 556.
168 Atticus wealth (Birley, *Marcus Aurelius*, p. 63); haughtiness (Grant, *The Antonines*, p. 131).
169 Philostratus, *Lives of the Sophists*, 559–560.
170 Ibid., 560; Birley, *Marcus Aurelius*, pp. 180f.
171 Philostratus, *Lives of the Sophists*, 560.
172 Ibid., 554–555.
173 Ibid.
174 Tobin, pp. 32, 76.
175 Ibid., p. 34.
176 Philostratus, *Lives of the Sophists*, 560.
177 Ibid., 560–561.
178 Ibid., 561.
179 Ibid.
180 Ibid.
181 Bowersock, p. 95; Birley, *Marcus Aurelius*, p. 191; Fronto, Loeb Vol. II, pp. 295f.
182 Philostratus, *Lives of the Sophists*, 562–563; Birley, *Marcus Aurelius*, p. 192.
183 Historia Augusta, *Marcus Aurelius*, 3.5–9.
184 Philostratus, *Lives of the Sophists*, 562.
185 Birley, *Marcus Aurelius*, p. 194; Tobin, pp. 2, 41.
186 Marcus Aurelius, *Meditations*, 7.22.
187 Philostratus, *Lives of the Sophists*, 565; Tobin, p. 47.
188 Philostratus, *Lives of the Sophists*, 562.
189 Victor, 16.12; Tertullian says Sirmium (*Apologia*, 25).
190 Victor, 17.
191 Dio, 72.36.4, 73.4.1; Herodian, 1.8f.
192 Dio, 73.4.5–6; Herodian, 1.8.3–8.
193 Julian, *The Caesars*, Loeb Vol. II, p. 359.
194 Grant, *The Roman Emperors*, p. 91.
195 Dio, 73.10.3; Herodian, 15.1–9; Historia Augusta, *Commodus*, 19.1f.
196 Dio, 73.20.1–2; Herodian, 1.13.8, 1.15.7.
197 Grant, *Gladiators*, p. 97; Barton, p. 66.
198 Eutropius, 8.15; Historia Augusta, *Commodus*, 5.5–6; Grant, *Gladiators*, p. 98; Dio, 73.10.3, 73.19, 73.22.3; Herodian, 1.15.9.
199 Dio 73.17.2–3, 73.18.3.
200 Ibid., 73.17.2–3.
201 Ibid., 73.21.1–2.
202 Grant, *Gladiators*, p. 97.
203 Historia Augusta, *Commodus*, 17.1–2; Dio, 73.22.5–6; Herodian, 1.17.10–11.
204 Herodian, 2.14.3.
205 Dio, 75.3.1; Birley, *Septimius Severus*, p. 76.

206 Herodian, 3.10.5.
207 Historia Augusta, *Caracalla*, 11.6–7.
208 Philostratus, *Lives of the Sophists*, 607, Loeb, pp. xxxviii–xl; Birley, *Septimius Severus*, pp. 137, 198.
209 Historia Augusta, *Marcus Aurelius*, 25.8–12.
210 Dio, 78.16.6; Herodian, 4.6.3.
211 Herodian, 1.13.1–5.
212 Birley, *Marcus Aurelius*, pp. 247–248.
213 Dio, 62.36.4.
214 Birley, *Marcus Aurelius*, p. 225, Grant, *The Roman Emperors*, p. 90; Balsdon, *Roman Women*, p. 144; Giacosa, p. 50.
215 Women gladiators (Juvenal, *Satires*, 6.246–267; Grant, *Gladiators*, 34–35; Petronius, *Satyricon*, 45).
216 Seneca, *Epistles*, 7.2–6; Kiefer, pp. 102–103.
217 Seneca, *Epistles*, 95.33.
218 Seneca a solitary voice (Kiefer, p. 105); Marcus limited gladiatorial contests (Historia Augusta, *Marcus Aurelius*, 11.4); blunt weapons (Dio, 72.29.3, Loeb, p. 51).
219 Dio, 72.29.3, Loeb, p. 51.
220 Cicero, *Tusculanae Disputationes*, 2.17.
221 Barton, pp. 66, 81; Petronius, *Satyricon*, 126; Juvenal, *Satires*, 6.82–83, 103–113, 352; Grant, *Gladiators*, pp. 96, 101.
222 Grant, *Gladiators*, p. 7.
223 Petronius, *Satyricon*, 126; Barton, pp. 47–49, 79–81.
224 Kiefer, p. 100; Barton, p. 13.
225 Valerius Maximus, 2.4.7.
226 Kiefer, pp. 99, 101.
227 Julius Caesar (Plutarch, *Caesar*, 5; Kiefer, p. 101); Trajan (Dio, 68.15.1, Loeb Vol. VIII, p. 389; Kiefer, p. 101).
228 Kiefer, p. 102; Grant, *Gladiators*, pp. 30–31.
229 Kiefer, p. 102; Grant, *Gladiators*, pp. 30–31; Barton, pp. 12, 46.
230 Barton, p. 14, citing Ville, *La Gladiature*, p. 227.
231 Grant, *Gladiators*, p. 11; Barton, pp. 13, 80.
232 MacMullen, pp. 88–89.
233 Suetonius, *Claudius*, 2.6.
234 Petronius, *Satyricon*, 117.5; Seneca, *Letters*, 71.23; Grant, *Gladiators*, p. 31.
235 See Barton, pp. 11–46.
236 Ibid., pp. 40–45.
237 Cicero, *Tusculanae Disputationes*, 2.41, translation by James R. Burns.
238 Barton, p. 13.

10 JULIA DOMNA: THE PHILOSOPHER

1 Dio, 76.7.4; Historia Augusta, *Geta*, 2.2–3; Grant, *The Antonines*, pp. 79, 182.
2 Birley, *Septimius Severus*, p. 35; Kleiner, *Roman Sculpture*, p. 319.
3 Epitome, 21.3, 23.2; Millar, p. 119 (Julius Bassianus); Turcan, p. 177; Kleiner *et al.*, *I Claudia*, p. 81.
4 Millar, pp. 82, 119, 303; Scarre, p. 133; Birley, *Septimius Severus*, pp. 70–72.
5 See Herodian, 6.1.4.
6 Birley, *Septimius Severus*, p. 72; Millar, p. 302.
7 Millar, p. 300.
8 Ibid., p. 306.
9 Birley, *Septimius Severus*, p. 71.

10 Grant, *Guide to the Ancient World*, p. 236; Herodian, 5.3.5.

11 Avienus, *Descriptio Orbis Terrae*, 1075–81.

12 Herodian, 5.3.6.

13 Ibid., 5.3.8.

14 Lucian, *De Dea Syria*, 30–33, 41, 44, 45, 54, 55.

15 Grant, *The Severans*, p. 45.

16 Birley, *Septimius Severus*, p. 72.

17 Date of birth (Dio, 77.17.4; Birley, *Septimius Severus*, p. 220); Paccia Marciana (Birley, *Septimius Severus*, p. 72; Historia Augusta, Loeb Vol. I, p. 374, note 2); daughters (Grant, *The Severans*, p. 45; Kleiner, *Roman Sculpture*, p. 318); no daughters (Birley, *Septimius Severus*, pp. 52, 75).

18 Historia August, *Septimius Severus*, 3.9; Birley, *Septimius Severus*, p. 76.

19 Grant, *The Severans*, p. 45; Historia Augusta, *Septimius Severus*, 3.2; Birley, *Septimius Severus*, p. 52.

20 Historia Augusta, *Septimius Severus*, 3.2–3, 14.4–5; Birley, *Septimius Severus*, p. 52.

21 Historia Augusta, *Septimius Severus*, 3.9; Historia Augusta, *Severus Alexander*, 5.4.

22 Historia Augusta, *Septimius Severus*, 3.9.

23 Birley, *Septimius Severus*, p. 222.

24 Historia Augusta, *Caracalla*, 10.1–2; Victor, 21; Birley, *Septimius Severus*, p. 76.

25 Interpretation of dreams (Historia Augusta, *Geta*, 1.5); craftiness (Dio, 78.10.2).

26 Kleiner *et al.*, *I Claudia*, p. 81.

27 Kleiner, *Roman Sculpture*, p. 378.

28 Birley, *Septimius Severus*, p. 76.

29 Ibid.

30 Millar, p. 118.

31 Dio, 77.16.1.

32 Decisive, competent (Herodian, 2.9.2); interested in the occult (Dio, 76.13.1–2); energetic (Dio, 77.16.1).

33 Victor, 20; Eutropius, 8.19.

34 Birley, *Septimius Severus*, p. 83; Herodian, 2.9.2.

35 Birley, *Septimius Severus*, p. 215.

36 Ibid., p. 218; Scarre, p. 142.

37 Birley, *Septimius Severus*, p. 63.

38 Pertinax assassinated (Dio, 74.9); empire auctioned (ibid., 74.11).

39 Ibid., 74.11.5.

40 Grant, *The Severans*, p. 8; Herodian, Loeb Vol. I, pp. 204–205, note 2.

41 Herodian, 2.9.12, Loeb Vol. I, p. 204, note 1, p. 214, note 1; Scarre, p. 129.

42 Dio, 74.14.3–4.

43 Ibid., 74.14.3.

44 Ibid., 74.15.1–3.

45 Ibid., 74.17.5; Herodian, 2.12.6–7.

46 Praetorian Guard (Dio, 75.1.1–2); recognized by senate (ibid., 74.17.4–5).

47 Birley, *Septimius Severus*, p. 245, note 35.

48 Dio, 75.6.3–75.8.5; Ammianus Marcellinus, 26.8.15.

49 Birley, *Septimius Severus*, p. 115; Kondoleon, p. 127.

50 Honors and riches bestowed (Kondoleon, p. 127); tax exemption (Grant, *Guide to the Ancient World*, p. 236).

51 Dio, 79.30.3; Herodian, 5.3.2.

52 Millar, p. 119.

53 Murphy, p. 103.

54 Birley, *Septimius Severus*, p. 115; Herodian, Loeb Vol. I, p. 283, note 1.

55 Herodian, Loeb Vol. I, p. 289, note 1.

56 Herodian, 3.5.8; Scarre, p. 133.

57 Dio, 76.6; Herodian, 7.2; Birley, *Septimius Severus*, pp. 124–125; Scarre, p. 129.
58 Dio, 76.7.
59 Historia Augusta, *Albinus*, 9.5–7; Historia Augusta, *Septimius Severus*, 11.6–9; Birley, *Septimius Severus*, p. 125.
60 Historia Augusta, *Albinus*, 10.9–12, 11.1; Grant, *The Antonines*, p. 52.
61 Historia Augusta, *Albinus*, 12.2–4; Birley, *Septimius Severus*, p. 125; Potter, p. 193.
62 Historia Augusta, *Albinus*, 3.5; Grant, *The Severans*, p. 45.
63 Potter, p. 150; King, p. 173.
64 Herodian, 3.8.4; Dio, 78.9, 78.10.4; Grant, *The Severans*, p. 34.
65 Harl, p. 224.
66 Grant, *The Severans*, p. 6.
67 Dio, 76.9.
68 Herodian, 3.10.6.
69 Ibid.
70 Dio, 76.9.3–5.
71 Ibid., 76.10.1, 76.11–12; Ammianus Marcellinus, 23.8.5.
72 Dio, 76.13.1.
73 Grant, *The Severans*, p. 29.
74 Birley, *Septimius Severus*, pp. 135–139.
75 Serapis (Grant, *The Severans*, pp. 77–78; Birley, *Septimius Severus*, p. 138); Isis (Turcan, p. 238).
76 Birley, *Septimius Severus*, p. 137.
77 Ibid., p. 139; Scarre, p. 135.
78 Kleiner, *Roman Sculpture*, p. 321.
79 Birley, *Septimius Severus*, p. 144; Scarre, p. 134.
80 Grant, *The Severans*, p. 64.
81 Ibid.
82 Ibid., p. 66; Birley, *Septimius Severus*, p. 155.
83 Potter, pp. 193–194; Grant, *The Severans*, p. 65.
84 Victor, 113–114, note 6.
85 Fantham *et al.*, p. 366.
86 Cohen, 234.
87 Lanciani, p. 222.
88 Royal visit (Grant, *The Severans*, pp. 28, 68; Wheeler, p. 55); embellishment (Scarre, p. 136; Cunliffe, p. 126; Kleiner, *Roman Sculpture*, p. 340).
89 Wheeler, pp. 53, 57.
90 Grant, *The Severans*, p. 68; Wheeler, p. 155; Bandinelli, pp. 31–48; Strong, pp. 224f.
91 Historia Augusta, *Septimius Severus*, 15.7.
92 Grant, *The Severans*, p. 46; Balsdon, *Roman Women*, p. 151; Herodian, Loeb Vol. I, p. 367, note 2.
93 Grant, *The Severans*, p. 46.
94 Sear, p. 218.
95 Herodian, 3.8.5, Loeb Vol. I, p. 309, note 5.
96 Dio, 76.16.1.
97 Ibid., 76.15.5–7, 79.24.1.
98 Ibid., 76.15.6–7.
99 Historia Augusta, *Septimius Severus*, 18.8–9; Victor, 20.
100 Balsdon, *Roman Women*, p. 152.
101 Dio., 76.15.1–2.
102 Ibid., 77.1.1–2; Historia Augusta, *Caracalla*, 14.8–9; Historia Augusta, Loeb Vol. I, p. 404, note 1.

103 Dio, 77.1.2.
104 Ibid., 77.2.4–77.3.1; Herodian, 3.10.8.
105 Historia Augusta, Loeb Vol. I, p. 404, note 1.
106 Herodian, 3.10.6.
107 Dio, 76.14, 76.15.7; Herodian, 3.11.2–3.
108 Dio, 76.14.6–7, 76.16.2.
109 Ibid., 76.15.2, 76.16.3–4.
110 Ibid., 76.15.6–7.
111 Bowersock, pp. 101f.
112 Ibid., pp. 102, 108.
113 Galen (Bowersock, pp. 106–107); Gordian I (ibid., pp. 5, 102); Laertius (Diogenes Laertius, *Lives of Eminent Philosophers*, 3.47, 10.29; Hope, p. 7); Antipater (Philostratus, *Lives of the Sophists*, 607; Birley, *Septimius Severus*, pp. 137, 198; Bowersock, p. 5); Oppian (Oppian, *Cynegetica*, 1.7; Turcan, p. 178; Bowersock, pp. 102, 108); Aelian and others (Bowersock, p. 102; Kondoleon, p. 127).
114 Bowersock, pp. 101f.
115 Philostratus, *Life of Apollonius of Tyana*, 1.3; Philostratus, *Lives of the Sophists*, 622.
116 Philostratus, *Lives of the Sophists*, 622; *Life of Apollonius of Tyana*, 1.3.
117 Philostratus, *Lives of the Sophists*, 622.
118 Ibid., 626, Loeb, p. 306, note 1.
119 Ibid., p. x.
120 Kleiner, *Roman Sculpture*, p. 328; *I Claudia II*, pp. 5, 52–53, 57.
121 Kleiner, *I Claudia II*, pp. 5, 53.
122 Kondoleon, p. 93; Wheeler, p. 167; Grant, *The Visible Past*, p. 209; Kleiner, *Roman Sculpture*, p. 343.
123 Wheeler, p. 167.
124 Philostratus, *Life of Apollonius of Tyana*, 1.3.
125 Iamblichus from Emesa (Birley, *Septimius Severus*, p. 71); others (Grant, *The Severans*, p. 5).
126 Reardon, pp. 35–351; Lamb, pp. xxvi–xxvii, 288f., 299; Grant, *The Climax of Rome*, p. 130; Franz, *The Golden Ass*.
127 Grant, *The Climax of Rome*, pp. 126f.
128 Lamb, p. xvii.
129 Heliodorus, *Aethiopica*, 10.41.
130 Grant, *The Climax of Rome*, p. 129.
131 Grant, *Roman History from Coins*, p. 43.
132 Philostratus, *Life of Apollonius of Tyana*, 1.3.
133 Various sources (ibid.); published after Domna's death (Bowersock, p. 5).
134 Philostratus, *Life of Apollonius of Tyana*, 1.7, 1.8, 1.32, 3.23, 4.16, 6.11.
135 Gladiatorial contests (ibid., 4.22); cruelty to animals (ibid., 1.31, 5.25, 8.7); prophesies (ibid., 5.30, 8.26); resurrecting the dead (ibid., 4.45).
136 Ibid., 2.22, 2.38, 6.10; Grant, *The Climax of Rome*, pp. 176, 182.
137 Philostratus, *Life of Apollonius of Tyana*, 5.28, 6.30, 7.32, 8.27.
138 Tigellinus (ibid., 4.44); Domitian (ibid., 8).
139 Ibid., 3.18.
140 Initiation (Philostratus, *Epistles of Apollonius*, 78, Loeb Vol. II, p. 475); quote (Philostratus, *Life of Apollonius of Tyana*, 3.15, 6.11).
141 Philostratus, *Life of Apollonius of Tyana*, 4.40.
142 Caracalla's temple (Dio, 78.18.4); other temples (Philostratus, *Life of Apollonius of Tyana*, Loeb Vol. I, p. xii).
143 Philostratus, *Life of Apollonius of Tyana*, 7.14.
144 Ibid., 2.5.

145 Ibid., 1.33.
146 Ibid., 6.2.
147 Philostratus, *Epistles of Apollonius of Tyana*, 26, to the priests in Olympia.
148 Philostratus, *Life of Apollonius of Tyana*, 5.35.
149 Philostratus, *Epistles of Apollonius of Tyana*, 58, to Valerius.
150 Philostratus, *Life of Apollonius of Tyana*, 8.30.31.
151 Grant, *The Climax of Rome*, pp. 182f.
152 Grant, *The Severans*, p. 74; Conybeare in Philostratus, *Life of Apollonius of Tyana*, Loeb, pp. xii–xiii.
153 Eusebius, *The Treatise of Eusebius*, ch. 1, in Philostratus, *Life of Apollonius of Tyana*, Loeb Vol. II, p. 487.
154 Grant, *The Climax of Rome*, p. 226.
155 Brauer, pp. 43, 45–51.
156 Philostratus, *Lives of the Sophists*, Loeb Vol. I, p. x.
157 Grant, *The Severans*, p. 84.
158 Eusebius, *Historia Ecclesiastica*, 6.21.3–4; Herodian, Loeb Vol. II, p. 119, note 2.
159 Grant, *The Severans*, p. 74; Fraser, p. 110; Turcan, p. 93.
160 Turcan, pp. 138–139; Vermaseren, pp. 138–139, 180; Michon.
161 Kleiner, *Roman Sculpture*, p. 328.
162 Grant, *The Severans*, pp. 5, 74; Turcan, p. 140.
163 Grant, *The Severans*, p. 61.
164 Balsdon, *Roman Women*, p. 153.
165 Herodian, 3.8.10.
166 Herodian, Loeb Vol. I, p. 315, note 1; Birley, *Septimius Severus*, pp. 158, 160.
167 Dio, 77.2.4; Grant, *The Severans*, p. 16.
168 Dio, 77.3–4; Herodian, 3.2.4f.
169 Dio, 77.2.4–5; Herodian, 3.11.3.
170 Dio, 77.3.
171 Caracalla made joint-emperor (Birley, *Septimius Severus*, p. 130); resented Plautianus (Herodian, 3.11.3–4).
172 Grant, *The Severans*, p. 16.
173 Dio, 77.4.3–4; Herodian, 34.11.11–12.
174 Dio, 77.4.4.
175 Ibid., 77.6.3; Herodian, 3.13.3.
176 Herodian, Loeb Vol. I, p. 348, note 1; Historia Augusta, *Caracalla*, 8.2–3; Grant, *The Severans*, p. 49; Birley, *Septimius Severus*, pp. 133, 164; Grant, *The Climax of Rome*, p. 79 (related to Julia Domna).
177 Grant, *The Severans*, p. 52.
178 Grant, *The Climax of Rome*, pp. 50, 81.
179 Ibid., p. 79.
180 Grant, *The Severans*, p. 49.
181 Dio, 77.7; Herodian, 3.10.3–4.
182 Herodian, 3.13.1–6.
183 Dio, 77.7; Herodian, 3.10.3.
184 Dio, 77.7.2.
185 BMCRE, V, 92; Herodian, Loeb Vol. I, p. 356, note 1; Howgego, pp. 86, 169: no. 163; Balsdon, *Roman Women*, p. 153.
186 Geta's resemblance to Severus (Dio, 78.1.3); Geta less violent than Caracalla (Julian, *The Caesars*, Loeb Vol. II, p. 359; Historia Augusta, *Geta*, 4–5).
187 Historia Augusta, *Geta*, 5.1.
188 Herodian 4.3.2–4, Loeb Vol. I, p. 367, note 3.
189 Dio, 77.7.
190 Ibid., 77.11.1; Herodian, 3.10.3, 3.13.1.

191 Dio, 77.7.1–2; Herodian, 3.10.4, 3.13.6.
192 Dio, 77.7.1; Herodian, 3.14.1–3, Loeb Vol. I, p. 357, note 2; Salway, p. 167; Balsdon, *Roman Women*, p. 153.
193 Herodian, 3.14.1–3.
194 Salway, p. 170.
195 Herodian, 3.14.9; Salway, p. 167.
196 Dio, 77.16.5.
197 Ibid., 77.14.1.
198 Gout (Historia Augusta, *Septimius Severus*, 16.6); arthritis (Herodian, 3.14.2); smallpox (Grant, *The Severans*, pp. 3, 19).
199 Dio, 77.13.4; Herodian, 3.14.2–3.
200 Herodian, Loeb Vol. I, p. 361, note 2.
201 Herodian, 3.15.2.
202 Dio, 77.14.3–7.
203 Herodian, 3.15.1–3; Dio, 77.17.4; Birley, *Septimius Severus*, p. 187.
204 Dio, 77.15.2.
205 Ibid., 78.1.3–4.
206 Partial reconciliation (Herodian, 3.15.6–8); trip to Rome (ibid., 3.15.7; Dio, 77.15.4).
207 Herodian, 4.1.1–2
208 Ibid., 4.2 (see Dio, 74.5, for comparison on the apotheosis of Pertinax).
209 Herodian, 4.2.2.
210 Ibid., 4.2.3–4.
211 Ibid., 4.2.4.
212 Ibid., 4.2.4–5.
213 Ibid., 4.2.7–8.
214 Ibid., 4.2.9–10.
215 Ibid., 4.2.10.
216 Ibid., 4.2.11.
217 See coin in Cohen (Faustina II), 69, 80.
218 Dio, 78.1; Herodian, 4.3.1–2, Loeb Vol. I, p. 369, note 2.
219 Herodian, 4.1.5.
220 Ibid., 4.3.4–8.
221 Ibid., 4.3.8–9.
222 Dio, 78.2.2.
223 Soldiers (ibid., 78.2.3); Caracalla himself (Herodian, 4.4.3, Loeb Vol. I, p. 391, note 2); wounded hand (Dio, 78.2.4).
224 Dio, 78.2.3–4.
225 Herodian, 4.6.
226 Dio, 78.4.1; Historia Augusta, *Caracalla*, 8.
227 Dio, 78.12.6; Harl, p. 364: no. 107.
228 Dio, 78.2.5–6.
229 Herodian, 4.6.3; Dio, 77.16.6; Historia Augusta, *Caracalla*, 3.3; Historia Augusta, *Geta*, 7.3–4.
230 Grant, *The Severans*, p. 47.
231 Dio, 78.13.1–2; Herodian, 4.3.4, 4.7.4–7.
232 Grant, *The Severans*, pp. 21–22.
233 Ibid., p. 46.
234 Ibid.; Fantham *et al.*, p. 352.
235 Dio, 79.23.2.
236 Ibid., 78.18.2–3.
237 Turcan, pp. 237–238.
238 Grant, *The Severans*, p. 70.

239 Grant, *History of Rome*, p. 382.
240 Dio, 78.9.5; Grant, *The Severans*, p. 31.
241 Grant, *The Severans*, p. 31.
242 Dio, 78.9.5–6; Grant, *The Severans*, p. 31.
243 Grant, *The Severans*, pp. 28–30, 49.
244 Dio, 78.13.4, 78.14.1–3; King, p. 170.
245 Sharing hardships (Dio, 78.13.1–2); increasing pay (Grant, *The Severans*, p. 34).
246 Dio, 79.3.3; Herodian, 4.7.3.
247 Herodian, 4.7.3.
248 Financial subsidies (Dio, 78.14; Grant, *The Roman Emperors*, p. 119; King, p. 170); loved by Germans (Herodian, 4.7.3).
249 King, p. 170.
250 Dio, 78.15.3.
251 Ibid.
252 Ibid., 78.15.4–5, 78.16.1–4.
253 Ibid., 78.15.2.
254 Ibid., 78.16.6; Herodian, 4.8.3.
255 Dio, 78.15.6, also, Dio, Loeb Vol. IX, p. 319, note 1; King, p. 142.
256 Dio, 78.22.1–24.1; Herodian, 4.8–9.8.
257 Germany (Dio, 78.13.5); Pergamon (ibid., 78.16.8); Alexandria (ibid., 78.22.1–24.1; Herodian, 4.8–9.8); Parthia (Herodian, 4.11.1–7).
258 Burns, "Was Caracalla Guilty of Human Sacrifice?".
259 Philostratus, *Life of Apollonius of Tyana*, 1.31, 5.25, 8.7, Loeb Vol. II, pp. 325, 345f.
260 Dio, 78.18.2.
261 Ibid., 78.18.3.
262 Ibid., 78.16.8, 78.23.4.
263 Kleiner, *Roman Sculpture*, p. 325.
264 Violent temper (Herodian, 4.3.4); savage expression (Dio, 78.11.1–2).
265 Dio, 78.11.2.
266 Ibid., 78.15.2.
267 Obstinate (ibid., 78.11.5); sound judgment (ibid., 78.11.3–4).
268 Herodian, 4.7.2, 4.7.7; Victor, 21.
269 Grant, *The Roman Emperors*, p. 120.
270 Dio, 78.7.2; Herodian, 4.8.1–3.
271 Dio, 78.19.
272 Burns, "Was Caracalla Guilty of Human Sacrifice?," p. 6.
273 Troy (Dio, 78.16.7; Herodian, 4.8.4); Pergamon (Herodian, 4.8.3).
274 Dio, 79.4.2–3.
275 Birley, *Septimius Severus*, p. 69.
276 Herodian, 4.11.1–7.
277 Ibid., 4.10.2–4.
278 Dio, 78.18.2–3.
279 Ibid., 79.4.2–3.
280 Ibid., 79.4.3–4.
281 Grant, *The Severans*, p. 22; Herodian, 4.13.3–4; Dio, 79.5; Herodian, 4.13.5–7.
282 Dio, 79.11.4.
283 Ibid., 79.11.1–2.
284 Grant, *The Severans*, p. 22.
285 Herodian, 4.13.4–7.
286 Dio, 79.23.1, 79.23.6.
287 Ibid., 79.23.1.
288 Ibid.

289 Ibid., 79.23.1–3.
290 Burial (Herodian, 4.13.8); deification (Grant, *The Severans*, p. 23).
291 Dio, 79.23.2–6.
292 Ibid., 79.23.6.
293 Ibid.; Herodian, 4.13.8.
294 Heliodorus, *Aethiopica*, 6.9.
295 Deification (Grant, *The Severans*, pp. 45–46; Kleiner, *Roman Sculpture*, p. 326; Balsdon, *Roman Women*, p. 160); burial (Dio, 79.24.3, Victor, 21).
296 Historia Augusta, *Septimius Severus*, 21.6–8; Historia Augusta, *Caracalla*, 10.1–4; Victor, 20.
297 Herodian, 4.9.3.
298 Historia Augusta, *Caracalla*, 10.1–4; Historia Augusta, *Septimius Severus*, 21.6–8; Eutropius, 8.20.
299 Kleiner *et al.*, *I Claudia II*, p. 80.
300 Grant, *The Severans*, p. 46; Herodian, Loeb Vol. I, p. 367, note 2; Kleiner *et al.*, *I Claudia II*, p. 22.
301 Kleiner *et al.*, *I Claudia*, p. 57.

11 JULIA MAMAEA: A WOMAN IN CHARGE

1 Herodian, Loeb Vol. II, p. 16, note 1; Birley, *Septimius Severus*, p. 192.
2 Birley, *Septimius Severus*, pp. 134, 192, 217; Victor, 115, 23 note 1; Dio, 79.30.2–4.
3 Dio, 79.30.2–4; Birley, *Septimius Severus*, p. 175.
4 Grant, *Roman Emperors*, p. 126.
5 Herodian, 5.3.2; Historia Augusta, *Macrinus*, 9.2.
6 Herodian, 5.3.9.
7 Dio, 79.31–32.
8 Death of Julius Avitus Alexianus (ibid., 79.30.4; Birley, *Septimius Severus*, pp. 192, 223); death of Julia Soaemias' husband (Birley, *Septimius Severus*, p. 175; Dio, 79.30.3; Herodian, Loeb Vol. II, p. 17, note 2).
9 Herodian, 5.3.3, 5.3.6; Historia Augusta, *Macrinus*, 9.3; Historia Augusta, Loeb Vol. II, p. 164, note 1.
10 Birley, *Septimius Severus*, p. 194.
11 Dio, 79.30.3; Historia Augusta, *Severus Alexander*, 5.1; Victor, 24; Herodian, Loeb Vol. II, p. 19, note 3, p. 186, note 4.
12 Birley, *Septimius Severus*, p. 217.
13 Ibid., p. 222.
14 Mamaea's married daughter (Dio, 79.31.4); Mamaea's second son (Birley, *Septimius Severus*, p. 217; Historia Augusta, *Two Maximini*, 29.1–5).
15 Historia Augusta, *Severus Alexander*, 13.1.
16 Star (ibid., 13.5); purple snake (ibid., 14.1).
17 Defeat (Dio, 79.26.5); payment to Parthian king (ibid., 79.27.1–2).
18 Ibid., 79.28.1–2.
19 Herodian, 5.3.11, 5.4.2.
20 Ibid., 5.3.9, 5.4.1–2.
21 Ibid., 5.3.10; Historia Augusta, *Macrinus*, 9.4.
22 Historia Augusta, *Elagabalus*, 2.1; Herodian, Loeb Vol. II, p. 24, note 1.
23 Dio, 79.32.2.
24 Historia Augusta, *Macrinus*, 9.5–6.
25 Dio, 79.34.3–4 (date); Herodian, 5.3.11; Historia Augusta, *Macrinus*, 9.6.
26 Herodian, 5.3.12; Historia Augusta, *Macrinus*, 9.6.
27 Grant, *Roman Emperors*, p. 125.

28 Dio, 79.38.1.
29 Ibid., 79.31.4; Historia Augusta, *Macrinus*, 9.1–2; Herodian, 5.5.4.2, Loeb Vol. II, p. 27, note 1.
30 Dio, 79.31.4.
31 Ibid., 79.32.3, 79.33.1–2; Herodian, 5.4.3–4; Historia Augusta, *Macrinus*, 9.3.
32 Herodian 5.4.4; Dio, 79.32.3.
33 Dio, 79.34.4–5.
34 Ibid., 79.34.
35 Herodian, 5.4.5–10; Dio, 79.37.3–79.39.1; Historia Augusta, *Macrinus*, 9.3.
36 Dio, 80.6.2.
37 Ibid., 79.38.3–4.
38 Ibid.
39 Elagabalus' appearance (ibid.); victory (Herodian, 5.4.7; Dio, 79.38.4).
40 Shaving of hair and beard (Herodian, 5.4.7; Dio, 78.39.2–4); capture and execution (Herodian, 5.4.11; Dio, 79.40.1–2; Historia Augusta, *Macrinus*, 9.3).
41 Herodian, Loeb Vol. II, p. 16, note 1, also p. 41, note 3.
42 Dio, 79.30.3; Herodian, 5.3.2, 5.8.3.
43 Dio, 80.20.2; Herodian, Loeb Vol. II, p. 19, note 2.
44 Herodian, 5.3.3–4.
45 Turcan, p. 178; Herodian, 5.3.8–10; Historia Augusta, *Elagabalus*, 18f.
46 Herodian, 5.6.10, 5.8.1; Historia Augusta, *Elagabalus*, 5.4, 23.3–5, 26.5; Dio, 80.14–16, 80.11.1, 80.16.7.
47 Dio, 80.5.5, 80.13–14, 80.15–16; Historia Augusta, *Elagabalus*, 5.2–5, 6.5, 10.2–7.
48 Dio, 80.13.1, 80.9.4; Historia Augusta, *Elagabalus*, 24.2.
49 Herodian, 5.3.6–7; Dio, 80.11.2; Historia Augusta, *Elagabalus*, 23.2–5, 26.1–2.
50 Dio, 80.11.1.
51 Kiefer, p. 347; Herodian, 5.3.5.
52 Historia Augusta, *Elagabalus*, 7.3; Herodian, 5.6.4–5.
53 Historia Augusta, *Elagabalus*, 7.1–3.
54 Ibid., 28.2.
55 Balsdon, *Roman Women*, p. 158; Herodian, 5.5.3–4; Dio, 80.3.1; Historia Augusta, *Elagabalus*, 5.1.
56 Herodian, 5.53–6.
57 Dio, 80.6.3.
58 Ibid.; Birley, *Septimius Severus*, p. 193.
59 Herodian, 5.5.6–7.
60 Ibid., 5.5.7–10.
61 Historia Augusta, *Elagabalus*, 11.1–3; Herodian, 5.7.6–7, Loeb Vol. II, p. 57, note 4.
62 Herodian, 5.7.6; Historia Augusta, *Elagabalus*, 12.1.
63 Dio, 80.18.4.
64 Ibid., 80.9.1.
65 Ibid., 80.9.3; Herodian, 5.6.1.
66 Historia Augusta, *Elagabalus*, 6.6; Herodian, 5.6.2; Dio, 80.9.3–4.
67 Dio, 80.9.4.
68 Ibid., 80.5.1–4.
69 Herodian, 5.6.2, Loeb Vol. II, p. 48, note 1.
70 Dio, 80.9.4.
71 RIC, Elagabalus: Julia Paula 210, 211, 212; Aquilia Severa 225, 228, 434; Annia Faustina 232, 399.
72 Historia Augusta, *Elagabalus*, 3.4, 17.8; Herodian, 5.5.8; Herodian, Loeb Vol. II, pp. 52–53, note 1.

73 Herodian, 5.6.6–8.
74 Historia Augusta, *Elagabalus*, 3.4, 6.9.
75 Herodian, 5.6.9–10; Historia Augusta, *Elagabalus*, 8.3.
76 Herodian, 5.5.1, Loeb Vol. II, p. 16, note 1.
77 Ibid., 5.7.1.
78 Dio, 80.15.4–80.16.1.
79 Herodian, 5.7.1–2.
80 Ibid., Loeb Vol. II, p. 58, note 1.
81 Dio, 80.17.2.
82 Alexander's coins (e.g. RIC IV, 2, 3, 383); Mamaea's coins under Elagabalus (Grant, *Severans*, p. 100; BMCRE, pp. ccxxx, 571, 614).
83 Herodian, 5.3.10, 5.7.3.
84 Ibid., 5.7.3.
85 Ibid., 6.1.6; Historia Augusta, *Elagabalus*, 13.4–4; Historia Augusta, *Severus Alexander*, 20.4; Eutropius, 8.23; Victor, 24; Historia Augusta, *Severus Alexander*, 26.9.
86 Herodian, 6.1.5; Historia Augusta, *Severus Alexander*, 3.1, Loeb Vol. II, p. 182, note 2.
87 Alexander's virtues (Historia Augusta, *Elagabalus*, 13.2–3; Historia Augusta, *Severus Alexander*, 66.1); Alexander dominated by his mother (Herodian, 6.1.10; Julian, *The Caesars*, Loeb Vol. II, p. 361).
88 Historia Augusta, *Severus Alexander*, 3.
89 Ibid., 27.5–9.
90 Herodian, 5.7.5–6; Historia Augusta, *Severus Alexander*, 3.1, 27.10.
91 Herodian, 5.7.4–6.
92 Historia Augusta, *Elagabalus*, 19.2–5.
93 Ibid., 20.5–7.
94 Historia Augusta, *Severus Alexander*, 37.2–12.
95 Dio, 80.19.1.
96 Herodian, 5.8.2; Dio, 80.18.4, 80.19.1–2; Historia Augusta, *Elagabalus*, 5.1, 10.1.
97 Herodian, 5.7.5–6; Dio, 80.19.1; Historia Augusta, *Elagabalus*, 13.1.
98 Herodian, 5.8.2.
99 Ibid., 5.8.3; Dio, 80.19.1–2; Historia Augusta, *Elagabalus*, 15.3; Herodian, 5.8.3.
100 Herodian, 5.8.4–5, Loeb Vol. II, p. 69, note 2; Dio, 80.20.1.
101 Herodian, Loeb Vol. II, p. 72, note 1.
102 Historia Augusta, *Elagabalus*, 4.1–2, 12.3–4, 13.6; Dio, 80.17.2.
103 Herodian, Loeb Vol. II, p. 72, note 1.
104 Dio, 80.20.1.
105 Historia Augusta, *Severus Alexander*, 66.1; Eusebius, *Historia Ecclesiastica*, 6.
106 Grant, *Severans*, p. 48; Brauer, p. 119.
107 Historia Augusta, *Elagabalus*, 2.1, 18.2–3.
108 Ibid., 4.3–4.
109 Herodian, 5.8.4–5; Historia Augusta, *Elagabalus*, 13.1, 15.5–6.
110 Dio, 80.19.1, 80.20; Herodian, 5.8.3; Historia Augusta, *Elagabalus*, 13.5–8.
111 Dio, 80.19.2–4; Historia Augusta, *Elagabalus*, 13.5–15.3.
112 New plot against Alexander (Dio, 80.20.1; Historia Augusta, *Elagabalus*, 16.1); murder of Elagabalus (Historia Augusta, *Elagabalus*, 17.1).
113 Herodian, 80.1.1; Historia Augusta, *Elagabalus*, 17.1–3, 18.2–3.
114 Dio, 80.21.3; Historia Augusta, *Elagabalus*, 17.5.
115 Grant, *Severans*, p. 47.
116 Historia Augusta, *Severus Alexander*, 6.2; Herodian, Loeb Vol. II, p. 74, note 1; Historia Augusta, Loeb Vol. II, p. 188, note 3.

117 Historia Augusta, *Elagabalus*, 25.1–3.
118 Age at accession (Herodian 6.1.7; Historia Augusta, Loeb Vol. II, p. 204, note 3); held in check (Herodian 6.1.1–2; Historia Augusta, *Severus Alexander*, 14.7).
119 Herodian, Loeb Vol. II, pp. 74–75, note 1; Historia Augusta, Loeb Vol. II, p.198, note 2.
120 Coin portraits (Grant, *The Climax of Rome*, p. 92); simple dress (Historia Augusta, *Severus Alexander*, 4.1–3); simple lifestyle (ibid., 4.3, 34.1, 5–8).
121 Grant, *The Roman Emperors*, p. 129; Scarre, p. 153; Herodian, 6.1.3, Loeb Vol. II, pp. 80–81, note 2; Turcan, p. 184.
122 Dio, 80.17.2, Herodian, Loeb Vol. II, p. 72, note 1; Historia Augusta, *Elagabalus*, 18.3.
123 Dio, fragment, Loeb Vol. IX, p. 489; Birley, *Septimius Severus*, p. 222.
124 Herodian, Loeb Vol. II, p. 78, note 2.
125 Ibid., 6.1.2; Dio, fragment, Loeb Vol. IX, p. 489.
126 Historia Augusta, *Severus Alexander*, 16.1–3; Grant, *The Climax of Rome*, p. 75.
127 Historia Augusta, *Severus Alexander*, 21.1–2, 26.1–4, 32.5, 39.6.
128 Herodian, 6.1.3–4; Historia Augusta, *Severus Alexander*, 15.1–2, 16.3.
129 Historia Augusta, *Elagabalus*, 6.1–6; Historia Augusta, *Severus Alexander*, 15.3–4, 41.3–7; Grant, *Severans*, p. 43.
130 Herodian, 6.1.
131 Ibid.
132 Ibid., 6.1.1.
133 Dio, 80.1.1; Victor, 24; Eutropius, 8.23; Historia Augusta, *Severus Alexander*, 15.6, 26.5–6, 51.4; Historia Augusta, Loeb Vol. II, p. 138, note 2.
134 Historia Augusta, *Severus Alexander*, 31.2–3; Historia Augusta, *Elagabalus*, 16.4; Grant, *History of Rome*, p. 380.
135 Grant, *History of Rome*, p. 382; Grant, *Severans*, p. 51.
136 Dio, 80.2.2; Grant, *History of Rome*, p. 382; Grant, *The Roman Emperors*, p. 132.
137 Lack of political bloodshed (Herodian, 6.1.6–7; Historia Augusta, *Severus Alexander*, 52.2); new laws (Historia Augusta, *Severus Alexander*, 43.1).
138 Historia Augusta, *Severus Alexander*, 52.1–2.
139 Historia Augusta, *Elagabalus*, 17.9; Historia Augusta, *Severus Alexander*, 25.6.
140 Lanciani, pp. 534–540.
141 Grant, *The Roman Emperors*, p. 132.
142 Historia Augusta, *Severus Alexander*, 24.6; Scarre, p. 156.
143 Dio, 79.25.3; Historia Augusta, *Severus Alexander*, 24.3–4; Lanciani, pp. 370–371.
144 RIC IV, 410; Cohen, 468.
145 Historia Augusta, *Severus Alexander*, 26.9.10; Lanciani, p. 339.
146 Date of (Grant, *Severans*, p. 51); praetorian mutiny (Dio, 80.2.2–3).
147 Dio, 80.2.2–3.
148 Ibid.; Grant, *The Roman Emperors*, p. 131; Historia Augusta, *Severus Alexander*, 51.4.
149 Herodian, 6.1.4.
150 Herodian, Loeb Vol. II, p. 85, note 4.
151 Herodian, 6.1.5.
152 Ibid., 6.2.1; Dio, 80.3–4.
153 Grant, *The Roman Emperors*, p. 133.
154 Dio, 80.3.1.
155 Grant, *The Roman Emperors*, p. 133.
156 Dio, 80.3.1; Grant, *Severans*, p. 37.
157 Historia Augusta, *Severus Alexander*, 51.4; Herodian, Loeb Vol. II, p. 85, note 4.

158 Historia Augusta, *Severus Alexander*, 49.3–5; Herodian, 6.1.9, Loeb Vol. II, p. 87, note 3.
159 Herodian, 6.1.9.
160 Balsdon, *Roman Women*, p. 163.
161 Grant, *The Roman Emperors*, p. 131.
162 Herodian, 6.1.9; Historia Augusta, Loeb Vol. II, p. 214, note 2.
163 Herodian, 6.1.9; Historia Augusta, *Severus Alexander*, 49.3–5.
164 Sallustius' military career (Historia Augusta, *Severus Alexander*, 58.1, Loeb Vol. II, p. 294, note 4); adoption (Grant, *The Roman Emperors*, p. 131).
165 Suspicion (Grant, *The Roman Emperors*, p. 131; Scarre, p. 154); jealousy (Herodian, 6.1.9); Orbiana banished (ibid., 6.1.10).
166 Herodian, 6.1.9.
167 Ibid., 6.1.10.
168 Ibid.
169 Historia Augusta, *Severus Alexander*, 51.1–3.
170 Dio, 80.2.1.
171 Ibid., 80.4.2.
172 Ibid., 80.5.1–2.
173 Ibid., 80.4.1; Herodian, 6.2.1–5; Millar, p. 149.
174 Herodian, 6.2.2; Dio, 80.4.1.
175 Herodian, 6.4.2, Loeb Vol. II, p. 103, note 2.
176 Millar, p. 149.
177 Herodian, Loeb Vol. II, p. 103, note 4.
178 Ibid., 6.5.1.
179 Ibid., 5–6.
180 Illness (ibid., 6.6.1); over-protectiveness (ibid., 6.5.8–9).
181 Historia Augusta, *Severus Alexander*, 55.1, Loeb Vol. II, pp. 288–289, note 2; Eutropius, 8.23, p. 133, note 66; Millar, p. 150; Herodian, 6.6.6.
182 Historia Augusta, *Severus Alexander*, 55.1–2.
183 Herodian, 6.6.6–6.7.1.
184 Boardman *et al.*, p. 859.
185 Historia Augusta, *Severus Alexander*, 56; Herodian, Loeb Vol. II, p. 125, note 3.
186 Games and largess (Historia Augusta, *Severus Alexander*, 57.6–7); title (Grant, *The Roman Emperors*, p. 133).
187 Historia Augusta, *Severus Alexander*, 57.7.
188 Millar, p. 149; Daly, p. 21; Herodian, Loeb Vol. II, p. 119, note 2.
189 Eusebius, *Historia Ecclesiastica*, 6.30.
190 Origen's date of birth (Crouzel, p. 11); family history (Daly, p. 2).
191 Eusebius, *Historia Ecclesiastica*, 6.8.1–5; Crouzel, pp. 8–9.
192 Diogenes Laertius, 8.9.
193 Crouzel, p. 9, note 32.
194 Grant, *The Climax of Rome*, p. 210; Daly, p. 3.
195 Origen, *On Prayer, Part 1*, 17.2; Greer, p. 117.
196 Origen, *First Principles*, 4.9.
197 Origen, *Dialogue with Heraclides, etc.*, 18.15–20.
198 Origen, *An Exhortation to Martyrdom*, 32.
199 Origen, *On Prayer, Preface*, 2.1.
200 Respect for Plato (Crouzel, p. 157; Grant, *The Climax of Rome*, pp. 210–211); interpretation (Grant, *The Climax of Rome*, pp. 210–211).
201 Grant, *The Climax of Rome*, p. 181.
202 Ibid.; Hanfmann, p. 242.
203 For example, RIC IV, 109, 123, 528, 541.

204 Crouzel, p. 17.
205 Orosius, 7.18.7; Herodian, Loeb Vol. II, p. 61, note 3.
206 Crouzel, p. 17.
207 Historia Augusta, *Severus Alexander*, 51.6–8.
208 Ibid., 28.7.
209 Ibid., 26.8; Grant, *The Roman Emperors*, p. 134.
210 Historia Augusta, *Severus Alexander*, 29.1–2, 31.4–5.
211 Giacosa, p.120, no. XLVIII; Grant, *Severans*, plate 26.
212 Historia Augusta, *Severus Alexander*, 22.4–5; Giacosa, p. 64.
213 Historia Augusta, *Severus Alexander*, 66.1; Balsdon, *Roman Women*, p. 164; Orosius, 6.15; Eusebius, *Historia Ecclesiastica*, 6.15; Gibbon, p. 480.
214 Grant, *The Roman Emperors*, p. 139; Grant, *The Climax of Rome*, pp. 210–211; Toynbee, p. 298.
215 Herodian, 6.7.2–3; Historia Augusta, *Severus Alexander*, 59.1–3; King, p. 170.
216 Herodian, 6.7.5, Loeb Vol. II, p. 125, note 3.
217 Ibid. 6.4.7; Dio, 80.4.1–2.
218 Herodian, 6.7.3.
219 Historia Augusta, *Severus Alexander*, 52.3; Herodian, 6.8.4, Loeb Vol. II, p. 136, note 1; Scarre, p. 156; Grant, *Severans*, pp. 38, 43.
220 Herodian, 6.6.1–2, 6.7.3; Grant, *The Roman Emperors*, p. 133.
221 Herodian, 6.7.3.
222 Ibid., Loeb Vol. II, p. 125, note 3
223 Ibid., 6.7.6, Loeb Vol. II, p. 127, note 3.
224 Ibid., 6.7.9; King, p. 170.
225 Herodian, 6.7.9.
226 Ibid., 6.7.10.
227 Historia Augusta, *Severus Alexander*, 63.5; Historia Augusta, *Two Maximini*, 7.5; Herodian, Loeb Vol. II, p. 123, note 3, p. 130, note 2.
228 Herodian, 6.8.
229 Ibid., 6.8.3, 6.9.5.
230 Illiterate (Victor, 25); origins (Herodian, 6.8.1; Historia Augusta, *Two Maximini*, 1.5).
231 Historia Augusta, *Two Maximini*, 6.8–9.
232 Herodian, 6.8.1–3.
233 Historia Augusta, *Two Maximini*, 2–3.
234 Grant, *The Roman Emperors*, p. 137; Herodian, 6.8.1, Loeb Vol. II, p. 133, note 2.
235 Herodian, 6.8.2; Historia Augusta, *Severus Alexander*, 59.7.
236 Herodian, 6.8.5.
237 Ibid., 6.8.7–8; Eutropius, p. 133, note 67.
238 Herodian, 6.9.1–2.
239 Ibid., 6.9.3–4.
240 Ibid., 6.9.5–6.
241 Ibid., 6.9.6.
242 Ibid., 6.9.6–7; Historia Augusta, *Severus Alexander*, 59.7–8, 60.1–2.
243 Historia Augusta, *Severus Alexander*, 61.6; Birley, *Septimius Severus*, p. 195; Eutropius, p. 133, note 67.
244 Ammianus Marcellinus, 26.6.19; Scarre, p. 155.
245 Bonus (Herodian, 6.8.8); campaign (Historia Augusta, *Two Maximini*, 12).
246 Herodian, 7.1.2; Historia Augusta, *Two Maximini*, 12.2–3.
247 Herodian, 7.2.8; Historia Augusta, *Two Maximini*, 12.10–11.
248 Maximinus, Gordianus I, Gordianus II, Balbinus, Pupienus, Gordianus III.

249 Killed in his tent (Historia Augusta, *Two Maximini*, 23.6; Herodian, 8.5.8–9); suicide (Historia Augusta, *Two Maximini*, 32.4–5).
250 Historia Augusta, *Severus Alexander*, 14.7, 63.1–2.
251 Feast day (ibid., 63.4); deification and burial (ibid., 63.3).
252 Herodian, 6.1.8, 6.9.4, 6.9.8; Julian, *The Caesars*, Loeb p. 361; Historia Augusta, *Severus Alexander*, 14.7, 69.8.
253 Herodian, 6.1.8.
254 Grant, *The Roman Emperors*, p. 133
255 Ibid., p. 139; Scarre, p. 161.
256 Grant, *Severans*, p. 48.
257 Victor, 24; Grant, *The Roman Emperors*, p. 139.
258 Turcan, p. 49; Witt, p. 238.

12 EPILOGUE: THE LATER ROMAN EMPRESSES

1 Grant, *The Climax of Rome*, p. 62, p. 270, note 50.
2 BMCRE (Maximinus), 126–129.
3 Grant, *The Roman Emperors*, p. 150.
4 Eutropius, 9.2; Scarre, p. 165.
5 Historia Augusta, *Three Gordians*, 26–27.
6 Ibid., 28.6.
7 Ibid., 29–30; Victor, 27.
8 Bought peace (Harl, p. 129); turned west (Grant, *The Roman Emperors*, p. 152).
9 Crouzel, p. 40; Scarre, p. 167.
10 Scarre, p. 167; Grant, *The Roman Emperors*, p. 155.
11 Historia Augusta, *Three Gordians*, 33.1–2; Victor, 28.
12 RIC IV, 200a.
13 Grant, *The Roman Emperors*, p. 155.
14 Victor, 28; Eutropius, 9.3.
15 Grant, *The Roman Emperors*, p. 157; Scarre, p. 170.
16 Grant, *The Roman Emperors*, p. 157.
17 Ibid., p. 156; Scarre, p. 170.
18 Grant, *The Roman Emperors*, p. 156.
19 Victor, 29; Eutropius, 4.5; Ammianus Marcellinus, 31.13.13; Grant, *The Roman Emperors*, pp. 157–158; Scarre, p. 170.
20 Grant, *The Roman Emperors*, p. 160.
21 Victor, 30.
22 RIC IV (Aemilian), 30; Biaggi, p. 275.
23 Eutropius, 9.6.
24 Ibid., 9.6–7; Scarre, p. 171.
25 Biaggi, p. 279.
26 Bray, p. 49.
27 Victor, 32.
28 Scarre, p. 173.
29 Ibid.; Epitome, 32.5–6; Victor, 135, note 6; but see Bray, p. 115.
30 Grant, *The Roman Emperors*, p. 173; Scarre, pp. 175–182; Historia Augusta, *Thirty Pretenders*, 3.
31 Historia Augusta, *Two Valerians*, 6.2–4; Historia Augusta, *Thirty Pretenders*, 15; Grant, *The Roman Emperors*, p. 170.
32 Julian, *The Caesars*, 313; Ammianus Marcellinus, 16.1.9; Historia Augusta, *Two Gallieni*, 3.6–8, 5.7, 7.4–8.7, 16–18; Bray, pp. 206–209, 217–222; Blois, p. 153.

33 Historia Augusta, *Two Gallieni*, 14; Bray, p. 299.

34 Bray, p. 30; Grant, *The Roman Emperors*, p. 172.

35 Bray, pp. 231–244.

36 Plotinus (ibid., pp. 162, 217, 244–245, 247); Mysteries (ibid., pp. 239–244, 251).

37 Ibid., pp. 153–164; Grant, *The Climax of Rome*, p. 231; Grant, *The Roman Emperors*, p. 165; Scarre, pp. 173–174.

38 Historia Augusta, *Two Gallieni*, 11.6.

39 Ibid., 11.8; see Loeb Vol. III, p. 40, note 1 – additional text from *Codex Bellovacensis* of Binetus, translation by James R. Burns.

40 Scarre, p. 178.

41 Kleiner, *Roman Sculpture*, p. 381, fig. 350.

42 Historia Augusta, *Two Gallieni*, 21.3; Victor, 33.

43 Historia Augusta, *Two Gallieni*, 21.3; Victor, 33.6; Epitome, 33.1; Bray, p. 31.

44 Victor, 33.6; Bray, pp. 122, 188–189.

45 Grant, *The Roman Emperors*, p. 172.

46 Bray, pp. 67, 73.

47 Ibid., p. 95.

48 Ibid., pp. 94, 161–164.

49 Historia Augusta, *Two Gallieni*, 12.5; Bray, p. 227.

50 Bray, pp. 124, 217, 298, 308.

51 Historia Augusta, *Two Gallieni*, 13.1.

52 Balsdon, *Roman Women*, p. 164; Vaughan, pp. 9–10; Scarre, p. 182.

53 Historia Augusta, *Thirty Pretenders*, 30.2; Historia Augusta, *Two Gallieni*, 13.1–5.

54 Scarre, pp. 180–181.

55 Historia Augusta, *Thirty Pretenders*, 15, 30.15, 17–18.

56 Ibid., 30.2; Balsdon, *Roman Women*, p. 169; Vaughan, pp. 9, 120.

57 Historia Augusta, *Thirty Pretenders*, 30.20–22; Balsdon, *Roman Women*, p. 165.

58 Vaughan, p. 52.

59 Historia Augusta, *Thirty Pretenders*, 30.3.

60 Eutropius, 9.13.

61 Historia Augusta, *Thirty Pretenders*, 30.3, 24–27.

62 Ibid., 30.27; Vaughan, pp. 224–236; Fraser, p. 126; Grant, *The Roman Emperors*, p. 186.

63 Sayles, p. 103.

64 Historia Augusta, *Aurelian*, 6.2, 21.5–9.

65 Ibid., 45.5, translation by James R. Burns.

66 Ibid., 49.6.

67 Historia Augusta, *Tacitus*, 1–5; Victor, 35–36; Scarre, p. 189; Vagi, p. 369.

68 Balsdon, *Roman Women*, p. 166; Grant, *The Roman Emperors*, pp. 204, 209; Scarre, pp. 203–205.

69 Kleiner, *Roman Sculpture*, p. 418, fig. 386.

70 Balsdon, *Roman Women*, pp. 165–169; Grant, *The Roman Emperors*, p. 209; Giacosa, pp. 69–71.

71 Giacosa, p. 70.

72 Balsdon, *Roman Women*, pp. 167–168; Grant, *The Roman Emperors*, pp. 208, 222; Giacosa, pp. 70–71.

73 Grant, *The Roman Emperors*, p. 285; Scarre, pp. 214, 216.

74 Balsdon, *Roman Women*, p. 166; Grant, *Constantine*, pp. 16–17, 19.

75 Grant, *Constantine*, pp. 139–141.

76 Grant, *The Roman Emperors*, pp. 230–231; Scarre, pp. 216–217.

77 Grant, *The Climax of Rome*, pp. 233, 238; Bray, p. 90.

78 World Factbook 2000.
79 Grant, *The Climax of Rome*, p. 240.
80 Giacosa, p. 74.
81 Ibid., pp. 74–75; Scarre, pp. 215–216; Grant, *Constantine*, pp. 113–115.
82 Giacosa, p. 72.
83 Grant, *Constantine*, p. 204.
84 Ibid., pp. 202–205; Balsdon, *Roman Women*, pp. 166, 169; Giacosa, pp. 76–77; Kleiner, *Roman Sculpture*, pp. 442–443.
85 Ammianus Marcellinus, 31.12.10–19.
86 Grant, *The Roman Emperors*, p. 264.
87 Ibid., p. 273; Scarre, p. 229.
88 Grant, *The Roman Emperors*, p. 272.
89 Campbell, *Masks: Oriental*, pp. 326–327.
90 Grant, *The Roman Emperors*, p. 272.
91 Giacosa, pp. 90–96; Scarre, p. 230.
92 Giacosa, pp. 81–87; Scarre, p. 231.
93 Giacosa, pp. 88–90; Scarre, p. 231.

BIBLIOGRAPHY

Ancient and medieval sources

Adamantius Judaeus, *Scriptores physiognomici Graeci et Latini*, R. Foerster, Leipzig, 1893.

Aelius Aristides, Oration 26 (To Rome), translation by C. A. Behr, *Aristides in Four Volumes*, Harvard, Cambridge, Mass.

Ammianus Marcellinus, translation by John C. Rolfe, Loeb edition, 3 volumes, Harvard, Cambridge, Mass., 1986.

Appian, *Civil Wars*, translation by Horace White, *Roman History*, Loeb edition, 4 volumes, Harvard, Cambridge, Mass., 1972.

Aulus Gellius, *The Attic Nights of Aulus Gellius*, Loeb edition, 3 volumes, translated by John C. Rolfe, Heinemann, G. P. Putnam's Sons, London, 1927.

Avienus, *Descriptio Orbis Terrae*, translation in Martin Jessop Price and Bluma L. Trell, *Coins and Their Cities: Architecture on the Ancient Coins of Greece, Rome, and Palestine*, V. C. Vecchi and Sons, London, 1977.

Cicero, *Tusculan Disputations*, translation by J. E. King, Harvard, Cambridge, Mass., 1989. See also translations by Carlin Barton in *Sorrows of the Ancient Romans: The Gladiator and the Monster*, Princeton University Press, Princeton, 1993.

Corpus Inscriptionum Graecorum, edited by A. Boeckius, Olms, Berlin, 1825–1877.

Crinagoras, *Epigrams in Greek Anthology*, translation by W. R. Paton, Cambridge, Mass., 1918.

(Digest) Justinian, *The Digest of Roman Law*, Penguin, Harmondsworth, 1986.

(Dio) Cassius Dio, *Roman History*, translation by Earnest Cary, *Dio's Roman History*, Loeb edition, Volumes V–IX (1917, 1924, 1925, 1927), Harvard, Cambridge, Mass. (Book numbers in the notes conform to the principal system used in Loeb.)

Diogenes Laertius, *Lives of Eminent Philosophers*, translation by R. D. Hicks, Loeb edition, 2 volumes, Harvard, Cambridge, Mass., 1972.

(Epitome), Anonymous, *Epitome de Caesaribus* (translation in preparation by H. W. Bird, Translated Texts for Historians Volume 14, Liverpool University Press, Liverpool).

Eusebius, *The Treatise of Eusebius*, translation by F. C. Conybeare, in *Philostratus: The Life of Apollonius of Tyana*, Loeb edition, Volume II, Harvard, London, 1921.

Eusebius, *Historia Ecclesiastica*, translation by Kirsopp Lake and J. E. L. Oulton, *Ecclesiastical History*, Loeb edition, 2 volumes, Harvard, Cambridge, Mass., 1984; also translation by A. S. Worrall in Henri Crouzel, *Origen*, Harper and Row, San Francisco, 1989.

Eutropius, *The Breviarium ab Urbe Condita*, translated by H. W. Bird, Translated Texts for Historians Volume 14, Liverpool University Press, Liverpool, 1993.

Fronto, Marcus Cornelius, translation by C. R. Haines, *The Correspondence of M. Cornelius Fronto*, Loeb edition, 2 volumes (1919, 1920), Harvard, Cambridge, Mass.

Heliodorus, *Aethiopica*, translation by B. P. Reardon, *Collected Ancient Greek Novels*, University of California Press, Berkeley, 1989; and by Sir Walter Lamb, *Ethiopian Story*, J. M. Dent, London, 1997.

Herodian, *History of the Empire*, translation by C. R. Whittaker, *Herodian*, Loeb edition, Harvard, Cambridge, Mass., 1969, 1970.

(Historia Augusta), translation by David Magie, *Scriptores Historiae Augustae*, Loeb edition, 3 volumes (1921, 1924, 1932), Harvard, Cambridge, Mass., 1982; also Anthony Birley, *Lives of the Later Caesars: The First Part of the Augustan History, with Newly Compiled Lives of Nerva and Trajan*, Penguin Books, London, 1976.

Josephus, Flavius, *Antiquities of the Jews*, translated by William Whiston, *The Works of Flavius Josephus*, David McKay Publisher, Philadelphia, 1896.

Josephus, Flavius, *Life of Flavius Josephus*, translated by William Whiston, *The Works of Flavius Josephus*, David McKay Publisher, Philadelphia, 1896.

Josephus, Flavius, *Wars of the Jews*, translated by William Whiston, *The Works of Flavius Josephus*, David McKay Publisher, Philadelphia, 1896.

Julian, *The Caesars*, translation by Wilmer Cave Wright, *The Works of the Emperor Julian*, Loeb edition, Volume II, Harvard, Cambridge, Mass., [1923] 1992.

Julius Caesar, *The Gallic War*, translation by H. J. Edwards, Loeb edition, Harvard, Cambridge, Mass., 1984.

Juvenal, *Satires*, translation by G. G. Ramsay, *Juvenal and Persius*, Loeb edition, Harvard, Cambridge, Mass., 1940.

Livy, *History of Rome*, translations by B. O. Foster, F. G. Moore, Evan T. Sage, and A. C. Schlesinger, Loeb edition, 14 volumes, Harvard, Cambridge, Mass., 1970.

Lucian, *Affairs of the Heart*, translation by M. D. MacLeod, Loeb edition, Volume VIII, Harvard, Cambridge, Mass., 1967.

Lucian, *De Dea Syria*, translation by Harold W. Attridge and Robert A. Oden, Scholars Press, Missoula, 1976.

Lucian, *The Passing of Peregrinus*, translation by A. M. Harmon, *Lucian*, Loeb edition, Volume V, Harvard, Cambridge, Mass., 1936.

Lucretius, *De Rerum Natura*, translation by W. H. D. Rouse, revised by Martin F. Smith, *Lucretius: On the Nature of Things*, Loeb edition, Harvard, Cambridge, Mass., 1992.

Macrobius, *Saturnalia*, translated by Percival Vaughan Davies, *Records of Civilization Sources and Studies* 79, Columbia University Press, New York, 1969.

Marcus Aurelius, *Meditations*, translations by C. R. Haines, *The Communings With Himself of Marcus Aurelius Antoninus, Emperor of Rome*, Loeb edition, Harvard, Cambridge, Mass., 1987; also George Long, *Meditations*, Classics Club edition, Walter J. Black, Roslyn, N.Y., 1945.

Martial, *Epigrams*, translation by D. R. Shackleton Bailey, Loeb edition, 2 volumes, Harvard, Cambridge, Mass., 1993.

Musonius Rufus, translation in Mary R. Lefkovitz and Maureen B. Fant, *Women's Life in Greece and Rome: A Source Book in Translation*, The Johns Hopkins University Press, Baltimore, 1992.

Oppian, *Cynegetica*, translation by A. W. Mair, *Oppian, Colluthus, Tryphiodorus*, Loeb edition, Harvard, Cambridge, Mass., 1928.

Origen, *An Exhortation to Martyrdom*, translation by Rowan A. Greer, *Origen: An Exhortation to Martyrdom, Prayer and Selected Works*, Paulist Press, New York, 1979.

Origen, *Contra Celsum*, translation by Henry Chadwick, *Origen, Contra Celsum, Translated with an Introduction and Notes by Henry Chadwick*, Cambridge University Press, Cambridge, 1980.

Origen, *Dialogue with Heraclides*, translation by Robert J. Daly, *Origen: Treatise on the Passover and Dialogue of Origen with Heraclides and His Fellow Bishops on the Father, the Son, and the Soul*, Paulist Press, New York/Mahwah, N.J., 1972.

Origen, *First Principles*, translation by Rowan A. Greer, *Origen: An Exhortation to Martyrdom, Prayer and Selected Works*, Paulist Press, New York, 1979.

Origen, *On Prayer*, translation by Rowan A. Greer, *Origen: An Exhortation to Martyrdom, Prayer and Selected Works*, Paulist Press, New York, 1979.

Orosius, Paulus, *Historiae Adversus Paganos*, translated by Roy J. Deferrari, *The Seven Books of History Against the Pagans*, Washington, Catholic University of America Press, 1964.

"Ovid," *Consolatia ad Liviam*, translation by J. H. Mozley, *Ovid: The Art of Love and Other Poems*, Loeb edition, Volume II, Harvard, Cambridge, Mass., 1979.

Ovid, *Epistulae Ex Ponto*, translation by A. L. Wheeler, revised by G. P. Goold, *Tristia and Ex Ponto*, Loeb edition, Harvard, Cambridge, Mass., 1988.

Ovid, *Fasti*, translation by Sir James G. Frazer, revised by G. P. Goold, Loeb edition, Harvard, Cambridge, Mass., 1988.

Pausanias, translation by W. H. S. Jones, *Description of Greece*, Loeb edition, Volume I, Harvard, Cambridge, Mass., 1998.

Petronius, *Satyricon*, translation by Michael Heseltine, revised by E. H. Warmington, *Petronius, Seneca: Apocolocyntosis*, Loeb edition, Harvard, Cambridge, Mass., 1987.

Philo, *Embassy to Gaius*, translation by F. H. Colson, Revd G. H. Whitaker, and Revd J. W. Earp, Loeb edition, 10 volumes, Harvard, Cambridge, Mass., 1962.

Philostratus, *Epistles of Apollonius of Tyana*, to the priests in Olympia, translation by F. C. Conybeare, *Philostratus: The Life of Apollonius of Tyana*, Loeb edition, Volume II, London, 1912.

Philostratus, Flavius, *Life of Apollonius of Tyana*, translation by F. C. Conybeare, *Philostratus: The Life of Apollonius of Tyana*, Loeb edition, Volume II, Harvard, Cambridge, Mass., 1921.

Philostratus, Flavius, *Imagines*, translation by Arthur Fairbanks, *Philostratus: the Elder, the Younger: Imagines, Callistratus: Descriptions*, Loeb edition, Harvard, Cambridge, Mass., 1931.

Philostratus, Flavius, *Lives of the Sophists*, translation by William Cave Wright, *Philostratus and Eunapius: The Lives of the Sophists*, Loeb edition, Harvard, Cambridge, Mass., 1989.

Pliny the Elder, *Natural History*, translation by H. Rackham, W. H. S. Jones, and D. E. Eichholz, Loeb edition, 10 volumes, Harvard, Cambridge, Mass., 1942–1983.

Pliny (the Younger), *Pliny: Letters and Panegyricus*, translation by Betty Radice, Loeb edition, 2 volumes, Harvard, Cambridge, Mass., 1969.

Plutarch, *Antony*, translation by Bernadotte Perrin, *Plutarch's Lives*, Loeb edition, Volume IX, Harvard, Cambridge, Mass., 1988.

Plutarch, *Numa*, translation by Bernadotte Perrin, *Plutarch's Lives*, Loeb edition, Volume I, Harvard, Cambridge, Mass., 1914.

Plutarch, *Caesar*, translation by Bernadotte Perrin, *Plutarch's Lives*, Loeb edition, Volume VII, Harvard, Cambridge, Mass., 1919.

Procopius, *Secret History*, translation by H. B. Dewing, *The Anecdota or Secret History*, Loeb edition, Volume VI, Harvard, Cambridge, Mass., 1993.

Seneca, *Epistles Morales*, translation by Richard M. Gummere, Loeb edition, 3 volumes (IV–VI), Harvard, Cambridge, Mass., 1925.

Seneca, *On Anger*, translation by John W. Basore, *Moral Essays*, Loeb edition, Volume I, Harvard, Cambridge, Mass., 1928.

Seneca, *On Firmness*, translation by John W. Basore, *Moral Essays*, Loeb edition, Volume I, Harvard, Cambridge, Mass., 1928 (Seneca, On Mercy, 1.9.6).

Seneca, *On Providence*, translation by John W. Basore, *Moral Essays*, Loeb edition, Volume I, Harvard, Cambridge, Mass., 1928; also, translation by James R. Burns.

Seneca, *To Marcia on Consolation*, translation by John W. Basore, *Moral Essays*, Loeb edition, Volume II, Harvard, Cambridge, Mass., 1932.

Seneca, *On Tranquillity of Mind*, translation by John W. Basore, *Moral Essays*, Loeb edition, Volume II, Harvard, Cambridge, Mass., 1932.

Seneca, *On Benefits*, translation by John W. Basore, *Moral Essays*, Loeb edition, Volume III, Harvard, Cambridge, Mass., 1935.

Seneca, *Apocolocyntosis*, translation by Michael Heseltine, revised by W. H. D. Rouse, *Petronius, Seneca: Apocolocyntosis*, Loeb edition, Harvard, Cambridge, Mass., 1987.

Silius Italicus, *Punica*, translation by J. D. Duff, Loeb edition, Heinemann and G. P. Putnam's Sons, New York, 1934.

Statius, Publilius Papinius, *Silvae*, translation by J. H. Mozley, *Statius*, Loeb edition, 2 volumes, Harvard, Cambridge, Mass., 1982.

Statius, Publilius Papinius, *Achilleid*, translation by David R. Slavitt, in *Broken Columns*, University of Pennsylvania Press, Philadelphia, 1997.

Suetonius, *The Twelve Caesars*, translation by Robert Graves, Penguin Books, Harmondsworth, 1957.

Tacitus, *Annals*, translation by Michael Grant, *Tacitus: The Annals of Imperial Rome*, Penguin Books, New York, 1989, and by Alfred John Church and William Jackson Brodribb, *The Complete Works of Tacitus*, The Modern Library, New York, 1942.

Tacitus, *Agricola*, translation by H. Mattingly, revised by S. A. Handford, *Tacitus: The Agricola and the Germania*, Penguin Books, New York, 1983.

Tacitus, *Germania*, translation by H. Mattingly, revised by S. A. Handford, *Tacitus: The Agricola and the Germania*, Penguin Books, New York, 1983.

Tacitus, *The Histories*, translated by Kenneth Wellesley, Penguin Books, London, 1991.

Tertullian, *Apologia*, translation by T. R. Glover, *Apologia and De Spectaculis*, Loeb edition, Harvard, Cambridge, Mass., 1931.

Valerius Maximus, translation by D. R. Shackleton Bailey, *Valerius Maximus: Memorable Doings and Sayings*, Loeb edition, 2 volumes, Harvard, Cambridge, Mass., 2000.

Velleius Paterculus, *Res Gestae Divi Augusti*, translation by F. W. Shipley, Loeb edition, Harvard, Cambridge, Mass., 1924.

(Victor), Sextus Aurelius Victor, *Liber de Caesaribus*, translated by H. W. Bird, Translated Texts for Historians Volume 17, Liverpool University Press, Liverpool, 1994.

Zonoras, translation by Earnest Cary in *Dio's Roman History*, Loeb edition, Volume VIII, Harvard, Cambridge, Mass., 1925.

Modern sources

Alexander, Paul J., *Scriptiones Latinae Liberae Rei Publicae* II.7784.4–17, based on 1938:161, "Letters and Speeches of the Emperor Hadrian." *Harvard Studies in Classical Philology* 49:141–78.

Balsdon, J. P. V. D., *Roman Women: Their History and Habits*, Barnes and Noble, New York, 1962.

Balsdon, J. P. V. D., *Romans and Aliens*, University of North Carolina Press, Chapel Hill, 1979.

Bandinelli, Ranuccio Bianchi, *et al.*, *The Buried City: Excavations at Leptis Magna*, Frederick A. Praeger, New York and Washington, 1966.

Barrett, Anthony A., *Caligula: The Corruption of Power*, Yale University Press, New Haven and London, 1990.

Barrett, Anthony A., *Agrippina: Sex, Power, and Politics in the Early Empire*, Yale University Press, New Haven and London, 1996.

Barrett, Anthony A., *Livia: First Lady of Imperial Rome*, Yale University Press, New Haven and London, 2002.

Barton, Carlin A., *Sorrows of the Ancient Romans: The Gladiator and the Monster*, Princeton University Press, Princeton, 1993.

Bennett, Julian, *Trajan: Optimus Princeps*, Routledge, London, 1997.

Biaggi, Elio, *Le Preziose Patine dei Sesterzi di Roma Imperiale*, Collana, I Grandi Libri, 1992.

Birley, Anthony R., *Lives of the Later Caesars: The First Part of the Augustan History, with Newly Compiled Lives of Nerva and Trajan*, Penguin Books, London, 1976.

Birley, Anthony R., *Septimius Severus: The African Emperor*, Yale University Press, New Haven and London, 1988.

Birley, Anthony R., *Marcus Aurelius*, B. T. Batsford, Ltd, London, 1993.

Birley, Anthony R., *Hadrian: The Restless Emperor*, Routledge, London, 1997.

Blois, Lukas de, *The Policy of the Emperor Gallienus*, Brill, Leiden, 1976.

(BMCRE) Mattingly, H., *et al.*, *Coins of the Roman Empire in the British Museum*, London, 1932–1962.

Boardman, John, Griffin, Jasper, and Murray, Oswyn, *The Oxford History of the Classical World*, Oxford University Press, Oxford, 1986.

Bowersock, G. W., *Greek Sophists in the Roman Empire*, Oxford, at the Clarendon Press, 1969.

Brauer, George C., *The Decadent Emperors: Power and Depravity in Third-Century Rome*, Barnes and Noble, New York, 1967.

Bray, John, *Gallienus: A Study in Reformist and Sexual Politics*, Wakefield Press, Kent Town, 1997.

Brion, Marcel, *Pompeii and Herculaneum: The Glory and the Grief*, Paul Elek, London, 1960.

Bryant, E. E., *Reign of Antoninus Pius*, Cambridge, 1895.

Burke, John, *Roman England*, Artus Books, London, 1983.

Burkert, Walter, *Ancient Mystery Cults*, Harvard University Press, Cambridge, Mass., 1987.

Burns, Jasper, Was Nero the Natural Son of Claudius? *The Celator: Journal of Ancient Art and Artifacts*, January 1996.

Burns, Jasper, Was Caracalla Guilty of Human Sacrifice? *The Celator: Journal of Ancient Art and Artifacts*, February 1997.

Burns, Jasper, Vipsania on Roman Coins? *The Celator: Journal of Ancient Art and Artifacts*, May 2004.

Campbell, Joseph, *The Masks of God: Occidental Mythology*, Penguin, New York, 1976.

Campbell, Joseph, *The Masks of God: Oriental Mythology*, Penguin, New York, 1976.

Campbell, Joseph, *Transformations of Myth Through Time*, Harper and Row, 1990.

Carson, R. A. G., *The Birth of Western Civilization*, edited by Michael Grant, McGraw Hill, New York, 1964.

Cohen, H., *Description Historique des Monnaies Frappées sous l'Empire Romain*, 8 volumes, Rollin et Fenardent, Paris, 1880–1892.

Connolly, Peter and Dodge, Hazel, *The Ancient City: Life in Classical Athens and Rome*, Oxford University Press, Oxford, 1998.

Costa, Virginia M. da, The Consecration Phenomena of Faustina the Elder, *The Celator: Journal of Ancient Art and Artifacts*, February 1994.

Crouzel, Henri, *Origen*, translation A. S. Worrall, Harper and Row, San Francisco, 1989.

Cunliffe, Barry, *Rome and Her Empire*, McGraw-Hill, New York, 1978.

Curchin, Leonard A., *Roman Spain*, Barnes and Noble, New York, 1991.

D'Ambra, Eve, *Private Lives, Imperial Virtues: The Frieze of the Forum Transitorium in Rome*, Princeton University Press, Princeton, 1993.

Daly, Robert J., *Origen: Treatise on the Passover and Dialogue of Origen with Heraclides*, Paulist Press, New York/Mahwah, N.J., 1972.

Deiss, Joseph Day, *Herculaneum: Italy's Buried Treasure*, Harper and Row, New York, 1985.

Embleton, Ronald and Graham, Frank, *Hadrian's Wall in the Days of the Romans*, Barnes and Noble, New York, 1984.

Fantham, Elaine, *et al.*, *Women in the Classical World*, Oxford University Press, New York and Oxford, 1994.

Ferrill, Arther, *Caligula: Emperor of Rome*, Thames and Hudson, London and New York, 1991.

Franz, Marie-Louise von, *The Golden Ass of Apuleius: The Liberation of the Feminine in Man*, Shambhala Publications, London and Boston, 1992.

Fraser, Antonia, *Boadicea's Chariot: The Warrior Queens*, Weidenfeld and Nicolson, London, 1988.

Frazer, Sir James George, *The Golden Bough: A Study in Magic and Religion* (one-volume, abridged edition), Macmillan Company, New York, 1950.

Galinsky, Karl, *Augustan Culture*, Princeton University Press, Princeton, 1996.

Giacosa, Giorgio, *Women of the Caesars: Their Lives and Portraits on Coins*, translation by R. Ross Holloway, Edizioni Arte e Moneta, Publishers, Milan, n.d.

Gibbon, Edward, *The Decline and Fall of the Roman Empire*, Modern Library, 3 volumes, Vol. I, Random House, Inc., New York, n.d.

Glob, P. V., *The Bog People: Iron-Age Man Preserved*, Ballantine Books, New York, 1969.

Grant, Michael, *Roman History from Coins*, Barnes and Noble, New York, 1958.

Grant, Michael, The High Art of Portraiture on Roman Coins, *Horizon: A Magazine of the Arts*, Vol. 5, No. 7, September 1963.

Grant, Michael, *History of Rome*, Charles Scribner's Sons, New York, 1968.

Grant, Michael, *Nero: Emperor in Revolt*, American Heritage Press, New York, 1970.

Grant, Michael, *Cities of Vesuvius: Pompeii and Herculaneum*, Penguin Books, New York, 1971.

Grant, Michael, *Cleopatra*, Simon and Schuster, New York, 1972.

Grant, Michael, *The Twelve Caesars*, Charles Scribner's Sons, New York, 1975.

Grant, Michael, *The Roman Emperors*, Charles Scribner's Sons, New York, 1985.

Grant, Michael, *The Visible Past: An Archeological Reinterpretation of Ancient History*, Collier Books, New York, 1990.

Grant, Michael, *The Climax of Rome*, Weidenfeld and Nicolson, London, 1993.

Grant, Michael, *Constantine*, Charles Scribner's Sons, New York, 1994.

Grant, Michael, *The Antonines: The Roman Empire in Transition*, Routledge, London, 1994.

Grant, Michael, *Art in the Roman Empire*, Routledge, London, 1995.

Grant, Michael, *Gladiators*, Barnes and Noble, New York, 1995.

Grant, Michael, *The Severans: The Changed Roman Empire*, Routledge, London, 1996.

Grant, Michael, *A Guide to the Ancient World*, Barnes and Noble, New York, 1997.

Grant, Michael and Mulas, Antonia, *Eros in Pompeii: The Secret Rooms of the National Museum of Naples*, William Morrow and Company, New York, 1975.

Graves, Robert, *I Claudius*, Modern Library, New York, 1934.

Greer, Rowan A., *Origen: An Exhortation to Martyrdom, Prayer and Selected Works*, Paulist Press, New York, 1979.

Griffin, Miriam T., *Nero: The End of a Dynasty*, Yale University Press, New Haven and London, 1985.

Hanfmann, George M. A., *Roman Art: A Modern Survey of the Art of Imperial Rome*, Norton, New York and London, 1975.

Harl, Kenneth W., *Coinage in the Roman Economy: 300 B.C. to A.D. 700*, Johns Hopkins University Press, Baltimore, 1996.

Henig, Martin, *A Handbook of Roman Art: A Survey of the Visual Arts of the Roman World*, Phaidon, London, 1983.

Hope, Richard, *The Book of Diogenes Laertius: Its Spirit and Its Method*, Columbia University Press, New York, 1930.

Hopkins, K., On the Probable Age Structure of the Roman Population, *Population Studies* 20, 1966.

Hopkins, K., Death and Renewal, *Sociological Studies in Roman History, Volume 2*, Cambridge University Press, Cambridge, 1983.

Howgego, Christopher, *Ancient History from Coins*, Routledge, London, 1995.

Huzar, Eleanor Goltz, *Mark Antony: A Biography*, University of Minnesota Press, Minneapolis, 1978.

James, Simon, *Eyewitness Books: Ancient Rome*, Alfred A. Knopf, New York, 1990.

Jones, Brian W., *The Emperor Domitian*, Routledge, London, 1992.

Kähler, Heinz *The Art of Rome and Her Empire*, Greystone Press, New York, 1965.

Kiefer, Otto, *Sexual Life in Ancient Rome*, Abbey Library, London, 1976.

King, Anthony, *Roman Gaul and Germany*, University of California Press, Berkeley, 1990.

Kinsley, David, *The Goddesses' Mirror*, SUNY, Albany, 1989.

Kleiner, Diana E. E., *Roman Sculpture*, Yale University Press, New Haven and London, 1992.

Kleiner, Diana E. E. and Matheson, Susan B., editors, *I Claudia: Women in Ancient Rome*, Yale University Art Gallery, New Haven, Conn., 1996.

Kleiner, Diana E. E. and Matheson, Susan B., editors, *I Claudia II: Women in Roman Art and Society*, University of Texas Press, Austin, 2000.

Kokkinos, Nikos, *Antonia Augusta: Portrait of a Great Roman Lady*, Routledge, London, 1992.

Kondoleon, Christine, *Antioch: The Lost Ancient City*, Princeton University Press, Princeton, and Worcester Art Museum, Worcester, Mass., 2000.

Lamb, Sir Walter, *Ethiopian Story*, edited by J. R. Morgan, J. M. Dent, London, 1997.

Lambert, Royston, *Beloved and God: The Story of Hadrian and Antinous*, Viking, New York, 1984.

Lanciani, Rodolfo, *The Ruins and Excavations of Ancient Rome*, Bell Publishing, New York, 1969.

Lefkovitz, Mary R. and Fant, Maureen B., *Women's Life in Greece and Rome: A Source Book in Translation*, Johns Hopkins University Press, Baltimore, 1992.

Levick, Barbara, *Claudius*, Yale University Press, New Haven and London, 1990.

Levick, Barbara, *Tiberius: The Politician*, Routledge, London, 1999.

Levick, Barbara, *Vespasian*, Routledge, London, 1999.

Lyttleton, Margaret and Forman, Werner, *The Romans: Their Gods and Their Beliefs*, Orbis Publishing, London, 1984.

McDermott, William C. and Orentzel, Anne E., *Roman Portraits: The Flavian Trajanic Period*, University of Missouri Press, Columbia and London, 1979.

MacDonald, William L. and Pinto, John A., *Hadrian's Villa and Its Legacy*, Yale University Press, New Haven, 1995.

MacMullen, Ramsay, *Paganism in the Roman Empire*, Yale University Press, New Haven, 1981.

Massa, Aldo, *The Phoenicians*, Minerva, Geneva, 1977.

Mayo, Adrienne, *The First Fossil Hunters: Paleontology in Greek and Roman Times*, Princeton, Princeton University Press, 2000.

Mazzolani, Lidia Storoni, *Empire Without End: Three Historians of Rome*, Harcourt Brace Jovanovich, New York and London, 1976.

Michon, d'Etienne, *Le Louvre: Sculpture Romaine*, L'Illustration, Paris, 1936.

Millar, Fergus, *The Roman Near East: 31 BC–AD 337*, Harvard University Press, Cambridge, Mass., 1993.

Murphy, Gerard J., *Reign of Septimius Severus from Evidence of Inscriptions*, University of Pennsylvania, Philadelphia, 1945.

Mylonas, George E., *Eleusis and the Eleusinian Mysteries*, Routledge and Kegan Paul, London, 1961.

Perowne, Stewart, *Hadrian*, Hodder and Stoughton, London, 1960.

Pollitt, J. J., *The Art of Rome: c. 753 B.C.–337 A.D.*, Prentice-Hall, Englewood Cliffs, 1966.

Potter, T. W., *Roman Italy*, University of California Press, Berkeley and Los Angeles, 1987.

Price, Martin Jessop and Trell, Bluma L., *Coins and Their Cities: Architecture on the Ancient Coins of Greece, Rome, and Palestine*, V. C. Vecchi and Sons, London, 1977.

Reardon, B. P., *Collected Ancient Greek Novels*, University of California Press, Berkeley, 1989.

(RIC) Mattingly, Harold *et al.*, *The Roman Imperial Coinage*, 10 volumes, Spink, London, 1923–1994.

Rohrman, Douglass F., Mater Castrorum: The Coinage of Faustina the Younger, *The Celator: Journal of Ancient Art and Artifacts*, July and August, 1999.

Roller, Lynn E., *In Search of God the Mother: The Cult of Anatolian Cybele*, University of California Press, Berkeley, 1999.

Rutland, Jonathan, *An Ancient Greek Town*, edited by R. J. Unstead, Kingfisher Books, Ltd, London, 1986.

Salway, Peter, *The Oxford Illustrated History of Roman Britain*, Oxford University Press, Oxford and New York, 1993.

Sayles, Wayne, *Ancient Coin Collecting III: The Roman World – Politics and Propaganda*, Krause Publications, Iola, 1997.

Scarre, Chris, *Chronicles of the Roman Emperors*, Thames and Hudson, London, 1995.

Sear, David R., *Greek Imperial Coinage*, Seaby Publications, Ltd, London, 1982.

Serviez, Jacques Roergas de, *The Roman Empresses: History of the Lives and Secret Intrigues of the Wives of the Twelve Caesars*, Vol. II, Walpole Press, London, 1899.

Shuckburgh, E. S., *Augustus Caesar*, Barnes and Noble, New York, 1995.

Southern, Pat, *Domitian: Tragic Tyrant*, Indiana University Press, Bloomington, 1997.

Spaeth, Barbette Stanley, *The Roman Goddess Ceres*, University of Texas Press, Austin, 1996.

Strong, Donald, *Roman Art*, Penguin Books, New York, 1976.

Syme, R., Domitius Corbulo, *Roman Papers: Volume 2*, edited by E. Badian, Oxford University Press, Oxford, 1979–1988.

Tameanko, Marvin, The Evolution of the Empresses' Hairdos on Roman Coinage from Augustus to Constantine, *The Celator: Journal of Ancient Art and Artifacts*, June 1997.

Tameanko, Marvin, *Monumental Coins*, Krause Publications, Iola, 1999.

Tobin, Jennifer, *Herodes Attikos and the City of Athens: Patronage and Conflict Under the Antonines*, J. C. Gieben, Amsterdam, 1997.

Toynbee, Arnold, editor, *Crucible of Christianity: Judaism, Hellenism, and the Historical Background to the Christian Faith*, World Publishing Company, New York and Cleveland, 1969.

Turcan, Robert, *The Cults of the Roman Empire*, Blackwell, Oxford and Cambridge, 1996.

Vagi, David L., *Coinage and History of the Roman Empire*, Volume I, Coin World, Sidney, Ohio, 1999.

Vaughan, Agnes Carr, *Zenobia of Palmyra*, Doubleday, Garden City, 1967.

Vermaseren, Maarten J., *Cybele and Attis: The Myth and the Cult*, Thames and Hudson, London, 1977.

Veyne, Paul, *et al.*, *A History of Private Life from Pagan Rome to Byzantium*, Belknap Press, Harvard, Cambridge, Mass. and London, 1987.

Ville, Georges, *La Gladiature en Occident des origines à la mort de Domitian*, École Française, Rome, 1981.

Von Hagen, Victor W. and Tomeucci, Adolfo, *The Roads That Led to Rome*, World Publishing Company, Cleveland and New York, 1967.

Walker, Susan, *Roman Art*, British Museum, London, 1991.

Wheeler, Mortimer, *Roman Art and Architecture*, Oxford University Press, Oxford and Toronto, 1964.

Witt, R. E., *Isis in the Ancient World*, Johns Hopkins University Press, Baltimore, 1971.

Woodford, Susan, *Cambridge Introduction to the History of Art: Greece and Rome*, Cambridge University Press, Cambridge, 1982.

World Factbook 2000, CIA. Online: <http://www.odci.gov/cia/publications/factbook/> (accessed 12 January 2005).

Wright, F. A., *Marcus Agrippa: Organizer of Victory*, George Routledge and Sons, Ltd, London, 1937.

INDEX

Page numbers in **bold** indicate references within figures and tables.

Valerian 232–3; coin
of **241**
Marius Maximus, Roman
historian 134, 170, 189
Mark Antony 5–6, 8, 30,
38, 42, 49, 59, 107; and
Cleopatra 20, 26, 49;
coins of **21, 22, 37**;
described 25; marries
Octavia 25; revered in
eastern provinces 31; rule
by descendants of 20
marriage: Augustus' laws
regarding 9–10, 28–9
Martial, Roman poet 91–2,
95
Masada 88
massacres: by Caracalla
197–8, by Germans under
Arminius 43, 46
Mater Castrorum: Faustina the
Younger as 164; Julia
Domna as 186, 197; Julia
Maesa as 210; Salonina as
234
Mater Deum, Cybele as
Mother of the Gods 146,
204
mater familias female head of
Roman *familia* 2, 11, 19,
33, 35; Antonia as 33, 35;
Faustina the Elder as 144;
Livia as 11, 19
Mater Patriae, Mother of the
Fatherland 2; Livia as 18
Mater Senatus, Mother of the
Senate 214
Matidia the Elder, mother of
Sabina 111, 116, 125,
136; coin of **120, 137**;
deification of 136; district
of Antinoopolis named for
136; named Augusta 115;
praised by Hadrian 136
Matidia the Younger, sister
of Sabina 111;
accompanies Sabina on her
travels 128; coin of **137**;
and Eleusis 132; remains
unmarried 125, 128
Matthew, book of 219
Mauretania, Africa 30,
148

mausoleum 23, 33, 291; of
Augustus 17, 28, 35, 51,
54, 62; of Diocletian 236;
of Hadrian 136
Maximianus, or Maximian,
Roman emperor 236; coin
of **243**
Maximinus I, Roman
emperor 222–4, 231; coin
of **228, 240**
Maximinus II, Roman
emperor 236
medicines: and Livia 18
Mediolanum (Milan), Italy
185
Meditations, of Marcus
Aurelius 143, 156, 157,
167, 169; quoted 143,
163, 167, 169
Memnon, Colossi of 132–3,
187
Memnon, Greek hero 132
Memphis, Egypt 187
Meroe, Ethiopia 191
Mesopotamia 115–16, 200,
219, 221, 223; conquered
by Trajan 115; overrun by
Persians 218; uprising in
217
Messalina, Roman empress
30, 66–7, 76; attempts to
kill Nero 68–9; coins of
80; compared to Faustina
the Younger 155; death of
64; descended from Mark
Antony 20; described
62–4, 68–9; influence
over Claudius 64; lovers of
64; no imperial Roman
coins minted for 35
Metamorphoses, by Lucius
Apuleius 190
Milvian Bridge, Rome:
Constantine the Great's
vision there 237
Minerva 77; Domitian's
devotion to 94, 97–8
Misenum, Italy 77
misogyny: of ancient writers
220, 239
Mithras 132
Moesia, Lower, Roman
province 185

Moguntiacum, modern
Mainz, Germany 223
mosaics 98, 131
mother of three children
8–9, 12, 30
Mucianus, Caius Licinius,
lieutenant of Vespasian 88
mulberry 113
mushrooms: and Claudius'
death 70–1
mutiny of the Rhine legions
44–6

Nabatea 49
Naples, Italy, ancient
Neapolis 6, 17, 29, 77
Napoleon: imitation of
Roman hairstyles in court
of 155
Narcissus, advisor to
Claudius 64–66
Nemausus, modern Nimes,
France 42, 107–8, 118,
142; coin of **21**; Pont du
Gard, 42, **106**, 107
Neptune 35, Caligula as 61
Nero, brother of Caligula 33,
49, 51; birth of 42;
charged with perversity
52; coin of **56**, 60–1;
exiled by Tiberius 53
Nero, Roman emperor 20,
29, 42, **58**, 59, 60–79,
85–7, 88, 90, 98, 126,
156, 159, 191, 216, 233;
accession of 70; and Acte
75; adopted by Claudius
67, 69; and the arts 71–4,
76; baths of 216; birth of
60; character of 68, 71–2,
73–4, 76; coins of **80, 81,
82, 83**; death of 79, 87;
and death of Agrippina
the Younger 76–8;
designated Claudius' heir
67; and the fire in Rome
85; hairstyle of 126;
incest with Agrippina the
Younger 68, 75, 201; as
natural son of Claudius
67–70; and Octavia 70,
76, 156; and Otho 87;
nocturnal rambles of 76;

Germanicus 48; of Lucius
Verus 160; of Severus
Alexander 219
Trojan War 132, 199, 221
trompe l'oeil: in Livia's palace
18
Troy 85, 199
Turkey 112, 116, 128,
142–3, 165, 191, 199,
211, 238–9
Tyre, Phoenicia 184

Ulpian, Roman jurist 194,
216–17
Ulpii, Trajan's family 108
Ulysses, Greek hero:
compared to Livia by
Caligula 14
univira, woman of one man
8–9; Antonia as 29
Urgulania, friend of Livia,
Roman empress 16
Ursus, Lucius Julius, relative
of Domitia Longina,
Roman empress 94

Vabalathus, son of Zenobia
234–5; coin of 242
Valentinian III, Roman
emperor 238; coin of 245
Valerian I, Roman emperor
233; coin of 242
Valerian II, son of Salonina;
coin of 242
Valerius Asiaticus 30
Valerius Maximus, Roman
writer 97; on Livia's
chastity 15; praises
Antonia 26
Varius Avitus Bassianus, see
Elagabalus 207
Varus, Publius Quinctilius
46; killed in Germany 43;
site of defeat visited by
Germanicus 47
Vatican 145, 149
vegetarians 191
Velleius Paterculus, Roman
writer 15
Venus 7, 16, 35, **180**;
Caligula as 61; on coins,
157, 193; Livia as 9;
pearls dedicated to by

Severus Alexander 218;
temple of in Rome 170
Venus Genetrix: Antonia as
35
Vespasian, Roman emperor
32, 87–93, 97, 99, 108,
132, 170, 191; accessibility
of 90; appearance of 90,
91; and Britain 90;
character of 87, 90–2;
coins of **102**; death of 92;
humor of 90–1, 92; and
Judaea 87–8; and Nero 90;
origins of 90; and Senate
97; and technological
innovation 148
Vespasianus, Domitian's heir
99
Vesta 15; Temple of in Rome
17, 188, **204**
Vestal Virgins: Antonia
given rights of 34;
Caligula's sisters honored
as 59; described 15;
Elagabalus marries one
212; importance in
Roman state religion, 5;
Livia as 15; punished by
Domitian 96; rights of 15
Vicus Britannicus, modern
Bretzenheim, Germany
223
Vindex, governor of Gaul:
rebels against Nero 87
Vindobona, modern Vienna,
Austria: death of Marcus
Aurelius there 169
vineyards 18, 29
Vinicianus, Annius, son-in-
law of Corbulo 86
Vipsania, wife of Tiberius,
Roman emperor 10, 53, 92
Virgil, Roman poet 26, 221
Visigoths: victory at
Hadrianopolis 238
Vistilia, cousin of Domitia
Longina, Roman empress
86
Vistilia, grandmother of
Domitia Longina 86
Vitellius, Aulus, Roman
emperor 30, 87–8, 90, 97;
coins of **39, 102**

Vitellius, Lucius, Roman
senator 30, 64
Volusian, son of Trebonianus
Gallus: coin of **241**

Wall: Antonine 148;
Hadrian's 129, 148
wigs: worn by Julia Domna
184
wine 18, 63, 213
women 1–3, 5, 9–10, 15,
19–20, 35, 48, 93, 107,
111–12, 125, 128,
129–30, 131, 142, 157,
158, 184, 194, 196, 208,
219, 238, 239; adoration
for gladiators 172; as
concubines of soldiers
188; decline of rights
during 3rd Century crisis
224, 231; divinity of 13;
and the fall of dynasties
171; in funerals 196;
German, fought as
soldiers 162; as gladiators
172, 189, 294; Hadrian's
attitude toward 129–30;
hairstyles of, 220; high
status and economic
power of 3, 35; in
literature 191; and
marriage 2, 8, 112; on
portrait coins 210;
protection of under law
3, 216; in the Saecular
Games 193; senate of
214, 235; in senate
house 71, 74, 214–15;
sexual freedom in
Scotland 195; and
sports 94; status in
Judaism 220; status in
Roman vs. Greek society
2, 128, 131; status of in
Stoicism 157; under-
privileged, state support
for 15, 146, 166

Zeno, Stoic philosopher 156
Zenobia, Septimia, Queen of
Palmyra 234–5; coin of
242
Zeus, Greek god 69